SHAPING THE IDEAL CHILD

Shaping the Ideal Child

Children and Their Primers in Late Imperial China

Limin Bai

The Chinese University Press

Shaping the Ideal Child: Children and Their
Primers in Late Imperial China
 By Limin Bai

© **The Chinese University of Hong Kong**, 2005

ISBN 962–996–114–8

THE CHINESE UNIVERSITY PRESS
The Chinese University of Hong Kong
SHA TIN, N.T., HONG KONG
Fax: +852 2603 6692
    +852 2603 7355
E-mail: cup@cuhk.edu.hk
Web-site: www.chineseupress.com

Printed in Hong Kong

∽ **Contents** ∽

⌒ Foreword ⌒

Ruth Hayhoe

In his contribution to the volume *Confucian Traditions in East Asian Modernity*, William Theodore de Bary comments on the long lasting influence of the Four Books and Five Classics as a core curriculum in premodern East Asia. He also notes how there was greater variety and change over time in the educational content of the earliest stage of traditional schooling.[1] It is this earliest phase of teaching material, the primers used for children's learning, that is the focus of this fascinating volume. The fact that there was considerable change in the character of these primers over the centuries makes for an interesting study, one that gives insight into the foundations of Chinese civilization. In all of the rich literature on classical patterns of education in China, much has been written about pedagogy and content in traditional schools of various types, in academies or *shuyuan*, and most of all, in the preparation for the famous civil service examinations. However, little has been written about children themselves, how they were viewed in traditional society, how their learning was structured, and what kinds of experiences they were exposed to in their earliest years. This book thus does an admirable job of filling a gap in our knowledge about education in traditional Chinese society at the most basic level.

The author notes how the study of childhood, as it has been carried out in various Western societies since the 1960s, reveals many different aspects of the character and expectations of different societies. One of the themes that emerges throughout this volume is the strong focus on moral development in the Chinese context, as the most important aspect of a child's growing up within the community. A second theme is the importance of the social and natural environment to the healthy development of the child, from its pre-birth experience as a foetus right up through its early childhood years. One of the most inspiring aspects of traditional Chinese philosophy is the affirmation of human potential, and the belief that every child has an inner self which can blossom, given a supportive environment and the right kinds of education. While the intellectual demands of learning a complex written language called for concentration and hard work, this was only one aspect of the lessons given in these primers. The ways in which the learning of characters was made enjoyable and understandable, also the links between language learning and simple mathematics are also interesting aspects of the learning experience. Finally, the link between knowledge and action in education is illustrated beautifully in the discussion of how children were taught to participate in various "rites" relating to their social responsibilities to parents, siblings, teachers and various important others. The concept that a child can become a fully human person only in relationship to others is fundamental to Chinese thought, and the ways in which various types of ritual or symbolic action made this knowledge real in the mind and feelings of the child is dealt with at several different junctures in the book.

Another important part of the story is the exploration of the educational revolution that took place under the influence of the great Ming Neo-Confucian scholar, Wang Yangming, whose educational theories had a profound impact. His belief that every individual could become a sage, if they took the step of commitment, opened up new possibilities in education to a much wider number of children. In addition, he understood the importance of play and story-telling in children's development, and encouraged the incorporation of an array of stories drawn from Taoist and Buddhist sources as well as Confucian, into the early curriculum. Education was no longer limited to a small elite who could suppress selfish desire and discipline themselves to master the huge collection of literature about society and nature that had built up over long history, but became more accessible, with the recognition that every person could become a sage. All of the knowledge needed for sageliness could be found within, in Wang's view, with action and reflection on action as the real fount of knowledge and understanding. No wonder when Chinese scholars and educators of the twentieth century came in touch with John Dewey, and enthusiastically introduced many of his ideas into Chinese schools and teacher education programs, they came to feel that China had its own Dewey, in the heritage of pedagogy left by Wang Yangming.

Chapter eight of this book deals with efforts of scholars such as Liang Qichao to bring about reforms in education that would strengthen China in face of the incursion of foreign powers. Liang's efforts to develop new textbooks that would integrate China's own pedagogical tradition with patterns and ideas being introduced from the West are analysed in detail, as are some of the early textbooks developed by missionary educators. With the May 4th Movement of 1919, which is beyond the scope of this book, traditional pedagogy was left behind, as new ideas of science and democracy were embraced wholeheartedly. In a sense, therefore, this task of integration still faces educators in China today. In the chapter cited at the beginning of this foreword, William Theodore de Bary commented on how China was influenced by Western assumptions abut the unlimited value of science, technology and industrialisation, and how these have led to the almost total predominance of specialized training in technical disciplines in the twentieth century. In this process, he notes "centrifugal forces have created a vacuum in public discourse, into which liberationist philosophies have rushed."[2]

Now in the early twenty-first century, in a period which the United Nations has defined in terms of a "dialogue among civilizations" and a period where China is rapidly becoming a global power, understanding the roots of her civilization in terms of centuries of tradition in the education of her children is increasingly important. If China's contribution to the global community is to be more than a mirror of what she received from the West — from liberal ideologies to Marxism-Leninism — it will have to be rooted in an authentic and profound re-assessment of her own cultural and educational heritage, and a weaving of some of its threads into the present and future curriculum of her schools. Veteran Chinese educator, Li Bingde, who was born in 1911, studied in Switzerland and France in the 1940s, and has been the leading figure in curriculum and pedagogical theory in China's Northwest since the 1950s, made an assessment similar to that of de Bary, in a recent book chapter. He defined the period from the 1840s to 1979 as one of a "half open door" and noted how the influx of ideologies and patterns from abroad had "delivered highly charged cultural shocks to traditional Chinese society." "In only one and a half centuries," Li went on to remark, "Chinese scholars have imported, imitated and copied foreign cultures, often with no regard for the unique conditions of their own country. Before 1949, they copied the example of America and Europe; after that, they copied that of the Soviet Union. During all those years, borrowing and copying was the basis of the relationships they built with foreign cultures."[3] Since 1979, Li sees some hope for a new integration of external influences into a pedagogy rooted in a thorough knowledge of China's own cultural traditions and social context.

This volume provides a wonderful starting point for such a reassessment, with its detailed overview of the primers prepared for children's learning throughout China's long history of traditional education, and its subtle insights into Chinese ways of thinking about children and childhood.

⌒ Introduction ⌒

This book examines an extensive range of primers circulated and used in late imperial China. Preparation for this book has involved three areas of scholarly research: the history of traditional Chinese primers, the early Chinese perceptions of childhood, and intellectual movements and their impact on the education of children. The book analyses the contents of the primers, looking at how Chinese children in pre-modern times learned to read and write; and considers whether and how they studied arithmetic, history and other subjects besides the Confucian classics. It probes the unique characteristics of the traditional Chinese pedagogical approach to children, and the substantial differences in educating children of the gentry and those of the peasantry. An investigation of the motivations of some Confucian scholars, who devoted themselves to the writing of primers, leads to a study of the involvement of different intellectual movements in educating children and the role of elementary education in shaping traditional Chinese culture and society.

This study of traditional Chinese primers, focusing particularly on their relationship to the theory and practice of elementary education in late imperial China, and their underlying philosophical premises, aims to reveal the elite attitudes towards children and childhood apparent in these texts.

While the study of Chinese attitudes to children has just begun to attract scholarly attention, the history of childhood in other cultures has been of great interest to scholars in the West since Philippe Aries published his pioneering work *Centuries of Childhood* in 1960.[1] Aries focuses on the emergence of concepts of childhood, and argues that there was no such concept until the mid-eighteenth century. This conclusion and some of his historical methods have stimulated research on the subject, and since then many works on childhood in

Western countries, such as France, England and the United States, have been produced to either challenge or support Aries's claim.[2] The inter-disciplinary involvements in the study of childhood have resulted in diversity in the use of materials, methodological approaches, interpretations of sources and perspectives. As Chris Jenks summarises,

> The idea of childhood is not a natural but a social construct; as such its status is constituted in particular socially located forms of discourse. Whether the child is being considered in the common-sense world or in the disciplined world of specialisms, the meaningfulness of the child as a social being derives from its place, its purpose, within the theory.[3]

From the 1970s onward scholars have been interested in adult attitudes to children and the changes in their attitudes through time rather than simply in Aries's argument about whether there was a concept of childhood in the Middle Ages. From aspects such as the child-parent relationship,[4] history and structure of family[5] and education,[6] historians, anthropologists, sociologists and psychologists, among others, have attempted to construct a conceptualized childhood as well as to reveal the actual treatment of children in certain periods and against certain cultural settings in the West.

So far research on Chinese attitudes to children has rarely been divorced from the education of children, which often functioned as a significant force that shaped a child's development. Thomas Lee, who claims that his article "The Discovery of Childhood: Children's Education in Sung China (960–1279)" was the first on the subject of Chinese childhood published in English, links elementary education in Song China with Neo-Confucian educators' attitudes to childhood.[7] However, Lee's notion of the discovery of childhood in the Song dynasty is challenged by Ann Kinney's study of Han educational theory and historical writing. She finds that the Han thinkers "were the first to focus on childhood in philosophical discussions," and the metaphor "dyed silk" vividly illustrates the Han educators' emphasis on the important role of education in the child's intellectual and moral development.[8]

In his comments on Kinney's finding, Thomas Lee begins to see "childhood" in traditional China as "a vision and an intellectual construct," relating less "to how children were treated than to how they could serve as a reminder of the self-image of adults." Since both writers' findings are based on the Confucian interest in educating children, Lee then concludes that "there was not a time when China did not have education in some form," so simply stating "that childhood was discovered at any point in Chinese history" appears meaningless.[9]

It is true that Han thinkers left a wealth of data about medical and philosophical views of children. It is equally true that in Song Neo-Confucian education children received greater attention than before, as it was strongly believed that moral cultivation should begin with children, and the earlier the better. Therefore, there is really no point in arguing whether childhood was first discovered in the Han or in the Song, but it is important to see how Song Neo-Confucian thinkers created their formulas for child-rearing, specifying how to shape the child in accordance with their ideals. The key focus of this study is not whether children were dramatically shaped through education, but what Neo-Confucian educators believed they were doing and how they attempted to achieve their goal.

The elite attitudes to children and childhood in traditional China are analysed in this study in the context of the very nature of Confucian education. Here the term "Confucian education" is defined in a broader sense. It is generally agreed that non-Confucian schools of thought, such as Taoism and Buddhism, had a great impact on the course of traditional Chinese education in both theory and practice. Especially in the late imperial period, Buddhism and Taoism arose to challenge the monopoly of Confucianism in education and found their own way to influence the content and even the form of education. Meanwhile, Confucianism in the process of development incorporated some Buddhist and Taoist elements into its doctrines. This mutual assimilation and incorporation can be seen as an internal factor contributing significantly to the combination, formation and emergence of the Three Teachings in the Ming-Qing period. As analyses and discussions of the content of primers in this book show, some texts were written by Confucian scholars but contained considerable Buddhist and Taoist material. As a matter of fact, even some of the twenty-four examples of filial piety, well-known to almost every household in Ming-Qing China as illustrative guidelines for people to practise Confucian virtues in daily life, actually originated in Buddhist preaching. The common ground of the Three Teachings was built on "what Eugen Weber has called 'official culture,'"[10] which reflected the interests of the ruling class, and permeated the whole of society through the promotion of basic education. Based on this broader definition, traditional Chinese literacy primers in this study are understood exclusively as reflections of Confucian ideals of childhood and Confucian debate about the education of children.

There were two basic phases in the traditional Chinese educational system: full classical education that would allow a small proportion of males to compete in the civil service examinations; and basic education that would permit children of commoners to attain either functional or very limited literacy skills, depending on their financial resources. Generally speaking, the spectrum of literacy levels corresponded to social groups. Both Evelyn Rawski and David Johnson state that members of the *shi* or literati class, including both successful and failed candidates in the civil service examinations, were classically educated and attained "full literacy."[11] Those who succeeded in the civil service examinations would become legally privileged scholar-officials and members of the ruling class; those who failed in the examinations would be in various strata in society according to their financial situations.[12] For the group of commoners, their literacy levels and social status varied: affluent people, such as "respectable merchants, artisans, shopkeepers, landlords, and well-to-do peasants," who attended schools for several years but did not sit the civil service examinations, were normally equipped with "functional skills in reading and writing," while less fortunate and less wealthy commoners could only enjoy much briefer periods of schooling provided by either community or charitable schools, and obtained rudimentary literacy skills. Below them come the most disadvantaged people, who were illiterate.[13]

Among these three social groups, highly educated scholar-officials, as a single elite body "controlled all national institutions."[14] They themselves were the product of traditional Chinese education, and they in turn became part of the authoritarian body controlling educational institutions as well as the purpose and the content of education. Through promoting basic education for all layers of society, they helped create and propagate the "official culture" and "conventional morality," which dominated "popular consciousness" and made a large number of ordinary people "become willing partners in their own subjection."[15] At this point elementary education was viewed and used as a very significant and convenient instrument for the ruling class to accomplish the moral transformation of society and among individuals. This power of education, as discussed in Chapter Seven, even reached the illiterate group through children's songs.

Such moral, social and political effects of primers developed gradually through the centuries. The first traditional Chinese primers were *xiaoxue* books (*xiaoxue zhi shu*), a term which, in the Han, mainly referred to word-books, listing selected characters, and were used for teaching and learning characters. Books produced specifically for children after the Han varied in both content and form, and by the Song almost all genres had appeared. According to their contents, traditional Chinese primers can be categorized into history, literature, learning characters, classical learning and Neo-Confucianism, rituals and regulations. *Mengshu*, a very general term, was employed to refer to any books relating to education for children. Strictly speaking, however, children's primers were only part of *mengshu*, and not all *mengshu* were textbooks for children. Some *mengshu* concentrated on teaching philosophy and pedagogy, or on rudiments of specific knowledge, such as astronomy and mathematics. The subject of this study is children's literacy primers, not *mengshu* in general.

Furthermore, although the content of popular primers, such as *Sanzi jing* (*Trimetrical Classic*), *Baijia xing* (*One Hundred Surnames*) and *Qianzi wen* (*One Thousand Characters*) (abbreviated to *San Bai Qian* in Ming-Qing China), reflected the elite attitudes to childhood and Confucian views of the education of children, this does not necessarily indicate that they were intended only for elite boys. Firstly, a brief history of traditional primers outlined in Chapters Two and Three points to their very humble origins and their links with village books. Before the Ming, literati attitudes to such popular primers were very negative. Instead of adopting *San Bai Qian* and other similar primers for beginners, many scholars preferred the direct use of the Confucian *Four Books* and *Five Classics*, as well as other Neo-Confucian writings in the first stage of elementary training. Thanks to social and economic changes and shifts in intellectual trends, the popularity of such primers in the Ming-Qing period increased. In particular, when Ming-Qing educators employed the primers in vernacular forms to integrate elementary education into their far-reaching social reform programme, the social effects of these primers went far beyond the elite circle.

Secondly, from a pedagogical perspective, during the first phase of literacy education, the elite educational curriculum and basic literacy education had overlaps and common ground. These popular primers could be used either for children from the elite families who were inspired to compete in the civil service examinations; or for children from the families of affluent commoners whose parents had enough means to send them to school to attain functional literacy skills or climb the examination ladder; or for children who came from less fortunate families and were either willing or persuaded to attend village or charity schools. Of course, as is well known to students of Chinese history, only boys would be sent to school, and consequently the audience for primers examined in this study, generally speaking, were boys.[16] The point here is that no matter what motivations parents had for their sons' education, while these boys were learning their very first 2,000 characters by reading and chanting the sentences from these primers, Confucian values were being instilled into their young minds. Moreover, when illiterate people outside the classrooms heard these children's chanting, they were then also included in the process of indoctrination. In this way some traditional literacy primers were widely circulated and reached almost every corner of society. In this process children, through chanting these primers, inadvertently acted as Confucian messengers. At this point the process of basic education mingled with social indoctrination. This perhaps can account for the motivations of many Ming-Qing scholars who not only changed their negative attitudes toward popular primers but also devoted themselves to the composition of textbooks for children.

Evidently, Confucian writers of primers showed their interest in children, and represented their image of the ideal child in their writings. The childhood they construed and imaged reflected an essential element of the duality in traditional Chinese conceptions of childhood. On the one hand, the child was perceived as an ideal, symbolizing future and hope; on the other, children of non-elite families, especially the poor, were seen as unstable factors threatening the safety of the empire. This duality then determined the purpose of Confucian education for the poor, which aimed to train them to be "willing partners" of the ruling class and law-abiding subjects before anything else. Vocational education, as this study suggests, was absent from traditional Chinese education. Confucian scholar-officials might have carried out skills training among poor people in order to help them improve their lives, but training as such was not considered part of education in pre-modern China. Therefore, primers that concentrated only on functional literacy skills without indoctrination appear not to represent the main feature of traditional literacy primers. Some *zazi*, or glossary primers, as Rawski suggests in her study, may contain very limited terms and vocabulary relating to the Confucian Classics and Confucian doctrines. She also admits, however, that such glossary primers rarely appear to have been used solely in the first stage of elementary education.[17] From this perspective, we can conclude that by and large the basic feature of traditional Chinese literacy primers was to convey various kinds of knowledge, but with Confucian indoctrination at its core.

Studies in English on the education of Chinese children have all devoted some attention to the materials used in teaching children, but few have studied traditional Chinese primers systematically.[18] In China, a systematic introduction to traditional primers is Zhang Zhigong's work, which provides extensive information about the formation, development and use of primers in the traditional Chinese education of children.[19] However, Zhang concentrates only on pedagogy and linguistic teaching in pre-modern China, and his study is informative rather than critical.[20] Recently traditional primers have received much greater attention within China than ever before, but it appears that scholars and publishers are only interested in reprinting the popular ones.[21] This phenomenon might have granted some particular primers the status of "best sellers," but analytical research is almost absent, as the focus is on gathering historical commentaries and translating the classical texts into a modern form so as to make them easily understood by a modern audience.[22]

This study examines the possible role of elementary education in shaping traditional Chinese society and culture by seeking a link between Confucian efforts to create the ideal child and to construct a Confucian society. It is from this perspective that I explore the contents of primers and trace their historical origins which, in turn, reveal the Confucian ideal of childhood and elite attitudes to children. I argue that the desire "to construct a Confucian society" strongly motivated Confucian scholars' devotion to children's education. And at this point, the contents of primers, traditional Chinese attitudes to children and intellectual involvement are integrated into one single history.

C. John Sommerville, a noted historian of Western childhood, warns us to be cautious when studying childhood:

> But *literature* of all sorts only supports a cultural history of 'childhood' — a construct comprised of adult expectations, hopes, and fears concerning the rising generation as opposed to a social history of the actual treatment of children.[23]

This advice I have taken as a guiding principle in my own treatment of childhood.

Thomas Lee applies the same idea to the case of Chinese childhood: "in traditional China 'childhood' was imaged, ... it has been understood more in term of ideal, dream and abstraction. The study of 'childhood' is the study of the history and historiography of this mental construct and its moment of change, ... but not the study of how children have been treated."[24] In the light of this insight, we must interpret the contents of primers and other relevant Confucian writings studied in this book not as the Chinese treatment of children but only as an aspect of the elite view of childhood and elementary education, since this literature reveals more about what a child ought to be than what it was like to be a child.

Since this study intends to connect the contents of primers and the underlying philosophical notions of childhood to the theory and practice of elementary education, Chapter One is devoted to a theoretical exploration of medical writings, philosophical works and other historical documents, aiming to indicate that early Chinese notions of the child, attributes of childhood and the stages of children's development laid a significant foundation for Confucian educational theory.

Chapters Two and Three present a concise history of traditional Chinese primers — their origins, development, genres and role in the education of children. The content of primers and the underlying elite views of children are examined, along with a historical investigation of the various uses and meanings of the term *xiaoxue* (elementary education/elementary learning) in the three dominant Chinese schools of thought — Han Learning, Song Neo-Confucianism and the School of Evidential Research in the Qing. The specifying of this particular term aims to depict the relevant historical conditions within which to explore the changes in the conception of elementary education and the school system; and in turn their impact on the writing of primers. Chapter Two is focused on the origin and the development of wordbooks that mainly served literacy education, and then on Neo-Confucian treatises for moral cultivation. By examining some influential elements other than Neo-Confucianism, such as popular literature and Wang Yangming's teaching, the changes in the format and content of Ming-Qing primers are clarified in Chapter Three. Through this outline history we may see that the writers of primers might have differed in their approaches to the understanding of the essentials of Confucianism, but they held similar views about what the ideal child ought to be, and how elementary education could possibly be effective in fulfilling adults' aspirations for children. Whilst the special format of primers reveals a Chinese acknowledgment of the special nature of children and distinct stages in their physical, intellectual and social development, their contents indicate that the basic nature of primers was sober, aiming to shape the ideal child in accordance with Confucian virtues.

Perhaps in other cultures, even all societies, traditional education was devoted to the achievement of ritualized behaviour. The unique contribution which Song Neo-Confucians made to the Chinese ideas of childhood and education, however, is that they differentiated "elementary education" from "elementary learning" — whilst learning basic literacy skills was the main task of elementary education, elementary learning concentrated on "ritualizing the body." Here "ritualizing the body" referred to a process of controlling the external and then nourishing the internal. The principles involved in this process were also emphasized in a preparatory study for *daxue* (advanced learning) and were practised to promote the process of self-cultivation. This apparently shifted the focus in Han primary schooling from the teaching of characters to moral cultivation. Therefore, it is not surprising that by drawing on sources from the *Record of Rites* (*Liji*), Confucian writers of primers in the late imperial period created numerous guidelines and rules for the practice of rituals and good manners. Moral prescriptions for ritual performance and good manners are examined in Chapter Four, and exemplary figures described in primers are discussed in Chapter Five. An analysis of the primers in this category illustrates a Confucian image of the proper child and the careful design of the Confucian education of children. These two chapters clearly indicate a general Confucian attitude to childhood: to treat children as little adults or perhaps adults-in-training. The final section in Chapter Five looks at exemplary children and childish traits, suggesting that this approach to children even persisted into the Confucian perception of play which, generally speaking, was integrated into the Confucian educational programme rather than being for purely recreational purposes.

To further demonstrate the Confucian efforts to shape the ideal child through education, the primers which serve the requirements of basic training in literacy and numeracy skills are examined in Chapter Six. A textual discussion of the meaning of *xiaoxue* in the School of Evidential Research reveals the Qing evidential scholars' attempts to combine Han Learning with Neo-Confucianism. Reflected in elementary education, this intellectual approach can be interpreted as a reconfirmation of a Chinese pedagogical tradition in which literacy training was by and large integrated with moral and religious instruction. This integration was related to the main task of elementary education: basic training in literacy skills and in "good manners," and underwent little change from the Song through the Qing dynasties.

In the Confucian design, the purpose of shaping the ideal child was to construct an ideal society, so the child was seen as the key to social reform. This can be illustrated by Ming-Qing educators' attempts to educate peasant children as part of their far-reaching social reform programme. In Chapter Seven, the information generated from both literati writings and agricultural manuals points to the fact that, by and large, children of the peasantry were less restricted by Confucian norms than those growing up in elite families. Some Ming-Qing official-scholars were worried about this "childhood freedom," as in their opinion these uneducated peasant children might cause instability in society. Therefore, they devoted themselves to composing primers in colloquial language and to extending education to children in the lower layers of society. In their primers, moral cultivation and the performance of rituals in Song Neo-Confucianism were translated into a more pragmatic approach and the education of children in the peasantry became crucial to the maintenance of social order.

In the second half of the nineteenth century, the traditional practice in education was challenged by reformers and scholars who were sympathetic to reforms. In the face of Western aggression, these reformers also viewed the child as the key to China's survival, but they questioned the effectiveness of traditional education and its contribution to China's future. Information about Western education and the theory of social Darwinism stimulated criticism of the education of children and the traditional Chinese treatment of children. Liang Qichao's (1873–1929) argument that "China ruined children" physically, intellectually and psychologically expresses this intellectual climate well. In the May Fourth era cultural reformers went even further, as they saw children "more dead than alive"; and filial piety, Lu Xun (1881–1936) charged, sacrificed children for the sake of their parents' happiness.[25]

In attempting to demonstrate a late nineteenth-century intellectual search for an alternative education for children, the primer written by Lin Shu (1852–1924), and Liang Qichao's proposal for the reform of children's education and his design for a new type of primer on the eve of the 1898 Reform are examined in Chapter Eight. This approach is defined by the fact that works on modern Chinese intellectual history have looked into the intellectual mood of the May Fourth era, revealing a denial of Confucian teaching, especially the virtue of filial piety.[26] How the intellectual minds of this period were formed is also illustrated in the stories about a generation of Chinese intellectuals from 1890 to 1920 who received a Confucian education, but who, in the face of China's problems, began to re-appraise what they had been taught.[27] Both Lin Shu and Liang Qichao certainly belonged to this generation, but this study does not cover May Fourth history. The aim here is to illustrate how the search for a modern education for children was linked closely to China's struggle for survival in a social Darwinist sense; an analysis of Lin Shu's primer and Liang's proposals prior to the 1898 Reform serves this purpose well.

Unlike modern scholars who often use historical comparisons to test the validity of existing theoretical hypotheses and to reach new causal generalizations, Chinese intellectuals of the late nineteenth century, such as Lin Shu and Liang Qichao, saw Western achievements in modern sciences and technology as factual references, and they pointed to them in an attempt to establish factors affecting China's adaptation to modern civilization. Of all the Western nations, Liang Qichao admired England most; before the 1898 Reform his term "Western education" often referred to English education. This seems to coincide with a modern scholarly approach in which England is usually used as a bench-mark in the study of industrialization. This study thus ends with a discussion focusing on Liang's vision of a modern Chinese education that synthesized Western ideas and practice with Chinese tradition. It is from this specific perspective and through the critical eyes of Liang and his generation of intellectuals that we see the characteristics of the traditional Chinese education of children. It is also through their insightful accounts that we begin to understand how children and the education of children were closely linked to the fate of China, as at that particular time Chinese traditional child-rearing and education were challenged by a crisis that threatened the survival of the whole nation.

Chinese Historical Chronology

The Three Dynasties:
  Xia dynasty   *c.* 2100–1600 B.C.
  Shang dynasty   *c.* 1600–1100 B.C.
  Zhou dynasty:
    Western Zhou   *c.* 1100–771 B.C.
    Eastern Zhou: 770–256 B.C.
      Spring and Autumn Period   770–476 B.C.
      Warring States Period   475–221 B.C.

Qin dynasty   221–207 B.C.

Han dynasty:
  Former (or Western) Han   206 B.C.–A.D. 24
  Later (or Eastern) Han   25–220

Three Kingdoms   220–280

Western Jin dynasty   265–316

Eastern Jin dynasty   317–420

The Northern and Southern Dynasties:
  Southern Dynasties:
    Song   420–479
    Southern Qi   479–502
    Liang   502–557
    Chen   557–589
  Northern Dynasties:
    (Northern) Wei   386–534
    Eastern Wei   534–550

~ *Chapter 1* ~

The Education of Children: The Chinese Approach

Vulnerability and innocence were perceived as the basic characteristics of children, so a major purpose of education in traditional Chinese society was to protect children. This overall conception of children was well embedded in conventional beliefs and common practice in rearing children in the past and even in present-day Chinese society. This chapter examines this Chinese understanding of children and attributes of childhood as it was closely linked to Confucian educational theory. The early Confucian concept of man are brought into this discussion, along with medical views of human development, as a philosophical framework within which conventional beliefs and philosophical notions of children's development are interpreted and analysed.

The Vulnerable Child: Its Biological Characteristics

To the ancient Chinese, the vulnerability of the child was clearly indicated in the means used to protect newborns, such as swaddling clothes. Wrapping newborns in swaddling clothes was a traditional practice in most societies, and was believed to mould then protect the infant's body. The ancient Chinese practice was reflected in words such as zi 子, one of the most common words for children. One interpretation for the early form of this character emphasises the two arms of a new-born child but not two legs, as Chinese scholars generally agree "that the undivided line downwards suggests the enwrapping swaddling clothes confining and concealing the infant's legs."[1] Furthermore, two Chinese words referring to swaddling clothes are associated with the word meaning protection (*bao* 保).[2]

The ancient Chinese also observed some aspects of a newborn's helplessness, such as not being able to walk and needing to be carried and cuddled. The word meaning "carry" or "cuddle" sometimes also referred to infancy.[3] This extended meaning of the word indicates to a certain extent the ancient Chinese understanding of the different stages in a child's development.

The infant's inability to walk was well recognised in both medical and historical documents before and during the Han period. For instance, the *Book of the Rites by the Elder Dai* (*Da Dai Liji*) clearly stated that newborns were not able to walk until they reached one year old.[4] Ancient Chinese medical authorities clarified more specifically the stages of the newborn's development. It was recorded that six months after birth the infant ought to be starting to sit up, as by then its buttocks had become firm enough; two hundred days after birth the infant ought to be able to crawl, due to the development of its hands; a three-hundred-day-old infant ought to be able to stand without support, due to the development of its kneecaps; a one-year-old infant ought to be able to walk, as its knees were fully developed.[5] In modern judgement, an infant can be helped to sit up at six months old by being supported in a pram or a high chair. It seems the ancient Chinese view was similar to that of modern paediatrics, but the latter regards the ability of an infant to sit as a certain stage of the development of the head and back rather than only the buttocks. Also the infant's ability to crawl, in the modern view, may be attributed to its ability to bear weight on one hand; at forty-four weeks, a modern infant is able to crawl on hands and knees and stand; at fifty-two weeks it is able to walk with one hand held.[6] At this point, the observations made by the ancient Chinese on early child development do not conflict with modern medical opinions at all. More significantly, the ancient Chinese medical specialists urged wet nurses to teach infant babies how to sit, crawl, stand and walk in accordance with each stage in growth and maturation, and not to spoil them by carrying and cuddling them all the time. The implication was that if the appropriate time to teach the infant these essential steps was missed, this would stop it growing strong, as its bones and muscles would not be strengthened properly without learning these basic skills. Worst of all was the possibility that the infant might be disabled due to weak muscles in its legs and lower back.[7]

Other physical characteristics of the infant and the young child, such as its teeth and hair, were also observed by the ancient Chinese. *The Yellow Emperor's Classic of Internal Medicine* (*Huangdi neijing*), the most authoritative source of traditional Chinese medical doctrine, regarded the transition from primary to permanent dentition as an important stage in a child's growth and maturation, closely connected with the full development of the kidney system. In *Basic Questions* (*Suwen*), we read: "When a girl enters the seventh year of her life, her kidney *qi*[8] is abundant and therefore her teeth start to change [from primary to permanent dentition] and her hair is growing [longer and thicker].... When a boy enters the eighth year of his life, his kidney *qi* is abundant, so his hair is growing and his teeth enter a transition period."[9] Although the title of this medical work ascribes its authorship to the legendary Yellow Emperor (2697–2597 B.C.), modern scholarship believes that this is the work of several authors, compiled in the first century B.C. or early first century A.D., and "a great part of the text existed during the Han Dynasty."[10] This suggests that by the Han period this dental developmental stage was seen by the Chinese medical world as a part of a child's total development.

This early Chinese understanding of the development of the human body was accepted without any challenge throughout the entire late imperial period, and was close to modern medical views. Modern dentistry, however, relates the factors affecting the eruption pattern to "heredity, systematic disease or localised pathologic conditions"[11] rather than only to the development of the kidney system.

What is more important to our study of the traditional Chinese view of childhood is that the terms used to describe this dental process and movement were borrowed to refer to childhood and to children at the age of seven or eight *sui*.[12] This integration of professional terminology into daily language is an indication of the Chinese recognition of children's characteristics in classical times.[13]

In traditional Chinese medical theory, hair too was seen as a significant index of young children's growth and development, and thus words relating to the characteristics of the child's hair were also used for childhood. The classical example is the word *tong*, which generally stands for children under the age of fifteen.[14] Yet *tong* in its original use refers to bare hills, and young lambs and calves which have not yet grown horns.[15] The bare hill was used as a metaphor to illustrate the status of the infant's hair, as the ancient Chinese believed that full-growing hair had to wait till a girl reached seven and a boy eight, when their kidney system was fully developed. Yet the analogy between young children's hair and the ungrown horns of lambs and calves gives the word the meaning of young and not yet grown-up, which was further extend to refer to children in general.

The shaving of the infant's head a month after its birth was one of the important rituals of infancy, as both medical rationale and conventional belief then held that getting rid of "foetal hair" would contribute to the growing of thicker hair and prevent it from falling out in later life. Furthermore, the first shaving of an infant's head was seen as a signal of its entering the social world for the first time, and was therefore conducted in a very serious way, for instance, the ceremony had to be carried out on an auspicious day.[16] After the first shaving, later hair cuts usually shaved the crown but left two circles of hair, one above each ear, or even a whole ring on the top or at the back of the shaved head. This style was derived from the analogy between the child's tufts and the ungrown horns of lambs and calves, as mentioned above. An ungrown horn in Chinese was called *jiao*, so the tufts of hair on the heads of children were given a similar name (*zongjiao*), which was often used in Chinese literature as a general term for childhood.[17] The particular terms used for the child's hair, hairstyle and the shaving of the head were all used in literature and historical documents to refer to children and some of the attributes of childhood.[18] This can be seen as a recognition of the attributes of childhood in ancient China.

This kind of recognition is also represented in traditional Chinese paintings of children. In his pioneering work on the history of childhood, Aries sees the naked body of a child in pictures as a very important signal of the discovery of childhood in the West. He argues that before the seventeenth century children in paintings often appeared as "miniature adults" — depicted fully dressed, without any characteristics of childhood, and looking more like adults, only on a reduced scale. This rejection of the special features of children, Aries concludes, is one indication that it was not until the seventeenth century that there was an identifiable concept of childhood in the West.[19] Many scholars are opposed to this argument, pointing out that the way a child's body was depicted has more to do with technical improvements in art than changes in attitudes towards children.[20] In Chinese literati painting, the child's body, by and large, was not proportioned and shaped in a distinctive manner. This refusal to accept child morphology stemmed not only from moral concerns but also from the characteristics of Chinese figure painting, which never paid attention to human morphology. The three-dimensional techniques used in Western figure painting did not exist in traditional Chinese painting before the influence of Western realism.[21] Consequently, the Chinese scholar-painters (*wenren huajia*) of the child made no distinction between children and adults, avoiding the naked body where the accurate proportions of that body would have to be portrayed. Rather, they focused on children's charms. Here the term "children's charms" refers to special features of childhood, including particular hairstyles. However, some presentations of the child in Chinese folk art, such as fat babies in New Year's prints, not only display "children's charms" but are also distinct from images of adults.

The Early Chinese Concept of Man and the Innocence of Children

Apart from the lack of physical competence, the intellectual limitations of children were perceived by the ancient Chinese as special features in which "young" and "ignorant" were naturally connected. The word *tong* therefore also stands for ignorance and stupidity.[22] This seems to suggest a very negative attitude toward children. For example, as early as the pre-Qin era, children's ignorance was used as a metaphor to mock those adults who were too stupid to discuss any serious business.[23] Expressions such as "Your intelligence is at a child's level" were often used to pour scorn on an adult's intellectual inferiority. An adult's naivety or poor judgement was also regarded as childish,[24] and all uneducated people were seen as ignorant as a child.[25] Children's intellectual shortcomings are also illustrated in the compounds formed with *tong*, such as *tongmeng*, meaning ignorant, uneducated and unenlightened.

In the early Chinese concept of man, however, children's intellectual incompetence and physical imperfections were seen as their special traits and the prerequisites for human growth and development. The early Chinese philosophers saw man as one of the creatures of Nature, and thus while the human infant shared animal characteristics, such as the need to eat, drink and sleep, the human mind was a unique attribute of man. Because of this unique attribute, an ignorant baby was destined to develop its potentiality.[26] Its potential to develop was expressed by Xun Zi in the word *sheng* 生.[27] There are two meanings of this word: the first means life and the second, to produce. In Chinese philosophy, the first meaning of *sheng* was an acknowledgement of man's innate endowment that was not acquired but gifted from Heaven. It was from this perspective, that the early philosophers argued that man shared his characteristics with animals. Yet the second meaning of *sheng* referred only to man, whose ability to produce and to learn differentiated him from other animals.

Nevertheless, in the early Confucian classics the human species' unique ability was vaguely linked with the heart, as the ancient Chinese thought that the heart was the organ for thinking, and the brain, like the marrow and the bones, was one of the storing organs produced by the earth.[28] Accordingly, the early Chinese philosophers used the term *xin* or mind-and-heart loosely and sometimes confusingly — referring either to mind, or feelings, or to innate behaviour — and as a result their views of human nature (*xing*) differed.

In Mencius' philosophy, human nature contained not only five senses (hearing, sight, smell, taste and touch) but also four innate feelings — pity (*ceyin zhi xin*), shame (*xiu e zhi xin*), respect (*gongjing zhi xin*), and the sense of right and wrong (*shifei zhi xin*) — which were interrelated with the virtues of humanity (*ren*), justice (*yi*), the rites (*li*) and wisdom (*zhi*). Mencius stated that all these feelings and their related virtues were natural endowments — "we have them within ourselves."[29] For example, said Mencius, "seeing a child about to fall into a well, everyone has a feeling of horror and distress (*chuti ceyin*)" that was, he asserted, "the first sign of humanity."[30]

Xun Zi disagreed with Mencius, arguing that this kind of spontaneous response to stimulus was human physiological nature which, like the five senses (human biological nature), was not acquired or learned but inherent. Likes and dislikes, delight and anger, grief and joy, were human emotions (*qing*), not human nature; the activity of the mind-and-heart (*lü*) enabled man to make a choice from these emotions. Xun Zi concluded that human nature, emotions and the use of the mind were different in terms of their nature and functions, and should not be confused.[31] After clarifying these terms and their uses, Xun Zi further explained that *zhi*, the capacity to know, was the special faculty of the human species. According to him, the mind possessed an over-all understanding, but it had always to rely on the senses to receive data.[32] To use human beings' special capacity to acquire knowledge was where human wisdom came from.[33]

This philosophical debate on human nature and Xun Zi's efforts to discriminate between innate human capacity and virtue, feelings and knowledge were due in part to the confusion between ideas about the functions of the heart and the brain in classical times. It was not until the late sixteenth century that some Chinese scholars, after encountering Western knowledge of the human body, realised that man's intellectual capacity was not stored in the heart but connected with the development of the brain. For example, Fang Yizhi (1611–1671) clearly stated that man's intelligence had much to do with the quality of the brain.[34] Wang Fuzhi (1619–1692) made an explicit comparison between the human infant and the newborn animal, pointing out that the infant's incompetence at walking, eating, speaking and its need to be taken care of were actually unique to man, as these imperfections provided human beings with the potential to develop (*ke jin zhi neng*). This was because, Wang continued, man possessed the intellectual organ — the brain — which would allow human beings to outgrow all the limitations they shared with animals.[35] Based on this knowledge, Wang Fuzhi further developed Mencius' and Xun Zi's concepts of human nature, but placed the emphasis on man's capacity to learn, saying that this element of human nature enabled man to develop every day and to transform himself from imperfection to perfection through learning.[36] This process, which Wang Fuzhi expressed as *risheng richeng*, or producing and developing everyday, is similar to a certain extent to the theory of Erik Erikson (1902–1994) who believes that "people continue to grow and change right through their lives, from birth to death."[37]

In the view of Mencius, the child's spontaneous responses to its parents were innate human social tendencies which, he believed, were inherently good. Therefore he advocated returning to the child's innocence of mind (*chizi zhi xin*)[38] so as to seek humanity, justice, wisdom and reverence.[39] According to him, the child's mind or innocence was a natural endowment, differentiating man from animals. Although he admitted that a man could be made to do evil, he argued that this had nothing to do with his nature but only happened under the pressure of some exterior force.[40] Here Mencius' appreciation of the child's innocence appears similar to Taoist teaching, which held that only the ignorant baby lived a truly natural life. Yet Mencius' thesis that "human nature is good" is opposed to Xun Zi's view.

Xun Zi, too, noticed the original simplicity and naivety of the child which, he agreed with Mencius, was good. However, speaking of human nature in general, he argued that "man's nature is evil," because man "is born with a fondness for profit"[41] which, in his view, was the origin of desires and caused disharmony. This was why, Xun Zi further maintained, the ancient kings established ritual principles to "curb it, to train men's desires and to provide for their satisfaction."[42]

In brief, the early Chinese concept of man and the essential acknowledgement in both medical and philosophical writings of the special capacity of human beings present a positive attitude towards children's physical and intellectual limitations. Although Mencius and Xun Zi differed in their views of human nature, both of them appreciated the child's innocence and reached the same conclusion that education and environment were the two significant factors in human moral development. These views contributed significantly to the Confucian outlook on children and the attributes of childhood.

"Foetal Education" and the Early Development of the Child

Along with the belief in the natural equality of all men and man's unique abilities, Confucian writers also saw the significance of environmental factors in the child's intellectual and especially moral development. Although Xun Zi believed that "man's nature is evil," he noticed that "children born among the Han or Yüe people of the south and among the Mo barbarians of the north cry with the same voice at birth, but as they grow older they follow different customs. Education causes them to differ."[43] He went on to use analogies, such as pigweed growing up straight without any support because it was in the midst of hemp, white sand turning black as the result of being mixed up with mud, and the unpleasant smell of the root of a certain orchid (*zhi*)[44] due to contamination by urine, to emphasise the power of external forces.[45] Xun Zi's view represents the early Chinese way of thinking in which external forces included foetal environment, the community the child lived in, and the socio-economic setting.

The foetal environment was believed by the ancient Chinese to have a significant impact not only on the developing foetus but also on the child's temperament and moral status after its birth and in its later life. This idea is known as "foetal education" (*taijiao*), and was said to have originated in the legendary period. Yet the thesis was well elaborated in the Han period, when pre-Han examples were frequently quoted in scholarly writings to confirm and develop the theory. Among these examples, the mothers of the legendary kings of Wen and Cheng in the Zhou dynasty and the mother of Mencius are the three most noteworthy cases. During pregnancy these three mothers were all said to have applied strict discipline to their own behaviour, maintaining correct posture while standing and sitting, and seeing, hearing and speaking no evil. This was believed to have contributed to the formation of the personality and moral character of Mencius and the two sage kings.[46]

These stories appear very foreign or even absurd to modern minds, yet they are linked with a medical theory called *waixiang neigan*, namely that the senses perceive external phenomena and then transmit them to inside the body, and influence the body's system. This theory is related to the traditional Chinese knowledge of the human body, which was closely connected with traditional Chinese cosmogony. The creation of the universe was attributed to the Yin and the Yang, which were responsible for "the transformation to parenthood," and were the "root and source of life and death."[47] These two cosmic forces were also held to be the two regulators under which the human body, in response to the five elements (water, wood, metal, fire and earth), had five viscera (*zang*)[48] and six bowels (*fu*). Both intellectual[49] and emotional functions were held to depend on the five viscera, in which the five climates (rain, fine weather, heat, cold and wind) were transformed to create the five sentiments (joy, anger, sympathy, grief and fear).[50] This theory emphasized a natural bond between the mother's womb and the foetus. Zhu Zhenheng (1281–1358), a prominent medical practitioner of the Yuan dynasty, elaborated this idea. He pointed out that the foetus shared the same body with the mother, so if the mother had an unsuitable diet or suffered from illness (including mental instability) this was very likely to contribute to foetal poisoning. Foetal poisoning would be transmitted inside the body to "contaminate" the life energy and blood; then the "contaminated" life energy and blood would damage the five viscera which, as the "environment" for the foetus, would in turn affect not only the developing foetus but also the child's health in its first two years.[51]

The idea of "foetal education" was widely accepted as an authoritative theory as well as a conventional belief; but some doubts were raised to challenge this thesis: if the mother's encounters with external phenomena were so powerful and important in shaping a child's future character, how could Shun and Confucius have become great sages, since Shun's parents were intractable, and Confucius' father was an adulterer? Also, if an illegitimate child like Confucius could grow up to be a sage, it might be suggested that "foetal education" was not after all so vital to a child's future.[52]

Nevertheless, foetal poisoning was no doubt a serious threat to children's lives and health, so the theory of foetal education often urged pregnant women to be cautious about their diet and lifestyle. This theory also laid the foundation for serious concerns about the physical and moral qualities of wet nurses, as it was believed that after giving birth, the life energy and blood of a woman went to form her milk, which then became a crucial channel for the transmission not only of physical attributes or diseases but also of moral character from the mother or wet nurse to the child. Therefore, from the Han through to the Qing dynasty writers about infant care repeatedly urged parents to examine the physical and moral qualities of wet nurses very carefully.[53]

The serious concerns about the moral character of wet nurses were also attributed to the Confucian emphasis on the social world into which the infant was born. This social world in a narrow sense referred to the people around the infant, including parents, kin, wet nurses and servants (if in a wealthy family). This definition of the social world for a neonate is based on the ancient Chinese timetable for the infant's biological and cognitive development. The early Chinese medical specialists reckoned that "at sixty days the infant's eyesight is formed, and it will smile and identify people. Wet nurses must not let strangers hold or carry it. Don't allow it to see strange things."[54] This theory, originating in an ancient medical text and quoted by Zhu Duanzhang of the Song, was adopted by later generations of medical advisers.[55] On the surface this advice seems only to place stress on giving the infant a tranquil and protective environment.[56] Yet bearing in mind the Chinese understanding of the human body, one may see that the advice actually acknowledged a milestone in the infant's development — visual maturation. By modern standards, "few normal full term babies reach eight weeks of age without having begun to smile," otherwise they may prove to be "mentally subnormal," or blind or autistic.[57] And more importantly, in the modern view smiling at this stage differs from the neonatal smile, as the infant is looking at its mother while smiling — a sign of the beginning of social interactions,[58] and a good indicator of the infant's emotional state. Modern medical specialists also agree that once the infant can identify people, this perception provides a prerequisite for social responsiveness, although they still argue over whether the infant's smile at this stage should be taken as a specifically social gesture.[59] From this point of view, we may see the logic behind traditional Chinese medical advice that parents should be cautious about the infant's very first encounter with its social surroundings. This effort to prevent the infant from being disturbed by strangers and strange things was meant to prevent any psychophysical instability in the early months, as the ancient Chinese were aware of the possible impact of external perceptions on the infant's emotional and moral development, as well as its biological growth.

The Significance of *Xi* or "Practice" in the Child's Moral Development

The above discussion suggests that the ancient Chinese caution about external forces was rigorously put into practice in rearing children in traditional Chinese society. This was clearly highlighted by the introduction of both the concept of *xi* or "practice" and the philosophical notion of human nature into education for children. Confucius said: "By nature, men are nearly alike; by practice, they get to be wide apart."[60] Mencius believed that all men at birth were good and that evil actions did not emanate from nature but were due to different circumstances.[61] As discussed earlier, Xun Zi regarded external phenomena as one of the most crucial factors in a child's growth, and stressed the need to employ rites to "construct" the social man. This early Confucian teaching became accepted as a conventional belief and dominated the Chinese mind for centuries. In one of the most popular primers in premodern China, *The Trimetrical Classic*, this Confucian dictum was simply adopted as the opening sentence: "When men are first born, their nature is nearly the same; but their practice [later] grows wide apart."[62] "Practice" here can be interpreted as perception of external phenomena, including the surroundings where the child was brought up, and the things the child encountered in its day-to-day life.

Both philosophers and medical specialists in classical times agreed that the continuous interaction of the dual forces of Yin and Yang lay behind all natural phenomena, including the constitution and functioning of the human body. Ancient Chinese philosophers, however, placed more emphasis on *xi* or "practice" in the development of men's moral character, while medical authorities attributed the differences in personality and moral character to an individual's biological difference which, from a medical point of view, was determined by the Yin and Yang forces in the human body. According to *The Yellow Emperor's Classic of Internal Medicine*, a greedy person was one whose Yin force was too strong; a jealous person was one whose Yin force was too weak; a headstrong person was one whose Yang force was too strong, which caused the person to talk too much but do little; a self-centred person was one whose Yang force was weak which made him/her feel self-important all the time. These four types of character deficiency were attributed to the imbalance of the Yin and Yang forces in the human body, and the perfect person was one whose Yin and Yang were well balanced, so that he/she was quiet but pleasant, brave but modest.[63] According to this statement, the blending and adjusting of the two forces in the human body was therefore essential not only for physical health but also for moral perfection.

However, philosophers believed that moral differences were not a result of natural differences conferred by Heaven but a result of living conditions. Mencius said: "In good years the children of the people are mostly good, while in bad years most of them abandon themselves to evil."[64] Mencius emphasized that in an economically insecure environment, no man was likely to perceive and perform the right actions.

Han Ying, an eminent philosopher of the Han period, held the same view: "In peaceful years, people have no need to work overtime, men and women are able to get married at the appropriate time, dutiful sons are able to take care of their parents. There are no men and women who reach the age for marriage but are not able to marry. There are no violent fathers or undutiful sons. The relationships between father and son, husband and wife are in harmony, and therefore the whole of society is at peace, and the country is secure — there are no wars or rebellions."[65] But Han Ying knew what ordinary people were afraid of — hunger and thirst, which would affect their life energy and blood; and bad weather conditions, that would damage their skin and muscles. With this understanding of what people desired and feared, Han Ying went on to point out that a man would not be able to act like a man with virtue if he did not have clothes to cover his body; and he would not be able to behave like an upright gentleman if he did not have enough to eat. This was why, Han Ying reckoned, the legendary kings worked in the fields while their wives were responsible for sericulture, as they regarded feeding and clothing people as the most important jobs in government.[66]

Han Ying went on to address the relationship between education and man's moral development. From the perspective of human nature, Han Ying realised that everyone liked to see beautiful colours, to hear pleasant music, to taste delicious food, to be able to rest and enjoy leisure time, and to wear good clothes, which were not only light and warm but also beautifully embroidered. These needs, he said, were human desires (*qing*); ancient kings educated people by satisfying their basic needs first and then guiding them to conduct in accordance with the rites.[67] Han Ying concluded that education would be effective only when people were guaranteed a secure livelihood.[68]

These early philosophical notions were inherited and developed through the centuries. Yet it was not until the seventeenth century that the discovery of the function of the brain and the encounter with some Western medical knowledge enabled the thinkers of the time to clarify more precise the relations between the material force (*qi*), the material form (*zhi*), and "practice" (*xi*). To Wang Fuzhi, what *The Yellow Emperor's Classic of Internal Medicine* said about the connection between the Yin and Yang forces in the human body and man's moral character was only partly true, as it took into account only the material forms and ignored the material force, which Wang regarded as the creative principle and in which everything in the universe was contained. This point was not new but a philosophical heritage which Wang explored further. He said that there was only one principle of the material force, but under this principle, there were multiple material forms. More importantly, Wang Fuzhi saw the process of change as the characteristic of this material force and the potential for multiple forms to develop. Based on this theory, Wang Fuzhi addressed the relationship between the human body and man's moral character, saying that human biological nature was the same but the form it took varied, and this form was set from birth and could not be changed. Yet the material force was in a daily process of change, which thus provided the potential to transfer from the stupid to the intelligent, the weak to the strong. At this point, human nature was connected with the material force, not the material form, and the principle of the material force expressed in the process of change was an inalienable characteristic, which in turn gave human nature the potential to change, and "practice" was involved in this process of change. From this point of view, Wang Fuzhi reached the conclusion that the ability to undertake such "practice" was the potential to develop within the change of the material force. Although the human body was a given, man's moral character was formed after birth and developed in the process of growth and maturation that were characterised by daily practice.[69]

The concept of "practice" in Chinese philosophy was consistently defined as environmental factors and learning activities. By the seventeenth century, thinkers had further broadened the definition. Such elements as the changing times, social customs, family history and background, parents' personality and interests were all thought to contribute to the environment the child was born into, and to become decisive factors in the child's moral development.

To elaborate the connection between man's inherent nature and environmental influence, Huang Zongxi (1610–1695) used a simile in which man's inherent nature was like pure water and the environment where the man lived was like a vessel. Whether the water would remain clean was determined by whether the vessel was clean. If the vessel was filthy, the water would be contaminated by its unpleasant smell; and in a muddy vessel the water would naturally turn turbid.[70] In this metaphor, Huang Zongxi was referring to the mother's womb as well as the social environment as "the vessel" and its related "practice." Yan Yuan (1635–1704) also rejected the idea of the inherently evil character of human nature, maintaining that the evil acts of man were due to material "temptations," such as seductive music and sensual pleasures.[71]

Although the concept of man and human nature in Chinese philosophical thought differed to a certain extent from the medical view, Chinese thinkers, many of whom acted as teachers, never ignored individual physical differences in the teaching process. As mentioned earlier, *The Yellow Emperor's Classic of Internal Medicine* argued that the Yin and Yang forces determined personality and human character. The idea was borrowed by scholars in their search for a suitable approach to cultivating life energy and the mind-and-heart (*zhiqi yangxin*). For instance, Han Ying stated that a person with a strong personality should be taught to compromise; a suspicious person should be taught to trust people; a brave person should be encouraged to use his/her intelligence; meditation should be introduced to an active person, and lofty ideals to a person who was depressed or to a person who was too greedy. He also suggested teaching a sociable and generous person the relationship between teachers and students; comforting a person with low self-respect when he/she was in trouble; praising an agreeable person by using rites and music.[72] In sum, the content and methods of teaching should be varied in accordance with different personalities.

By the seventeenth century, philosophers had identified the biological body and its relationship with moral character more specifically. In the theory of the time, the biological body as the material carrier of the moral character contained two directions in moral development, e. g., a person with too much Yang in him could be either brave or violent; whether he turned out to be brave or violent entirely depended on the "practice" or *xi* after birth. Furthermore, the inherent imperfection could also be improved through "practice."[73]

The Appropriate Age for the Beginning of Children's Schooling

The ancient Chinese debate on the appropriate age for children to start school is associated with the different understandings of the stages in children's growth. The *Record of Rites* is the most authoritative source concerning education programmes for children at different stages. According to this text, the childhood of a boy spans from birth to the age of twenty when he is given a capping ceremony, called *guanli*, symbolising entry into adulthood and the end of childhood. Within these twenty years, there are ten stages for boys: (1) in the first year when the baby can eat food, he should be taught to use his right hand; (2) in the third year when the baby boy has just learned how to speak, he should be taught to reply appropriately to adults; (3) in the sixth year the child should be taught numerals and the names of the points of the compass; (4) in the seventh year, the child should be taught to separate himself from girls; (5) in the eighth year the child should be taught to respect his elders, for example, always walking behind them and sitting at table only after they have been seated; (6) in the ninth year, the child should be taught dates; (7) in the tenth year, a more formal education starts, namely the child is sent out to a teacher and learns the basic skills such as reading, writing and calculating, as well as children's rituals; (8) in the thirteenth year, the child should be taught music and songs as well as the ritual dance called *shao*; (9) the fifteenth year is the beginning of the last stage of childhood, in which he starts to learn the dance called *xiang* as well as shooting and driving a carriage; and (10) when the child reaches twenty, he is given a "courtesy" name at his capping ceremony, signifying his entry into adulthood, and has the privileges of learning adult rituals and dressing like an adult, in fur or silk clothes.[74]

For a girl the first six years are very similar, but in the seventh year she is supposed to lead a separate life. In the tenth year, she is supposed to learn skills in sericulture and textiles; and in the fifteenth year she is given a capping ceremony (*ji*) if she is already engaged to be married; otherwise she may not be given such a ceremony until she reaches twenty.[75]

The dynamic of these ten stages of childhood lies in its formulation of a fundamental framework for the theory of the child's education and development in pre-modern China. For more than two thousand years traditional Chinese educational theory and practice rarely went beyond this framework. From a linguistic perspective, we may merge these ten stages into four periods: the first six years after birth, the seventh year, the tenth year and the fifteenth year. A set of vocabulary can be found to correspond to each specific stage.

The ancient Chinese saw the first six years after birth as early childhood, and paid special attention to the attributes of infants and toddlers, as indicated in the words *ying* (infants) and *ru* (toddlers). The original meaning of *ying* was chest, from which the meaning that the infant was carried by the mother close to her chest and was breast-fed by her was generated, and then was further extended to refer to the infant. The word *ru*, originally meaning weak, characterised the toddler's physical state.[76] The emphasis on the child's physical weakness reflects ancient Chinese anxiety over the child's survival, as mortality rates at that time were high.

It was not until the seventh year that the child was considered to have passed the most dangerous period, so the word *dao* was used to express the grief over the death of a child at this age.[77] In the seventh year, the child started the transition from baby teeth to permanent teeth. The ancient Chinese also believed that in this year the child developed well not only in aspects of basic capacity, such as walking, eating and speaking, but also in its emotional progress, namely that it began to know shame and embarrassment. So this became another meaning of the word *dao*. Meanwhile, the child was believed to understand social gender, so the *Record of Rites* strongly recommended that separation between boys and girls should start at this stage. Evidently, in ancient China it was at this stage that the child began to be treated as an actual social being, with confidence in its physical, intellectual and emotional maturity. Before this age, according to Zhou law, the child did not have legal responsibility for any wrongdoing.[78] Clearly, the seventh year was a landmark in the child's development. It was based on this notion that the age of eight in Chinese terms was then considered an appropriate age for the beginning of elementary schooling.

The word *you* was used to mark the child's entry into the tenth year of its life. The linguistic explanation for the word was that *you* stood for few (*shao*), meaning the child had not been in the world for a long time.[79] Historically, as stated in the *Record of Rites*, a boy in his tenth year ought to be sent to an outside master where he might even take lodgings, while a girl started to be trained seriously for womanhood.[80]

In traditional Chinese understanding, the fifteenth year in a child's life marked a transitional period from childhood to adulthood. So the word *chengtong* was used to name this special period and to differentiate children of that age from children under fifteen in Chinese terms. According to *The Yellow Emperor's Classic of Internal Medicine,* when a girl reached fourteen and a boy sixteen, their kidney systems were well developed and they acquired their reproductive capacities.[81] Obviously, this medical canon measures the maturity of the human body from a biological perspective, so the acquisition of reproductive capacities was seen as a signal of entering adulthood. According to the *Record of Rites,* a capping ceremony in the Zhou symbolised the acceptance of the child into adulthood; yet a boy was given such a ceremony at twenty, and a girl at fifteen only if she was engaged, otherwise at twenty. After this ceremony, he or she was recognised as an adult and would be allowed to get married. However, as child concubines were often purchased by rich households even before they reached seven, an alternative was needed — child concubines would not be given a capping ceremony until they acquired reproductive capacities.[82]

There were different views regarding an appropriate age for marriage in the pre-Han era. One was that in very early days men got married at the age of fifty and women at thirty; and in mid-antiquity, men started a family at the age of thirty and women at twenty. Doubts about this were raised by scholars in the Han. For instance, Dai De (first century B.C.) argued that if this was the case, how could the sage King Wen in the Zhou have fathered King Wu when he was only fifteen?[83] According to the *Spring and Autumn Annals with Zuo's Commentary (Chunqiu zuozhuan),* kings could be married at the age of fifteen as they needed heirs; but ordinary people were supposed to have a family when men were thirty and women twenty.

The importance of the above argument to this study is that marriage was seen as a delimitation between childhood and adulthood. Although there were different proposals for an appropriate age for marriage, by the Han most scholars agreed that the *chengtong* referred to children between the ages of fifteen and twenty in Chinese terms, a stage for advanced learning and completing the transition from childhood to adulthood, while the age from eight to fifteen was considered to be for elementary schooling.

It was recorded by scholars in the Han and thereafter that in the Zhou dynasty the sons of the emperors and other aristocratic children started their schooling at eight.[84] In this ideal, aristocratic childhood children were under the system of protection and teaching (*baofu*) from the moment they were born. This system consisted of three male elders: one acted as *bao* to protect the child's health; the *fu* focused on its moral development and the *shi* concentrated on knowledge instruction.[85] As well as this system, the system of "three mothers" was employed both in the palace and among aristocratic families in the Zhou dynasty to nurse and teach children.[86] However, scholars in the Han were not interested in the details of these systems as they had ceased to be used in rearing and educating children. Most Han scholars adopted this ideal example simply to emphasise the importance of early education for children, and to seek out an appropriate age for starting schooling. It was generally agreed that children ought to go to school at eight.[87]

In brief, an appropriate age for children to start schooling was established in accordance with the ancient Chinese understanding of different stages in the child's development. The early Confucian concept of man brought into the discussion unfolds a positive Chinese attitude toward the child's physical and intellectual incompetence and imperfection, which were generally appreciated to be part of the child's innocence. This innocence, together with other special features of children, such as their hairstyles, was seen as an integral part of the child's characteristics. Furthermore, their confidence in the ability of man to learn helped the ancient Chinese perceive the child's limitations as the potential for development and prerequisites for education.

However, the child's potential for development was conditioned by "external forces" which, according to both philosophers and educators, were particularly vital to the child's physical, intellectual and moral development. The "external forces," broadly defined as "environmental factors," had multiple layers, including the "foetal environment," living conditions and the child's daily encounters with things and people, as well as the socioeconomic setting. The popularity of the theory of "foetal education" is indicative of Chinese faith in the power of external forces to affect the child's moral development in particular. This "foetal education" was believed to be effective as soon as the child was conceived.

It is also noticeable that the ancient Chinese made intellectual efforts to differentiate children from adults against the background of a philosophical debate on human nature. In other words, the child was comprehended as one stage in the whole development of the human being, promising an on-going process of change from imperfection to perfection, and from incompetence to competence. Both Mencius and Xun Zi's views about human nature constituted a basic framework for later schools of thought to carry on this philosophical discourse within which, generally speaking, inherent human nature was carefully distinguished from moral qualities and intellectual ability. Most thinkers agreed that moral character and intelligence were acquired and developed through the process of *xi* or practice. This notion not only justifies the child's potential to outgrow the limitations it shares with animals, but also highlights the two significant factors in human moral and intellectual development: education and environment. From this perspective, we may conclude that the ancient Chinese conceptions of children and the attributes of childhood laid a foundation for Confucian educational theory.

Chapter 2

Primers and the Establishment of Confucian Education

Traditional Chinese primers are of considerable significance to the study of the history of Chinese elementary education which, in pre-modern China, was never an isolated step in the whole process of education, but was associated with the development and evolution of scholarship in general. The earliest primers were called *xiaoxue* books. Historically, the term *xiaoxue* had a much broader meaning than its modern usage, as it changed with the main intellectual movements in Chinese history. In this chapter, through an analysis of *xiaoxue*, the origins and development of primers are traced, with a focus on the impact of Han scholarship and Song Neo-Confucianism on the establishment of Confucian education and the writing of primers.

Wordbooks: Their Origin and Development

"Wordbooks" here refers to a genre of primers created to teach children Chinese characters. The emergence and development of wordbooks paralleled the rise of Confucianism and curriculum development in Confucian education.

Learning Characters: A Focus in Both the Elementary Curriculum and Han Learning

In both pre-Han and Han times, the study of Chinese characters (named *xiaoxue*, or lesser learning) was the focus of the elementary education curriculum. Wordbooks, which emerged to teach basic literacy skills, were therefore the earliest form of traditional Chinese literacy primer.

The earliest wordbooks can be traced back to the pre-Qin (about 11th century–207 B.C.). According to historical records, at least four wordbooks were produced during this period.[1] Because the first emperor of the Qin had "burnt books and buried the Confucians alive" (*fenshu kengru*), scholars at the beginning of the Han dynasty had to gather and re-establish the Confucian classics as well as other literature, including wordbooks. For example, teachers who taught children characters collated the four wordbooks mentioned above, combined them into one volume, and entitled it *Cangjie.* As well as this wordbook, the period of 206–1 B.C. saw the production of other primers in this genre.[2]

Learning characters was the main focus of the elementary curriculum before and during the Han, and this was reflected not only in the earliest form of primers but also in various names of places for children's elementary schooling, such as *shuguan* (書館), meaning places for learning characters. Similarly, *shushi* (書師) were teachers who taught Chinese characters.[3] Since the first step of elementary schooling was to learn characters, elementary education was also called *shuxue* (書學), or the knowledge of words. The autobiography of Wang Chong (27–91) provides a glimpse of the life in a school at that time:

> [I] went to a place to learn how to read and write at eight. Other children there were punished because of their wrongdoing or were whipped for not writing characters properly. Only Chong made progress in learning characters every day and never did anything wrong.[4]

Schooling for children from farmers' families was less formal. According to Cui Shi,[5] the school terms coincided with quiet seasonal periods of farming activities, and in such schools children were divided into two groups: under and over fifteen. While the older children were learning the five Confucian classics at a more advanced level of school (*daxue*), the younger children were sent to learn the rudiments of literacy skills, including reading, writing and arithmetic.[6]

At the time (54–92) that Ban Gu (32–92) was writing the *History of the Former Han Dynasty* (*Hanshu*), about 5,240 Chinese characters were listed in wordbooks.[7] Jia Fang's wordbook *Pangxi*, which appeared in the middle of the Yong Yuan period (89–104), contained 7,380 Chinese characters. In Xu Shen's *Explanations of Words and Characters* (*Shuowen jiezi*),[8] there were 9,353 characters.[9]

While the study of Chinese characters was the main focus of elementary schooling, it gradually became associated with the development of Han scholarship. For example, the wordbook *Xunzhuan*, composed by Yang Xiong (57 B.C.–A.D.18),[10] contained the characters appearing in the six Confucian classics. Consequently, the book was of importance to all scholars.[11]

Gradually, increases in the number of characters and the development of the Chinese language, as well as the formation of Han scholarship, all demanded scholarly research on characters. So the method of *xungu*, or explaining archaic characters, was established. For instance, the *Cangjie* contained many archaic characters[12] and unqualified teachers frequently misread them. During the reign of Emperor Xuan (73–50 B.C.), the emperor found someone who was able to read these characters correctly, and from him Zhang Bi, a scholar of the time, learnt these archaic characters. Later, Zhang instructed his grandson Du Lin, who then wrote explanations of the characters. Du's explanations were put underneath these archaic characters as an aid to learners.[13] Xu Shen further developed this method and placed emphasis on these explanations in his *Explanations of Words and Characters*. Xu's work laid the foundation not only for the *xungu* method but also for what was called Han learning (*hanxue*).

Han wordbooks were thus divided into two types. The first type, for example Shi You's *Jijiu*, was used for elementary education. In this type of wordbook each sentence was comprised of three, five or seven characters. Later textbooks for children, such as the *San Bai Qian* series — *The Trimetrical Classic, One Hundred Surnames* and *One Thousand Characters*, all imitated this style. The second type, exemplified by Xu Shen's *Explanations of Words and Characters*, functioned as dictionaries and were used for the study of the Confucian classics. Obviously, wordbooks of this type were integrated into advanced learning. Children usually started with wordbooks of the first type, and then moved on to reading *The Analects* (*Lunyu*) and the *Classic of Filial Piety*, which occupied a place somewhere between wordbooks and the Confucian classics in the Han curriculum.[14]

Village Books and Changes in the School Curriculum

Right up to the Tang dynasty, Han primers were still being used to teach children. According to Gu Yanwu (1613–1683), one of the most popular primers to teach children characters was Shi You's *Jijiu*, and children would be highly regarded if they were able to recognise and to write the characters contained in the text at six years old. Gu attributed the popularity of this particular primer to the well-known calligraphists after the Han period, such as Zhong You (151–230), Huang Xiang, Madame Wei (272–349) and Wang Xizhi (303–379), who all demonstrated calligraphic beauty in making copies of the text. However, as Gu recorded, the growing use of the *San Bai Qian* series after the Tang reduced the popularity of *Jijiu*.[15]

The growing popularity of the *San Bai Qian* series in the late imperial period was attributed to changes in the school system and to curriculum development from the Tang onward. At the beginning of the Tang dynasty, Emperor Tai Zong (r. 627–649) attached great importance to education, and official schools were founded. There were six branches under the Imperial Academy (*guozi jian*), and another two educational institutions of the time named *guan*. The curriculum was dominated by the nine Confucian classics, but *shuxue* or the knowledge of words, and arithmetic and mathematics (*suanxue*) were also on the list. The subject "Knowledge of words," as recorded in *New Tang History* (*Xin Tangshu*), was similar in content to the elementary schooling of the Han dynasty, as is shown by the fact that wordbooks which were produced before and during the Han dynasty were listed as textbooks for the subject.[16] This suggests that the study of Chinese characters had shifted from being an elementary subject to being included in the curriculum for advanced learning, and it was then connected with the study of the Confucian classics.[17] In other words, the elementary learning of the Han dynasty became a specific subject in advanced education in the Tang educational system.[18]

At the beginning of the Song the court valued Confucianism highly and ordered schools to be founded in every county and prefecture. Local taxes were used to fund the schools and, according to Lu You (1125–1210), ordinary people at that time regarded educational taxation (*xueliang*) as a burden and their complaints were heard everywhere.[19] The term *xiaoxue* was still used as a general name for elementary schools,[20] which were recorded in *Song History* (*Songshi*), and some teachers were given the title "elementary school teacher" (*xiaoxue jiaoshou*),[21] although these schools did not appear to offer elementary education. However, the educational system of the Song followed that of the Tang, so it seems likely that the official *xiaoxue* in the Song, as in the Tang, were mainly concerned with the study of the Confucian classics, more than with teaching literacy skills.

The task of elementary education was therefore undertaken instead by private channels, and there emerged various places where teachers instructed children in literacy skills. For example, village schools (*xiangxiao*), family schools (*jiashu*), or places for learning characters (*sheguan* and *shuhui*), could be found in many locations.[22]

The village school terms, like those in the Han, were arranged according to the farming seasons. Lu You called village schools *dongxue*, or winter schools, because sons of farmers were sent there only in winter.[23] Some researchers have thought that this kind of school was "often nothing more than occasional gatherings of a teacher and a few pupils."[24] However, according to Cui Shi, *gengdu*, literally meaning "farming and study," characterised elementary education for ordinary people, as children from the families of farmers regularly had to help around the house or in the fields during the farming seasons and could only go to school during the relatively slack periods in farming.[25]

Cunshu, meaning "textbooks used in village schools," then emerged as a new type of wordbook to teach farmers' children basic literacy skills. It is commonly believed that the earliest textbook of this type was the *Tuyuan ce* (*The Pamphlet of the Rabbit Garden*). The term *tuyuan* referred to the garden owned by Emperor Jing (r. 156–141 B.C.), who rented the garden out to peasants. *The Pamphlet of the Rabbit Garden* was originally a book-keeping notebook, written in colloquial language. Because it contained vocabulary most relevant to the daily life of village people, the book was thus used as a primer to teach basic literacy skills to children from peasant families.[26] It was said that this pamphlet served as a popular textbook in village schools in the Five Dynasties period, but opinions about its authorship and content have varied.[27]

The text of *The Pamphlet of the Rabbit Garden* did not survive,[28] yet some other books used in Song village schools, as Lu You recorded in his poem, not only survived but also became popular throughout the late imperial period. In Lu You's account, these village textbooks were *One Hundred Surnames* and *Zazi* (*Miscellaneous Characters*).[29]

These two books are obviously wordbooks. *One Hundred Surnames* became popular in China at the end of the Tang and the early Song.[30] The author was not a well-known scholar, and we have no clue as to his/her name or life-history. *Zazi*, as the title suggests, usually listed Chinese characters or words for daily use; but the various versions often differed in content. In this sense, *zazi* refers to a type of manual rather than a particular text.[31]

San Bai Qian: A Popular Series and a Genre for Primers

The series of primers known as *San Bai Qian* were widely accepted and used in late imperial China.[32] Only one of them, *One Thousand Characters*, is by a known author. Legend has it that Emperor Liang Wu (r. 502–549) attempted to teach his sons how to write with a brush (*maobi*) in the style of Wang Xizhi. The Emperor first ordered Yin Tieshi to make rubbings of one thousand characters which were listed at random, and no character was allowed to appear more than once. Then the Emperor summoned Zhou Xingsi (?–520), a bureaucrat-scholar,[33] and said to him: "You have a good imagination, please make rhymes for me with these characters." The very next day the Emperor was presented with the book, and Zhou's hair was said to have turned grey overnight.[34] The story illustrates the fact that elementary training before the Tang still laid stress on the exercises of reading and writing, and penmanship was given special attention.

The thirty-two different editions of *One Thousand Characters* discovered in the Dunhuang caves may well serve as proof of the widespread distribution of the book. Among them are two copies written in both Chinese and Tibetan.[35] This suggests that *One Thousand Characters* helped meet the Tibetan people's demands for basic literacy in both languages.

The popularity of the book can also be demonstrated by the following story. Gu Meng, a scholar in the Tang dynasty, went to Guangzhou as a refugee because of the chaos in the areas of Huai and Zhe. He knew nobody there and was in dire financial straits. In order to survive, he made a hand-written copy of *One Thousand Characters* and sold it.[36]

This was not merely a wordbook that listed words or characters. The thousand characters were meaningfully linked by Zhou Xingsi to convey Confucian ideas, a knowledge of history and so on. For example, there were eight characters (*tui wei rang guo, you yu tao tang*) telling a short historical story in which neither of the sage kings, Yao and Shun, allowed their own sons to inherit the throne but gave it instead to respected men who were loved by the people.[37] There were also some aphorisms encouraging certain values for children, such as "A large piece of jade is not the most precious; a very short time should be cherished."[38]

The Trimetrical Classic too was a wordbook with a very rich content. It has been assumed that this little book was written by Wang Yinglin (1223–1296), a prominent scholar of the Song. Yet there is little evidence to prove who was the real author.[39] Possibly someone started to compose this book in the Song dynasty and then, from the Song onward, many other literati contributed to it. The book provided information about nature, such as the seasons and the five elements; general knowledge, such as the names of grains, domestic animals and kinship terms; knowledge of history; the titles of the Confucian classics; Confucian ethical values and many good models for children. As Zhang Binglin (1869–1936) pointed out, this primer for children successfully imparted the general rudiments of Chinese culture.[40]

Between the Tang and the Five Dynasties a primer entitled *The Essentials for Beginners* (*Kaimeng yaoxun*) was as popular as *One Thousand Characters*. Although there is no record of this book in Chinese history, twenty-five copies of it were found in the Dunhuang caves.[41] It was said that the author was a person named Ma Renshou, who lived in the region. The note under the title indicates that the text was composed during the period of the Six Dynasties (222–589), but many copies were made by people of later generations. Out of the twenty-five copies found in the Dunhuang caves, three clearly indicate that they were made in 851, 929 and 958 respectively. These dates suggest the use and the wide dissemination of the book between the Tang and the Five Dynasties, but its popularity did not continue after this period. Without the copies discovered in the Dunhuang caves the book would not have been known to us.

Nevertheless, these surviving copies have provided information about the nature, structure and content of the book. First of all, the book clearly indicated that it was intended for children who had just started to learn Chinese characters. With this in mind, the author endeavoured to make the entire text easy to understand and to memorise. The structure of the book was similar to that of *One Thousand Characters*: each sentence consisted of four characters, and all sentences were in rhyme. Its content was also somewhat similar to that of *One Thousand Characters*. The beginning of the text introduced the words for sky, earth, the four seasons and other natural phenomena; then came the words conveying some basic knowledge of astronomy and human beings. There were 1,400 characters in the text, arranged according to their radicals. This is a traditional device for teaching Chinese characters. Characters with the same radicals often indicated things (such as names of utensils, vegetation and animals) in the same or relevant categories. So radicals were often used as indexes in a dictionary and were very convenient for children to learn characters in groups or in categories. Although the text focused mainly on the learning of characters, orthodox Confucianism was conveyed where the combinations of characters allowed.[42]

Whilst *The Essentials for Beginners* was no longer used in elementary education after the Five Dynasties, the *San Bai Qian* series gradually became well known to almost every household in the late imperial period. In response to this popularity, many primers were produced with the same or similar titles and a particular genre of primers became established and attracted a wide audience. For instance, following the format and style of *The Trimetrical Classic*, later generations of writers composed *The Classic of Filial Piety in Three Characters* (*Sanzi xiaojing*), *The Classic of Current Affairs in Three Characters* (*Shiwu sanzi jing*) and *The Enlarged Trimetrical Classic* (*Guang sanzi jing*).[43] The titles of these three primers suggest that they all adopted the form of *The Trimetrical Classic*, namely that each sentence consisted of three characters and the whole text was rhymed. However, the content of these primers was not constrained by the original work.

Within this genre there were also primers which were simply based on *The Trimetrical Classic* in both content and form. Some of them added more sentences to the original text,[44] while others made commentaries on the original text,[45] or even provided illustrations.[46] In the Qing period, the format of *The Trimetrical Classic* also served the study of Confucian classics well. For example, the classics *Book of Documents* (*Shangshu*) and *Spring and Autumn Annals* (*Chunqiu*) were re-written in a three-character-sentence form and were even engraved on stones.[47]

Similarly, the forms of *One Hundred Surnames* and *One Thousand Characters* were imitated by many writers. For example, the titles of primers with the term *qianzi wen* usually contained one thousand characters in total and each sentence consisted of four characters. They were also rhymed. However, these primers varied in content. For instance, *Ancient History in One Thousand Characters* (*Xugu qianziwen*), written by Hu Yin (1098–1156) of the Song,[48] elaborated on history; and *One Thousand Characters on Human Nature and Principles* (*Xingli qianzi wen*), by Xia Taihe of the Ming, centred on Neo-Confucian doctrines. *Rectifying One Thousand Characters* (*Zhengzi qianzi wen*), a book intended to help children to distinguish between similar characters, was written by Li Deng, a professional teacher in a primary school during the Ming. In his teaching experience, Li Deng noticed that many characters looked similar and confused his pupils,[49] so he compiled this book to help children learn how to distinguish one from another carefully in their reading and writing.[50]

Mengqiu: Its Impact on Popular Primers

Another type of primer used in village schools was called *mengqiu*, a term derived from the *Book of Changes*: "Children ask me [for knowledge] (*Tongmeng qiu wo*)."[51] The first book entitled *Mengqiu* was written by Li Han, a scholar who gained the *jinshi* degree in the Later Tang dynasty (923–936). The primer's title clearly indicated the aim and readership of the book. In rhymed verses, the whole text consisted of 596 four-character phrases in two chapters (*juan*), and each phrase contained one allusion. In most cases, the first two characters were the name of the person alluded to, and the next two characters summed up the story. Most allusions were derived from historical books or legends.[52]

The survival of the book was attributed to the commentaries on it made by scholars of later generations, as in such a concentrated form it was impossible for children to understand the text. There were several commentaries written before the Song, but only the commentary of Xu Ziguang of the Song was handed down. In Xu's work, the original text was at the beginning and was then followed by a long explanation and the identification of the original sources. The phrases were arranged in pairs which sometimes were two connected stories. The beginning of the text reads: "Wang Rong, simple and efficient; Pei Kai, honest and liberal-minded." Both Wang Rong and Pei Kai lived in the period when Ruan Ji (210–263), Ji Kang (223–263) and other members of "Seven Sages of the Bamboo Grove" (*zhulin qixian*), faced with chaos and disunity in China, turned to wine, music and the consolations of Taoism. Wang Rong was a friend of Ruan Ji; Pei Kai was well-versed in the *Laozi* and *The Book of Changes*. The comments "simple and efficient" (*jianyao*) and "honest and liberal-minded" (*qingtong*) were made by Zhong Hui, the chancellor of the court, in responding to Emperor Wen's enquiry about which of the two men was more suitable for a particular office.[53]

In some cases, the phrases in pairs provided different stories but were related by topic. For example, "Kuang Heng chisels a hole in the wall, Sun Jing shuts his door." Kuang Heng of the former Han was from a poor peasant family but he was very diligent in study and eventually passed the civil service examination and entered officialdom. The literal translation of the first phrase seems to make no sense, but what it refers to is that Heng's family was too poor to provide him with a lamp to read by at night, so he chiselled a hole in the wall connecting with his neighbour's house, so as to read his books by the light coming through the wall. The second phrase refers to the story of Sun Jing of the state of Chu, who always kept his door closed and spent all the time studying. The commentator provided more information about Sun Jing, relating how, when he felt drowsy, Sun Jing would tie a rope around his neck and loop it over the rafters so he would be able to stay awake and continue studying.[54] These two independent stories address the same theme: the importance of studying hard.

The above examples also indicate that the content of Li Han's *Mengqiu* appeared to blend Confucianism with Lao-Zhuang Taoism. The text mentioned the names of 596 personages and their deeds, some of which conveyed Confucian doctrines such as filial piety — ten out of the twenty-four examples of filial piety, for instance, were contained in the text. Many exemplary models, such as the stories of Kuang Heng and Sun Jing, also constituted a significant part of the text. At the same time, however, many episodes were not orthodox in Confucian terms, such as allusions about the Three Kingdoms,[55] and stories about the Wei-Jin figures which were unambiguously Taoist.[56]

Later, the title *mengqiu*, its form of verbal parallelism (*dui'ou*) and incorporation of rhyme (*yayun*) were adopted in writing primers. However, unlike other popular primers, such as *The Trimetrical Classic* and *One Hundred Surnames*, the popularity of Li Han's primer did not continue into the late imperial period. Burton Watson attributes this to its unorthodox contents and to the traditional Confucian scholars' dignity that did not allow them to admit their erudition derived from such a children's primer.[57] However, Song scholarly criticism of Li Han's work mainly focused on its lack of clear criteria (*tili*) in its selection of material from historical books, and the textbook was characterised as being *za*, or "miscellaneous."

To avoid this "miscellaneous" label, writers of later times preferred to concentrate on a specific branch of knowledge. For example, *The History of Seventeen Dynasties* (*Shiqishi mengqiu*), by Wang Ling (1032–1059) of the Song, was exactly that.[58] Between the Song and the Yuan dynasties, there emerged quite a few primers with the title *History of Past Dynasties* (*Lidai mengqiu*), some of which only had their titles recorded, such as the one composed by Zheng Deyu of the Song, known by later generations through the *Record of Books* in the *History of the Song* (*Songzhi*); another written by Wang Rui of the Yuan, documented by the book collector Qian Zeng (1629–1701) in his *The Search for the Origins of Books* (*Dushu minqiu ji*).[59] According to Qian Zeng, Wang Rui's book was a chronological narrated history and was succinct in style. In addition, the commentary (by Zheng Zhensun) provided the audience with all the historical details. Therefore, Qian Zeng concluded that as a primer, Wang Rui's work was much better than Zhou Xingsi's *One Thousand Characters* which, Qian Zeng complained, was structured according to the arrangement of characters instead of in chronological order.[60] Nevertheless, it was not this version of the *History of Past Dynasties* but the one written by Chen Li of the Yuan which appeared to be more popular. The popularity of Chen Li's book was perhaps attributed to Zhu Sheng (1299–1370) who collected it together with three other primers in one volume under the title the *Four Little Books* (*Xiao sishu*).[61] By echoing the title the *Four Books*, Zhu Sheng emphasised the importance of these four primers in elementary schooling.

Furthermore, some primers in this genre focused on only one of the Classics. For instance, Yang Yanling of the Song composed the *Zuoshi Mengqiu*, which converted the classic *Zuo Commentary on the Spring and Autumn Annals* to this format.[62] This primer did not survive, although another, with the same title, but written by Wu Hualong (f. 1195) is still extant. The survival of this book was due to the commentary on it made by the Qing scholars Xu Naiji (f. 1798) and Wang Qinglin (f. 1807).[63] Meanwhile, the *mengqiu* form was also employed by scholars to convey various kinds of knowledge. For instance, *The Names and Descriptions of Things* (*Mingwu mengqiu*), by Fang Fengchen (1211–1291), contained general knowledge conveyed through descriptions of various things.[64]

Of course, there were also writers who were keen to write commentaries on Li Han's book, while others claimed their writings as sequels to Li Han's.[65] Quite a few of them, however, did not claim authorship at all, and in most cases only the names of their textbooks were recorded in book catalogues, or in the records (*zhi*) of historical works.

Evidently, the influence of Li Han's *Mengqiu* on the primers in this genre was not through its own popular use in elementary education during the late imperial period but through the wide adoption of its form and title, which was thought to provide an effective way to teach children all kinds of knowledge, including history and even the classics. In the form of anecdotes and with rhymed phrases, this genre of primers clearly identified its audience, even though some Qing primers, such as Wang Yun's (1784–1854) *Explanations of Characters for Children* (*Wenzi mengqiu*), abandoned verbal parallelism and rhythm, while still keeping the word *mengqiu* in their titles.

Song Neo-Confucian Treatises as Primers

The revival of Neo-Confucianism in the Song brought about a significant change in the concept of education. In Song Neo-Confucianism, the term *xiaoxue* had a very ambiguous meaning: in the sense of elementary learning, it formed the foundation of advanced learning; in the sense of elementary education, it offered detailed rules for rites and good manners. Accordingly, there were two types of Neo-Confucian treatises for children: one focused on preaching abstract ideas, which were generally derived from the classics and Neo-Confucian works; the other mainly established certain behavioural patterns for children's daily practice. By analysing the Neo-Confucian treatises intended for children, this section indicates how Neo-Confucian writers combined elementary education with advanced learning which, to some extent, ignored the attributes of children.

The Song Neo-Confucian Concept of Elementary Education

The term *xiaoxue* was originally linked with "small skills" (*xiaoyi*). In classical times, the "six arts" (*liuyi*) were regarded as the main content of education. Reading and writing characters (*shu* 書) and counting numbers (*shu* 數) were two of the "six arts," and they usually stood together as one term *shushu*, which was sometimes used to refer to elementary schooling instead of the term *xiaoxue*. The skills of reading, writing and counting were thought of as "small arts," as compared to the "great arts" (*dayi*) which were the other four items: ritual (*li*), music (*yue*), archery (*she*) and charioteering (*yu*). These four items were considered to be learning for aristocrats and the main content of advanced learning (*daxue*).[66] This suggests that the concept of education before the Han actually focused on utility. Elementary learning provided the basic knowledge needed in daily life; advanced learning mainly dealt with the art of governance.

In late Zhou times (c. 770–221 B.C.), many noble houses declined or disappeared, and the gentry (*shi*) class emerged.[67] This Chinese gentry class were "men of good birth but without titles of nobility, who served as warriors, officials, and supervisors in the state governments and noble households, or who lived on the land, which in some cases they may even have cultivated themselves."[68] Most thinkers and schools of thought at that time originated from this class and their attention was given to the political and social problems of the time.[69] Under these circumstances, the old "great arts" no longer met the needs of the time, although Confucius (551–479 B.C.) and his disciples had endeavoured to restore the Zhou system and to defend the "six arts." During the Han period, the "six arts" were sometimes used to refer to the six Confucian classics, and elementary education focused on learning characters while the study of the five classics was the core of the curriculum of education at an advanced level.[70]

By the end of the Tang, institutional and political developments brought about changes in society. The examination system made it

possible for people who were not from provincial aristocratic families
or the pre-eminent clans to attain the very highest positions in the
government.[71] In the Song, while a new elite continued to emerge
through the civil service examinations, the school of Neo-
Confucianism began to establish itself. Some thinkers of this school
advanced the revival of original Confucian learning with a new
intellectual awareness. They paid great attention to re-examining the
concept, content and function of education. Through education,
they attempted to promote Confucian ethical values and modes of
civilising behaviour throughout the whole of society.

In the first place, they reinterpreted the concept of *xiaoxue* on the
basis of their belief that their school had captured Confucian
orthodoxy and continued Confucian education. This belief was
embodied in the so-called *daotong*, or "the lineage of legitimate
transmission of the orthodoxy."[72] Three great Neo-Confucianists,
Cheng Hao (1032–1085), his brother Cheng Yi (1033–1107) and Zhu
Xi (1130–1200) represented this belief. According to them, the line
of orthodox legitimacy of Confucianism went from Confucius to
Zeng Zi to Zi Si to Mencius. In the Northern Song, the Cheng
brothers drew special attention to two chapters in the *Record of Rites*
— *Great Learning (Daxue)* and the *Doctrine of the Mean (Zhongyong)*.
They believed that Zeng Zi wrote the *Great Learning* and Zi Si
compiled the *Doctrine of the Mean*. Of the three thousand disciples of
Confucius, only Zeng Zi and Zi Si inherited the essence of
Confucianism and transmitted it through these two treatises.
Mencius was the successor to Zi Si and conveyed the Confucian
legitimacy through his work *Mencius (Meng Zi)*. After the death of
Mencius, however, this lineage of legitimacy faltered in the face of
heterodoxy.[73] The Cheng brothers attempted to perpetuate this line
by creating a new series of classics. Hence, they produced commentaries on the *Great Learning* and the *Doctrine of the Mean* and put them
together with the *Analects* and *Mencius*. However, it was not until 1212
that the *Analects* and *Mencius* were accepted as classics by the
Directorate of Education. In the Southern Song, Zhu Xi reaffirmed
the Cheng brothers' ideas and contributed his own commentaries on
these four books. After Zhu's death, the government recognized
these four books with Zhu Xi's commentaries. Together with the *Five
Classics*, the *Four Books* thus became the dominant texts in the
curriculum after the Song.[74] The appearance of the *Four Books*

illustrates how the Neo-Confucians in the Song tried to rediscover original Confucianism and how education as an accessible instrument helped perpetuate the orthodox lineage.

The content of elementary learning in Neo-Confucian education focused on "sweeping the ground, greeting and replying" (*sasao yingdui*). This concept originated from Confucius's *Analects* and hence from the orthodox lineage. In the *Analects*, easy tasks such as sprinkling and sweeping the ground (*sasao*), greeting and replying (*yingdui*), and advancing and receding (*jintui*) were claimed to have prime importance in the Way of being superior men.[75] The content of advanced learning was drawn from the *Great Learning* and included eight items: investigation of things, extension of knowledge, authentication of the will, rectification of the mind, cultivation of personal life, regulation of the family, governance of the state and peace-making throughout the world.[76] Zhu Xi used his explanation of the educational system and the content of education in classical times to show what he saw as true Confucian education. He stated:

> During the flourishing Three Dynasties, the educational system gradu-ally improved. Then schools were located in the palace, capital and alleys. At eight, children of the nobility as well as ordinary people went to el-ementary school (*xiaoxue*) and were taught to perform tasks such as sprin-kling and sweeping the ground, greeting and replying, and advancing and receding. Then they learned rituals, music, the arts of archery and charioteering, as well as characters, numbers and counting. At fifteen, children of *tianzi* (the son of heaven), nobility, officials, gentlemen (*shi*) and excellent students from ordinary families entered advanced educa-tion and were taught the Way, the search for principles, rectification of the mind, self-cultivation and governance of the people. This was the school system in classical times and the content of advanced learning and elementary learning.[77]

Obviously, Zhu Xi's description of the education system in classical times was different from those of other records. Firstly, Zhu Xi put the "six arts" into the curriculum of elementary education, in contrast to the accepted division of "small arts" and "great arts." Secondly, elementary schooling now concentrated on sweeping the ground and greeting, which stood for "ritualisation of the body." The principles involved in ritualisation of the body were also emphasised in a preparatory study for advanced learning and were practised to promote the process of self-cultivation. Hence, his concept of education as a whole focused on individual commitment to moral transformation. The learning of characters, knowledge of arithmetic and others of the "six arts" were not ignored in Zhu Xi's theory, but became secondary. Thus, the term *xiaoxue* in the Neo-Confucian concept of education appeared to have two meanings: elementary learning and elementary education. Zhu Xi signified this new definition by using this term as the title of his treatise *Xiaoxue*, or *Elementary Learning*, which addressed children as well as adults.[78]

The change in the definition of *xiaoxue* was also influenced by the Neo-Confucian idea that education should be available for everybody. In Zhu Xi's *Elementary Learning*, the concrete modes of behaviour were mainly drawn from the *Analects*, *Record of Rites*, *Book of Etiquette and Ceremonial* (*Yili*) and *Book of Rites by the Elder Dai* (*Dadai liji*), and the virtue of filial piety was centred on the rules of propriety. In the *Classic of Filial Piety* (*Xiaojing*), filial piety was regarded as "the root of virtues and also the starting point of education."[79] In the Cheng brothers' opinion, filial piety was the practice of the virtue of benevolence. They thought that benevolence stressed love (*ai*), and nothing could be more important than to love one's parents.[80] As the *Classic of Filial Piety* indicated: "Filial piety commences with the service of parents, then proceeds to the service of the ruler, and finally is completed by the establishment of the character."[81]

However, filial piety in this canon was divided into five categories according to the different social strata: filial piety of the son of heaven, nobility (*gongqing*), officials (*dafu*), gentlemen (*shi*) and ordinary people (*shuren*). In Neo-Confucian terms, Confucius's "learning for the sake of the self"[82] meant that education could carry on under any conditions, because sprinkling and sweeping the ground, answering and replying were all carried out in everyone's daily life, and the virtue of filial piety was embodied in such activities. This can be exemplified from the following quotations.

1. To love parents:

   For all sons it is the rule: in winter, to warm [the bed for their parents], and to cool it in summer; in the evening, to adjust everything [for their parents' repose], and to inquire [about their parents' health] in the morning.[83]

2. To respect elders:

> In going to take counsel with an elder, one must carry a stool and a staff [for the elder's use]. When the elder asks a question, to reply without acknowledging one's incompetence and to try to decline answering, is contrary to propriety.[84]

3. To venerate teachers:

> When one is following one's teacher, one should not quit the road to speak with another person. When one meets one's teacher on the road, one should hasten forward to him, and stand with one's hands joined across one's breast. If the teacher speaks to him, one will answer; if the teacher does not, one will retire with hasty steps.[85]

4. To be "friendly" with friends:

> A man keeps behind another who has his father's years; he follows one who might be his elder brother more closely, but still keeping behind, as geese fly after one another in a row. Friends do not pass by one another, when going the same way.[86]

Zhu Xi adopted these ceremonial rules in the classics and intended to show children as well as adults the way of ritualisation of the body. In the sense of elementary education, all the ceremonial rules had to be practised in childhood. In the sense of elementary learning, the practice of filial piety, and the performance of sprinkling and sweeping the ground, replying and walking properly, involved individual cultivation in morality as well as the social order. Zhu Xi regarded this practice and performance as "the roots of self-cultivation, regulation of family, governance of the state and peace-making throughout the world."[87]

As discussed earlier, the endeavour of the Neo-Confucians was to remake a Confucian society, in which everyone ought to be involved. The orthodox lineage of Confucianism, which was emphasised by the Cheng-Zhu school, represented the ideas of the gentry class (*shi*) in the last three centuries of the Zhou dynasty. The gentry class urged that the rulership ought to be based not only on good birth but also on an educated class; and rulers ought to be complemented by those with moral and intellectual qualifications. In the Song, scholars could gain access to government posts through the examination system. This implies that the ideal in classical times was realised in the Song. However, many tricks were used to cheat at examinations. Intellectuals, such as the Cheng brothers and Zhu Xi, saw the paradoxical results of the examination system. For the purpose of reforming society and establishing a good government, they attempted to advocate Confucian morals by promoting sound education. This is why the concept of education in Neo-Confucianism emphasised "learning for the sake of the self" rather than for status or profit, and self-cultivation became the basis of a good government and of a harmonious society. In this sense, classical usages assumed a new importance. The "distinction" of people, in theory, was determined less by social strata than by manners, which were embodied in one's behaviour in such areas as greeting, speaking and walking. As individuals, Zhu Xi and other Neo-Confucianists belonged to a certain social circle, but their educational treatises presented general human rules.

However, Zhu Xi did not provide much specific information about how to instruct children in aspects of literacy skills. His *Methods of Study* (*Dushu fa*),[88] with six items in twenty-four characters, mainly addressed adults and was only suitable for advanced learning.

Cheng Duanli (1271–1345), a Confucian instructor (*ruxue jiaoshou*) of an official school in Quzhou Lu, compiled *The Daily Schedule of Studies* (*Dushu fennian richeng*), a schedule of study or a teaching scheme on the basis of Zhu Xi's *Methods of Study*. In this schedule, there were three periods in the whole course of learning: (1) the very beginning of learning, for children under the age of eight; (2) the commencement of formal schooling, or the stage of elementary education from the ages of eight to fifteen; and (3) the advanced period or the stage of advanced education from the ages of fifteen to twenty-two.

In the first stage, children started learning characters and good manners. Cheng tried to combine the teaching of Neo-Confucianism with the learning of characters even at the earliest stage. For this purpose, he advocated that children should study *Explanations of Neo-Confucian Terms* (*Xingli zixun*).

Explanations of Neo-Confucian Terms, compiled by Cheng Duan-meng (1143–1191) and supplemented by Cheng Ruoyong,[89] was in total thirty lines but contained all the basic concepts of Neo-Confucianism, such as fate (*ming*), nature (*xing*), mind (*xin*), reverence (*jing*), the principles of heaven (*tianli*) and human desires (*renyu*).[90] In Cheng Duanli's opinion, children younger than eight had to learn this manual before starting formal schooling, and study Zhu Xi's *Children Should Know* (*Tongmeng xuzhi*) every day instead of other popular primers.[91] However, *Explanations of Neo-Confucian Terms* focuses mainly on the terms in Neo-Confucian metaphysics, which are abstract and difficult for children to understand, and it is not surprising that the book was not used as widely as other popular primers.

Cheng Duanli's book-list for the second stage included original texts of Zhu Xi's *Elementary Learning*, the *Four Books*, the *Five Classics* and the *Classic of Filial Piety*. In the stage of advanced education, students were required to read most of the same texts with Zhu Xi's commentaries, *A General Mirror for Aid in Government* (*Zizhi tongjian*), other Neo-Confucian works and specimens of the prose and poetry of Han Yu (768–824) and Qu Yuan (343–277 B.C.). Yet Zhu Xi's *Elementary Learning* and the *Classic of Filial Piety* were not listed in the curriculum of the advanced stage. Instead, students had to learn how to compose "the eight-legged essay" (*bagu wen*) for the civil service examinations.[92]

Clearly, Cheng's curriculum aimed at meeting the practical demands of the new examination system in the Yuan dynasty. On this basis, elementary training was also given much attention in Cheng's curriculum. For example, with respect to penmanship, Cheng advocated that children ought to practise brush writing by imitating Zhi Yong's calligraphic work of *One Thousand Characters*.[93] After this, children continued their reading course. Then they practised brush writing for another one or two months. Upon finishing this basic training, children could write four thousand characters. In the process of teaching penmanship, teachers had to teach children how to hold a writing brush and the order of the strokes in writing each character.[94]

Cheng's curriculum was highly praised by some Neo-Confucian scholars in the Ming and Qing periods. For example, Lu Longqi (1630–1693), an esteemed scholar-official in the early Qing, thought of Cheng's schedule as a standard curriculum for teaching and learning. He said that Cheng's schedule showed scholars how to practise Zhu Xi's *Methods of Study* and integrate book-learning with personal moral cultivation. According to Lu, Cheng's curriculum was adopted in schools in the Yuan and the early Ming periods. In the middle of the Ming, however, elementary education by and large was undertaken privately, at family schools or through private tutoring. Under these circumstances, Cheng's curriculum was rarely used. To

Lu Longqi, the use of Cheng's curriculum was primarily a matter of defending Zhu Xi's orthodoxy, and the idea of elementary training was insignificant.[95]

Neo-Confucian Treatises Intended for Children

Zhu Xi's *Elementary Learning* established a framework for Neo-Confucian treatises for children. Here these treatises are treated as a particular genre of primer, so as to identify different scholarly views of childhood and elementary education, and how these views are reflected in the composition of primers.

After the Song dynasty both Zhu Xi's *Elementary Learning* and Lü Benzhong's *Instructions for Children* (*Tongmeng xun*) were accepted by many Confucian educators as classical primers. However, the content of these treatises suggests that they addressed children as if they were adults. As Zhu Xi's *Elementary Learning* has already been discussed, here we take only Lü's *Instructions for Children* as an example.

Judging from its title, Lü's book was a primer for a family school.[96] However, the focus of the book was mainly on self-cultivation (*lishen*) and the art of governance. The author cited ideas from the Confucian classics and the works of authoritative writers and famous Neo-Confucians of the time, such as the Cheng brothers, Zhang Zai (1020–1077) and Zhu Xi. For example, in the discussion of the significance of *li*, or ritual, in learning, Lü Benzhong cited what Zhang Zai, Cheng Yi and a disciple of Cheng Yi said, instead of expressing his own opinions directly.[97]

With regard to the steps of learning, Lü shared the Cheng brothers' and Zhu Xi's ideas. In his opinion, students should firstly study classical treatises on etiquette and ceremony, such as the *Details for Ceremonial* (*Quli*), the *Rituals for Youths* (*Shaoyi*) and the *Book of Etiquette and Ceremonial*, and ritualise their bodies through sweeping the ground and greeting people. Secondly, they should study classical wordbooks, such as *Literary Expositor* (*Erya*). These two steps were thought of as the basic training in Neo-Confucian education.[98]

The *Details for Ceremonial* and the *Rituals for Youths*, two chapters in the *Record of Rites*, were listed separately by Lü Benzhong. In Neo-Confucian ideology, these two chapters, with the *Book of Etiquette and Ceremonial*, provided the principles for self-cultivation. Later treatises on manners were mostly derived from these three texts. The *Literary*

Expositor was a Han wordbook in the style of a dictionary[99] and was listed together with the *Analects* and the *Classic of Filial Piety* in the educational curriculum.[100]

From Lü's ideas, we can see that elementary training in Neo-Confucian education consisted of two aspects: self-cultivation and learning characters. These two parts were closely linked with the main doctrine of Neo-Confucianism: "abiding in reverence and the search for principles" (*jujing qiongli*). The performance of rituals in daily life was the foundation for practice in reverence; and book learning was the way to attain principles. In this sense, elementary training was also elementary learning as part of advanced education, and the line between elementary education and advanced education thus became very ambiguous. In the case of Lü's *Instructions for Children*, the style of language seem to be addressed to adults, and a book-list that he provided for children included the Confucian classics, other scholarly books and historical works, and showed few differences from advanced learning.[101] The book included quotations from the Confucian classics and writings of the Neo-Confucians, examples of virtuous behaviour, records of good government, and advice about learning and on choosing friends. The text appears more suitable for educating adults rather than young children, though the author claimed that his intention was to enlighten children (*youxue qidi zhi zi*).[102]

Lü's text reflects a Neo-Confucian approach to children: it is concerned only with the child's moral cultivation and ignores the stages in its development. It appears that in the Neo-Confucian understanding children were miniature adults or perhaps adults-in-training, so it was normal for scholars like Zhu Xi and Lü Benzhong simply to employ the classics as their only sources for compiling primers. Yet Zhu Xi's *Elementary Learning* gathered together some detailed regulations which could guide children's behaviour. In this sense, this manual, along with *Children Should Know*, another treatise that Zhu Xi composed to teach children good manners, was more like a primer than Lü's *Instructions for Children*.

Children Should Know was intended for children at the beginning of elementary schooling. Zhu Xi emphasised that the first step in education was to teach children "how to dress properly; then how to talk and walk in accordance with the rules; then how to sweep the floor, and tidy their books and stationery; then how to read and write."[103] Centuries later, some Song Neo-Confucian treatises were still being imitated, with slight modification. For example, Wan Huquan (1808–1904), a scholar of the late Qing dynasty, rewrote Zhu Xi's work *Children Should Know* in rhyme.

Some scholars, however, with a more defensive attitude to these treatises, rejected the popular primers which were produced before and during the Song. As mentioned earlier, Cheng Duanli in his *Daily Schedule of Studies* rejected the use of popular primers such as the *Mengqiu* and *One Thousand Characters* in elementary schooling. So did Xiong Danian of the Yuan, as clearly indicated in his *Great Instructions for Children* (*Yangmeng daxun*).[104]

Xiong firstly stated the purpose of his book by quoting what five great Song scholars had said about education for children.[105] After the quotations, he claimed that the entire book was based on these great scholars' principles. Then he listed the names of ten Song Neo-Confucianists, giving their home towns, official positions (if any) and their scholarly affinity,[106] so as to justify his inclusion of their treatises in his book.

These ten Neo-Confucian treatises basically contain philosophical concepts and abstract theory quoted directly from Song Neo-Confucian writings, as well as doctrines derived from the Confucian classics. This clearly illustrates the Neo-Confucian educators' intention that children be indoctrinated through language learning, although the texts are apparently beyond the level of elementary schooling, and would not be easily understood by children.

However, most of these ten treatises are in the form of four-character phrases, or are poems. This suggests that although these Neo-Confucian educators were not very efficient at selecting suitable content for children, they at least noticed that texts in four-character phrases or in a poetic form were easy for children to chant and memorise. Take Zhu Xi's *Instructive Poetry for Children* (*Xunmeng jueju*) as an example.[107] This volume contains one hundred poems which, according to Zhu Xi himself, were written while he was ill. Because of his illness, he felt that the only thing he could do was to recall the *Four Books* and their commentaries, and think about them. Afterwards he recorded his thoughts in the form of poems, of which there were several hundred. Two years later, he used these poems to teach his child, who was just starting to speak. Zhu Xi made it very clear that he wanted to teach his child using his own poems rather than the popular Tang poetry. To him, there was no such thing as art for art's sake, and poetry was a kind of vehicle to convey the Principles of the Way. This idea is clearly presented in his *Instructive Poetry for Children* where the poems can be catalogued into four groups: (1) Neo-Confucian metaphysics; (2) moral cultivation; (3) learning and officialdom, and (4) the way to nurture goodness. Clearly, all these contents are beyond the elementary level. Zhu Xi's teaching method was to push children to memorise these poems but not necessarily to understand them. In his poem entitled *Elementary Learning* (*Xiaoxue*), he clearly stated:

> Sweeping and cleaning the hall is every child's duty;
> Walking, replying and appearance should be well polished.
> No need to search for Principles behind the practice,
> As reverence and carefulness are well embodied in one's demeanour.[108]

Traditionally, the Chinese believed children could learn how to compose poetry simply by memorising poems. This may be one of the reasons that Tang poetry began to be used in elementary schooling. In this sense, Zhu Xi was adopting the same strategy, but in contrast to the popular Tang poetry, most of Zhu Xi's poems are philosophical and abstract, and could hardly be used in elementary teaching.

The final part of *Great Instructions for Children* is Zhu Xi's *Collation and Correction of the Classic of Filial Piety*. This arrangement represents Xiong Danian's idea about what should be used in teaching young children. Xiong believed that Zhu Xi's treatise *Elementary Learning* was as important as the six Confucian classics. Yet Xiong was fully aware that Zhu Xi's *Elementary Learning* was not able to compete in teaching practice with popular primers such as *The Trimetrical Classic* and *One Thousand Characters*. Like Cheng Duanli, Xiong Danian despised the popular primers which, in his opinion, led young children away from Neo-Confucian orthodoxy and caused them to lose their original good nature (*liangzhi liangneng*). Therefore, he put together this volume by collecting the texts written by Song Neo-Confucian scholars in a poetic form. This volume, he stated, was to help children understand Zhu Xi's *Elementary Learning*. In this sense, Xiong's *Great Instructions for Children* set out to promote the use of Zhu Xi's work in elementary education. His idea was that, after reading through all these texts, children would be ready to be transferred to a higher level — a level at which they were supposed to read the original Confucian classics. The *Classic of Filial Piety*, together with the *Five Classics* and *Four Books*, were the texts recommended for them.[109]

In brief, the development of wordbooks indicate that elementary schooling was originally designed on the basis of the Chinese understanding of different stages in childhood. Generally speaking, in both the pre-Han and the Han periods, elementary education was intended for children between the ages of eight and fifteen in Chinese terms, and the main focus of the curriculum was on literacy skills, although there were different names for the physical institution in which such teaching took place. Han wordbooks, the earliest format of Chinese primers, were produced as a response to this curriculum. Yet with the development of Han learning, some of the Han wordbooks became associated with the study of the *Five Classics*. By the Tang dynasty, official schools were flourishing and the Chinese education system had become more structured. At that time, the study of Chinese characters was no longer considered a part of the rudiments of literacy skills but a specific subject in the curriculum of advanced education. In the Song dynasty, private schools were very popular and the official schools existed in name more than in reality. Therefore, elementary training was undertaken through private channels, and village books were developed into a new form of wordbook as a response to new demands of social and business activities. The wordbooks in this popular format served the needs of learning and teaching characters, teaching various branches of knowledge and instructing children in morals and ethical values. These newly developed primers were usually written in verse, a form particularly suitable for children to chant and memorise. This ensured the use of these wordbooks in teaching basic literacy skills in the private sector or within communities in the Ming-Qing period, whilst all the formal educational institutions seemed only to serve the demand for preparation for the civil service examinations.

Neo-Confucian treatises presented a rather stern approach to elementary education. This approach, on the one hand, expressed the Neo-Confucian educators' great interest in children; on the other hand, however, their overwhelming anxiety about children's moral development, as shown in their treatises, to a certain extent meant that they ignored the nature of children and the differences between children and adults. Yet the detailed rules and regulations they included, which were mainly derived from the etiquette and rites in the classics, laid the foundation for a genre of later primers on good manners.

⌒ *Chapter 3* ⌒

The School of Wang Yangming and Ming-Qing Primers

In her pioneering work on education and popular literacy in Qing China, Evelyn Rawski regards the *San Bai Qian* as textbooks designed for "boys from elite families," who needed to acquire 2,000 characters "before enrolling in formal studies with a tutor."[1] Alexander Woodside holds the same view in his study of the relationship between literacy and modernisation in China.[2] However, as discussed in Chapter Two, prior to the Ming, scholars such as Cheng Duanli and Xiong Danian had considered popular primers to be of little value. Their opinions reflected those of the educated elite (*shidafu*)[3] with regard to the kind of books which were appropriate for the very beginning of children's schooling. Wang Fuzhi later recorded this discourse:

> With the lack of classical books, the ancient teaching method disappeared. In the schools for ordinary people's children, Zhou Xingsi's *One Thousand Characters* and Li Han's *Mengqiu* were used as textbooks at the beginning of schooling. The educated elite, however, thought of these primers as useless texts and abandoned them. At the very beginning of elementary schooling, children from elite families were taught *Elementary Learning* and the *Classic of Filial Piety*. The sentences in these two books were uneven, and hence it was very difficult for children to read them. If young children were forced to learn these books, how could they enjoy their studies?[4]

From the Ming onward, however, popular primers were no longer despised by the intellectual community, and many scholars were involved in composing them. At the same time, *San Bai Qian*, as a series of primers, was widely used in the teaching of basic literacy.

This changed attitude can be attributed to the influence of the teachings of the Wang Yangming school and a movement to combine the "Three Teachings" of Confucianism, Buddhism and Taoism into one syncretic religion.

Children and Their Education in the School of Wang Yangming

The concept of elementary education in the Wang Yangming school was to some extent much more modern than that in the Cheng-Zhu school. Wang Shouren (1472–1528), whom the scholars of the time called Master Yangming (*Yangming xiansheng*), was one of the greatest philosophers of the late Ming. His theory of "innate knowledge" (*liangzhi*)[5] attempted to provide a direct way of returning to the essence of Confucian teaching. This was quite different from the Cheng-Zhu school, which was characterised by a balance between intellectual enquiry and moral cultivation. In the eyes of the Wang Yangming school, intellectual enquiry had led the Cheng-Zhu school to overindulge in bookish pursuits. Wang Yangming preferred to see Confucius and other ancient sages as men of action rather than scholars.[6] The pursuit of book-learning in the Cheng-Zhu school suggested that the way to attain sagehood was actually only open to scholars and scholar-officials, although Zhu Xi and his contemporaries strove to establish principles (*li*) for all human beings and the whole of society. By comparison, Wang Yangming was less interested in book-learning. He believed that everyone could become a sage through instinctive moral sense. There were no critical conflicts between the Cheng-Zhu school and the Wang Yangming school with respect to moral ethics and social ideals. The main difference between them was that they understood the essence of Confucius's teaching and the path to sagehood in different ways.[7]

In relation to education for children, Wang Yangming, like Zhu Xi and other Neo-Confucians in the Song, placed emphasis on teaching young boys "the fundamental principles of human relations," "filial piety, brotherly respect, loyalty, faithfulness, propriety, righteousness, integrity, and the sense of shame."[8] In Wang Yangming's schedule, the first task in the daily teaching process was *kaode*, meaning "to examine the pupils' moral conduct."[9] This included determining:

Whether at home [students] have been negligent and lacked sincerity and earnestness in their desire to love their parents and to respect their elders, whether they have overlooked or failed to carry out any details in caring for their parents in the summer or the winter, whether in walking along the streets their movements and etiquette have been disorderly or careless, and whether in all their words, acts, and thoughts they have been deceitful or depraved, and not loyal, faithful, sincere, and respectful.[10]

If we compare the above items with the content of Zhu Xi's *Elementary Learning* cited earlier, we find that they are identical. As moral teaching, the regulations that Wang Yangming established for both teachers and pupils were as strict as Zhu Xi's. Wang said that in the process of examining moral conduct, "all boys must answer honestly. If they have made any mistake, they should correct it. If not, they should devote themselves to greater effort." For the teachers, they "should at all times, and in connection with anything that may occur, use special means to explain and teach" the pupils morals and good manners.[11]

What was unusual about Wang Yangming's ideas on elementary education was his understanding of the nature of children: "to love to play and to dislike restriction." Based on this understanding, Wang Yangming suggested attracting young pupils by singing. He said that singing was an important means of releasing children's energy, which they normally "[expressed in] jumping around and shouting," and "to free them through rhythm from depression and repression." On the basis of this concept of the nature of children, Wang Yangming also believed that to teach children "to practice etiquette is not only to make their demeanour dignified." More importantly, it was concerned with children's good health. The practice of "bowing and walking politely" would improve children's "blood circulation." Through the activities of kneeling, rising, and extending and contracting their limbs, children could "strengthen their tendons and bones."[12]

Certainly, Wang Yangming's ideas were in contrast to the orthodoxy of the Zhu Xi School in the Ming period. In theory, the emphasis on restraint and discipline in ritualization of the body was regarded as essential in Neo-Confucian education. In reality, the early sixteenth century saw formalistic education treat young pupils like prisoners. Wang Yangming criticised the way in which teachers "beat the pupils with a whip and tie(d) them with ropes." The cruel punishment caused the youngsters to "look upon their school as a prison and refuse to enter."[13] Wang Yangming thought that this was not true Confucian education. The subtle purpose of Confucian education was to nourish children's goodness and remove their weakness smoothly and silently. If teaching activities were aimed at adjusting and regulating children's "nature and feelings," children would "gradually approach propriety and righteousness without feeling that it is difficult to do so." The essence of Wang Yangming's proposal was to keep children "happy and cheerful at heart."[14]

Wang Yangming also disapproved of the curriculum of formal education in the Ming. At that time, children were forced to "recite phrases and sentences and imitate civil service examination papers" every day.[15] Wang Yangming sharply pointed out that this hampered children's development. In his opinion, reading and reciting should also be based on the nature of children, especially on their "natural endowments," so that they could always have "surplus energy and strength" and would not "suffer or feel tired."[16] Only when children felt easy and relaxed in their reading and reciting would their intelligence gradually broaden and unfold. In such a teaching process, children's minds would be preserved "through absorption in repeating passages" and their will would be expressed "through recitation."[17]

It is clear that Wang Yangming was urging that children be allowed to grow freely and naturally through education. The spirit of freedom in his ideas reflected the influence of increasing social fluidity on scholarship. During the sixteenth and seventeenth centuries, cultural activities, which had only been enjoyed by scholar-officials or literati in the past, were now often sponsored by merchants and artisans in economic and commercial centres such as the lower Yangtze valley.[18] Social mobility was especially evident not only in the fact that many merchant families went into the bureaucracy, but also in the phenomenon that some old gentry families were involved in commerce.[19] Class distinction thus became less significant. Economic affluence allowed more people to participate in education, and education was associated with social reform. Under these circumstances, consciousness of individualism and humanitarianism arose and attitudes towards children changed. Wang Yangming's ideas on educating children represented this tendency and had a strong impact on later generations. This can be exemplified by Lu Shiyi's idea of elementary education.

Lu Shiyi (1611–1672), a teacher during the late Ming and the early Qing period, appreciated Wang Yangming's ideas on educating children and criticised Zhu Xi's *Elementary Learning*. In his opinion, there were at least four defects in Zhu's book. Firstly, the content of the book was more suitable for advanced learning than for elementary education, because it involved seeking principles (*qiongli*). He said that the content of elementary education should be differentiated from advanced education, i.e. elementary education ought to focus on instructing children how to do things, while advanced education was a matter of understanding abstract theory and philosophy. Secondly, the content of *Elementary Learning* was not novel, because it was mostly derived from the *Four Books* and the *Five Classics*. Thirdly, the rites in *Elementary Learning* were adapted from those in classical times and were so far from the current custom that it was meaningless to practise them. Fourthly, in respect to teaching the language, the characters in *Elementary Learning* were too difficult for youngsters. Lu Shiyi agreed with Wang Yangming that a textbook for children should consider the nature of children. It was very difficult for youngsters who were five or six to read long sentences, because they could not pronounce clearly at that age. Where moral education was concerned, book learning was less important for youngsters than action. Lu therefore planned to compile a primer in which the rites were from the *Details for Ceremonial* in the *Record of Rites* but were modified according to contemporary customs, and the style of language would be plain and in verse. The book was to be named the *Rites for Youngsters in Rhyme* (*Jieyun youyi*). He suggested that reading and acting should not be separated in the teaching process. For example, when a teacher taught children the sentence "heads must be upright" (*tourong zhi*), he had to teach them how to hold their heads up.[20] In fact, the book never appeared. However, Lu's plans and his opinions about elementary education were very close to the spirit of Wang Yangming's thought.

Primers Under the Influence of the "Three Teachings"

In Chapter Two we pointed out that Li Han's *Mengqiu* presented a mixture of Confucianism with Taoism and Buddhism, a reflection of the so-called "tripartite balance of religions." Prior to the Tang dynasty China had experienced disunity for about four hundred years. During this chaotic period, official education existed only in name and Taoism and Buddhism arose to challenge the prestige of Confucianism. As a Tang scholar, Li Han witnessed the restoration of Confucian education and the state, as the Tang government made efforts to standardise the annotations of the nine Confucian classics, and "mastery of the Confucian classics" (*tongjing*) was set up as a major requirement in the civil service examinations. However, Taoism and Buddhism were still able to influence intellectual circles as well as the court. Consequently, the monopoly of Confucianism in education was challenged and all three religions had a strong following among the people, although theoretically and officially Confucianism still dominated education and scholarship.[21]

As a response to the challenge from Taoism and Buddhism, Confucian scholars established the "lineage of legitimate transmission of the orthodoxy" (*daotong*). This lineage had been advocated by Han Yu and inherited and authorised by Song Neo-Confucians, such as the Cheng-Zhu school. In Chapter Two, we saw how Song Neo-Confucian educators attempted to bring about a revival of what they saw as original Confucianism and to promote it through education. However, Lu Jiuyuan (1139–1192), a Song Neo-Confucian scholar and Zhu Xi's contemporary, borrowed ideas from Buddhism and Taoism openly, placing emphasis on the "direct unity between mind (*xin*) and principles (*li*)."[22] Lu's philosophy of mind (*xinxue*) was developed by Wang Yangming. Our earlier discussion of Wang Yangming's thought indicated that his approach to "respecting moral character" differed from Zhu Xi's "learning of the way." Wang's approach, reflected in his attitude to children, appeared to show more understanding of their nature. This is perhaps also an example of why and how the philosophy of mind was "kept alive over a period of three hundred years through informal channels among the people," and "became the vessel for some freedom of thought."[23]

The teachings of the Wang Yangming school provided a more convenient way for ordinary people to reach a high level of Confucian ethics. Especially with the efforts of the Taizhou school and "its primary engagement in education," as Professor de Bary points out, Confucianism was really brought down to the lowest class of society and "for the first time became heavily involved in the sphere traditionally occupied by the popular religions."[24] Meanwhile, the common ground for the three religions was a sense of morality appreciated by the scholars-official as well as the common people. In the Song, the emphasis in Neo-Confucian morality on the performance of classical ceremonies had met the requirements of the ruling class rather than the common people, because of the expense involved. The combined practice of the Three Teachings enabled the common people to perform meritorious deeds without any additional expense. Popular educational texts named *shanshu* (morality books) were produced and were aimed at persuading the common people that personal fulfilment could be achieved regardless of economic circumstances and social status.[25]

Under these circumstances, some texts, such as the *Collection of Wise Sayings* (*Mingxian ji*) and the *Enlarged Collection of Wise Words* (*Zengguang xianwen*), emerged to promote social norms and conventional beliefs which derived from Buddhism and Taoism as well as Confucianism; sometimes it is hard to identify whether they were social treatises, popular literature or primers. Take the *Collection of Wise Sayings* as an example.

The author of the text is unknown to us, but its content suggests that it was not produced before the Southern Song dynasty and it appears to have been widely used throughout the late imperial period. The entire text was composed of common sayings, some of which came from classics such as the *Analects*, while others originated in popular literature or were simply created by ordinary people.

Like the morality books, many sayings collected in the text persuaded people to accumulate virtue and to avoid misfortune by storing up merit, such as "Just do good things and never consider whether you will gain from what you do; good works you do to others actually are done to yourself."[26] Another similar saying is: "Often doing good things for other people, [you] will not bring calamity upon yourself."[27] Like many popular primers, some sayings also encouraged children to study hard and establish themselves while still young. For instance, one saying urged youths to master some useful skills: "It is not too much if a character is priced at one thousand pieces of gold; one cannot go wrong if one masters the skills of writing and counting. With such skills one would be useful to the country even if physically small; only having a well-built body [but without any skills] is useless."[28]

Although the text did not focus solely on Confucian teachings, it included a significant number of social norms established by Song Neo-Confucianists, such as "A loyal official will not serve two sovereigns; and a faithful widow (*lienü*)[29] will not marry a second husband."[30] This saying actually transferred Neo-Confucian teaching to a commonly accepted rule which, in pre-modern China, deprived women of freedom in this matter and was responsible for many women's deaths.

As well as the examples mentioned above, many sayings are concerned with the ways of the world, for instance

> Praising others is like bringing warmth to people in deep winter,
> Verbally abusing others is like making people feel chilly in summer.[31]

and

> Don't do things you are afraid that other people might know about;
> Study hard if you want to win respect from people.[32]

and

> Troubles come from talking too much,
> Vexations result from striving for fame.[33]

As a mixture of the Three Teachings, the text inevitably contains material about fatalism, Buddhist Karma and retribution, which had been secularised and translated into conventions and had become a well accepted life philosophy.[34]

The *Enlarged Collection of Wise Words*, also entitled *Wise Words from the Past* (*Xishi xianwen*) and *Wise Words from Both the Past and Present* (*Gujin xianwen*), is believed to have been first mentioned in the well-known Ming drama *Peony Pavilion* (*Mudan ting*), by Tang Xianzu (1550–1616), but its author is unknown. It was believed that the text was gradually accumulated in the late Ming period and throughout the Qing, and that during the process different versions were produced. Few scholars, however, claimed to have made contributions to it. The text appeared to be a collection of conventional beliefs, and its sources varied. Any sayings revealing wisdom and a philosophical approach to daily life were collected, no matter whether they came from the Confucian classics, or derived directly from popular literature such as Yuan-Ming plays (*zaju*), Buddhist writings or Taoist works. For instance, "You should only tell people a

third of what you know and never approach anyone unreservedly."[35]
The origin of this expression was a Song Buddhist work entitled
Jingde chuandeng lu (Transmission of the Lamp Composed in the
Jingde Era), yet since it had come into common usage, no one
seemed to feel the need to trace its original context and meaning; it
was taken as a piece of philosophical advice on being prudent in
speech and communication.

Texts of this type were widespread in Ming-Qing society, as they
expressed the wisdom and experience of ordinary people rather than
drawing only upon sources in the classics and scholarly writings.
Although these texts enjoyed the same popularity as *The Trimetrical
Classic, One Hundred Surnames*, and *One Thousand Characters*, they were
more likely to be used for adults than for children. Children's
primers, even those of unknown authorship, were generally
commentated, collated and corrected by scholars who either had an
interest in primers or were directly involved in teaching. Yet such
scholarly contributions were mostly absent in texts like *Collection of
Wise Sayings* and *Enlarged Collection of Wise Words*. In this sense, these
texts were genuine folklore. This may well suggest overlaps between
elementary education, popular literacy education and public
education in Ming-Qing China.

At the same time, folklore and primers did sometimes overlap.
For example, *Collection of Ancient Worthies' Deeds* (*Guxian ji*), an
important piece of folk literature in the late Tang, demonstrates that
children's books and popular literature sometimes shared the same
sources and bore some resemblance to each other.[36]

This book contained tales, *bianwen*,[37] materials from primers and
leishu (reference books arranged according to subject). It was
composed in the form of poems with seven-character lines, and the
whole work contained forty pairs of sentences. In this form, the text,
like most children's primers, could be read and memorised easily.
Furthermore, many of the stories about heroes and good deeds (e.g.
the story about Kuang Heng, who studied very hard while living in
poverty) were exactly the same as those in popular primers such as
the *Mengqiu* and *The Trimetrical Classic*. Stories about some of the
twenty-four examples of filial piety were also presented in this
volume.[38] Because of these similarities, some scholars believe that
Collection of Ancient Worthies' Deeds was as one of the primers
circulating in the Dunhuang region in the late Tang period.[39]

Parallel to popular educational texts, primers in the *gushi* genre were produced to stand between the sober Neo-Confucian treatises and the poetic primers. The term *gushi* literally means (1) events in the past; (2) precedents; and (3) allusions. Allusions were not only frequently used in literature, they were also the origins of many phrases and idioms, so they became an indispensable part of language learning. The *gushi*-genre type of primer provided explanations and stories within each selected allusion. This type of primer, like Neo-Confucian treatises, drew its contents mainly from archaic sources. Under the circumstances of a "tripartite balance of religions," however, allusions selected in the primers of this genre were not constrained by Confucian orthodoxy but accommodated Taoism and Buddhism too. Furthermore, not only Confucian classics but a far broader range of historical documents — from literary masterpieces to anecdotes — were collected to explain particular terms.

The emergence of this genre was perhaps also related to the flourishing of popular literature. Here "popular literature" refers to (1) a form of literature which was appreciated by the court, the literati and the lower classes as well, such as Tang poetry; and (2) a form of literature which was prevalent among the lower classes, such as story-telling or oral literature (*shuochang wenxue*).

In the Tang, poetry flourished, and this allowed village school teachers to select some popular poems to instruct children. Yuan Zhen (779–831), a famous poet of the time, described this situation:

> I saw village children learning poems in the market at Pingshui. I walked toward them and enquired about this, they all answered: "Our teacher taught us the poems of Letian and Weizhi." They apparently did not know that I was Weizhi.[40]

"Letian" was the literary name of Bai Juyi (772–846), the great Tang poet. In the middle of the Tang dynasty, "Yuan and Bai" were often bracketed together because of their widely loved poems, and thus it was not surprising that their poems were used for teaching children in their early years of schooling. Later, *One Thousand Poems* (*Qianjia shi*) emerged and was popular in the Ming-Qing period.[41] It was widely accepted in late imperial China that students could learn to compose poems through memorising Tang and Song poetry.

By the end of the Tang, historical poems were appearing. One of the most popular was Hu Zeng's *Historical Poem* (*Yongshi shi*),[42] which was used as a primer from then until the end of the Qing dynasty.[43] Its popularity was related to the interest in historical story-telling which arose during the Five Dynasties and the Song periods. According to Su Shi (1037–1101), some parents who were tired of their naughty children gave them money and let them go and listen to stories such as the *Three Kingdoms* (*Sanguo zhi*). The children would laugh or cry as they followed the story.[44] Historical poems were tidier in style of language than this oral literature and traced a more orthodox historical line in content. For example, *Ancient History in One Thousand Characters* by Hu Yin, as mentioned in Chapter Two, was written in the form of short and simplified annals. The history of thousands of years — from the beginning of the world to the Five Dynasties, was all contained in one thousand characters. However, it was hard for children to understand because of its dense language. Generally each historical event was described by only eight characters, but the commentaries on these eight characters were very long.[45]

Although Song Neo-Confucian educators endeavoured to establish a monopoly for Confucianism in the education of children, the writing of primers was influenced by popular literature and the "tripartite balance of religions." Consequently, primers in the *gushi* genre emerged as children's storybooks.

The earliest primer using the term *gushi* in the title was *Shuyan gushi* (*Stories from Ancient Books*), by Hu Jizong of the Song dynasty. The book was arranged into twelve chapters (*juan*) according to subject, and the names of the twelve earthly branches (*dizhi*) were used to label the chapters. It included knowledge of astronomy, geography, rituals and etiquette, ancient medicine and alchemy, architecture and forests, insects and flora, music and arts, as well as of the legal system and government administration. In a 1464 preface, Cheng Wanzhi claimed that the book would help young students enrich their minds with knowledge. However, the whole primer was compiled by quoting ancient books out of context, which made it difficult to understand. In addition, many errors occurred in the reproduction of the text. Therefore, Chen Wanzhi felt it necessary to collate the text and then comment on it. Otherwise, he said, using the original text would be like walking in the dark without a candle, and the book would be too difficult to be used as a primer.[46] Thanks to Chen Wanzhi's efforts, the book survived and was passed down to later generations. In 1589, Cheng Juanzhi recalled in his preface to the book that he had studied the text in his elementary schooling.[47]

The book contained a broader range of subjects, including content relating to Taoism and Buddhism. For example, under the term *waidan neidan,* the book explained that *waidan* referred to the alchemical activities of Taoists while *neidan* referred to deep breathing exercises.[48] To explain the term *xiaosi,* the book traced it back to the time when Buddhism was first introduced into China. It recorded that many Buddhist temples were established in the Liang (502–519) and called *Xiaosi* or Xiao temples, because Emperor Wu was very interested in Buddhism and his surname was Xiao.[49] Furthermore, the fourth chapter appears to contain a great deal of heterodox material, covering as it does various deities, witchcraft and witch doctors. What is also worth noting is that the author only quoted documents from the original texts but made no critical comments on anything contained in the book.

Yet the book did not reject Confucian doctrine and exemplary models. For instance, there were stories derived from the twenty-four examples of filial sons, such as that of Zi Lu who purchased rice for his parents although he had to walk hundreds of miles.[50] Stories of industrious study, such as that of Kuang Heng, who made a hole in the wall so as to read his books by light from his neighbour's house, were also recorded in the book.[51]

With such a variety of content, it is hardly surprising that contradictions are to be found in the text. Along with the stories of industrious students, for instance, there is an extract from a poem by Su Shi which says that human worries result from the ability to read and that therefore education should cease once one has mastered basic reading skills.[52] The poem as a whole expresses Su's views on calligraphy and also reveals his feelings of frustration at being frequently banished during his official career, but because only two lines are included in the book, without any context or comments, it appears to be denying the value of education.

There are many stories in this primer, which makes it more appropriate for young children, although the text is not written in rhyme. This is because explaining all kinds of knowledge through stories makes learning easier and more interesting to children. For instance, the book uses a story from the *Master Lie* (*Liezi*)[53] to explain the concept of the sky (*tian*). It tells of a man from the state of Qi who was scared that the sky might collapse, and was worrying about where he could live if it did. The man was so tormented by this thought that for a long time he was not able to eat or sleep. Upon hearing of this, someone said to him: "The sky consists of air. [Air can never collapse], so why are you worried about it?" The man felt relieved and happy as soon as he heard this simple fact.[54] The story teaches the basic concept of the sky in an interesting way (Figure 3.1).

The suitability of the book for children is reinforced by the way it groups relevant terms together. For instance, the term *duanwu*, referring to the fifth day of the fifth month in the lunar calendar, occurs in the section on "months." The book gathers together all the terms relating to this specific day so as to provide children with knowledge of history, festivals and customs, as well as the seasons.

By quoting from *The Records of Years and Seasons* (*Suishi ji*), the author informs children that the term relates to the activity of commemorating Qu Yuan, a great patriotic poet of the state of Chu. Based on historical resources, the author tells how, on the fifth day of the fifth month of the lunar calendar, Qu Yuan committed suicide by throwing himself into the Miluo River because he was so despondent over the corruption of the court, his own inability to maintain the trust of the king and the collapse of his country. The local people were very sad about his death, so every year on that day they put rice into bamboo tubes and then threw them into the river to feed his spirit. Later, someone in Changsha saw Qu Yuan's spirit, which complained that a type of water monster (*jiaolong*) was eating his rice and leaving him to go hungry. To prevent this, spirit asked people to use five coloured threads to wrap over the bamboo tubes, as the water monster was scared of these five coloured threads.

After narrating the story of Qu Yuan, the author starts to explain the term *jiaoshu*, which was actually better-known as *zongzi*, a pyramid-shaped dumpling made of glutinous rice wrapped in bamboo or reed leaves. However, the author does not relate this to the worship of Qu Yuan as other stories usually do, but provides another source, saying that the pyramid-shaped dumpling originated in the games played on the fifth day inside the Tang Palace during the Tianbao reign-period (742–756).

Then the author returns to the theme of Qu Yuan by looking into the word *longzhou* (dragon boat). He first points out that these were

Figure 3.1 A man from the state of Qi was scared that the sky might collapse, *Stories from Ancient Books* (*Shuyan gushi*). Ming Wanli edition.

used for the boat races (*jingdu*) of that time. Quoting from *The Records of Years and Seasons*, he says that on the day Qu Yuan died people hurried to save him by boat, but failed to find his body. However, in order to commemorate Qu Yuan, this activity was perpetuated in the form of the Dragon Boat Festival.[55]

Throughout the book, the author uses stories to illustrate the meanings as well as the origins of the idioms. For phrases or words, he usually provides simple explanations first, which are then followed by stories which reveal the origins of the phrases or the words. Take the word *fujing* (carrying a birch-rod) as an example. The author first uses a simple sentence to explain the meaning of the word: to apologise for an offence. Then comes the story of Lian Po and Lin Xingru, to explain where the word came from. The story originated in *Records of the Historian* (*Shiji*), and tells how, during the period of the Warring States, Lian Po, a general of the state of Zhao, was unhappy that Lin Xiangru, who was only a persuasive talker (*shuike*), held a position higher than his. Lian Po thus often insulted Lin Xiangru who, however, seemed scared and always avoided Lian Po instead of confronting him. Xiangru's subordinates were not able to understand why he behaved like a coward and asked for an explanation. Xiangru replied: "It is only because of me and General Lian Po that Qin does not dare to invade our country. If we two fought each other, both of us would be destroyed in disputes, and then in turn our country would be in danger. I have to think about the safety of our country first and personal grief second." Lian Po felt shamed after hearing of this. To apologise for his offence, he went to see Xiangru carrying a birch-rod on his bare back — a gesture of his willingness to accept punishment. They then became friends who would die for each other.[56] Clearly, through reading this story, children would learn not only the meaning of the term but also history and good examples.

This primer also traced the origins of the words that had already come into common usage at the time the author compiled the book. For instance, it recorded that the first use of the word *mantou* (a type of Chinese bread) was by Shu Xi of the Jin (265–420) in his *Poetic Prose on Cakes* (*Bingfu*);[57] and such words as *xiaoxi* (news) and *ping'an* (safe) were all from Du Fu's poems.[58] These examples indicate that *Stories from Ancient Books* served the needs of both popular literacy and the study of the classics.

Gushi **Primers in the Ming-Qing Period**

Many Ming-Qing writers of primers were enthusiastic about the *gushi* genre. Perhaps this is because primers of this type appear richer in content than those in other forms. For instance, *The Young Horse and the Shadow of a Whip* (*Longwen bianying*) was originally written by Xiao Liangyou (1550–1602), a scholar in charge of the National Academy (*guozi jian*), the highest educational institution in the Ming.[59] Although he held such a high academic position, Xiao paid special attention to elementary education and was personally involved in compiling a primer. The original title of the book was *Stories for Young Children* (*Mengyang gushi*). The word *meng*, as mentioned earlier, referred to young children who were ignorant and innocent; and the word *yang* meant to nourish. *Mengyang* in the title clearly indicated that the aim of the book was to nourish ignorant and young children. This title also specified the content and the readers for whom the book was intended. At the beginning of the book, the author used only eight characters to tell his readers: "[Each sentence] is made of four characters; [the aim of this book] is to instruct you young children."[60]

Like *Stories from Ancient Books*, the content of this book originated from historical texts and touched upon many subjects, including history, politics, the military, arts, alchemy and alchemists, Confucian scholars, moral examples, treacherous officials at court and unusual phenomena. Yet unlike *Stories from Ancient Books*, this book was arranged in rhyme, and verbal parallelism (*dui'ou* or *duizhang*) was observed in every couplet which, with four-character lines, narrated a story.

Later scholars like Yang Chenzheng (dates unknown) regarded this book highly. In his opinion, this book could help children learn twice as much with half the effort. With this book, children (even those who were not very bright) could easily memorise a few sentences and receive some knowledge of Chinese history every day. To him, children were like the *longwen*, a fine young horse, which runs fast as soon as it sees the shadow of a whip. With this in mind, he changed the title of the book to *Longwen bianying*, implying that the book would function as a whip.[61] Yang's contribution to the book was not limited to this. He enriched the book and corrected many errors in Xiao Liangyou's edition.

The format of *Longwen bianying* was appreciated by many scholars during the Qing. For instance, two scholars made a sequel to it. Meanwhile, an abridged edition with the title *Siyan biandu* (*Four Characters for Reading Convenience*) was distributed by some booksellers. In 1883, Li Enshou, a teacher, thought that the plain language and rich content of *Longwen bianying* would benefit children, but agreed that there were many repetitious sentences and mistakes. So he revised the book again.[62]

The appearance of illustrated primers marked another important development in the history of Chinese primers. This was a result of the development of woodcuts, which were employed to illustrate a wide variety of books, ranging from Confucian classics to technical manuals. In the history of Chinese painting, woodcuts were mainly produced by artisan painters. "Artisan painters," in a traditional Chinese sense, were not regarded as artists but as skilled craftsmen, who often belonged to a guild or a family (sometimes regional) organisation. Consequently, artisan painters did not usually leave their names on their products, and were called *huagong* in order to differentiate them from scholar-artists and court artists (and later professional artists). Within this tradition, "high art," as exhibited in the standard works of the scholar-artists, was confined to a limited range of subjects, typically landscape scenes, and rarely touched on the reality of society. In contrast, artisan painters, who were responsible for most woodcuts, favoured themes which were more "profane," such as scenes where children were often represented as part of the daily life of ordinary people. Court artists or professional painters lay somewhere between these two groups. Thus in painting landscapes, works by court artists or professional artists followed the practice of scholar-artists, though their style often differed. In Ming and Qing times, some professional painters collaborated with artisan painters and created some very artistic woodcuts.[63] At that time, woodcuts became popular not only among ordinary people but among the educated elite as well. Because fine and artistic woodcuts made books more marketable, they appeared in a wide variety of books illustrating a broad range of subjects.[64] These illustrations were similar to anecdotal painting, in that the subject matter was often the main factor in determining how characters were to be depicted. As for primers, woodcuts made these specific texts more interesting and appealing to children. However, in most illustrations for primers children were depicted as small-scale adults, which is perhaps consistent with the contents of the primers that were designed, according to Confucian ideals, as instruction manuals to teach children adult behaviour.

The most impressive example is *Stories for Daily Learning* (*Riji gushi*)[65] which, according to *The Book Catalogue of Qianqing Hall* (*Qianqing tang shumu*), was written by Yu Shao of the Yuan. However, the various versions passed down to the present were all produced in the Ming and afterwards. A brief discussion of the 1542 edition may demonstrate how Ming-Qing writers used and reproduced the primers from previous dynasties.

The 1542 version of *Stories for Daily Learning* was created by Xiong Damu (fl. 1542), a teacher at elementary level (*guanmeng*). In his preface to the book, Xiong clearly stated that in the course of teaching children this book, he found so many errors in it that he could not even punctuate (*judou*) the text. Therefore, in his spare time he started to edit and comment on the book. After many years' hard work, he eventually completed the book, and with his permission, his neighbour published it.[66] According to the catalogue of the Qianqing Hall, the original edition of *Stories for Daily Learning* consisted of ten chapters, but Xiong's version had only nine covering (1) those born with knowledge and those obtaining knowledge through learning; (2) filial piety; (3) respecting elders and teachers; (4) making friends and maintaining friendship in a proper way; (5) virtues such as generosity, sincerity, chastity, thrift and integrity; (6) family relations; (7) pertinent conduct in social life; (8) charity; and (9) royalty and righteousness. Each example was presented with a four-character title, followed by the details. Not every case had an illustration, as only two pictures were located in the upper part of each page while in the lower part the text might contain three or more cases (*shangtu/xiawen* format). Each picture was accompanied by a couplet or a four-sentence poem, highlighting the meaning of the picture as well as the text.

There were a few editions of *Stories for Daily Learning* that differed not only in illustrations but also in content. Some were circulated and survived in Japan. For instance, a 1669 Japanese version was based on a Ming edition collated by Zhang Ruitu (of whom no biographical details are known). Compared to other versions circulating in Japan at the time, Zhang's version was considered a complete text.[67] It contained only seven chapters, of which the first chapter was entirely devoted to the twenty-four examples of filial piety, and the second included the first two chapters of the 1542 edition. From the third chapter onward, some texts resembled those of the 1542 version, but many parts appeared entirely different. As for illustrations, only the first chapter in this 1669 edition adopted the half-illustration and half-text style, and had all twenty-four examples illustrated. From the second to the seventh chapter, only the beginning of each chapter had a full-page illustration. It is not clear whether this 1669 version was derived from a 1591 copy when woodcuts had changed in style, and the full-page illustrations were preferred to the half-illustration and half-text format.[68] Nevertheless, it is clear that these versions of *Stories for Daily Learning* differed in content and illustrations. This was perhaps determined by the experience the editors or the commentators had had in their teaching as well as by their artistic tastes.

In sum, the appearance of the Wang Yangming school in the late Ming period challenged formalistic education and signalled an awareness of the distinctive characteristics of children. The concept of elementary education in Wang Yangming's teaching appeared more liberal than that in the Song Neo-Confucian definition. Also, the writing of primers during the Tang-Song period was influenced not only by Neo-Confucianism but also by the flourishing of literature. Under these circumstances, poetic primers and texts in the form of story-telling were produced to serve youngsters not only as their textbooks but also as more enjoyable literature. Most of the Ming-Qing primers, generally speaking, were descendents of the genres which appeared before and during the Song. This means that some earlier texts were directly adopted in the teaching process; and even new productions stayed within the previous framework. However, illustrations made many primers not only more marketable but also more appealing to children.

By and large, traditional Chinese education was dominated by Confucianism, so the terms "Confucian education" and "traditional Chinese education" are often used interchangeably. This understanding, however, is based on a very broad definition of "Confucianism," namely that anything which is not Buddhism or Taoism is Confucianism. This is determined by the fact that the so-called "tripartite balance of religions" in the late imperial period influenced interpretations and definitions of Confucian theories and concepts, and then a process of incorporation of non-Confucian elements into Confucianism inevitably brought divisions within Confucian schools. Some unorthodox content represented in primers reflected this complexity. Nevertheless, Confucian moral ethics in education were emphasised by all schools, despite their different approaches to the understanding of the essentials of Confucianism, and this ensured the popularity of some primers over many centuries.

~ *Chapter 4* ~

Shaping the Ideal Child:
Ritualising the Body

Chapter Two pointed out that Song Neo-Confucian educators differentiated "elementary education" from "elementary learning," and the focus in education shifted from the learning of characters, emphasised in Han learning, to moral cultivation. This chapter will concentrate on how this educational theory was further developed into a philosophical pursuit of the relationship between the mind (or the internal) and its embodiment in behavior (or the external). Reflected in education, this pursuit was translated into "ritualising the body," a process of controlling the external and then nourishing the internal.

The term "ritualising the body" in this chapter is defined as behaving in accordance with rules of demeanour and deportment derived from the *Record of Rites*. Indeed, from the Song and throughout the Qing, by drawing upon sources from the *Record of Rites*, Confucian writers of primers established numerous guidelines and rules for the practice of rituals and good manners. Similar rules or rituals were often adopted and repeated in either independent texts, school regulations, or family rules. This repetitive feature can be interpreted as a reflection of intellectual attempts to shape children's personalities into the ideal Confucian mould.

To provide a theoretical framework for examining these detailed rules and guidelines, this chapter first probes the concept of *li* (ritual) and Song Neo-Confucian notions of human nature. Within this framework the second section elaborates the Song Neo-Confucian approach to the education of children by analysing two educational treatises, written by Zhu Xi and Chen Chun respectively. The third section then centres on the Ming-Qing primers in this genre, discussing further how actual behavioural patterns were established to shape the ideal child and thence an ideal Confucian society. Finally the chapter concludes with a focus on information about actual teaching practice at a late-Ming school, so as to help us understand primers of this type and highlight the nature and aim of elementary education in pre-modern China.

The Dynamics of *Li* or Ritual in Primers

Li is a very significant concept in Confucianism. In English, the term "ritual" is very close to the meaning of *li*. From a religious perspective, some have seen "ritual" as "the origin of religion," or "a technique of magic, and worship." In anthropology, ritual has been seen as "a system of procedure, a form or pattern of social interaction."[1] In a more restricted sense, ritual is symbolic action related to the sacred. In a broader sense, ritual expresses cultural values which regularise a social situation. In ancient China, *li* in the restricted sense referred to religious and social ceremonies, such as ancestor worship. In the broader sense, *li* was basically regarded as decorum, and it provided an objective standard of conduct and governed social deportment and domestic relationships.[2]

Herbert Fingarette sees *li* in the *Analects* not only as "secular prosaic moralism"[3] but as a "holy rite" and "sacred ceremony"[4] as well. He argues that social etiquette and moral obligations are ritual and can be seen as "the ceremonial aspect of life that bestows sacredness upon persons, acts, and objects which have a role in the performance of ceremony."[5] Here, Fingarette interprets *li* as a combination of human convention and moral obligations with sacred symbolic action.

In Neo-Confucianism, the structure of *li* consisted very much of ritualised behaviour and rites. Ritualised behaviour in general meant the physical actions of the body and was restricted by social demands for conformity. The performance of rituals, such as weddings, funerals and ancestral rites, was human activity related to the sacred. Song Neo-Confucians such as Zhu Xi saw ritual first of all as giving "defined form to human relations and suitable expression to the feelings of mutual respect that attach to all specific relationships."[6] On this basis, they believed that, through education, Confucian ethical values and the modes of civilising behaviour could be promoted throughout the whole of society.

Both Confucius and Zhu Xi chose education as a significant means to pass on their messages to the whole of society and to carry out their ideals. In Confucianism everyone theoretically had an equal opportunity for education. Confucius said: "In teaching there should be no distinction of classes."[7] According to Zhu Xi, "classes" here did not refer to social strata but to the differences between good and bad. On the one hand, Zhu Xi proclaimed that the original nature (*xing*) of all human beings was good; on the other, he stressed that physical constitution and practice (*qizhi*) caused distinctions among people. Based on this idea, Zhu Xi asserted that the function of education was to bring men back to their original state.[8] Indeed, in Neo-Confucian theory everyone could attain sagehood through self-cultivation, in spite of their different social positions. In reality, however, Zhu Xi and other Song Neo-Confucian scholars distinguished themselves by practising etiquette and rituals strictly according to classical models. In other words, a high level of morality was not embodied only in everyday actions such as walking, speaking and greeting. Ethical observations were primarily emphasised in the performance of classical ceremonies. Many Song scholars, in order to defend real Confucian social ethics, objected to popular customs which they considered to be debased.[9] In Song Neo-Confucianism, the performance of classical ceremonies had no less importance than the ritualisation of the body. Hence, it is quite understandable that the two classics, the *Book of Etiquette and Ceremonial*, which describes the steps of various rites, and the *Record of Rites*, which provides the details of decorum, took on a new importance. Based on the *Book of Etiquette and Ceremonial*, Zhu Xi composed *Family Rituals* (*Jiali*);[10] and the *Record of Rites* became one of the main sources of his *Elementary Learning*.[11]

This emphasis on performing classical rituals and practising ritualised behaviour was closely interrelated with changes in the standards and structure of societies. In the Song, a new scholar-official elite (*shi*) emerged through the civil service examinations and replaced the old aristocracy. Further changes such as intensive economic growth,[12] "revolution" in the fields of science and technology,[13] the formation of a civilian absolutist court and the spread of schooling[14] accelerated the demand for a re-definition of nobility and gentility. Among the criteria for inclusion in the ruling class, moral and intellectual qualities became more important than good birth. Under these circumstances, the school of Neo-Confucianism chose education as an accessible instrument to help promote Confucian ethical values throughout society. Therefore, the concept of education as a whole in Song Neo-Confucianism focused on individual commitment to moral transformation; and the interest of its exponents in elementary education was mainly motivated by their moral and religious concerns. As for the aim of education for children, it was already expressed in one sentence from the *Book of Changes*:

> [The method of dealing with] the young and ignorant is to nourish what is correct (*meng yi yang zheng*); this accomplishes the service of the sage.[15]

The meaning of nourishing youths and leading them back to "correctness" was also embedded in the term *jiaoyu* (education) that, in classical times, referred to the enlightenment of people. *Jiao* alone meant to teach, to awaken, to make aware. We can find this meaning in the *Book of Documents* (*Shangshu*):

> [Pangeng] is making the people aware (*jiao*) of his teaching, ...[16]

In relation to *jiao*, the meaning of *yu* was to nourish. The *Book of Changes* said:

> The Superior man (*junzi*) strives to be resolute in his conduct and nourishes (*yu*) his virtue.[17]

These two quotations taken from the Confucian classics suggest that the concept of education in early China meant moulding a person's character, not just the acquisition of skills or knowledge. By applying this notion to elementary education specifically, Song Neo-Confucianists prescribed certain modes of behaviour and believed that the practice of such ritualised behaviour would nourish virtues and correctness.

The practice of ritualised behaviour was intended to repress desires (*yu*). The Neo-Confucianism of the Cheng-Zhu school represented the Principle of Nature (*li*) and material force (*qi*) as different forms of reality. The Principle of Nature was the ultimate substance of man and things, providing the paradigms of good; whilst material force gave rise to evil, for the endowment of material force in man might be impure and imperfect. "Desire" was a manifestation of the endowment of material force, so there was a moral opposition between the Principle of Nature and desire.[18]

The term "desire" was originally used in the *Laozi* as well as the *Mencius*. Mencius said: "To nourish the mind, nothing is better than to have few desires (*guayu*)."[19] Yet "having no desire" (*wuyu*) came from the *Laozi*.[20] Zhou Dunyi (1017–1073), one of the greatest Neo-Confucianists in the Song, absorbed the ideas of Taoism and stated that the way of becoming a sage was to have no desire.[21] Cheng Yi held the same opinion. He said that human desire was contrary to propriety, and only when there was no human desire, would all be the Principle of Nature.[22] The problem is that neither Zhou nor Cheng defined the term *yu* or desire, and "having no desire" obviously showed the influence of Buddhism as well as Taoism. Therefore, Zhu Xi felt it necessary to give the term a definition. At first, he admitted that the desire for food when hungry and desire for drink when thirsty were part of human nature and were proper desires.[23] Then he drew a line between proper desires and improper desires: "We follow our natural desires. But it is wrong to let these desires go to extremes."[24] Here the "natural desires" were proper desires, which were also recognised by Zhang Zai. Zhang Zai said that the original state of material force, such as the relation between the mouth and the stomach, was pure and good; yet "sensual desires," which became a burden to one's mind,[25] were improper. Zhu Xi further referred the "sensual desires" to the eye's desire for colour and the ear's desire for sound, which he regarded as "desires of material force."[26] With this definition, Zhu Xi agreed with Zhou Dunyi's view: "to nourish the mind one should not stop at having few desires and preserving one's mind. One should have fewer and fewer desires until there is none."[27] The word "desires," as Zhou used it here, was interpreted by Zhu Xi as meaning "selfish desires."[28]

The Way of repressing "selfish desires" and moving toward good was to refuse to look, listen, speak or make any movement in a way which was contrary to propriety.[29] Song Neo-Confucianists strongly believed that there was a close link between the rectification of the mind and its embodiment in deportment. Cheng Yi said: "What comes from within has its response outside. To control the external is to nourish the internal."[30] Zhu Xi further explained that "looking, listening, speaking and movement all proceed from the mind."[31] The relation of mind to body, as Mary Douglas points out, can be seen "as exchanges of condensed statements about the relation of society to the individual."[32] Body represents the wider society and mind refers to "the individual identified with the sub-group concerned."[33] According to this theory, bodily control usually corresponds with social norms, and bodily carriage is often restricted by social demands. In Cheng and Zhu's expression, to behave in accordance with propriety was "to nourish the internal" and "to overcome any selfish desires" embodied in one's "looking, listening, speaking, and Movement."[34] In Douglas' theory, this kind of nourishment can be expressed as "symbolic nourishment."[35] In the relation of mind to body, the process of "symbolic nourishment" is that "spiritual values are made effective through material acts, that body and mind are intimately united."[36] This theory is consistent with Neo-Confucian belief that the performance of bodily ritual would eventually shape a person's personality. In particular, if youths practised good manners when they were ignorant, correct manners would then become natural to them. This was called "nourishing one's nature."

Children from the ages of eight to fifteen, as discussed in Chapter One, were at the first stage of learning. The main purpose of education at this stage was not only the acquisition of literacy skills, but more importantly, to keep children away from all practice and sight of naughtiness. Therefore, the moral instruction and guidance of children's behaviour were of great concern and became the most important content in Neo-Confucian treatises on education.

To serve this aim of moral cultivation, the teaching of reading and writing integrated moral and religious instruction, and therefore the *Four Books* became the most important texts in elementary education. Zhu Xi pointed out that children should read the *Great Learning* first, for this book could help them gain a broad grasp of Confucian learning; secondly, they should read the *Analects*, in order to establish the fundamentals of learning; then they should read the *Mencius*, which would develop their minds and lead them to the way of the sages; finally, they should read the *Doctrine of the Mean* to discover the more subtle meanings of the Confucian classics.[37] This suggestion was adopted by many scholars and every dynasty after the Song dynasty.[38]

However, the *Four Books* were too difficult to teach young beginners. Only a few very bright children were able to learn them at the very beginning of their schooling. Therefore, from the Tang dynasty onward some simple textbooks were produced. Generally, children started learning characters from these books before they started on the *Four Books* and other Confucian classics. Such primers provided both the rudiments of literacy skills and Confucian teachings.

To Neo-Confucianists, rules for morality and social manners took precedence over other subjects in primers, as they believed that religion, morals and good behaviour were the three integral components of elementary education, and Confucian virtues were embodied in the practice of ritualised behaviour which was regarded as the basis of self-cultivation and as the way to sagehood.

The rules for rituals and guidelines for good manners mainly derived from the classic *Record of Rites*. It was the Song Neo-Confucian educators who regarded remarks on demeanour and deportment in the *Record of Rites* as a suitable source for educating children. For example, Zhu Xi cited these principles in his *Elementary Learning*. However, the original text of the *Record of Rites* was too difficult for children. Some Song Neo-Confucianists thus realised the necessity of developing an appropriate set of regulations for young children. Zhu Xi and Lu Zishou (1132–1180) discussed this issue seriously. Both of them noted the difference between education in the Song and in classical times. According to their dialogue, in classical times, young children were taught cleaning, sweeping and polite conversation as soon as they were able to talk and eat. In contrast, children in the Song were taught to compose couplets and showy prose. In their opinion, this kind of education ruined a child's originally good nature. Therefore, they planned to educate youths in accordance with the classical tradition and establish a set of regulations.[39] Though Lu composed nothing on this subject, Zhu Xi compiled *Children Should Know* which, together with *Rituals for Children in Rhythm* (*Xiaoxue lishi*) by Chen Chun (1159–1233), became a classical treatise for education of the young.

Modes of Behaviour in the Primers Written by Zhu Xi and Chen Chun

Zhu Xi and his contemporaries believed that virtues were embodied in behaviour and that a high level of morality could be reached through the practice of "ritual." They then chose education as an instrument to spread their concepts and approved modes of behaviour throughout society. As mentioned earlier, in the Song the demand for literacy and the use of literacy skills were inspired by economic development, and basic education was more prevalent than before. To Song Neo-Confucians, however, elementary education was not simply a stage in teaching the rudiments of literacy skills. They saw children as naturally ignorant and foolish, so in their design the main aim of elementary education was to nourish and mould children's personalities in their early years. For this purpose they transformed "rituals" in their treatises into rules for guiding children's manners and integrated them with moral instruction. To further demonstrate this Song Neo-Confucian approach to the education of children, this section examines Zhu Xi's *Children Should Know* and Chen Chun's *Rituals for Children in Rhyme*.

For the convenience of analysis, the contents of these two texts are classified into five categories: (1) demeanour of the body; (2) clothing; (3) manners in school; (4) table manners; and (5) behaviour in the bedroom.

1. Demeanour of the Body

First come instructions as to how to greet people. Zhu Xi instructed children how to give a reverent greeting to their superiors. He said:

> When he meets his superiors on the road, a boy must stand upright and make obeisance by cupping one hand in the other before his chest; or he should move quickly to be in front of them and make a bow with hands clasped.[40]

Second are the instructions as to how to talk to people.

In pre-modern China, the authority of a father in a family was equated with the authority of the sovereign in the state. Therefore, the rules concentrated on how to behave properly before the father:

> Children have to look at their fathers' feet when their fathers stand before them;
> They have to look at their fathers' knees when their fathers take a seat;
> They have to look at their fathers' faces when they answer their fathers' enquiries;
> They have to look beyond their fathers when they stand before them.[41]

The reason behind this is that one's eyes might reveal the disposition of one's mind.[42]

With regard to talking to adults, Zhu Xi instructed children how to speak in a suitable voice and to use proper words:

> As a son to his parents and a pupil to his teacher, he should speak with a soft and submissive voice. His speech should not be too fast; his voice should not be too high; he should not make a racket, neither speak lightly nor make jests.[43]

2. Clothing

In *Children Should Know*, Zhu Xi considered decency of apparel as a matter of prime importance in good manners. He said that youths should take care of their own scarves, clothes, socks and shoes, and keep them neat and clean. If youths were slovenly in dress, they would be underestimated by others.[44]

Why did decency of apparel have a place in this training? According to Chen Chun, a superior man had to dress neatly and properly to show his quality of nobility, then he might be respected by other people.[45]

3. Manners in School

In pre-modern China the authority of a teacher in school was equal to that of parents at home; sometimes the task of instruction was taken over by children's fathers or other elders of the family. Therefore, youths had to be obedient not only to their teachers but also to their fathers or other superiors, who all had authority to educate them. Zhu Xi particularly stressed that youths should not argue with teachers, parents and other superiors even if their instruction was wrong.[46]

With regard to study, both Zhu Xi and Chen Chun encouraged children to be industrious and diligent and to ask questions when they had doubts. Children were also instructed not to fight with fellow students and not to make a noise and disturb others. Furthermore, Zhu Xi required children to read books aloud without making any mistakes whatsoever. He said: "Only when they have read the book many times, can they recite it automatically and commit it to memory."[47] The overwhelming emphasis on repetition and memorisation was a characteristic of elementary training in traditional Chinese education, but in Zhu Xi's instructions repeating and memorising were not only a teaching method but also a sign of studying hard.

4. Table Manners

In pre-modern China, training in table manners also had a place in elementary education. For example, Chen Chun said:

> When a boy has a drink with his superior, he should kneel down to accept the drink given by the superior. If the superior has not started drinking, the boy should not dare to raise his glass. If the superior has not finished his drink, the boy should not finish first.[48]

Also from Chen Chun's book:

> At a banquet, ... a boy should neither gnaw a bone nor pick his teeth.[49]

Again, Chen Chun said:

> When you are seated with your elders, you should be silent and calm. You should never speak unless you are invited to do so or questioned by your elders.[50]

There were also instructions about technical skills, such as the use of chopsticks and spoons: "when one uses a spoon, one is not allowed still to hold his chopsticks; one has to put his spoon on the table while using chopsticks."[51]

5. Behaviour in the Bedroom

In his *Rituals for Children in Rhyme*, Chen Chun paid special attention to serving parents:

> To serve parents, a son should rise as soon as the cock crows, then wash himself. After combing his hair, putting on his hat and dressing himself properly, he should go to his parents' chamber.[52]

This instruction was derived from the *Record of Rites* and related to the practice of filial piety. This will be discussed further in the next section and in Chapter Five.

Evidently, teaching children the rules of good manners was of great importance in Song Neo-Confucian elementary education. The significance of these rules in elementary training was in the first place related to the practice of morality. In Confucianism, benevolence (*ren*) was a key term, referring to the virtues of goodness, humanity and love. It was impossible to become a superior man (*junzi*) or a complete man without the virtue of benevolence.[53] A good Confucianist had to conduct himself with reverence in any circumstance and practice the virtue of benevolence. Confucius gave his disciples this clear message:

> Zhong Gong asked about the virtue of benevolence. Confucius said: "Behave when away from home as though you were in the presence of an important guest. Deal with the common people as though you were officiating at an important sacrifice. Do not do to others what you would not want others to do to you. Then there will be no dissatisfaction either in the state or at home."[54]

Later, Neo-Confucianism, especially the Cheng-Zhu school, laid even greater stress on morality. For Neo-Confucianists, the goal of pursuing learning was to achieve moral transcendence. The term "the investigation of things and the extension of knowledge" (*gewu zhizhi*) stood for intellectual and moral cultivation. To a certain extent, this resembled the humanist concept of a complete man.[55] To young children, self-cultivation was firstly embodied in the activities of daily life, such as greeting people and undertaking light housework.

Furthermore, the rules in those five categories were in fact intended to guide children to practise the virtues of loyalty, piety and obedience, and the virtue of obedience was central to the other virtues. Only when children were obedient to their parents, schoolteachers and other superiors could they be regarded as having practised the virtues of loyalty and piety.

In addition, good manners were related not only to the practice of virtues but also to social stability. In the *Great Learning* "eight items" combined self-cultivation with keeping good order at home and dealing with the affairs of state. It was said that a person who was not cultivated would not be able to keep his family in good order. If his family was in chaos, he could not be expected to manage state affairs well.[56] In this sense, the virtue of obedience embodied two elements: loyalty to the emperor in the empire and filial piety towards parents at home.

To sum up, Song Neo-Confucians like Zhu Xi and Chen Chun placed great stress on moral education in order to bring up children with proper filial piety, loyalty, and especially obedience; *li* or ritual was in accordance with these virtues. In their design, the ritualisation of the body was the basis of self-cultivation, which was regarded as "an experience of the realisation of the true self"[57] as well as a way to attain sagehood. To a considerable extent, "ritual" not only had the function of guiding children's behaviour and leading children along a certain moral path, it also served the requirements of social order and security in the empire.

The Rules for Rituals and Good Manners in Ming-Qing Primers

The rules Zhu Xi and his followers established became the norms — what should be done, what should not be done — which prescribed children's social behaviour for centuries. During the Ming and Qing periods, the creation of regulations for children was taken as seriously as in the Song. There were three types: (1) rules for rituals and guidelines for good manners; (2) school precepts; and (3) family regulations. All of them shared a common characteristic in that they re-expressed the rituals in the *Record of Rites* in plain language.

The Rules for Rituals and Guidelines for Good Manners

Not all texts on rituals and good manners were devised directly for children. Some of them were actually intended for teachers who were expected to teach children basic etiquette at the beginning of schooling. This type of teaching manual existed as early as the Song, an example being *The Methods of Teaching Children* (*Xunmeng fa*) by Wang Rixiu (dates unknown). The text of this contained instructions on ritualised behaviour and the rudiments of literacy skills. Similar manuals were produced during the Ming and Qing period, for example *Rituals for Nourishing Children* (*Mengyang li*) by Lü Kun (1536–1618), and *Instructions for Young Children* (*Youxun*) by Cui Xuegu of the Qing.

  The first six parts of Lü Kun's *Rituals for Nourishing Children* were devoted to instructions about how to care for and nourish children before they started their schooling, and included such things as the way to handle a crying infant. There were also suggestions that parents should not feed young children elaborated food but simple food; and they should dress youngsters not in silk or fur but in plain clothes; and should not let young children slap anyone's face or swear at other people. However, the text did not elaborate on rituals as other manuals did. Instead, it focused on issues concerning reading and writing, such as how to make ink, how to use a brush and how to write characters. These matters, in Lü's opinion, were all associated with the cultivation of good conduct and demeanour.[58]

Cui Xuegu's *Instructions for Young Children* provided teachers with more detailed instructions on how to bow, stand, sit and eat than Lü's text. Besides this, it covered principles concerning the teaching of reading and writing. The author made it very clear that the manual was intended for teachers teaching children at the beginning of their schooling (*mengshi*). This is because he was fully aware of the difficulty of teaching children at this stage, which was so important for the child's future learning and moral development.[59]

The titles of the above two primers suggest that they were intended for children; but the contents indicate that they were actually addressed to teachers. Why were such teaching manuals listed as children's books (*mengshu*)? Perhaps it was due to the broad definition of children's education (*mengxue*). After all, they shared the same content as primers on rituals and good manners. Ming primers in this genre generally consisted of two parts: ritualised behaviour patterns and rudiments of literacy skills, and were intended for children to read and, at the same time, to practise. Among them are *Rituals for Children* (*Tongzi li*) by Tu Xiying (dates unknown) of the Ming, and *Elementary Learning in the Classics* (*Xiaoxue guxun*) by Huang Zuo (1490–1566).

Tu Xiying selected rituals for children from such classics as *Details for Ceremonial, Inner Rules* (*Neize*), *Rituals for Youths* and *Duties of Disciples* (*Dizi zhi*), as well as from primers produced in previous dynasties, and arranged these selections into three sections. The first section was about ritualising the body and cultivating the mind, centring on bodily deportment. There were instructions on daily practice, such as washing one's face in the morning, dressing and clapping hands; submissive behaviour, such as bowing and kneeling; and the proper postures for standing, sitting and walking. Apart from these, appropriate manners in speaking, reading books, listening to teachers' instruction and eating were also emphasised. The second part was about how to serve parents and elder brothers at home and teachers in school, including instructions on cleaning, replying, and comportment (*jintui*, literally meaning "coming forward and retreating") with regard to meeting elders, making parents feel cool during the summer, leaving home in the morning and returning in the evening. The appropriate manners for waiting on table, sitting with elders, greeting elders on the road, and serving elders were also detailed in the text. The third section dealt with ceremonial behaviour in school, such as how to behave in the ceremony of paying respect to teachers, in morning and evening assemblies, in the dormitory, and when meeting guests. Instructions on reading books and writing characters were also attached to this part.[60] In fact, there is nothing new in this primer. Nevertheless, it contained a complete set of guidelines for children to ritualise their conduct, to behave properly in school as well as at home, and to learn good manners in such areas as serving, receiving and greeting other people.

Huang Zuo's *Elementary Learning in the Classics*, as its title indicates, was based on Zhu Xi's *Elementary Learning* which, in Huang's view, was too broad in theme and too abstract and deep in content. Consequently, the book was abandoned by elementary teachers who, instead, chose other primers for the beginning of schooling. Huang Zuo criticised this practice, arguing that the way to steer children in their moral development was not to allow any instruction other than Confucian doctrine to enter children's minds, as children at this stage were so naive that they would accept whatever they were taught.[61] Thus, he decided to compile this manual by selecting materials from the Inner Chapters of Zhu Xi's *Elementary Learning* and some references from other books. The broad themes presented in Zhu Xi's book were reduced to twenty items which were classified into three parts: ritualising the body (*jingshen*), approaching the Way (*shidao*) and learning literacy skills and the six arts. The first part focused on the correct behaviour in moving, serving, and eating, and the appropriate ways of dressing, cleaning, replying and carrying oneself. The second part was concerned with the Way (*dao*). However, Huang Zuo avoided abstract concepts and principles. Instead, he concentrated on practical issues, such as human relationships, filial piety, respecting elders, prudence in deeds, sincerity in words, overflowing love to all, and benevolence. As these first two parts mainly concentrated on moral instruction, the third section then dealt with literacy and the six arts. Obviously, the content and the structure of the manual did not go beyond the Neo-Confucian framework, but Huang Zuo modified Zhu Xi's *Elementary Learning* and made it more like a primer and more suitable for children at the elementary level.

During the Qing, more primers on ritual were produced, such as Li Yuxiu's *Regulations for Disciples* (*Dizi gui*), which was acclaimed as one of the most popular primers in the middle of the Qing. The text expounded upon four abstract principles from the *Analects*: being filial and fraternal, being earnest and truthful, overflowing in love to all and cultivating the friendship of the good. Li Yuxiu collected instructions for behaviour from the *Record of Rites* and other classics and then instructed children how their behaviour was linked with Confucian virtues. He said that children should

> bow deeply, kneel down reverently; not leave shoes inside the door, nor stand with one foot raised nor lean on anything; not sit with knees apart, nor walk badly.[62]

This instruction included rules similar to those concerning demeanour and deportment in the *Record of Rites*, for example:

> Do not tread on shoes [left outside the door] (*bu jianlü*).[63]
> Do not stand with one foot raised. Do not sit with knees wide apart.[64]

Li Yuxiu's unique contribution was to tie certain behaviour patterns to specific teachings of Confucianism through his use of the *Analects*. He believed that bodily control was actually an expression of the inner virtue of a person, and for example the virtue of sincerity was embodied in bowing, kneeling, sitting and walking; and through these physical acts, one could achieve the fulfilment of sincerity. This helped children to understand and practise Confucian teachings. The format of the manual was suitable for children, in that each sentence was composed of three characters and the whole manual was rhymed.

Also based on the teachings in the *Analects*, Chen Hu (1613–1675) wrote the *Daily Practice of Elementary Learning* (*Xiaoxue richeng*) for his two sons. Like other primers of this type, this tiny manual contained moral instructions on filial piety, brotherhood, proper behaviour, sincere speech, respect and friendship, as well as literacy skills. In fact, nothing is new. Yet by using the contrast of synonyms and antonyms, the author arranged appropriate behaviour patterns via the improper, which made his instructions very clear to young children. For instance,

appropriate behaviour	improper conduct
All speeches are sincere;	all speeches are not sincere.
Never saying anything unlawful;	talking improperly.
Laughing infrequently;	laughing too often.
No mistakes in answering questions;	making mistakes in replying.[65]

The author did not apparently pay much attention to linguistic beauty as the text was written in a form of colloquial language. This was perhaps his attempt to integrate the teaching derived from Confucius' *Analects* into daily usage.

Another primer of this kind was *Poetry for Nourishing Children* (*Mengyang shijiao*), by Hu Yuan of the Qing. The title indicates its poetic format. In these poems with seven-character lines, the author focused on deportment in aspects of standing, walking, sitting, *longshou* (meaning "putting each hand in the opposite sleeve."), *gong shou* (meaning "to salute by cupping one hand in the other before one's chest"), bowing, kneeling, dressing, eating, greeting, remaining silent, sleeping, defecating, cleaning and wiping. There were also instructions about how to serve parents and older brothers; how to respect teachers, get along with friends, and receive guests. Instructions on reading, writing, and chanting poems were the last part of the manual.

Not surprisingly, each form of conduct presented in this primer only repeated what had already been cited in the classics and other manuals. However, the uniqueness of this primer was that the author addressed all possible problems that could occur in children's daily lives. For instance, urinating and defecating were everyday activities, and youngsters could be naughty, acting according to their needs and convenience instead of behaving in an appropriate way. This issue was not addressed in the classics but was a reality in school life. So the author instructed pupils:

If you are going out to empty your bowels,
you should choose an out-of-the-way place.
It is offensive if you leave excrement under the sun;
It is ghastly if you leave excrement in front of the door.
Take your coat off when you are going to the lavatory,
And wash your hands when you return from the toilet.[66]

Obviously, this is not an elegant poem but it would be so easy for children to chant and memorise.

Serving parents was a major issue in classical rituals, and instructions in most primers did not go beyond what was written in the *Record of Rites.* Yet there was a different presentation in this primer:

> Like the sky, parents' kindness cannot be measured;
> Even the most dutiful children won't be able to pay it back.
> Greet your parents as soon as you get out of bed;
> Say good-night to your parents every evening.
> Be grateful to your parents while you are eating fruit;
> Think of your parents while you are away.
> Don't be angry if sometimes your parents beat you;
> Instead, try even harder to please them.[67]

School Precepts

School regulations and family rules, strictly speaking, were not primers. Yet in regard to rules and guidelines for ritual performance and good manners, some school regulations and some parts of family rules were often used as primers.

Like his *Elementary Learning,* Zhu Xi's *Regulations of the Bailudong Academy* (*Bailudong shuyuan xuegui*) was regarded as a yardstick for all students as well as an established form for school regulations. However, Zhu Xi's regulations were not intended for elementary school. The text was very short, beginning with five teachings in human relations, such as love between father and son, righteousness among all officials, discrimination between husband and wife, order between the older and the younger, and trust between friends. Then followed the five steps for studying: reading widely, questioning meticulously, thinking carefully, discriminating clearly and acting sincerely. And the third part included instructions as to how to act sincerely: (1) *xiushen*, or self-cultivation (i.e. speaking and acting loyally and sincerely, repressing desires and correcting wrongdoing so as to be virtuous); (2) *chushi*, or managing business (i.e. focusing on principles rather than pursuing profits; following the Way rather than pursuing material gains), and (3) *jiewu*, or the way to conduct oneself (i.e. do not do to others that which you do not wish to be done to yourself).[68] It is doubtful whether children would be able to follow these abstract principles in their daily practice.

Another set of Song Neo-Confucian regulations is *School Regulations by Masters Cheng Duanmeng and Dong Zhu*[69] (*Cheng Dong er xiansheng xueze*), which focuses on rituals and manners in school. The first two items covered morning and evening ceremonial assemblies, and then there were eight items on ritualised behaviour which were derived from the *Record of Rites* but adapted to the school situation in particular. The eight items covered reading, writing, taking care of chairs and classrooms, appellations between classmates, receiving guests, playing with classmates and mutual help in moral cultivation among students.[70]

Lü Kun's *Essential Points for a Community School* (*Shexue yaolüe*) appears more suitable to schools at a lower level than the above two sets of regulations. Lü Kun was a scholar-official in the late Ming, who seemed to have a negative attitude towards Neo-Confucianism. Firstly, he dismissed or questioned many of the rules for ceremonies and behaviour which Song Neo-Confucians had stressed.[71] For example, he forbade his family to hold any ceremony for him after his death.[72] In his opinion, Neo-Confucian writings were not very helpful for self-cultivation and Neo-Confucian theory was far removed from the real life of ordinary people. Hence, he suggested ignoring the doctrines of Neo-Confucianism and instead proposed understanding Confucianism from the perspective of daily life and personal experience.[73] Lü Kun claimed not to be a member of any school and to be only himself,[74] but embodied Confucian ideals through his personal integrity and official responsibility, devoting himself to education for public morality while promoting ethical behaviour for officials.

The *Essential Points for a Community School* was an educational text, comprised of three sections: a statement which stressed the significance of education and tried to persuade all people to send their children to community schools (*shexue*); school regulations; and ideas about elementary education, teaching methods and curriculum. The second section, about school regulations, which taught children good manners in school, filial piety at home and certain other behavioural patterns, actually stands on its own as a primer.

1. Order in Schools

School order was first of all embodied in the forms of address used by pupils. Younger pupils had to call older pupils *xiong* (elder brother), and older pupils could directly use younger pupils' names. All pupils had to walk on the right side and sit in the right-hand seat. When elders stood up, all pupils had to stand up; only when elders left could pupils be dismissed. All pupils were forbidden to play in groups, to curse each other, to damage other pupils' books or stationery, to make mischief and to bully others. Any pupils who broke these five rules would be severely punished.[75]

There were also ten rules relating to morality. All pupils were forbidden: (1) to lie; (2) to be greedy; (3) to use rude words and spread rumours; (4) to covet other people's property; (5) to create gossip behind people's backs; (6) to stare at women; (7) to become wicked people's friends; (8) to wear expensive clothes; (9) to engage in blackmail, and (10) to lose their temper or be arrogant.[76]

The above rules actually drew on the rules in the *Record of Rites*, Zhu Xi's *Elementary Learning* and other classics, but Lü Kun expressed them in a different way. In Lü Kun's regulations, the rules were, to some extent, like laws and reflected Lü's ideas about the maintenance of social order. The guiding educational theory thus appeared to be that pupils would be unlikely to break the laws of society if they were trained to obey school rules at an early age.

2. Manners Relating to the Virtue of Filial Piety

Pupils were required to be filial to parents at home. If they were not, their fathers and elder brothers could report them to the schoolteacher, and they would be punished. For convenience of practice, Lü Kun gave detailed rules. He said:

> Children have to pay their respects to their parents every morning and ask their parents whether they slept well the previous night. When they go home for breakfast or for lunch, they should also pay their respects to their parents and ask them how much they have eaten. Every night, they should go to their parents' bedrooms and wait until their parents go to bed. They must kneel down and hang their heads when their parents reprimand them. They are not allowed to defend themselves verbally. While their parents are working, they should help them. They should offer chairs to their parents when they see their parents have been standing for a long time. When their parents are looking for somebody, they should help their parents find the person. When their parents are ill, they have to personally prepare medicinal herbs and taste them for

their parents. These events are all very trivial duties for sons, but all youths have to practise them every day. In addition, the general rule is to respect parents and the elders of a family and to be tolerant and quiet under all circumstances.[77]

These detailed rules were also derived from the *Record of Rites*. According to the *Record of Rites*, sons were required to enquire about their parents' health in the morning and to adjust everything for their parents' repose in the evening.[78] It was the duty of filial sons to please their parents through both their deeds for them and their behaviour towards them. Also, sons were not allowed to oppose their parents' wishes.[79] If parents did not love them, sons had to fear them but not to feel resentment.[80] Even when parents were displeased and beat them till the blood flowed, sons should not presume to be angry and resentful: instead, they had to be more reverential and more filial to their parents.[81] All these rules also appeared in Zhu Xi's *Elementary Learning*. As we have seen in the above quotation, however, Lü Kun did not cite these principles directly from the *Record of Rites*; instead, he expressed them in clear and plain language.

3. Behaviour Patterns

Like some primers which focused on children's manners, Lü Kun's school regulations also dealt with actions such as speaking, walking and standing:

> Walk peacefully; jumping and running are not allowed.
> Speak slowly and clearly; do not talk vaguely and hurriedly.
> Bow gracefully and deeply; do not do it superficially and hurriedly.
> Stand seriously and quietly; do not stand like a cripple.
> Keep the body balanced while kneeling down and standing up.
> Cherish clothes and shoes; do not ruin them.
> Control your eyes properly; do not let your eyes be busy coming and going.
> Put your hands close to the lower hem of your clothes or on the level of your chest; do not conduct yourself lazily.
> Sit with dignity; do not be seated with legs apart.[82]

All these rules were also drawn from the principles in the *Record of Rites* which states:

> Do not listen with the head inclined on one side, nor answer with a loud

sharp voice, nor look with a dissolute leer, nor keep the body in a slouching position.

Do not saunter about with a haughty gait, nor stand with one foot raised. Do not sit with your knees wide apart. [83]

Family Regulations

Strictly speaking, *jiaxun* or family regulations should not be listed as primers. In pre-modern China, however, family rule-books were special texts for educating children, since many children started their elementary training at home. The earliest family rule-book which functioned as a primer was *Family Instruction by Tai Gong* (*Tai Gong jiajiao*) which, as recorded by some scholars and supported by a surviving incomplete Tang edition discovered in the Dunhuang caves, was a very popular teaching manual from 750 to 1000 A.D. [84] According to Xiang Anshi (d.1206), a scholar of the Song dynasty, *Family Instruction by Tai Gong*, along with Li Han's *Mengqiu*, Zhou Xingsi's *One Thousand Characters*, and *The Trimetrical Instruction* (*Sanzi xun*), was listed as a primer. [85]

In the past, most scholars regarded *Family Instruction by Tai Gong* as a Tang village book because its language was rustic and vulgar. This might have somewhat affected its use in teaching children. From 1000 A.D. onward, *The Trimetrical Classic, One Hundred Surnames* and *One Thousand Characters* replaced many primers that had been popular, and were well accepted as the most suitable primers for children in the late imperial period. According to Wang Chongmin, however, *Family Instruction by Tai Gong*, while losing its dominant position in the South and among Han children, was still widely used as a primer among nations other than the Han in North and Northeast China (such as Liao, Jin, Korea and Manchuria). [86] Under these circumstances, like *Essentials for Beginners*, *Family Instruction by Tai Gong* was not well known to scholars after the Song. It was not until the beginning of the twentieth century that an incomplete copy found in the Dunhuang caves stimulated intellectual interest in it and Wang Chongmin has made an important contribution to the research on the text.

According to Wang, *Family Instruction by Tai Gong* was derived from *Six Strategies* (*Liu tao*), a work on military arts. In its original version, this text consists of the deeds and teachings of three Zhou sage-kings. Therefore, between the Han and the Tang many people used *Six Strategies* to promote Confucian ethics. Later, what Taigong said to the King of Wen was assembled under the title *Family Instruction by Tai Gong*, while what Taigong said to the King of Zhou Wu contributed to *Family Instruction by the King of Wu* (*Wuwang jiajiao*). Between 1078 and 1085 someone collected what related to the military arts and created a new version of *Six Strategies* which, from then on, became a work focusing only on such topics.[87]

Evidently, *Family Instruction by Tai Gong* was widely used as a primer for children before the Song, yet the earliest educational treatise bearing the word *jiaxun* in its title was *Yan's Family Precepts* (*Yanshi jiaxun*),[88] by Yan Zhitui (531–?595), who served different governments in the period of the Northern and Southern Dynasties. The book is assumed to have been completed in the Sui dynasty,[89] and covers many subjects such as customs, religion (Confucianism and Buddhism), literature, social mores, the business of managing a family, the importance of education, self-cultivation and various branches of knowledge. By modern standards, this is not a primer for children's early schooling but a treatise in which "education" is embodied in a very broad sense. However, from the Sui dynasty to the Qing, *Yan's Family Precepts* was reprinted many times. The book was used to teach children reading in some family schools or private tutorials.[90] In the early Qing, some scholars, such as Huang Shulin (1672–1756), omitted the chapters on phonology, philology and Buddhism, and produced an abridged edition for a family school.[91] In the middle of the Qing, some scholars of the School of Evidential Research, such as Zhao Jingfu (dates unknown) and Duan Yucai (1735–1815), made further contributions to the book through editing, annotation and commentaries. To them, knowledge of phonology and philology was a part of elementary training.[92]

From the Song onward, many family rule-books appeared. These later family rule-books all kept the framework of Yan's book, although they had different focuses. Some focused on manners in social life and the management of family property, while others stressed ethical values and the significance of classical learning. *Yuan's Precepts for Social Life* (*Yuanshi shifan*) was the most influential of them and was listed together with Zhu Xi's *Elementary Learning* and Lü Benzhong's *Instruction for Children* as officially recognised primers in the *Annotated Catalogue of the Four Treasuries*.[93]

Yuan's Precepts for Social Life was written by Yuan Cai (1140–1195) in 1178. Yuan Cai was in office for thirty years. Like other scholar-officials, he composed several works, but only *Yuan's Precepts for Social Life* survived. The book mainly dealt with family affairs, as the titles of these three chapters show: "Getting along with relatives," "Improving personal conduct" and "Managing family affairs." It is worth noting that Yuan Cai did not name this book "family rules" although it was within the framework of family rule-books. *Shi* means society; *fan* refers to norm, precept. The title of the book suggests that Yuan Cai was attempting to offer norms for the whole of society, not only for individual families.[94] Thus, unlike other family rule-books, this book concentrated neither on the rudiments of literacy skills nor on the rules for children's behaviour. The book set up rules for all people in society and instructed them how to keep a family in peace and harmony. In this sense, the book seemed unsuitable as a primer for children. The fact that it stood together with other primers was due to changes in the concept, content and purpose of education in the Song.

Unlike Yuan Cai's broad approach, Zhen Dexiu (1178–1235) produced a manual entitled *Daily Rites in Family Schools* (*Jiashu changyi*), indicating clearly that all regulations were intended for family schools.

The first two items in Zhen's text, resembling those presented in other primers, were about ceremonial assemblies in the mornings and evenings, and the text then addressed six issues — in theory concerning the study of ritual (particularly reverence and obedience), and in practice concerning the correct way of sitting, walking, standing, bowing and speaking. However, the content of this primer was uniquely designed according to the daily school schedule. The proper ways of casting one's eyes, listening, dressing and eating were considered morning practice, and therefore came before instructions on study and pastimes.[95]

Some family rule-books contain only one section relevant to children's education, such as *Family Rules* (*Jiaxun*) by Huo Tao (1487–1540). Like most scholar-officials Huo Tao attained government office through the civil service examinations;[96] and as with many wealthy families, there was a family school attached to his household. Yet only the fifth part of his *Family Rules*, entitled *Regulations for Youngsters* (*Menggui*) was intended for children in that school. The first part of his *Family Rules* was concerned with family business, such as the importance of farming, the storage of grain and the arrangement of income and expenses. The second part of his *Family Rules* concerned issues in daily life, such as the management of clothes and meals. The third was about weddings and funeral ceremonies. The fourth contained instructions for the younger generation. There were some materials relevant to education in this part, for example, it states that children above seven had to go to community schools; above ten, they had to join in farming after school; above fifteen, they should start to prepare for the civil service examinations and no longer work in the fields; by twenty-five, they had to come back to farming if they still had not passed the examinations.[97] While the fifth part, *Regulations for Youngsters*, was devoted to regulating children, the sixth provided general instructions, including an article and a poem to be read in the ancestral hall.

The contents of Huo's *Regulations for Youngsters* in the first place emphasised the importance of conduct, countenance and speech. Huo Tao believed that conduct was closely linked with rectification of the mind. The detailed items were as follows:

> Keep your head upright: do not listen with your head inclined on one side or squint.
>
> Keep your mouth composed: do not show your teeth or laugh loudly.
>
> Keep your hands reverently: do not put your hands in a slouching position or incline an arm on one side.
>
> Move your feet calmly: do not run or move your thighs hurriedly.
>
> Keep your face serious: do not show laziness in your expression.
>
> Keep your appearance grave: do not show irreverence in bodily carriage.
>
> Keep your breathing easy and slow: answer questions gently and unhurriedly.
>
> Keep your expression mild: do not have a stern countenance.
>
> Keep your eyes focused straight forward: do not turn your head to watch something or direct your eyes askance; do not look at anything which is not in accordance with rituals.
>
> Be mindful of what you listen to: do not listen to jokes, filthy language and vulgar songs.
>
> Be cautious in speech: do not make ugly noises or utter obscenities; do not speak of odd things; do not joke or lie.
>
> Have a feeling of awe while in action: be respectful in walking, moving hands, casting eyes and speaking.

Sit straight: do not lean on things; one would not feel tired if one sat
   upright and kept one's shoulders balanced.

Stand properly: do not stand with one foot raised or in a sloping position;
   do not face downward or upward.

Walk quietly: do not walk too fast or move your feet hurriedly; do not
   walk ahead of your elders.

Sleep scrupulously: do not sleep on your face or naked; do not get up
   late or sleep during the daytime.[98]

These sixteen rules also originated from the *Record of Rites* as is
shown by the following passages:

Do not move your feet lightly nor your hands irreverently. Look straight
forward, and keep your mouth composed. Do not break the stillness.
Keep your head upright and your breath easy and unhurried. Stand with
the appearance of virtue and keep your looks grave.[99]

Do not sleep on your face.[100]

Not only did Huo Tao gather together all the rituals of bodily
deportment in the classics and put them under these general
headings, he also related them to the rectification of the mind. He
justified this relationship: "One's head, mouth, hands and feet are
parts of one's body. One's appearance and expression are
indications of one's body. One's seeing, hearing, speaking, acting,
sitting, standing, walking and sleeping are the application of one's
body. One's mind controls one's organs and action." Youths had to
practise these rituals when they were ignorant; and correct manners
would thus gradually become natural to them. This was called
"nourishing correctness" and was the path to the attainment of
sagehood.[101]

There was nothing new in Huo's material. Song philosophers
and educationists wrote at length on the rectification of the mind
and its embodiment in deportment, as shown in the major popular
compendium *Reflections on Things at Hand* (*Jinsi lu*). For example,
Zhu Xi related *jingshi* (to be serious about things) to the *Record of
Rites*. The *Record of Rites* stipulated that a child should hold an elder's
hand with both of his hands while the elder held him with one hand;
when the child was asked a question, he had to cover his mouth with
his hand while he answered.[102] Zhu Xi said that this rule in ancient
times was to teach children to be serious about things. The way that

a child held an elder's hand and answered questions indicated that the child's attitude towards his elders was reverent and respectful. Hence, instruction in being serious about things in elementary education was to teach children "first to be quiet, careful, respectful and reverent"[103] through their physical experiences in daily life. Furthermore, this kind of physical experience, in Douglas' theory, as mentioned earlier, can be expressed as "symbolic nourishment," which is "developed to the extent that the social body and the physical body are assimilated and both focus the identity of individuals in a structured, bounded system."[104] In this sense, *li* or ritual expressed human relations in a certain social context; and the performance of *li* then ensured social stability.

Elementary Education in Practice

Primers on rituals and good manners, especially those in the form of school and family regulations, reflected to some extent the reality of primary education in traditional China. To highlight this point, Gui E's description of a late-Ming school is used here to provide more information about actual teaching practice, which in turn may help us understand the primers in this genre.

Gui E succeeded in the civil service examinations and received the *jinshi* degree in 1511. At the beginning of the Jiajing period (1522–1566), he was promoted from the Magistrate of Cheng'an county to a post in charge of the Justice Department (*xingbu*).[105] At that time, Gui E presented a memorial to the emperor expressing his opinions about elementary education. His memorial was recorded in the *Chit-chat of Hao'an* (*Hao'an xianhua*), composed by Zhang Erqi (1612–1677). Zhang Erqi was a student in an official school (*zhusheng*) of the late Ming, and after the fall of the Ming dynasty devoted himself to teaching.[106]

Gui E's memorial contains an invaluable record of the teaching process in a primary school in the late Ming. Gui E first described the school building that he set up when he was the magistrate of the county:

> There are two houses on the left and right sides, four halls in the middle, and doors both at the front and back of the halls.[107]

This construction was dictated by the requirement that "every morning and evening, two older teachers sat in front of the classroom and ordered the children to go through the door in a column."[108] This was to teach children to pay respect to teachers and maintain school order.

There were four subjects covered in a day. The first was ceremonies. Eight pictures were hung on the wall. They were: the ceremony for welcoming new babies, propriety for youths, propriety for scholars to greet each other, the wedding ceremony, the rituals of sons who served parents, the rituals of women who served parents-in-law, the ceremony for worshipping ancestors and the archery ceremony. A teacher was in charge of this course. All pupils first greeted their teacher according to propriety, then the teacher taught them about one of these pictures and let them practise the ceremony depicted.[109]

The second subject was reading. The illustrations of Guan Zhong's *Duties of Disciples* were on the wall. At the beginning of the course, the teacher explained one of these illustrations and then started to teach the children to read. The textbooks used in this course were the *Classic of Filial Piety* and Zhu Xi's *Elementary Learning*. Once familiar with the sentences in these two books, pupils were given explanations and encouraged to conduct themselves according to the teachings of these two books.[110]

The third subject was writing and counting. This course aimed at teaching pupils the six styles of calligraphy; but children needed to learn only one or two characters each day. Counting included the names of the points of the compass, the numbers from one to ten, and the names of the ten Heavenly Stems and the twelve Earthly Branches.[111]

The fourth subject was music and physical exercise. Pupils were taught to beat drums, or chant poems, or archery. After these four courses, it was afternoon. Pupils were required to revise all courses and then the class was dismissed.[112]

Gui E's memorial clearly indicated that rituals and certain behaviour patterns played a significant part in elementary education. Historically, the rituals were described originally in the classics and then perpetuated through the writings of Song Neo-Confucians. Based on the belief in the connection between the rectification of the mind and its embodiment in bodily carriage, Song Neo-Confucians regarded the practice of ritualised behaviour as a way to lead children back to their original good nature.

Furthermore, according to the Neo-Confucian ideal of "the true self," virtues, learning and good manners were integral to education, and the aim of elementary education was to mould children's personalities according to the new concept of man and to nourish children's virtues. The virtues of obedience, piety and loyalty were very much emphasised in the teaching of good manners. In this sense, elementary education in pre-industrial societies was in essence a religious and moral education rather than merely the transmission of literacy skills.

Ming-Qing primers in this genre reflected the scholarly inheritance and continuity of this tradition. Although the content was repetitive, these primers succeeded in re-expressing the rituals in plain language and in a variety of forms. The authors of these educational treatises might have had different approaches to the understanding of Confucianism, but there was no conflict among them about actual behavioural patterns. Through the endeavours of these authors, etiquette from the Confucian classics for the first time became accessible at an elementary level and permeated the whole of society.

Chapter 5

Shaping the Ideal Child:
Modelling on Exemplary Deeds

As mentioned in Chapter Four, Zhu Xi's *Elementary Learning* consists of two major sections: the first, from Chapter One to Chapter Four, is the "Inner Chapters" containing direct quotations from the classics; and the second section, Chapters Five and Six, is the "Outer Chapters" including "admirable sayings" and "exemplary deeds" of figures from the Han through the Song. The "admirable sayings" in the Outer Chapters are used to further elaborate the Confucian teachings quoted from the classics, while the "exemplary deeds" provide good examples for ordinary people as well as children to model themselves on. This structure presents a Neo-Confucian teaching device within which the original Confucian doctrine is embedded not only in book learning but also in daily practice.

While the previous chapter mainly examines moral instructions and prescriptions on ritual behaviour and good manners, this chapter will focus on the exemplary figures described in primers. These figures are not necessarily children; in fact most of them are adults. This perhaps confirms the conclusion drawn from the scholarship in this area that Confucian education "aimed at fostering in children as quickly and efficiently as possible the adult Confucian virtues of self-restraint, altruism, and sober and discriminating moral judgement."[1] Nevertheless, there are still some exemplary children portrayed in primers: some are presented together with adult examples whilst some stand alone as precocious or proper children. Exemplary children are analysed in this chapter in order to further demonstrate the Confucian effort to shape the ideal child. Firstly the childhood prodigies and the Confucian image of the proper child are examined; then the focus is placed on twenty-four examples of filial piety, as filial piety was a fundamental element of Confucianism and was considered the highest of all the virtues. Since most exemplary children presented in primers appear to have no childish traits, the final section then discusses the portraits of these "little adults" and Confucian perceptions of education and play.

Juvenile Precocity and Proper Children

In her analysis of the legend of Hou Ji and juvenile achievements throughout the Han, Anne Kinney points out that precocious children presented in early Chinese literature are "preternaturally wise or filial," or their "births are marked by the appearance of miraculous signs."[2] Childhood prodigies were not unique to Chinese culture but also existed in other civilisations. All stories of precocity were actually "a staple of myth and biography."[3] In the case of Chinese primers, however, the examples set up for children were all supposed to be easy for children to model themselves on. Therefore, in contrast to what was presented in early Chinese literature, Confucian writers of primers appeared to be interested more in exemplary deeds of real individuals than in mythical figures.

A prodigy in early China was understood to be the highest exemplification of wisdom, acknowledged in the *Analects* as *shengzhi* (born with knowledge), whilst people who obtained knowledge through learning were called *xuezhi*.[4] Confucius never regarded himself as one "born with knowledge" but as a person with great eagerness to learn.[5] He was not just being modest, but also rational, inasmuch as most people were not gifted with the highest form of wisdom, so "eagerness to learn" was a more appropriate and attainable quality to encourage in ordinary people, children in particular. Education in the Confucian context was a significant means to transform (*hua*) people; and "learning" (*xue*) was seen as power that "enables a man to become a better man morally," since morals, in the Confucian view, "can be transmitted from teacher to pupil."[6] Therefore, it is not surprising that primers contained ample stories about children who improved themselves through studying industriously.

Although the writers of primers placed much emphasis on obtaining knowledge through learning, they did not deny the existence of precocious ability or innate gifts. Kinney has shown in her study that the juvenile prodigy presented in early Chinese literature was often considered to be endowed with divine gifts and abilities. Yet in primers precocious children were often portrayed only as being more advanced in their intellectual development than other children. Take *Stories for Daily Learning* as an example.

In both the 1542 and the 1669 editions of *Stories for Daily Learning*, there were twenty stories about precocious children, though the examples contained in the two versions were not identical. Table 5.1 indicates that the juvenile achievements were mainly displayed in aspects of reading, writing and intellectual thinking, in which all the children reached an adult level. For example, six precocious children in the 1542 edition and nine in the 1669 edition were depicted as being able to compose poetry at the age of seven or eight, the age which, in the Chinese conception of children, was just the beginning of the child's learning life. However, the only indication of miraculous ability in *Stories for Daily Learning* was the story about Bai Juyi, who was said to be able to open a book and read it when he was only seven months old infant![7]

It is noticeable that the importance of mastery of the Classics, one of the most substantial aspects of juvenile achievement in the Han, was superseded in *Stories for Daily Learning* by the ability to compose poetry and prose. This was attributed to such factors as the

Table 5.1 Types of Precocious Children in *Stories for Daily Learning*

Categories	Numbers	
	1542 edition	1669 edition
1. Mastery of the Classics	2	4
2. Ability to compose poetry and prose	6	9
3. Wisdom shown in replying	5	3
4. Excellent memory	2	1
5. Ability to read at the age of seven months	1	1
6. Enquiries about philosophical questions	1	1
7. Ambitions shown in *zhuazhou*[8]	1	0
8. Wisdom shown in saving life	1	0
9. Lofty aspirations through reading history	1	0
10. Passing the civil service examination at seven	0	1
Total	20	20

establishment of the civil service examination system in the Tang, the changes in the concept of *shi* and the redefinition of learning. In the Han, Confucian classics were at the centre of learning, and "the Confucian literati had become an enormous and formidable social force." Under these circumstances, children precocious in mastery of the Classics were therefore exemplified "to validate the superior social position occupied by the elite," as well as to help "justify the social and political ascent of worthy but low-ranking individuals."[9] In the Tang, a Confucian scholar was required to be versed in both canonical knowledge and literary composition (*wenzhang*), as learning was linked not only to the Classics but also to *wen*, which included literature, literary forms, the textual tradition and culture. This broader definition of learning was intended to integrate Han learning, other scholarly traditions, and literary practice into one form — literary composition.[10] This change was endorsed by the Tang examination system, as all the candidates sitting for an examination in the Classics (*ming jing*) had to take an additional test in literary composition — involving one poem and one piece of rhymeprose (*fu*). This requirement drove the literati to devote themselves to literary compositions, and turned school into an instrument to help people attain official posts through study. It was under these circumstances that child prodigies in literary composition emerged. Poetry then became popular in primers, and instruction in literary compositions constituted a significant part of elementary education.

With the rise of Song Neo-Confucianism the original Confucian education, believed to place emphasis on individual moral cultivation rather than emoluments (*lu*), came back into favour. There were two major intellectual streams from the Song onward: one was characterised by a pragmatic approach to learning, with the pursuit of official appointments as a key focus; the other held to the Neo-Confucian ideal that "learning is for one's self." Precocious children presented in primers, with either superior intelligence or moral precocity, were actually influenced by these two different intellectual orientations. Some were potential earlier achievers in the civil service examinations and in literary composition; and others represented the Neo-Confucian image of childhood prodigy.

The most direct expression of the first category of precocious children can be seen in the widespread *Poetry by a Child Prodigy*

(*Shentong shi*). The author of this poetry anthology was Wang Zhu (fl. 1100) of the Song, who was regarded as a child prodigy because he composed poetry at the age of eight or nine. Later, the poems Wang Zhu wrote in childhood were collected and published in the form of a primer entitled *Poetry by Wang Zhu, a Child Prodigy* (*Wang shentong shi*), afterwards abbreviated to *Poetry by a Child Prodigy*.[11] However, some poems in this volume were not by Wang (Li Bai [699–762], the prominent poet of the mid-Tang, was the author of at least two of them) and it is doubtful whether all the poems by Wang were composed when he was only eight or nine years old.

In the first part of the volume, there are fourteen poems with the same title, *Encouraging Learning* (*Quanxue*), then comes one poem called *Zhuangyuan* (literally the number one scholar, referring to the candidate who came first in the highest imperial examination), one poem entitled *On Loyalty* (*Yan zhong*), two poems called *Imperial Capital* (*Didu*) and then *Four Great Joys* (*Sixi*). These nineteen poems appear not to extol preternatural power but to encourage children to enter officialdom through diligent study. The first poem clearly states this theme:

> Emperors always appoint talented persons to higher positions,
> Literary works (*wenzhang*) are used to educate you young people.
> No occupations can go beyond a low status,
> Unless you study to help you reach higher.[12]

The second poem tells children the purpose of studying hard:

> [You] have to study hard from childhood,
> Both classics and literary compositions enable you to become
>   accomplished.
> Look at those wearing higher-official robes in the court,
> They all reached there through the civil service examinations.[13]

The third poem urges children to study hard:

> You can only obtain knowledge through diligent study,
> So read thousands of volumes day and night.
> Then you will be well versed in classics in three years,
> And no-one will dare to ridicule you as having no knowledge.[14]

The fourth poem tells children that pens are as good as generals' swords, so they have to become very learned scholars even though

they are still children. The fifth poem further explains the benefits of
learning for gaining official emoluments and social status:

> In the morning [he] is still a farmer's son,
> But by evening he ascends to the palace.
> Nobody is born a general or chancellor,
> A good man should be ambitious.[15]

These poems apparently consider diligence in study more
important than innate gifts, encouraging people of low social rank to
raise their status through the civil service examinations.

The sixth poem employs similes (for example, knowledge is
likened to the most precious part of the body, and scholars to
delicacies presented at banquets) to further explain the usefulness of
learning, and then relates the benefits of study to the position of
chancellor. However, the competition for official careers was fierce,
and the majority of candidates would fail to pass the civil service
examinations and might end up only as private teachers. This crucial
reality was most likely to discourage youths from pursuing official
positions in this way. The seventh poem therefore addresses this
issue. It says the pursuit of knowledge in whatever situation is not a
waste of one's life, and poetry and books disappoint nobody, as
successful scholars can enter officialdom through the examinations,
and even those who fail to pass the examinations can at least become
well-educated gentlemen.[16]

As in the Han dynasty, too in the late imperial period juvenile
achievements were what parents wanted for their children. The
eighth poem thus tries to persuade parents that instead of leaving
their children only gold or other material treasures, they should
teach them to be proficient in the Confucian classics so as to pass the
civil service examinations at an early age. The ninth poem once again
emphasises the importance of teaching children the Classics from
childhood, and the tenth describes the joy of a juvenile achiever who
has an audience with the emperor on the way to pay the chancellor
a call.[17] This set of poems expresses the same idea: that children,
regardless of their different social statuses and family backgrounds,
should all have the same goal — to master the Confucian classics and
the skill of literary composition so as to succeed in the civil service
examinations. These poems advise both children and parents that
the earlier children start to strive for this goal the better. This idea is

further reiterated in the next four poems through the description of the feelings of delight experienced after having succeeded in the examinations at an early age, for example "obtaining a *jinshi* degree as a youth, returning from the capital with pride and triumph."[18] The attainment of success in traditional China was often vividly depicted in a metaphor — a carp leaping over the dragon-gate (*li yue longmen*).[19] The accomplishment of this "leaping" at an early age greatly honoured one's parents, family, clan and even the entire region. Consequently, success in the examinations became the only criterion in judging whether a boy had grown into a real man. As stated clearly in one poem:

> The day [you] attain the highest degree,
> [Your] parents are still young.
> Returning home in a glamorous official robe,
> Hi! You are really a good man.[20]

The poem here is an illustration of gender criteria of the time. As is well known to students of China, men traditionally played "outer roles" and women "inner roles." This different role-play design shaped not only the traditional husband-wife relationship but also the criteria for entering adulthood and being adults. Boys were encouraged to succeed in careers; and under the civil service examination system the "career" primarily meant success in the examinations, since such success could ensure a promising future in officialdom. Women's "inner roles" were to help their husbands to achieve this goal, or to teach their sons to work towards this goal (*xiangfu jiaozi*).

After the fourteen poems with the title *Encouraging Learning*, the poems *Zhuangyuan* and *On Loyalty* stress the honour achieved after being successful in the examinations and urge children to study hard so as to honour their family through obtaining first place in the examinations and being chancellor later.[21]

All the poems in this volume appear only to encourage children to be ambitious, competitive and assiduous as early as possible, and there is no stress on preternatural abilities. Children's intellectual capacity was measured by their ability to pass the civil service examinations at an early age. These stories suggest that through the examination system the door to officialdom was open to everybody, regardless of their family backgrounds. This ideal was also presented in other primers through exemplary children from disadvantaged backgrounds, such as Ouyang Xiu (1007–1072). Ouyang's father died when he was only four years old, and his mother had to raise him alone. They lived in poverty, but that did not discourage his mother from teaching him characters, though he had to use a kind of reed as a pen. Later he not only survived the hardship but also achieved success in both literature and his official career.[22]

However, as discussed in the Introduction to this book, in reality only a very small proportion of males were able to attain a full classical education and to compete in the civil service examinations. The educational levels of children of commoners varied according to their financial resources, and accordingly their career paths differed. As for children living in poverty, many of them were deprived of educational opportunities altogether and remained illiterate all their lives. Some Ming-Qing scholars were aware of this reality and endeavoured to promote basic education to the lowest layer of society. Their aim of educating the children of the peasantry, however, was to train them as law-abiding subjects rather than to encourage them to raise their social status through the examination system. This will be discussed further in Chapter Seven.

Unlike *Poetry by a Child Prodigy*, *Stories for Daily Learning* achieved a balance between learning for one's moral cultivation and for the pursuit of an official career. For instance, during the reign of the emperor Xuanzong (712–756), Liu Yan was officially selected as a "gifted child" (*shentong*) through an examination for child prodigies (*tongzi ke*) at seven. In the Tang, all gifted children were given particular official posts, and Liu Yan was given the post called *zhengzi* (lit. "to correct characters"). One day, the emperor and his favourite concubine Yang Guifei summoned Liu Yan, and Yang Guifei put him on her lap, blackening his eyebrows and putting his hair into tufts. The emperor started to tease Liu Yan and asked: "Your official title is *zhengzi*. How many characters would you be able to correct?" Liu Yan replied: "All the characters are already correct, except for the character *peng* (clique)." The answer implied that Yang Guifei and her relatives had formed a clique and the emperor was being manipulated by them.[23] The story, which also appeared in other primers such as *Pure Mengqiu* (*Chunzheng mengqiu*) by Hu Bingwen,[24] suggests that the "gifted child" not only had intellectual superiority but also had a clear idea of right and wrong.

As both precocious and proper children were supposed to begin to become accomplished through learning at an early age, they sometimes shared the same attributes. The only difference between them may have been that intellectually precocious children reached their goals easily while most children had to make more effort to realize their dreams. Many examples were provided to encourage young children to study hard on their own initiative. For example, Sima Guang (1019–1086) of the Song was said to have been taught the *Spring and Autumn Annals with Zuo's Commentary* (*Zuoshi chunqiu*) at seven, and to have liked it so much that he could not stop reading it. As he was so immersed in his study, he did not even notice when he felt hungry or when the weather changed. Consequently, he mastered all the classics at the age of fifteen.[25] With this achievement, Sima Guang could actually also be perceived as a gifted child. Yet *Stories for Daily Learning* regarded him as an example of *xuezhi* or "obtaining knowledge through learning," aiming to encourage children with an average intellectual ability to study diligently.

In Chapter Four instructions, regulations and guidelines for children to practise Confucian rites in their daily life were discussed. Many exemplary children were used for this purpose in a more explicit way; they were pictured as normal children rather than precocious juveniles. One of the best-known stories is about Kong Rong, a four-year-old child of the Han, who chose a smaller pear when eating with his older brothers. When he was asked to give an explanation, he replied: "I am younger and smaller than my brothers, so I should eat a smaller pear." People admired him for this answer.[26] The story illustrates the principle of brotherly submission (*di*). In this case, Kong Rong should not be viewed as an extraordinary filial child, as the example was meant to teach all normal children to act this way.

The story of Wang Sengru indicates a similar approach. Wang was taught the *Classic of Filial Piety* at the age of four. As a child, he naturally asked his tutor about the main theme of the text. The tutor replied: "The main theme is about loyalty and filial piety." The child was inspired by this answer and vowed to read this classic more often. One day, someone came to give his father some plums, and asked Wang Sengru to taste one of them first. Normally, a child would have taken it, but Wang Sengru refused it, saying: "My parents have not seen these plums, so I do not dare to taste them first."[27] This story illustrates the principle in filial piety that a filial child was not supposed to touch food and wine before setting them in front of his parents.

The virtuous children presented in these primers conveyed a Neo-Confucian idea that the practice of the Confucian principles was more important than the pursuit of success in the examinations and book learning. Above all else, filial piety was the main focus of Neo-Confucian education for children.

Twenty-Four Examples of Filial Piety

The importance of filial piety was clearly stated in the *Classic of Filial Piety*: those who accepted filial duty in family life would feel the same responsibility in their social obligations, and those who paid reverence to their parents would show the same affection to their sovereign.[28] As well as the *Classic of Filial Piety*, other classics such as the *Analects* and the *Record of Rites* covered the principles of the virtue of filial piety and guidelines for practice in daily life. In the wider society, however, most people did not come to understand filial piety through reading these classics but through popular sources. As the research of Hui-chen Wang Liu shows, in the traditional Chinese clan rules, filial piety was the most frequently mentioned virtue.[29] Also, during the Ming and Qing periods, the stories of the twenty-four examples of filial piety were widely known. This may suggest that the leading role of filial piety among all the Confucian virtues was founded in the classics, but its dissemination can be attributed more to literature in a variety of forms other than the original classics. In this section, an analysis of some stories which were included among the well-known twenty-four examples of filial piety but which were presented in some primers as well as in Neo-Confucian treatises on education, will demonstrate how Confucian orthodoxy became conventional belief and how these exemplary children helped to promote the Confucian effort in the shaping of the ideal child.

The earliest work we know of which was devoted entirely to examples of filial piety was the *Poetry of Filial Piety* (*Xiaoshi*), written by Lin Tong of the late Song. Lin Tong and his brother was said to have sacrificed their lives out of loyalty to the Song when the Yuan took over.[30] Many of the Lins' works did not survive, but *The Poetry of Filial Piety* can be found in both official and unofficial collections. This book contained three hundred poems which extolled the deeds of the sages in classical times (10 poems), people who exhibited the virtue of filial piety before the Song (240 poems), foreigners (10 poems), women (20 poems), Buddhists (10 poems) and even animals (10 poems).[31]

It was before the Song that the term *ershisi xiao* (twenty-four examples of filial piety) was first used. According to the Dunhuang *bianwen*, in his public preaching, Master Yuan Jian used this term to promote the virtue of filial piety. As mentioned in Chapter Three, *bianwen*, a literary form emerging in the Tang, usually contained complete stories based on anecdotes from the sutras but did not quote the sutras directly; stories were written in the vernacular. Since story-telling was a characteristic of the *bianwen*, later some non-Buddhist *bianwen* appeared, focusing on secular themes and historical events. Gradually, this type of non-Buddhist *bianwen* developed into a significant part of Chinese popular literature.[32] However, Buddhist preachers felt that they needed to deal with challenges from Confucian believers. For instance, the term *wufuwumu* (without parents) was often used to characterise and to criticise Buddhism, as the Han Chinese were not able to accept that young people should become monks and serve Buddha instead of their parents. To counteract this rejection, popular Buddhism began to secularise Buddhist teaching and to accommodate Confucian beliefs such as filial piety. Therefore, it is not surprising that the term "twenty-four examples of filial piety" occurs in Master Yuan Jian's sermon, in what appears to be the earliest use of the term we can find in any surviving written documents today. The whole text of Master Yuan Jian's sermon did not survive, but the *yazuowen* (alternate prose and verse) at the beginning of the text was found in the Dunhuang caves. This surviving section suggests that the term "twenty-four examples of filial piety" must have appeared before the Five Dynasties, as Master Yuan Jian died in 951.[33]

Nevertheless, Buddhist incorporation of the Confucian virtue of filial piety does not necessarily mean that all twenty-four examples were the same as those presented in Confucian writings. According to this surviving *yazuowen*, only six examples (sage-king Shun, Wang Xiang, Guo, Lao Laizi, Meng Zong and Huang Xiang) in Master Yuan Jian's sermon were the same as those in the twenty-four Confucian examples which have been passed on to the present. This surviving text also reveals that Master Yuan Jian paid much attention to the examples consistent with Buddhist doctrine, such as the story about Mu Lian (Moginlin).

The story originated in a sutra text which was translated into Chinese during the period of the Western Jin (265–316) and was entitled *The Yulanpen Sutra* (*Yulan pen jing*). *Yulan* is a Sanskrit term, literally meaning "to hang upside down." *Pen*, understood as a Chinese word, refers to bowl. In combination and in the context, the title of this sutra in popular Chinese understanding means "filling the Buddhist monks' begging bowls in order to rescue [people] who suffer from being hung upside down in Hell." It was said that Mu Lian, a disciple of Shakyamuni (Buddha), travelled to Hell to see his recently deceased mother. He found her in the Road of the Pratas or hungry ghosts (*e'guidao*)[34] where she was hungry and in torment. He tried to feed her, but the food turned to ashes as soon as it touched her lips. Mu Lian himself was not able to rescue his mother, so he asked Buddha to help. Buddha replied that his mother was sinful and Mu would need help from monks around the world. Mu Lian asked for further instruction about how to gather together the monks around the world. Buddha told him that the fifteenth day of the seventh month was the day monks emerged from their summer retreat, and Mu Lian should lay out a grand banquet (*Yulan pen hui*) for all the monks who would then use their spiritual power to pray for his mother and enable her to escape from the netherworld and to ascend to heaven. Mu Lian followed Buddha's instructions and as a result his mother was saved. Afterwards, Mu Lian asked Buddha whether other disciples could also hold such a grand banquet to rescue their parents. Buddha approved Mu Lian's proposal.[35]

Obviously the idea of filial piety presented in this story did not conflict with that in Confucian teaching, so it was well received by the Han Chinese. In the reign of Emperor Liang Wu (502–549), a grand banquet of this kind was officially held by the emperor himself; from then on this became a grand event among the Han Chinese, and reached its peak during the Tang, when the grand banquet was moved from temples to the palace. Yet in the Song, this festive event became an opportunity for worshipping ghosts, and was no longer held solely to praise dutiful behaviour. This Song variation was well preserved throughout the late imperial period and became the Zhongyuan Festival (which fitted in with the Taoist Ghost Month) and is still celebrated today. Meanwhile, Mu Lian's story was performed on the stage and became well-known in almost every household.

In this context, we may conclude that the Buddhist use of the term "twenty-four examples of filial piety" indicates a kind of cultural accommodation within which Buddhism was transformed into a Chinese version which later was integrated into the Chinese indigenous religion, Taoism, and into conventional beliefs, exhorting ordinary people toward virtuous behaviour. As indicated in Lin Tong's *Poetry of Filial Piety*, the virtue of filial piety in the Song and afterwards was well accepted by society, regardless of race, religion or sex.

The literature of the twenty-four examples we see today, however, generally illustrated Confucian filial piety, though the examples still varied in different editions. As for the authorship of the extant literature, there are at least three different claims: one refers to Guo Jujing of the Yuan; the second to Guo Juye of the Yuan and the third to Guo Shouzheng, the younger brother of Guo Shoujing, the eminent astronomer of the Yuan.[36] Although its authorship cannot be confirmed, the three claims above at least established the fact that the surviving edition of the *Poetry of Twenty-four Examples of Filial Piety* (*Ershisi xiaoshi*) was produced in the Yuan and the author came from a family with the surname Guo. This tiny volume contained nineteen stories resembling those in Lin's *Poetry of Filial Piety*, and some had also appeared in Zhu Xi's work. This may suggest that a Confucian version of the twenty-four examples developed during the Song dynasty, as in the Song Neo-Confucian beliefs filial piety became more important in self-cultivation than ever. In the Yuan, this Confucian version was well received through presentations in folklore, children's primers and other forms of popular literature.

However, it is not clear when the twenty-four illustrations were put together with these poems. The earliest illustrations of these twenty-four stories we are able to see today may perhaps be those in various Ming editions of *Stories for Daily Learning*. As the brief introduction to *Stories for Daily Learning* in Chapter Three points out, these twenty-four examples were located in different sections in the 1542 edition (by Xiong Damu) while in a 1669 Japanese edition (based on a Ming edition collated by Zhang Ruitu) they were assembled with illustrations in the first *juan*.[37] Yet the *Poetry of Twenty-four Examples of Filial Piety* with illustrations is rarely seen as an independent book, as it was not a part of either of the two official collections (*congshu*): the *Yongle Encyclopaedia* (*Yongle dadian*) in the Ming and the *Complete Collection in the Four Treasuries* (*Siku quanshu*) in the Qing, nor included in unofficial collections of this period. During the Ming and Qing periods, the term "twenty-four examples of filial piety" was sometimes used to refer to the virtue of filial piety in general rather than as the title of a specific book.

Children in Ming-Qing China were probably familiar with these exemplary stories through primers that repeated them frequently. For instance, the Ming primer *Illustrations and Explanations for Children* (*Mengyang tushuo*) contained six stories that were in the *Poetry of Twenty-four Examples of Filial Piety*.[38] In the late Qing, one primer, *One Hundred Illustrated Examples of Filial Piety* (*Baixiao tu*), included all twenty-four examples.[39] As part of the content of primers, these examples were given to children at a very early age. As popular stories, they tried to persuade people to be filial to their parents, even under trying circumstances. Consequently, the ideal of filial piety was transmitted from the Confucian classics to conventional belief, and therefore was deeply rooted throughout society.

For the purpose of showing how elementary textbooks facilitated the permeation of filial piety into children's lives, I have chosen Zhu Xi's *Elementary Learning* as an example of classically-based Neo-Confucian treatises and *The Young Horse and the Shadow of a Whip* (hereafter referred to as *Horse and Whip*) as an example of popular primers in the Ming and Qing periods. According to the *Classic of Filial Piety*, a filial son had five duties: (1) to venerate his parents in daily life, (2) to make them happy in every possible way, (3) to give them extra care when they were ill, (4) to show great sorrow when they were dead and (5) to offer sacrifices to deceased parents with solemnity.[40] From Table 5.2, we can see how the five duties were presented in the stories of filial sons in *Elementary Learning* and *Horse and Whip*.

In the classics, the main duty of filial piety was to nourish parents. This idea was elaborated by these twenty-four exemplary stories in which no matter how old an ideal figure was, as long as his parents were alive, he was still considered a child. Lao Laizi of the Zhou dynasty, for example, was said to have still dressed in coloured baby garments to please his parents when he was already upwards of

Table 5.2 The Stories of Filial Sons in *Elementary Learning* and *Horse and Whip*[41]

The Five Duties	No. of Examples of Filial Sons	
	in *Elementary Learning*	in *Horse and Whip*
1. To venerate his parents in daily life	5	5
2. To make them happy in every possible way	5	3
3. To give them extra care when they were ill	1	0
4. To show great sorrow when they were dead	0	1
5. To offer sacrifices to deceased parents with solemnity	0	1

seventy and had lost almost all his teeth. With the purpose of amusing his parents, he carried buckets of water into the house, and then deliberately fell to the ground, wailing and crying like an infant in front of them.[42] The way Lao Laizi amused his parents may seem preposterous to us, but the point is that with the emphasis on filial piety, the attributes of children were not cherished for themselves but employed to serve parents. Hence, in these stories, children were often presented as an object for sacrifice, as in the well-known story of Guo Ju, who was prepared to bury his three-year-old child alive for his mother's sake. Guo Ju lived in poverty and his mother had to divide her portion of food with his son. Guo feared that his mother did not get enough to eat because of his child, so he decided to bury his son alive. When he started digging he saw a pot of gold, which was believed to be a reward from Heaven for being a dutiful son.[43] It seems a happy ending, but it is definitely not a story indicating that children were cherished and loved.

In fact, out of these twenty-four examples, fifteen characters are adults, and only four are recognised as children with clear indications of their ages, whilst five are indicated only as "youths." Not only adult sons but also young children were said to be obliged to make sacrifices for their parents. For instance, it was said that Huang Xiang, a boy of the Han dynasty, lost his mother at nine. For the comfort of his father, he cooled his father's pillow and the bed with a fan in summer and warmed the bed with his body in winter.[44] Another eight-year-old boy called Wu Meng was said to have voluntarily let mosquitoes bite him, as he thought they would not attack his parents after being fed with his own flesh and blood. In the

Confucian context these self-sacrificing examples were held up for children to follow as deeds of filial piety.

Confucius thought that giving parents only material support did not constitute filial piety, because even animals were able to act in this way. He said:

> Now filial piety means the support of parents. Dogs and horses, however, are able to do something in the way of support. Without reverence, what is the difference between these supports?[45]

He stressed the importance of reverence in the practice of filial piety. Mencius expanded on Confucius' idea and drew a line between "nourishing the will" and "nourishing the mouth and body" in the service of parents.[46] "To nourish the mouth and body" was merely physical and biological. Furthermore, it strongly suggested analogies with animal behaviour. "To nourish the will" was to transfer material or physical acts into the symbolic, that is, people should serve their parents in accordance with *li*, which was "the feeling of respect and reverence."[47]

There were various ways "to nourish the will." The first involved one's countenance. The *Record of Rites* pointed out that one's countenance was in fact related to one's affection for parents.

> A filial son who has a deep love for his parents will surely have a bland air. Having a bland air, he will show his parents a pleasant look. Having a pleasant look, his demeanour will be mild and compliant.[48]

The story of Lao Laizi was an excellent example of this doctrine in the classics that a filial son had to give joy to his aged parents.[49]

Secondly, "nourishment of the will" was shown by giving support to parents under difficult circumstances. The stories in which Zi Lu carried rice for his parents[50] and Jiang Ge supported his mother by labour[51] emphasise the utmost dutifulness (*zhixiao*), and Guo Ju's intention of burying his son alive demonstrates that a really filial son in ancient times would be willing to sacrifice everything to satisfy his parents.

Thirdly, "nourishing the will" was embodied in not touching food and wine before setting them in front of parents. The case of Lu Ji exemplified this teaching. In the time of the late Han, Lu Ji, a six-year old boy, met the general Yuan Shu who gave him a few oranges. Lu put two of them away instead of tasting them. When he was asked why he did so, Lu Ji answered that he wished to present these oranges to his mother because she was very fond of them.[52]

Confucius believed that filial piety was basically embodied in the above three aspects.[53] In other words, a filial son was required to give his parents all his personal attention and affection, that is, to provide his parents with spiritual support as well as material provisions.

However, if parents were unkind, should a son still show respect to them? The answer in the classics was in the affirmative. Sage-king Shun was depicted in the classics such as the *Book of Documents*, the *Doctrine of the Mean* and the *Mencius* as having perfect virtue. [54] His exceedingly filial disposition was embodied in his performing filial duties even though his father was stupid, his mother perverse and his younger brother conceited. Shun's virtue was widely spoken of and a miracle occurred. As he cultivated the hills of Li (Lishan), elephants came to help plough his fields and birds came to help weed the grain. Eventually, Emperor Yao heard of him, and then sent his nine sons to serve him and married his two daughters to him. Afterwards, Yao gave the empire to him instead of to his own sons.[55] This story was frequently used in the classics as well as in many primers as an example of perfect virtue. In Zhu Xi's opinion, the parents of Shun were unusual. He said that most parents had "the nature of an average person" and their love and hate would not "violate principle," so sons should obey them.[56]

In other exemplary cases of filial piety, the virtue of filial piety was stressed in the sense that a dutiful son had to be obedient to his parents even if he was abused. The case of Min Sun expresses this idea.

Min Sun was a disciple of Confucius. He lost his mother early in his life and his stepmother disliked him because she had two children of her own. In winter, she clothed him in garments which were made of rushes; in contrast, her own children wore fine clothes. One day, Min Sun was driving a chariot for his father but was too cold to hold the reins. When his father discovered how his second wife treated his son, he determined to divorce her. Min Sun stopped his father, because although he was suffering from cold and hunger, he was concerned about his two stepbrothers. He said to his father: "If she remains, only one son is cold; if she departs, all sons will be destitute." His stepmother was touched and repented. Eventually, she became a virtuous parent.[57] Min Sun's virtue was widely reported and even reached the ears of Confucius, who praised him and said: "Filial indeed is Min Ziqian!"[58]

The story of Wang Xiang (of the Jin dynasty) was also written to persuade people to maintain a good disposition and to endure oppressive treatment at the hands of their parents. Wang Xiang's stepmother maltreated him, and his father no longer regarded him with kindness because he had heard many evil reports about Xiang. Nevertheless, Xiang's filial devotion did not waver. His stepmother loved to eat fresh fish. It was very difficult to catch fish in winter because the rivers froze over. So Xiang took off his clothes and slept on the ice to warm it up. His filial disposition brought about a miracle: the ice opened of itself and two carp leapt out.[59]

In reality, it also happened quite often that a father was clearly in the wrong and did not listen to respectful advice. Under these circumstances, should a son still obey his father? Neither the classics, Neo-Confucian writings, nor other influential works such as Yuan Cai's *Yuan's Precepts for Social Life*[60] provided any direct answer, but they all insisted on the importance of the practice of filial piety even under trying circumstances. This suggests that the practice of filial piety was of significance to government authority and social order. As mentioned earlier, ritual behaviour in the service of parents was designed according to the demands of the social system. When a person acted in accordance with ritual, he/she was thus "identified as part of his/her immediate social world." This means that "personal and social integration are achieved together."[61]

The symbolic expression of human behaviour actively presents a particular view of society and is related to the solidarity of that society.[62] You Zi, one of Confucius' disciples, is said to have believed:

> One who is filial and fraternal will be unlikely to be fond of offending against his superiors. One who does not like to offend his superiors will not like to stir up confusion.[63]

You Zi's belief was passed on to later generations through philosophical explanations in scholarly works and records of exemplary deeds in historical documents. No matter whether parents were in the wrong, the most important thing was to prevent social turmoil from occurring. At the same time, the story of Min Sun, whose virtue even changed his stepmother, conveyed a Confucian wish that everyone could be transformed (*hua*) in the end and then the whole of society would achieve harmony. In this sense, the above stories of filial piety translated Confucian teachings into conventional belief.

In respect to self-cultivation, filial piety was considered the foundation of all virtues. Confucius said:

> The superior man bends his attention to what is fundamental. Once the foundation is established, the Way (*dao*) will be naturally produced. Filial piety and fraternal submission are the root of the virtue of humanity (*ren*).[64]

This argument derives from the Confucian conception of man. Humanity as an inner morality, Tu Wei-ming argues, is "basically linked with the self-reviving, self-perfecting and self-fulfilling process of an individual."[65] Yet originally *ren* stood for human beings in society, of which ritual was an outer expression. According to the Confucian concept of man, the truly human was social rather than isolated, and thus there was a need for reciprocity in human relations. Real humanity was in the first place embodied in the basic relation of sons to parents. If one was not able to relate to one's parents in the spirit of filiality, how could one be expected to be loyal to one's superior or ruler, faithful to one's friends and caring towards other people?

Neo-Confucians in the Song explored the concept of man on the basis of a new metaphysics. In this metaphysical system, man, Heaven and Earth were regarded as one body. Zhang Zai claimed:

> Heaven is my father and Earth is my mother, and even such a small creature as I finds an intimate place in their midst. Therefore that which fills the universe I regard as my body and that which directs the universe I consider as my nature.[66]

Zhang's argument presented a belief that a man was not just a son of his parents; rather, he was a son of Heaven and Earth. To extend this relationship to the whole of society, the emperor was the eldest son of Heaven and Earth and the ministers were his stewards.[67] The relationships between father and son and between ruler and minister were "definite principles of the world" and nobody under Heaven could "escape from them."[68] Cheng Yi also said that according to the Principle of Nature, one could "develop one's nature" and fulfil one's destiny "in the very acts of filial piety and brotherly respect."[69] Clearly, these Neo-Confucian scholars considered man the filial son of the universe and filial piety at its purest was "to rejoice in Heaven and to have no anxiety."[70]

How did a human being become one with Heaven and Earth? A general principle in Song Neo-Confucianism was that a person had to "put his moral nature into practice and bring his physical existence into complete fulfilment"; then he could "match [Heaven and Earth]."[71] Moral practice required ritual; ritual was needed to regulate activities such as "seeing, hearing, thinking, reflection and movement."[72] They were all natural activities and thus should be practised in accordance with the Principle of Nature. According to Mencius, the Principle of Nature was the harmony and order of things, which characterised sageness.[73] Song Neo-Confucians expounded this idea in terms of the *Book of Changes*: "The character of the sage is 'identical with that of Heaven and Earth; his brilliancy is identical with that of the sun and moon; his order is identical with that of the four seasons; and his good and evil fortunes are identical with those of spiritual beings.'"[74] In modern anthropology, ritualised behaviour is related to the harmony and order of a society. In Song Neo-Confucianism, the harmony and order of a society and of the universe were integrated. The rules of ritual were seen as manifesting the Principle of Nature. This may be why Chen Chun defined the term "rites" as "order" and music as "harmony."[75] As a filial son of the universe, one searched for self-fulfilment or a match with Heaven and Earth rather than only taking responsibility for one's parents. This was a line drawn between just "nourishing the mouth and body" and "nourishing the will" in a philosophical sense.

Exemplary Children and Childish Traits

The above sections appear to indicate that most exemplary children presented in primers did not show childish tendencies and this phenomenon, according to Kinney, became "most extreme" as early as "in Han times."[76] Take the child Zhu Xi as an example. Zhu Xi was proficient in the *Classic of Filial Piety* at eight. According to the story, even at this age Zhu Xi had already understood the true meaning of learning, as indicated in his statement: "I cannot even be regarded as a human being if I do not follow the principles in the *Classic of Filial Piety*." The story also reveals that even with a group of children playing around him, Zhu Xi was still able to draw the Eight Trigrams (*bagua*) in sand, and then sat up straight and stared at it quietly.[77] This portrait of a little adult was intended to prove the potential of Zhu Xi, who later became a great Neo-Confucian scholar (Figure 5.1).

This image of the child Zhu Xi represents the Neo-Confucian idealised child prodigy, who was often characterised by a distinct dislike of play. This image was actually created in Han times, as Kinney finds in her study.[78] In Song Neo-Confucianism, quietness or meditation (*jing*) were required in self-cultivation. Therefore, linked with "a dislike of play," a precocious child also had a sedate appearance, expressed as "young but mature" (*shaonian laocheng*), something which was highly respected in the Confucian images of a proper child. For example, the superior intelligence of the child Lu Jiuyuan was said to be displayed in his questions about Heaven (*tian*) at the age of three or four. His father was not able to answer his questions, so he indulged in deep thought and even forgot to eat and sleep. When he reached the age of ten, his behaviour had no childish traits and all people respected his sedate appearance.[79] This was not unique to Lu Jiuyuan, for all great scholars' childhoods seemed to meet such a criterion, as the story of Xu Heng shows.

Xu Heng (1209–1281), a distinguished Confucian scholar of the Yuan, was said to have an innate talent for behaving in accordance with Confucian rites. When he was playing with a group of children, his manners in sitting, walking and greeting all accorded with the Confucian norms, so the other children did not dare to bully him. When he was between the ages of seven and eight, he started to study under a village teacher, who was amazed not only at his intellectual precocity (such as his incredible memory), but also at his perfected manners and lofty ideals. The teacher felt unqualified to teach Xu Heng, and consequently he resigned within a week.[80]

These examples all indicate that both Confucian proper children and childhood prodigies seemed never to have been attracted to ordinary children's play. This can possibly be attributed in part to the format of official biographies, as Kinney has found in her study of early Chinese literature, which were interested in neither childish behaviour nor ordinary children's games or toys.[81] As has been pointed out in the study of primers in previous chapters and sections, Confucian writings, both about and for children, were by and large

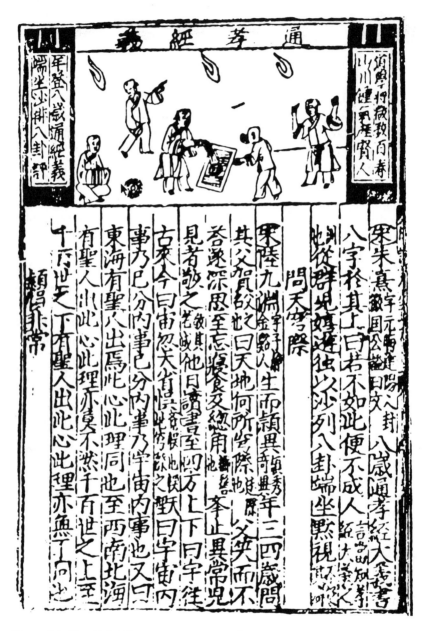

Figure 5.1 The Child Zhu Xi, being proficient in *The Classic if Filial Piety* at eight,
and drawing the Eight Trigrams in sand while children play around
him. *Stories for Daily Learning* (*Riji gushi*), 1542 edition.

intended to shape "the proper child" rather than to appreciate "the ordinary child." This approach originated in Confucian perceptions of play and education.

The earliest Confucian view of play can be traced back to a phrase in the *Analects*: "*you yu yi*" (7:6). James Legge translates the phrase as "let relaxation and enjoyment be found in the polite arts."[82] A more recent translation of this phrase by Arthur Waley is "seek distraction in the arts."[83] Apparently here the word *you* is related to relaxation and amusement, but *yi*, which in Confucian writings often referred to the six arts, has nothing to do with the modern concept of play and games. Parallel to *yi*, Confucius listed the Way (*dao*), virtues (*de*) and benevolence (*ren*), which later on were developed as the three important aspects in Confucian metaphysics. Compared to these three abstract concepts, the six arts were visible and practicable in daily life. In Neo-Confucian metaphysics, because of their visibility and practicability, they were called *wu*, referring to real things or affairs. Bearing this in mind, we may easily understand Zhu Xi's interpretation of *you* as "to practise the six arts according to one's personality" (*wan wu shi qing*). Zhu Xi regarded the six arts as things or affairs, and the Way, virtues and benevolence as principles (*li*). According to him, the relationship between the six arts and the principles was that the six arts accommodated the principles; and the practice of these six arts would not lead people to indulge themselves but to find satisfaction in pursuit of principles.[84] Evidently, in Zhu Xi's interpretation, the six arts were not related to the modern concept of amusement or entertainment but to self-cultivation in moral practice. The arts of music and driving a chariot were seen as part of the training that a Confucian gentleman ought to have.

However, the Chinese people in ancient times enjoyed playing, and many Chinese games can be traced back to as early as the Spring and Autumn and Warring States periods. In the *Analects*, games such as chess (*bo* and *yi*)[85] were mentioned. According to Confucius, playing chess was better than doing nothing all day but stuffing oneself with food.[86] Did Confucius here acknowledge a scholar's right to play? *Bo* in modern Chinese refers to gambling, but in ancient times it was only a type of chess, and was regarded as a harmless game (*yaxi*). It was in the fifth century that *bo* gradually became a gambling game. Apparently, many people of the time indulged in this gambling game: scholars discarded their study of Confucian classics, kings and princes neglected affairs of state, farmers set aside their farming operations, and merchants lost their businesses. Therefore, a serious campaign against this fashion was initiated. Yan Zhitui mentioned these games in his family regulations, on the one hand; but on the other, he noticed that indulgence in the game had a pernicious effect on society. Yan pointed out that Confucius did not regard games as part of serious learning but as occasional relaxation, which was better than eating, sleeping or sitting around all day without doing anything positive.[87] Most Confucian commentators of later generations translated this opinion into a more proscriptive attitude. For instance, Zhu Xi emphasised that Confucius meant only that there were worse things than playing games, and had not meant to encourage anyone to play chess or other games, but wanted to advise people that they should always apply their minds to something good.[88]

From the Song onward, most sober Confucian scholars used the phrase *wan wu sang zhi* (by trifling with "things" one would lose one's goal and energy) to express their hostile attitude to things beyond the Way. This phrase originated in the *Book of Documents*.[89] In the Song, Cheng Hao used it to comment on Xie Liangzuo's broad knowledge of things beyond the Way.[90] In Cheng Hao's criticism, *wu* referred to anything not relevant to the Neo-Confucian metaphysical Way, including not only curios and games but also literature such as poems, and practical skills such as mathematics. This hostile attitude to things beyond the metaphysical Way was one of the characteristics of Song Neo-Confucianism, which placed extreme emphasis on moral cultivation. However, this was not unique to Neo-Confucianism, and a similar attitude can be found in "the dominant Western epistemologies since Plato," which "emphasised philosophy, logic, and science as the sources of knowledge," and "discredited the arts, literature and play as such sources."[91]

Play in a Confucian definition, however, had a significant role in the education of children. As mentioned earlier, music in Confucian education was always regarded as having a magic power to nurture and shape one's personality. Basically this was due to the close link between music and the performance of ceremony. However, it could also be related to Confucius' particular interest in music, which originated in his childhood experience. The only childish trait recorded in Confucius' biography is his imitating adults' performance of ceremony when he was a little child. This childish play was interpreted in the Han biography as something which contributed to Confucius' permanent strengths.[92] To Confucius, music was not only an important means of education but also a significant part of education. Accordingly, "educating through music" (*yu jiao yu le* 寓教於樂) was developed as one of the basic principles in Confucian educational theories. Yet the words *yue* (music) and *le* (pleasure) share the same character 樂. To most orthodox Confucian scholars education was a rather sober matter, but the fact that the same character is used for *yue* and *le* provided liberal educationists with some space to criticise those rigid attitudes in educational practice. As discussed earlier, Wang Yangming presented a better understanding of children than did other Confucian scholars. He realised that children love to play and dislike regulations. By adopting the notion of "educating through music," Wang Yangming suggested that young pupils could be attracted to learning by singing and practising etiquette. At the same time, these more enjoyable aspects of education would, he believed, nurture children's innate goodness and, indirectly, remove their weaknesses. Although Wang Yangming sympathised with children, he, like other Confucian writers, never claimed that children had a right to enjoy themselves. So, while his approach was more creative than most Confucian educators, his writings reveal little about children's games and pastimes.[93]

The notion of "educating through music (or pleasure)" and Wang Yangming's proposal, are to a certain extent similar to what modern educational theory and psychological literature call "educational play and games." In Confucian theory, the term used to express this similar idea was *xi* (practice), which was discussed in Chapter One. The significance of play of this kind in a child's growth is well illustrated in the story of the mother of Mencius who changed her abode three times. Mencius was said to have been raised by his mother alone, for his father died when he was little. Their first house was near a cemetery, so young Mencius used to imitate the performance of obsequies. His mother thought that this was not good for the child, so she moved to a place near a market. In this environment, Mencius imitated a butcher's activities. His mother was again dissatisfied and moved to a place near a temple and school. Mencius thus learned to perform rituals and practise etiquette, for he often saw people doing so. His mother was happy and decided to stay there permanently.[94] The moral of the story is that Mencius' mother shaped not only Mencius' play but also his adult aspirations. The story also indicates a widely accepted conventional idea derived from the Confucian teaching that children's moral character was to a large extent influenced by their social environment and the things they perceived in everyday life.

Playthings particularly for children are also modern creations, associated with the emergence and development of the modern concept of childhood. In classical Chinese, no words specifically referred to children's playthings. The term *wanwu* referred both to curios and to things to be prized and played with. The modern concept of children's toys appeared in China at the beginning of the twentieth century when Froebel's ideas on early child education were introduced into China through Japanese translation.[95] The core of Froebel's theory is to assimilate education into play, and to give children "gifts" to play with. In Japanese translation, the word "gifts" was interpreted into two Chinese characters: *enwu*. At that time, the Chinese accepted Froebel's idea on the basis of Confucian educational theory, so "educating through music" became a very Chinese version of Froebel's thesis; and Confucius' childish play was once again used as a classical example for the interpretation of the relationship between play and education.[96]

However, some exemplary figures presented in primers display both childlike traits and a heroic personality. One of the most famous stories narrated in primers is the story of Sima Guang, who rescued one of his playmates from being drowned. Sima Guang was playing with a group of children when one of them fell into a big water vat. While the other children were all frightened and ran away screaming, Sima Guang calmly broke the vat so as to let the water flow out, and thus the child was saved.[97] In this story, Sima Guang was treated as a normal child, that is, like other children, he loved to play and his heroic performance was accomplished in the course of playing. In the 1542 version of *Stories for Daily Learning*, this story appeared under the category of child prodigy, which perhaps suggests a novel approach to child wisdom.

Also, Wen Yanbo of the Song is portrayed as a child rather than as a little adult-in-training. According to the story, Wen Yanbo was playing ball with other children. The ball fell into a deep hole, and none of the children knew how to get it out. Wen Yanbo poured water into the hole and the ball floated to the surface.[98] What we see here was not actually an exemplary child in the Confucian sense but an intelligent child who solved a problem occurring as he played with other children (Figure 5.2).

Summary

The exemplary children presented in the primers were intended primarily to show children how to grow into adulthood properly and quickly. Yet standards for the ideal adult varied depending on the differing perceptions of the structure of learning and criteria for a Confucian scholar. Intellectual precocity in the context of pursuing success in the civil service examinations referred to reaching adult achievements at an age when the majority of children were just beginning their schooling. In addition, the reliance on literary examinations for official appointments from the Tang onward steered both scholarship and education away from moral cultivation. Under these circumstances, child prodigies were portrayed not in order to illustrate preternatural ability but to stimulate youngsters to devote themselves to literary composition as early as possible.

Learning in Song Neo-Confucianism represented a moral approach, within which the ideal child was to be equipped with adult Confucian virtues at a very early age; and freedom from childish traits was often a characteristic of child prodigies of this kind. The stories of Confucius' and Mencius' childish imitation of adult activities were to a certain extent an acknowledgement of the existence of childish traits; but the childish traits as such were often used only to emphasise the important impact of environment and practice on children, and the aspect of children's play was ignored. The lack of attention paid to this aspect of even Confucius' and Mencius' childish acts of imitation was part of the traditional Confucian intention of shaping an ordinary child by creating a "precocious or proper child." However, in the 1542 version of *Stories for Daily Learning* two exemplary children were presented in the setting of playing with other children, and their heroic acts occurred during the course of play. This may suggest a more liberal recognition of the attributes of childhood under the influence of the Wang Yangming School.

Although many popular primers accommodated some content

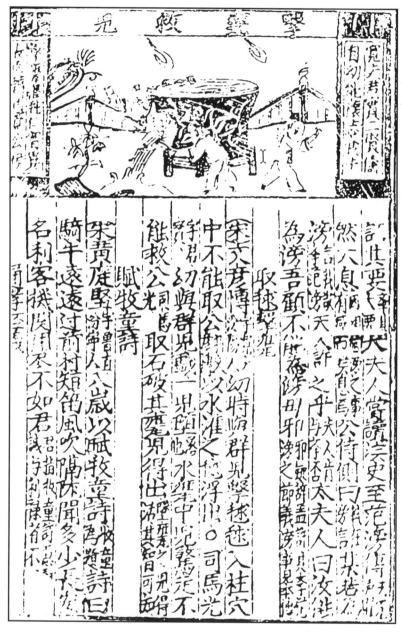

Figure 5.2 Wen Yanbo: getting a ball out of a deep hole by floating it. Sima
Guang: rescuing a child by breaking a big water vat. *Stories for Daily
Learning* (*Riji gushi*), 1542 edition.

other than Neo-Confucianism, most exemplary children were established to illustrate the Neo-Confucian image of what the proper child should be, such as in the twenty-four examples of filial piety. Children in these examples were by modern standards victims of Confucian adults — they either sacrificed themselves for adults or they were sacrificed by adults. Yet in the presentations of Neo-Confucianism, this was the way to practise the rites and to ritualise the body.

The Song Neo-Confucians were aware that abstract metaphysics would not be easily understood and accepted. Hence, they called metaphysics "the idea." Zhu Xi said that people should not "just hold on to the idea of filial piety"; they had to "know the way to practice it, for instance, the way to serve [their] parents and to take care of their comfort in both winter and summer."[99] Here Zhu Xi was drawing on an essential rule from the *Record of Rites*,[100] and the story of Huang Xiang, as narrated earlier, was often used to elucidate this rule.

According to the Cheng-Zhu school, "the direct understanding of such-and-such an affair" was the basic principle in elementary teaching (*xiaoxue*); at a higher level, education (*daxue*) focused on "the investigation of such-and-such a principle — the reason why an affair is as it is."[101] Therefore, filial piety in advanced learning was related to topics of Neo-Confucian metaphysics such as "the Principle of Nature" and destiny. At a lower stage, filial piety had to be practised in accordance with the rules in the *Record of Rites* and the other classics, and the exemplary stories provided illustrations of these rules. The whole process of fulfilment of filial piety was composed of these two stages (the "idea" and the "way"). This is why Zhu Xi collected the rules and examples of filial piety from the classics and other historical materials and compiled *Elementary Learning*. Meanwhile, in his other philosophical works, such as *Reflections on Things at Hand*, Zhu Xi saw both man (as an individual) and the universe (as a whole) as embodying the same Great Ultimate. Thus "the Great Ultimate in the universe as a principle is one and its manifestations are many."[102] Based on this interpretation, Zhu Xi regarded the idea of filial piety as a specific branch of the principle and a manifestation of the Great Ultimate. In the late Ming, Wang Yangming preferred a more direct way to reach a high level of morality. In Wang's concept of learning, the "idea" of filial piety became less important and the "way" of filial piety had greater significance. This was more realistic for educating young children. Nevertheless, filial children presented in Zhu Xi's *Elementary Learning* and in other primers all served to guide children in their moral development.

Chapter 6

Basic Elementary Training and the Instillation of Morals

The term *xiaoxue* basically has four meanings. Originally it referred to wordbooks and elementary schooling, and later it was developed to relate to the study of Confucian classics in Han learning. In Song Neo-Confucianism, the term was redefined with a focus on moral cultivation. In Qing evidential scholarship (*Kaozheng xue*), the term was used for the name of an auxiliary branch, as the Qing evidential scholars attempted to bridge the different intellectual approaches, and regarded the study of characters as an important step in the training of a Confucian scholar.

Dai Zhen (1724–1777) stated that learning characters was not only a matter of literacy education but was related to understanding the original meaning of the Confucian classics and defending Confucian orthodoxy.[1] What Dai Zhen believed reflected a commonly-held view among the evidential scholars: original Confucianism could be rediscovered and retrieved by tracing the archaic forms of characters. Ruan Yuan (1764–1849), as the patron of the School of Evidential Research and a distinguished scholar, carried this idea further by using a simile:

> The Way of the sages is like the house of a teacher. Learning primary and derived characters and their glosses is the entrance. If one misses the path, all steps will lead away from it. If this is the case, how can one reach the hall and enter the studio?[2]

Ruan Yuan clearly pointed to the importance of learning characters in the study of the Confucian classics. If one was not able to find the entrance, one would never "see what lay between the door and the inner recesses of the room." Also, if one sought only to "classify names and their referents" but not to consider the Way of the sages, one would only get to a place "between the gate and the entrance" and never "recall that there are still a hall and a studio to enter."[3] Ruan's message was very clear: the destination was to retrieve the Way of the sages by using the principles of Han learning. This suggests that Qing evidential scholars and Song Neo-Confucians might have used different methodology and had different "entrances" in reconstructing Confucianism, but they had the same goal. More importantly, there were no conflicts between Song Neo-Confucians and evidential scholars with respect to moral concepts and Confucian values.

The first section of this chapter focuses mainly on Wang Yun's *Explanations of Characters for Children* (*Wenzi mengqiu*), a representative Qing wordbook. The study of this primer helps us see how the educational ideas of the evidential school connected the study of characters to moral accomplishment. The second part then shows the link between basic training in numeracy and the instillation of morals through an investigation of how numerals and calculations were presented in primers. It confirms that literacy education in late imperial China was integrated into moral education, and the fundamental ideas of Confucianism were instilled in children's minds as soon as they started learning characters, numerals and basic calculating skills.

The Study of Characters and Moral Edification

An alphabetical language usually has a system of spelling that closely approximates the sounds represented by the letters, although a lack of correlation between spelling and pronunciation frequently exists in English and English-speaking children have to spend valuable time in their early years of schooling learning spelling.[4] The first section of elementary English textbooks during the sixteenth and seventeenth centuries normally focused on spelling, which was a basic step in learning to read and write.[5] However, because the letters express sounds,[6] in pre-industrial England, a child in his early schooling could start learning to read once he had mastered twenty-six letters.[7]

In contrast, Chinese characters represent whole words, or parts of compound words; and they represent concepts rather than "sounds." Because of this, in the early stages of their schooling Chinese-speaking children have to learn characters one by one before they can start reading. In pre-modern China, there was no phonetic alphabet to represent the sound of each character, and the phonetic symbols used still depended on prior knowledge of at least some characters.[8] School masters and scholars tried to find the best way to help children acquire literacy skills easily and quickly.

Wang Yun suggested that children at the ages of four and five should start learning about two thousand basic characters; only when children were able to master at least two thousand characters could they begin to study classics and other works.[9] He therefore compiled a textbook called *Explanations of Characters for Children*, to help children learn characters.

From a linguistics aspect, the importance of learning two thousand basic characters may be that, in earlier written Chinese, many words were independent units not modified according to their function in the sentence. Unlike English, Chinese is not an inflected language. Thus characters in Chinese elementary textbooks could be arranged according to how many basic characters children should learn, and would not be limited by the demands of inflection.[10] This is why Chinese elementary textbooks paid so much attention to the characters themselves. In contrast, the focus of attention in English textbooks of the sixteenth and seventeenth centuries was on grammar.[11]

In pre-modern China, the teaching of Chinese characters was guided by the six rules (*liushu*) for forming Chinese characters.[12] Following these rules, Wang Yun classified over two thousand (2,044) basic characters into four categories. In Wang's *Explanations of Characters for Children*, there are 264 characters (13%) which are pure pictographs (*xiangxing*). There are 129 characters (6%) which are simple ideographs (*zhishi*), conveying ideas by means of symbols. These two categories of characters are named *chunti* (pure structure) — they have only a single indivisible structure, compared with others which usually have two or more parts. The third category of characters (1,260, 62%) is compound ideographs (*huiyi*), which combine one or more pictographs to form characters with different meanings. The other 391 characters (19%) are phonetic compounds (*xingsheng*), which are usually comprised of two parts: one represents the meaning while the other determines the sound.[13] Evidently, many characters in standard textbooks were formed from pictographs and ideographs.

This may seem to confirm the traditional Chinese analysis in which characters were described as "pictographic" or "ideographic." However, as early as the twelfth century, scholars such as Zheng Qiao (1104–1162) found that many characters were formed on the basis of phonetics rather than ideographics. Some Qing evidential scholars also held the view that the majority of characters were composed using phonetic rules rather than ideographic combination.[14] This section will not deal with this linguistic controversy. Rather, it will look at the relationship between graphic inscriptions and points of reference by examining the six rules for creating characters and their links with Chinese philosophy.

According to modern linguistics, the relationship between graphic inscriptions and points of reference is absolutely arbitrary.[15] In traditional Chinese philology, however, characters were thought to have close links with nature and concrete objects. In Chinese philosophy, the whole universe was regarded as an all-pervasive unity: the way of "Heaven and Earth is perseverently visible"; and "all the dynamical activities in the universe are perseverently exhibiting the One."[16] According to this doctrine, characters were naturally connected with Heaven and Earth and were created to manifest the Way of the whole universe. As Xu Shen stated, Chinese characters were the classified images of natural phenomena (*yilei xiangxing*). However, Xu Shen continued, a pictorial element was not a character but a drawing. Only when this pictorial part was given a sound was a character formed.[17] According to this point of view, a Chinese character was a union of two elements: one pictorial and one audible. The six types of characters can actually be classified into three categories: (1) the pictographic; (2) the ideographic, including simple ideographs and compound ideographs; (3) the phonetic, including phonetic compounds, borrowed characters and characters used for new words by extension of meaning. The opinion of Qing evidential scholars was that the phonetic element played an important role in making characters and establishing their meanings. Therefore, they attempted to reconstruct ancient phonology and to decipher the original meaning of each character by means of the phonetic element.[18] However, the Chinese writing system was not alphabetic but graphic, and a sound was presented by graphic symbols, not by an alphabet or syllabary. The graphic symbols appeared to demonstrate some connections between characters and meanings, and between names and things. This allowed teachers in pre-modern China to employ the Chinese writing system as a convenient tool for language teaching, especially at an elementary level.

Wang Yun's *Explanation for Characters for Children* represented this traditional pedagogical method. In his preface, Wang Yun stated that he wrote this book to instruct two grandchildren of an old friend. In his opinion, the first step of learning was to recognise basic characters, as he believed: "It is not very difficult to recognise these two thousand characters when children are four or five years old."[19] It may sound incredible to us now that a child of four or five was able to master some two thousand Chinese characters. In ancient China, however, there was a belief that children had a very strong capacity for memory, and an emphasis was placed on memorising and reciting as the basic processes of elementary training. Nevertheless, at the same time, much serious criticism of Chinese education concentrated on this point. For example, Wang Yun stressed the necessity of mastering at least two thousand basic characters on the one hand; but on the other, he also realised that "students are human beings, not pigs or dogs,"[20] and teachers should not drive them to memorise and recite books and characters all day. Thus, Wang Yun strongly recommended teaching children original pictographs and ideographic symbols by analysing the structure of each character. He believed that this pedagogical method afforded an easy way to remember characters, and turned the hard job of learning characters into a test of wits.[21]

In addition, many Chinese characters are compounds consisting of one "phonetic" indicating pronunciation and one "radical" related to the meaning. The radicals became the key to mastering Chinese characters. A child could look up characters in a dictionary if he knew the radicals. He could also learn new phonetic compounds without a teacher if he had mastered the basic characters. Wang Yun stated that the two thousand basic characters in his book included most of the radicals and phonetics used in the composition of Chinese characters.[22] From a comparative point of view, tracing the original roots of Chinese characters had the same function as finding the stems of words and their prefixes and suffixes in English.

Wang Yun's ideas about literacy education were not altogether new. Firstly, his idea that children should learn two thousand basic characters at the first stage of learning had been practised in language teaching for many centuries. This can be demonstrated by looking at *The Trimetrical Classic, One Hundred Surnames,* and *One Thousand Characters,* the three most popular primers in late imperial China. As discussed in Chapter Two, these three primers were all produced before the Song dynasty, and in Ming-Qing times they were employed as a series for teaching and learning characters. There were 2,720 characters in these three books. Since some characters appeared more than once, they actually contained about 2,000 different characters,[23] the same number mentioned in Wang Yun's book. This is not a coincidence but demonstrates the idea, which gradually developed over the centuries, of just how many basic characters children should learn in their first stage of acquiring literacy skills.

Secondly, in these three textbooks, pictorial and ideographic elements were also of significance in choosing basic characters for beginners. This can be exemplified by *The Trimetrical Classic,* which contained 508 different characters in all. Of these characters, 278 were in the categories of pictographs, simple ideographs and compound ideographs (See Table 6.1).[24]

Furthermore, out of the 278 pictographic, simple ideographic and compound ideographic characters used in *The Trimetrical Classic* only 59 do not appear in the *Explanations of Characters for Children* (See Table 6.2).

These two tables illustrate that Wang Yun in fact followed earlier traditional views about elementary education and highlighted the significant role of pictographs and ideographs in selecting two

Table 6.1 Four Categories of Chinese Character in *The Trimetrical Classic*

Category	Number		%	
Pictographs	62		12.20	
Simple ideographs	24	278	4.72	54.72
Compound ideographs	192		37.80	
Phonetic compounds	230	230	45.28	45.28
Total	508	508	100	100

Table 6.2 Comparison between the Distribution of Three Character Types Listed in *The Trimetrical Classic* and *Explanations of Characters for Children*

Type	Sanzi jing		Wenzi mengqiu	
	Number	%	Number Present	Number Absent
Pictographs	62	22.30	60	2
Simple ideographs	24	8.64	23	1
Compound ideographs	192	69.06	136	56
Total	278	100	219	59

thousand basic characters for beginners. Knowledge, concepts and Confucian values could be instilled in the students through explanations of pictorial or ideographic symbols. In other words, those pictorial and ideographic elements could be employed as metaphors to convey certain ideas. On this basis, we may assume that through learning *Explanations of Characters for Children*, a child could not only recognise about 2,000 characters but also gain some general knowledge, such as a knowledge of history.[25] For instance, many of the key points of Confucianism were revealed by an analysis of the structures of various characters, as summarized below:

1. The Idea of Strata in Chinese Society

冏 同 君 *jun*, sovereign. The original form of this character depicts a seated prince.

臣 臣 *chen*, minister, subjects. The earlier form of this character depicts an official who is kneeing, meaning that he obeys his sovereign.

民 眾 民 *min*, people. All characters related to the form *ren* (man) face the left. *Jun* faces the front; *chen* and *min* both face towards the right, meaning that the officials and ordinary people have their faces towards the sovereign.[26]

2. The Concept of Loyalty and Obedience

望 望 *wang*, full moon. It is a combination of three parts: 月 the moon; 臣 the subject; 壬 the court. Wang Yun said that courtiers paying attention to a sovereign were just like the full moon facing the sun.[27]

臥 臥 *wo*, to lie. The original form of the character depicts both ministers (臣) and and ordinary people (人) performing the kowtow, as they were all required to do before their sovereign.[28]

3. The Concept of Filial Piety

弔 弔 *diao*, to condole. This ideogram comprises person (人) and bow (弓), which is intended to represent a person holding a bow and trying to help a dutiful son to protect his parents from animals.[29] Later the meaning "to condole" evolved, to express sympathy with someone whose parent(s) had passed away.

孝 孝 *xiao*, filial piety. It seems obvious that the son (子) is a product of the father (爻); thus the duty of a son is to be filial to his father.[30]

4. Attitudes towards Education

Confucianism also placed a positive value on education. This can be seen from an analysis of the following characters.

斅 學 *jiao* 教 and 學 *xue*, to teach and to learn. In their earliest forms, these two characters were one. The original character showed a child inside the "冂", which meant ignorant; and the task of education was to wake up ignorant youths. In the small seal (*xiaozhuan*) style of characters, the "攴" was omitted. In fact, the "攴" shows a hand gripping a stick or rod. This is perhaps the reason why the character was divided into two. The 斅, with the radical "攴", symbolises the authority of a master.[31]

The explanations of the following characters also reflect the popular idea of Confucianism that "official emolument may be found in one's learning."[32]

士 *shi*, literati. This is comprised of ten (十) and one (一), originally indicating that everything was contained in the numbers from one to ten. In the Confucian society, the literati were considered as the leaders of the ordinary people; here, ten (十) stood for ordinary people, and one (一) stood for the literati; so the character could also represent the literati.[33] From this, the character 仕 was produced, meaning "to enter official employment." Wang Yun simply said that the meaning of the word was "to learn."[34] It really expressed the relationship between learning and official employment in Confucian thought. Confucius said: "The officer, having discharged all his duties, should devote his leisure to learning. The student, having completed his learning, should apply himself to be an official."[35]

5. The Position of the Female in Chinese Society

女 女 *nü*, woman. The pictograph shows a kneeling woman, indicating Chinese women's submissive position.[36]

婦 婦 *fu*, woman, especially a married woman. The character consists of a woman (女) with a broom (帚), clearly indicating the meaning of this character.[37] The duty of women was to serve their husbands and their parents-in-law according to the teaching of Confucianism. If a woman (女) was beneath the roof (宀) and willingly did her duty at home, her whole family could enjoy the tranquil life. This is the meaning of *an* 安 — peace.[38]

That notions of Confucianism could be built into the structures of some characters was really a unique feature employed in the teaching of Chinese characters. An alphabetic writing system such as English did not have this kind of ideological advantage.[39] For example, *The A B C of Aristotle,* a popular manuscript circulating in England before the appearance of printing,[40] attempted to inject some moral conceptions of Christianity into children's minds by teaching the letters of the alphabet. For example, it stated,

> Be not —
> **A** too Amorous, too Adventurous, nor Argue too much.[41]

However, the letter *A* in isolation expressed nothing. The author could have used it to teach something totally different. As early as the seventeenth century, Eachard, a clergyman of the Church of England, pointed to this fact. He argued that one could use letters to preach religious ideas, for example, the letter *R* could be used to teach the word "repent": "Repent ye, for the Kingdom of Heaven is at hand." However, the letter *R* also could be used to teach other words which are not relevant to religion, e.g. *R,* "readily" or "roaring"; also, *A*: "why [is] not A apple-pasty?"[42]

This argument indicates that the bond between the graphic inscriptions and points of reference is arbitrary; the graphic inscriptions actually have no natural connection with the points of reference. The Chinese writing system with its "visual" symbols seems to have been used to lead people to believe that there was a natural connection between graphic inscriptions and points of reference. This belief is in conflict with the arbitrary nature of language. Yet it was convenient for teachers in pre-modern China to employ the

Chinese writing system as a vehicle for Confucian values in language teaching.[43]

Another kind of textbook, represented by *The Names and Descriptions of Things*, combined the teaching of characters with general knowledge.[44] The special feature of *The Names and Descriptions of Things* was that it attempted to teach characters through introductions to, and descriptions of, things. Take the character *shui* (water) as an example. Fang Fengchen used four sentences and sixteen characters to teach the word and other characters with the radical *shui*. He wrote:

> Moving forward in waves is water (*tao tao zhe shui*),
> Flowing in a thin stream is spring water (*juan juan zhe quan*),
> A rushing stream is rapids (*ji wei tan lai*),
> A deep pool is an abyss (*shen wei tan yuan*).[45]

Shui (water), *quan* (spring water), *tanlai* (rapids) and *tanyuan* (abyss) are nouns; *tao tao*, *juanjuan* are descriptors (functioning like adjectives); *ji* and *shen* are adjectives which were used to describe the specific nouns. Excluding the word *zhe*[46] and *wei*,[47] the other nine characters all have the radical *shui* (See Figure 6.1).

These four sentences reveal Fang's approach to elementary training. First, he taught characters systematically. Children did not learn the word "water" (*shui*) alone; from this basic character, they learned another nine characters. Secondly, he did not simply give

Figure 6.1 The Teaching of 水 and its Associated Characters

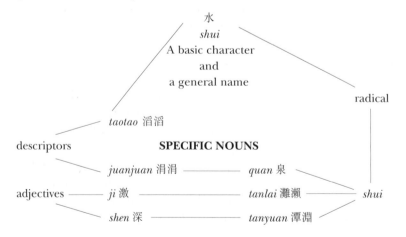

students a basic word and a general name for an object. Instead, he used adjectives to characterise specific items which were related to the general name. From this, students learned how to correctly use different words to name things precisely and how to compose a sentence to describe an object specifically. Thirdly, he organised these characters on the basis of radicals. Through learning these sentences and characters, children accepted the concept of radicals and knew how to use this kind of knowledge in their later studies. This indicates that a Chinese character in itself might give children a visual prompt; and building on the function of the radical, a basic character could generate a series of characters with connected meanings.

While teaching children both general and specific knowledge in his introduction to nouns, Fang never omitted the teachings of Confucianism. For example, when he introduced appellations, Fang stressed the qualities human beings should have. He said that people had to have education while living in groups; a sovereign had to have the virtue of benevolence, and an official had to be loyal to his sovereign; a father had to show his love to his son, a son had to be filial to his father; duties had to be divided between husbands and wives; friends had to trust each other; elders and youths had to be ranked according to their ages.[48] The main human relationships, according to Confucius, were between sovereign and officials, fathers and sons, husbands and wives, friends and friends, older and younger brothers. Fang arranged these terms in accordance with the teachings in the Classics. Thus, children were introduced to the Confucian doctrines at the same time as they learned these terms.

Furthermore, Fang also transmitted Confucian ideas in his explanations of why some objects had specific names. As an example, the word for almond is *xingren*. Fang said that the main reason for this was that only its inside was edible, and since benevolence (*ren*) was an inner virtue, so it was used as the name for almond.[49] This analysis of the word *xingren* represents a traditional practice in Chinese teaching.

Teaching children Confucian values through teaching them literacy gradually became a formal principle in traditional Chinese elementary education. For instance, Huo Tao said that teachers should teach pupils the basic concepts of Confucian ethics while they explained the meanings of characters such as *xiao* (filial piety).[50]

Both Wang Yun's *Explanations of Characters for Children* and Fang's *The Names and Descriptions of Things* indicate that, apart from some primers which aimed at teaching children the rules of rituals and good manners, the primers which focused on literacy skills were still involved in moral instruction. The tie between literacy education and moral instruction existed even in teaching the writing of characters.

Writing characters was a main issue in elementary training, and teaching characters usually went together with instruction in writing. Some primers and teaching manuals thus contained detailed instructions on how to write characters. For example, in his *Essential Points in Community School,* Lü Kun pointed out that in the course of teaching calligraphy, teachers should first instruct children how to clean their inkstones every day and to keep their body about ten centimetres away from their books.[51] In Ming-Qing China, calligraphy took on a new importance as a consequence of the civil service examinations. It was said that "the calligraphy of a script could play a very important part in the examiner's assessment of the candidate's ability."[52] Many scholars and educationists, such as Huo Tao, also believed that writing characters was closely linked with moral cultivation.

The emphasis on the relationship between writing characters and cultivation of mind originated with Cheng Hao. He said:

> When I practice calligraphy, I am very serious. My objective is not that the calligraphy must be good. Rather my practice is the way of moral training.[53]

Huo Tao elaborated this abstract idea and provided details as to how to practise moral cultivation in writing characters. For instance, the vertical stroke symbolised the virtue of being unbiased; a left-falling stroke or a right-falling stroke stood for the picture of a person raising his hands. Through the practice of writing a vertical, children learned to be impartial; and either a left-falling stroke or a right-falling stroke reminded children that they should move their hands reverently.[54]

This idea was accepted by Neo-Confucianists in later generations, as well as some scholars who were reluctant to call themselves Neo-Confucianists. Even Lü Kun, who referred to himself as an independent thinker, admitted that the practice of calligraphy actually helped to nourish a child's character.[55] Thus the role of moral cultivation in elementary education, which was emphasised by the Song Neo-Confucians, was reaffirmed by many scholars in Ming-Qing China. This can be seen in another statement of Huo Tao. He said:

> To cultivate children's minds is one of the main aims and functions of elementary education. If children keep correct ideas in their heart/mind, they are no doubt intelligent. Perhaps they might not have a good brain or ear, but if they can hold the Confucian teachings in their heart/mind, it could be said that they are intelligent, and they are able to hear well. If children do not have good thoughts in their minds, perhaps they might be very bright and their hearing might not be poor, but it could be said that they are stupid and they are deaf. Intelligence and good hearing come automatically when children cultivate their minds well. Literati who have merit can approach the level of sages even if they are not gifted with keen intelligence.[56]

This passage represents a strong belief that moral cultivation had precedence over other subjects in elementary education; and in judging a person, natural endowments and knowledge were of no consequence.

Numerals in Some Primers

It is important first to investigate the meaning of the English words "mathematics" and "arithmetic," since the terms, in a historical perspective, differed in meaning from their modern use. According to *The Oxford English Dictionary*, the term "arithmetic" means (1) "the science of numbers; the art of computation by figures; and (2) "arithmetical knowledge, computation, reckoning."[57] The first meaning refers to a division of mathematics and the second to arithmetic at an elementary level, as we use it today. The term "mathematics" was originally "the collective name for geometry, arithmetic, and certain physical sciences (as astronomy and optics) involving geometrical reasoning."[58] In modern usage, mathematics is divided into (1) pure mathematics in a strict sense, and (2) applied or mixed mathematics in a wider sense. The main divisions of pure mathematics are geometry, arithmetic and algebra. Applied mathematics emphasises concrete applications of pure mathematics in astronomy, various branches of physics, the theory of probability and so on.[59]

The term *suan* in classical Chinese was a collective noun which stood for both "mathematics" and "arithmetic" in English. As Needham points out:

> In ancient times the term arithmetic did not mean the simple computations which go by the name of arithmetic today, but concerned rather the elementary aspects of the theory of numbers.[60]

In many pre-modern Chinese books, the term *suan* referred to mathematics rather than to arithmetic as we understand it today. For instance, the *Suanjing shishu* is best translated as the *Ten Mathematical Canons*. Here, the terms "mathematics" and "arithmetic" are not interchangeable. *Shu* as one of the "six arts" embraced both mathematics and basic arithmetical knowledge. In modern Chinese, the term *shuxue*, meaning mathematics, is distinguished from *suanshu* which only refers to simple computation and is usually taught in elementary school.

In the discussion of the concept and content of *xiaoxue*, we have mentioned that in the records of educational documents arithmetic was part of elementary education. The earliest record occurs in the *Record of Rites*, which states that in the Zhou dynasty, children were taught numbers (*shu* 數), learning to count from one to ten; and the names of the points of the compass (*fangming*), learning to recognise north, south, east and west. Children also had to learn the traditional Chinese counting method — to count days and dates by using the "Heavenly Stems" and "Earthly Branches" (*shuri*).[61] Then a sexagesimal cycle was formed for recording years which used pairs from the ten Heavenly Stems and the twelve Earthly Branches, so that after sixty years the scheme repeated itself.[62] This elementary training was supposed to be carried out at home. After this beginning, children were sent to a teacher and learned reading, writing (*shu* 書) and basic calculation skills (*ji*).[63] Later educational documents rarely recorded the details of teaching and learning arithmetic in elementary education, but mathematics became a subject in advanced learning during the Sui and Tang periods.[64]

From the Tang onward, although the subject of mathematics was included in the curriculum of the Imperial Academy from time to time, it had no continuity of development. In relation to arithmetic in elementary training, we can find no more information than that provided by the *Record of Rites*.

A survey of the contents of elementary textbooks suggests that no particular textbooks were used for instruction in arithmetic at the beginning of elementary schooling from the Tang through the Qing. Numbers and numeration were sometimes taught together with Chinese characters. This can be exemplified by *The Trimetrical Classic*.

The Trimetrical Classic did not introduce the ten basic numbers in order but presented them in sentences. For example, for the number four the text reads:

> There are spring, summer, autumn and winter;
> These four (*si*) seasons revolve without ceasing.[65]

For the number six:

> Horses, oxen, sheep, roosters, dogs and pigs,
> These six (*liu*) animals are those which men keep.[66]

Numeration in *The Trimetrical Classic* was also contained in one sentence, a literal translation of which is:

> One — ten, ten — one hundred;
> One hundred — one thousand, one thousand — ten thousand.[67]

The meaning of the sentence is that the first number is one, and ten is the last of the ten basic numbers. One hundred is a multiple of ten; one thousand is a multiple of one hundred; and ten thousand is a multiple of one thousand. In modern terminology, the above sentence could be simply expressed in this way:

$$1 \times 10 = 10$$
$$10 \times 10 = 100$$
$$10 \times 100 = 1,000$$
$$10 \times 1,000 = 10,000$$

According to commentaries on the above sentence, the explanation that a teacher ought to give students included: (1) the basic numbers from one to ten; (2) the odd and the even numbers, which were usually associated with the two polar forces, that is, 1, 3, 5, 7, 9 were *yang*, and 2, 4, 6, 8, 10 were *yin*; and (3) the origin of numbers.[68] The explanation of the origin of numbers went back to the legendary period of history. The legendary Emperor Yu was said to have been presented with two diagrams by miraculous animals which emerged from the rivers. One was the *River Diagram* (*Hetu*) and the other the *Luo River Writing* (*Luoshu*). In ancient China, it was believed that the numbers from one to ten originated from the *River Diagram*. According to Zhu Xi's interpretation, the ten numbers in the two diagrams were arranged as *The Great Appendix* (*Xici*) to *The Book of Changes* put it: "heaven is one, earth is two, heaven three, earth four, heaven five, earth six, heaven seven, earth eight, heaven nine, earth ten."[69] In respect to teaching arithmetical knowledge, the numbers in this sentence were not merely semantic, as the examples mentioned above suggest. Basic numbers and simple calculation were encouraged while the meaning of the words was being taught.

The process of teaching arithmetic in elementary schools in the early Qing can be gleaned from the writing of various literati. For example, Yan Yuan's disciple Zhong Ling (dates unknown) recorded Yan's method of teaching children arithmetic:

> I witnessed the Master teaching young children arithmetic. At first he taught them nine basic numbers and did not teach addition and subtraction. It was not until the young children were familiar with the numbers that the Master began to teach them addition and subtraction. Multiplication was introduced to the young children only when they were good at addition and subtraction. After the children mastered the method of multiplication, they were then taught the method of division.[70]

The above quotation does not tell us which textbooks were used to teach calculation. In the early eighteenth century, however, we know that Li Gong (1659–1733) compiled a textbook called *An Elementary Text Collected from Classics* (*Xiaoxue jiye*)[71] for teaching his nephews at an elementary level,[72] and this included a section on arithmetic. In Li's writing, arithmetical computation was explained without using the modern mathematical signs. For example, he explained 1250×12.5 in a traditional Chinese way (see Figure 6.2).[73]

In modern mathematical writing, Li's explanation can be simply expressed in the following way:

		step 1:	step 2:	step 3:
	1250	1250	125	125
	$\times$ 12.5	$\times$ 0.5	$\times$ 2	$\times$ 1
	625	625	250	125
	250			
	+125			
	15,625			

Figure 6.2 1,250 × 12.5 = 15,625 presented in Li Gong's *Xiaoxue jiye* (An Elementary Text Collected from Classics). *Congshu jicheng* edition.

The above example indicates that Chinese traditional mathematics lacked technical words corresponding to symbols in modern mathematics, and mathematical signs were expressed by Chinese characters.[74] The counting-board[75] and the abacus were used in calculation, and they automatically became the tools for teaching arithmetical computing. As a result of the absence of any symbolic way of writing formulae, calculations in Chinese mathematics did not leave any records of "the intermediate stages by which the answer was reached."[76] Clavius' *Epitome of Practical Arithmetic,* translated into Chinese by Li Zhizao (1565–1630) and the Jesuit Matteo Ricci (1552–1610), under the title of *The Treatise on European Arithmetic (Tongwen suanzhi),* was published in 1631. This book systematically introduced Western methods of calculation using pen and paper (*bisuan*). Yet the Arabic numerals, 1, 2, 3, ... and 0 were not adopted in the book. Chinese characters for numbers and O (*yuan,* circle) were still used in the mathematical statements.[77]

The use of Chinese characters in calculation and recording numbers was perhaps one of the main reasons that arithmetic in Chinese elementary education was closely linked to language teaching. This also resulted in a difference between Chinese and English manuals for teaching arithmetic, as can be seen from Recorde's *The Grounde of Artes* (1542), the first arithmetical text written in English.

Robert Recorde (1510–1558) studied at both Oxford and Cambridge. *The Grounde of Artes,* the first volume of his four elementary mathematical textbooks, was intended for self-education by the new type of technician who did not understand Latin.[78] Written in the form of dialogue, the book covered numeration, addition, subtraction, multiplication and division. All examples were explained explicitly by statements, and calculations were performed with mathematical symbols. For example, the case $1{,}365 \times 236 = 322{,}140$ was given in all its intermediate stages (see Figure 6.3).[79]

It is clear that the Arabic numerals and other mathematical signs, missing in Li's treatise in the early eighteenth century, were already being used in the English manual in the middle of the sixteenth century. However, like some Chinese textbooks, a few English manuals during the sixteenth and seventeenth centuries also combined language teaching with instruction in numeration. For instance, Francis Clement's *The Petie Schole* was produced in 1587. The section on numeration and calculation occupied twenty-eight of its ninety pages. The book aimed to teach children "to reade perfectly within one moneth, & also the vnperfect to write English aright."[80] As well as this, Clement intended "to teach a childe in the trade of his way and when he is old he shall not depart from it,"[81] and hence numeration and calculation (limited to addition) became a part of the book. In the section on numeration and calculation,

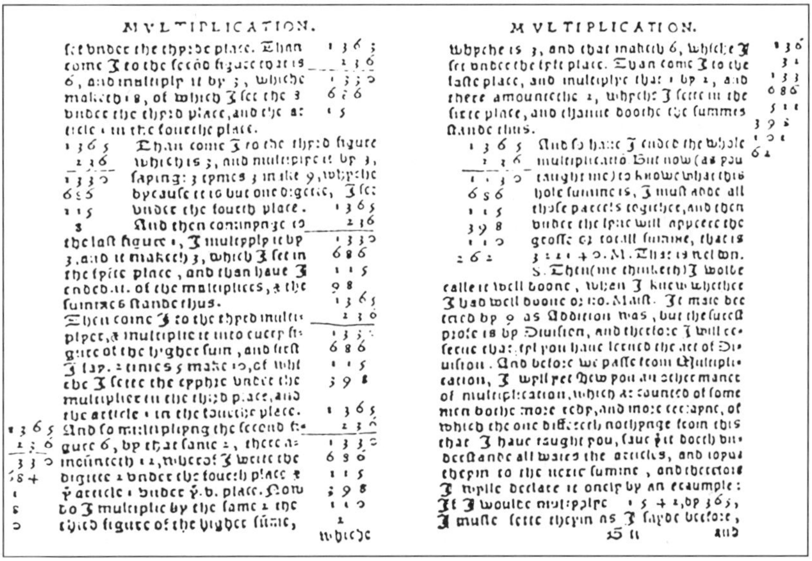

Figure 6.3 Robert Recorde's *The Grounde of Artes* (1542). Da Capo Press & Theatrum Orbis Terrarum Ltd., 1969.

Clement firstly introduced basic numbers from one to zero and presented them in both Latin letters and Arabic numbers, for example:

Latin letters: I, II, III, ...
Arabic numbers: 1, 2, 3, ...[82]

Then he introduced the place where the number stood, for example, in the number 8670532, the first place was for the unit (2); the second was for ten (3); ....[83] And "prickes"[84] should be used to help reckon the great sum.[85]

Finally, Clement taught students how to use counters to do simple addition or subtraction. It is worth noting that calculation in this book was performed by a combination of Latin letters and Arabic numbers in spite of the fact that the book was produced about forty-five years later than Recorde's *The Grounde of Artes*. The use of both Latin letters and Arabic numbers in computing resulted in errors. For instance, Clement added up six separate groups of figures but was not able to get the total correct.[86]

The above example may suggest that numeration and simple

calculation as an affiliated part of language teaching was not unique to arithmetic teaching in pre-modern China, although in England arithmetical calculation was already beginning to be written in modern mathematical signs by the sixteenth century, as Recorde's book showed. However, Recorde's book was not intended for elementary schooling but for technicians of the time. In other words, Recorde's book was an arithmetical treatise for the study of arithmetic outside formal schooling.

It was unusual that so many pages in Clement's book were devoted to arithmetic, compared to other textbooks which centred on language teaching. In 1596, Edmund Coote's *The English Schoolemaister* contained only two pages of numeration. In 1612, John Brinsley's *Ludus Literarius* also devoted only two pages to an explanation of numeration. According to Brinsley, the reason for the existence of these two pages was that many students in grammar schools were "almost ready to goe to the University, who yet can hardly tell you the number of pages, sections, chapters, or other divisions in their books, to find what they should."[87] Brinsley provided the explanation of numbers either in Arabic numbers or Latin letters, as Clement had. The recognition of numbers in both letters and figures was conducted in two ways, for example, students were asked "what the letter X stood for" and then "which letter stood for one."[88] Yet Brinsley supplied no further treatment of calculation. He regarded the knowledge of numbers as a part of reading skills, so these two pages were in Chapter III, to show how students might be taught to read English speedily to meet the requirements of grammar school. In other words, Brinsley hoped that students in grammar school would be able to count the pages of their school books properly and quickly through learning numbers in both letters and figures.

These illustrations of both Chinese and English textbooks show that arithmetical knowledge was not an independent part of elementary education but was joined to language teaching. Moreover, numeration sometimes also went with instruction in religion and morals, as demonstrated by the following passages from *The Trimetrical Classic*:

Dou Yanshan has good methods to teach his children;
His five (*wu*) sons raised the family reputation.[89]

(Huang) Xiang warmed the bed for his father at [the age of] nine (*jiu*);

Filial piety towards parents is something youths should hold firmly.[90]

At four (*si*), [Kong] Rong gave the bigger pear to his elder brother;
[Children] should know brotherly respect at an early age.[91]

The above examples indicate that instruction in numbers could be contained in stories that conveyed moral teachings.

The link between numeration and moral and religious instruction can also be found in English textbooks, such as Coote's *The English Schoole-maister* (1596). Its brief introduction to arithmetic included the basic nine numbers, and Coote's explaination of how to use these basic numbers to read the Bible. For instance, 1596 was the "present yeere from the birth of Christ."[92] He also said that the knowledge of numeration contained in his book was for students' "better understanding this brief Chronologie following," for example, "how long was it after the Creation? or how long after the Floud? how long after the departure out of Egypt and the Lawe given?"[93] Hence, there were another six pages containing lists of numbers concerning the chronology in the Bible.

While arithmetic was not excluded from the curricula of elementary education in either China or England, it was an insignificant subject, compared to others. In England, Brinsley criticised the poor level of numeration in the early part of the seventeenth century, as has been shown above. From Brinsley's complaint, we can assume that ignorance of arithmetic must have existed throughout the sixteenth and seventeenth centuries.

In China, mathematics was theoretically one of the "six arts" in Confucian learning. However, many documents show that mathematics was regarded as a trivial skill and was largely ignored. This attitude towards mathematics can be attributed to both government policy and intellectual interests. Some scholars were even discouraged from becoming too involved in mathematical studies.

Western mathematics was first introduced into China by missionaries at the end of the sixteenth century and the beginning of the seventeenth century. Some eminent scholars of the time, such as Xu Guangqi (1562–1633) and Li Zhizao, were very interested in using science and technology from the West for the purpose of strengthening the country. In the reign of the Kang Xi Emperor (1662–1722), the hitherto largely unfavourable attitude towards the learning of mathematics and astronomy was changed, to a certain extent, because these were subjects which interested the emperor. From then on, the intellectual fashion turned in favour of learning mathematics and astronomy in particular.[94]

This trend, however, did not have a strong impact on elementary education. Many proposals for educational reform advocated learning mathematics at an advanced level; but at the level of elementary education, learning characters and moral instruction were still considered the main tasks. Nevertheless, some thinkers reviewed the content of elementary education on the basis of the concept of the "six arts" and put forward the idea that children ought to acquire some knowledge of arithmetic before they entered the advanced stage of learning. For instance, Lu Shiyi pointed out that young students before the age of fifteen should learn some *gejue* (formulas written in verse) on mathematics, astronomy, geography and history as well as the Confucian classics.[95] Yet he did not produce any primers on these subjects. The school of Yan-Li (Yan Yuan and Li Gong), in particular, believed that children should start learning arithmetic at the beginning of their schooling. As mentioned already, according to his disciples, Yan Yuan instructed children in arithmetic, and Li Gong compiled a textbook, *An Elementary Text Collected from Classics.*

Li Gong was a disciple of Yan Yuan. Like his master, he advocated that all branches of learning, including elementary education, should be based on the "six arts." He noted that the classical methods in elementary education were lost and the only way to rediscover them was to reassemble the lost texts. Therefore, his book was a collection of materials from the classics in a total of five sections.[96] The first section was written in verse and generalised about the content of the following four sections, which gathered together materials which he believed had provided the content and method of elementary education in classical times.[97]

The second section of Li Gong's book included programmes for children between six and nine years old, such as learning numbers, names of the points of the compass and working out dates, and also a programme for ten-year-old children — "the behaviour of youth" (*youyi*).[98]

The third section focused on the skills of reading and writing and the history of the evolution of Chinese characters.[99] The fourth section was on calculation (*ji*) including: (1) a multiplication table (*jiujiu shu,* "nine times nine numbers"); (2) a table for abacus calculation; (3) a formula for multiplication; (4) a formula for division; (5) introductions to both multiplication and division; (6) introductions to both addition and subtraction; and (7) the content of the first chapter of the *Nine Chapters on the Mathematical Arts* (*jiuzhang suanfa*): field measurement (*fangtian*).[100] The fifth section concerned music and dance.[101]

Elementary education in Li Gong's book was in fact divided into two stages: before and after the age of ten. This apparently followed the principles recorded in the *Record of Rites.* By modern standards, the stage before ten was like pre-primary schooling; and the stage after ten was formal primary schooling. At the second stage, children were required to master the arts of writing characters and of calculation. *The Nine Chapters on the Mathematical Arts* was actually used as a textbook for mathematics students in the Imperial Academy in the Tang and afterwards. Perhaps this is why Li Gong adopted only the first part of the book, thinking that the rest of the book was too difficult for children at an elementary level. However, he said that pupils could learn it after they had gained basic arithmetical skills.[102]

An Elementary Text Collected from Classics set out Li Gong's ideas on education. Li Gong had a strong belief that the "six arts" were the content of original Confucian education,[103] which, he asserted, must be rediscovered; otherwise, China could not be strengthened.[104] In his time, formal education mainly prepared students for the civil service examinations and the "eight-legged essay" had become the main focus of the teaching process. Under these circumstances, Li Gong tried to run his teaching beyond the framework of formal education. He said that he would teach students the "six arts" if they were willing to learn and were capable of mastering these subjects.[105] On the basis of these ideas, arithmetic was thus to stand as an independent part of *An Elementary Text Collected from Classics.* According to a chronological biography, in 1703 Li Gong compiled *Mathematics for Elementary Education* (*Xiaoxue shuxue*),[106] but it does not appear to have been printed.

Li Gong's proposal for adopting the "six arts" was not just an exercise in returning to classical times (*fugu*), as he maintained that the practice of the "six arts" should both "discover its classical content and serve the requirements of the present as well (*kaogu zhunjin*)."[107] In the matter of mathematics, he suggested learning Western mathematics as well as Chinese classical mathematics.[108]

Li Gong's attitude towards mathematics actually represented a new intellectual trend during the late Ming and early Qing. As mentioned earlier, however, this new intellectual fashion focused on learning mathematics at an advanced level rather than at an elementary stage. In the Qing dynasty, some texts on astronomy and mathematics appeared with very similar titles to those of primers, such as research works on solar eclipses and lunar eclipses written by Mei Wending (1633–1721).[109] In fact, the term *mengqiu* used as part of the titles of these texts does not refer to the original meaning that primers adopted, but to an extended meaning of "preliminary research or discussion." Moreover, throughout his entire life, Mei Wending composed numerous treatises on mathematics and astronomy,[110] but none for learning and teaching arithmetic in elementary education. He himself never indicated that any of his writings were intended for children or elementary schooling.[111] As far as we know, Li Gong's *An Elementary Text Collected from Classics* was the only primer which devoted a whole chapter to the study of arithmetic during this period. However, there is no further information about whether or how his nephews used the book. Also, little has been discovered about the popularity of the book.

In brief, elementary education in late imperial China was characterised by the use of literacy education to instil morals and religious knowledge in children's minds. Although this was not unique to China, the Chinese writing system with its "visual symbols" was often employed conveniently and freely as a teaching device to promote moral education in the course of teaching characters.

An examination of the contents of some textbooks shows that arithmetical teaching at an elementary level was closely linked to language teaching rather than being an independent subject, and, as such, it was also able to serve the needs of moral and religious instruction on some occasions. The investigation of these textbooks also suggests that the insignificant role played by arithmetic in Chinese elementary education was paralleled by that which it played in English formal elementary education during the sixteenth and seventeenth centuries.

Chapter 7

Peasant Children and the Confucian Ideal Society

Research on Chinese peasant children is very much limited by the paucity of source materials. In his study of Chinese peasants in North China, Philip C. C. Huang points out that "large quantities of official sources, elite writings, and elite genealogies," as well as "elite biographies in local gazetteers," are all rich sources for the study of the elite but not yet of the "little people" in Chinese history.[1] Similarly, primers mainly represent elite attitudes to childhood, though they may have differed in form and in the language skills they displayed. Here "elite" is used to refer to the *shi* class — a broad category identified with scholar-officials but also including anyone with a traditional education from the Tang-Song period through the Qing. The views of the educated elite, combined with the treatment of children in the elite families, serve as a collective manifestation of elite attitudes to childhood, through which we can see the Confucian efforts to shape the ideal child. However, some Ming-Qing Confucian educators, as described in the second part of this chapter, were particularly concerned about education for children in lower levels of society. Their concerns may indicate their awareness of the different worlds of childhood.

As well as literati writings, illustrations in agricultural manuals (*nongshu*), such as the *Pictures of Tilling and Weaving* (*Geng zhi tu*), may provide a glimpse of children in the fields and peasant households. Of course, agricultural manuals are not an authentic peasant source, as they were produced by and for the educated elite. Also, artistic convention and the limitations of the artists in depicting children make us cautious about the degree to which the illustrations reveal what the actual child was like. However, as Philip Huang says, "the fact that China's peasant society remained intact into the mid-twentieth century means that China scholars have access to masses of modern ethnographic data,"[2] which may help us trace and reconstruct some aspects of peasant life in the Ming-Qing period. This method may also apply to the study of peasant children in the late imperial period. For instance, in his study of life in a Chinese village in the 1930s, Hsiao-Tung Fei (Fei Xiaotong) observes peasant children and their parents and relatives' attitudes towards them, their education and their economic values. Fei's findings, to some extent, corroborate the information generated from the *Pictures of Tilling and Weaving* and other sources.[3]

By using such source materials, the first section of this chapter examines images of children against the setting of peasant working life. This by no means suggests that these presentations of children reflect the actual treatment of children in the peasantry. The aim here is to indicate Confucian educators' anxiety over peasant children's "freedom" and their attempt to educate peasant children as part of a far reaching programme of social reform. This will be discussed extensively in the second section.

Children in the Peasantry

As already well known, pre-modern China was predominantly an agricultural country. Men working in the fields while women were weaving at home (*nan geng nü zhi*) was both an ideal and to some extent a reality. Accordingly, agricultural manuals were produced to restore and spread the knowledge both of tillage and the manufacture of textiles. From the Song to the Qing, however, traditional Chinese agricultural technology, by and large, underwent no significant changes. Thus, technical manuals were often illustrated by pictures produced centuries earlier. Such reproductions normally differed, however, in the style and quality of the printing.

From the Song onward, the theme of agriculture and sericulture became a traditional subject of Chinese painting. It was Lou Shu (1090–1162), at one time a county magistrate, who conducted a study into the whole process of sericulture — from silkworm breeding to spinning and weaving — and then had each step illustrated. These drawings were presented to Emperor Gao Zong (fl. 1127–1161) to illustrate the idea that, since ancient times, agriculture and sericulture had formed the fundamental occupations of men and women. The emperor was very fond of this series of pictures and showed them to Empress Wu (1115–1197) who ordered the court artists to make new copies. These differed slightly from Lou's work and the Empress herself wrote notes to accompany each drawing. Later, one of the greatest artists, Liu Songnian (active in the twelfth century), presented another series of pictures entitled *Pictures of Tilling and Weaving* to the court (the regime of Ning Zong, 1195–1224). Unfortunately, except for one version of the *Sericulture* (*Can zhi tu*) bearing calligraphy attributed to Empress Wu, neither Lou's nor Liu's original works remain extant.[4] However, it is believed that later editions of the *Pictures of Tilling and Weaving* or manuals which followed similar themes were based essentially upon those original works. For example, the *Collection of Pictures for Ordinary People* (*Bianmin tuzuan*), including fifteen pictures of tilling and sixteen of weaving, all originated in Lou's work.[5] Xu Guangqi's *Complete Treatise on Agriculture* (*Nongzheng quanshu*), composed between 1625 and 1628 and printed in 1639, also contained a few pictures derived from the *Pictures of Tilling and Weaving*. The 1696 version of the *Pictures of Tilling and Weaving* was the first Qing edition (in the Kangxi regime), upon which the later Qing editions (such as the editions of the Yongzheng regime and Qianlong regime) were all based.

While these illustrations were designed with only technical objectives in mind, they also included complex representations of working life during the late imperial period, and children were often presented in these scenes of tilling and weaving. The 1696 edition of the *Pictures of Tilling and Weaving* contained twenty-three pictures of tilling and twenty-three of weaving. In at least sixteen pictures children appeared among the characters: children with their family; children helping in the field; children playing while adults were busy working; children seeking maternal care and attention; children engaged in the ceremonies of ancestor worship.[6]

Including children in so many of these pictures did have the effect of promoting the traditional Chinese concept of *tianlun zhi le* which referred to the natural bonds and ethical relationships between family members as well as to family happiness, although this was not the prime objective of these technical manuals. Another Chinese saying — *fengyi zushi, ersun raoxi*, or "to have enough food and clothing, and to be surrounded by children" — expresses the same idea.

For instance, picture 12 from the section on tilling depicts two women with a child taking lunch to a field where men are busy weeding (Figure 7.1). One woman, probably the mother, holds a little boy's hand while she carries water and food. The child is wearing shorts and a short-sleeved shirt. Through the unbuttoned shirt we can see the child is also wearing a stomacher (*dudou*) — a typical article of children's clothing. His left hand holds a toy — a paper butterfly on a stick. The poem says:

> Sun burns our back as we loosen our clothing;
> We wear hats but the perspiration is not stopped.

Figure 7.1 Picture 12 from the section on tilling, *Geng zhi tu*, 1696

With the risk of being burned,
We desperately want to get rid of the weeds.
There come our women,
With a basket and burdened with water and food.
Even our child knows the farming business,
Who says he is only brought around to play?

Here, a child that is still very young and needs its mother's care, is included to demonstrate the bond between the mother and child. Furthermore, by bringing women with their children into the field where men are working, the author emphasises the hopes that peasants placed in their offspring as well as in the harvest. The child in this picture appears to be cherished by adults as the symbol of affection, family happiness and the purpose of life.

This idealised image certainly contrasts with the harsh reality of peasant society. First of all, socioeconomic factors often impeded peasant devotion to their children, who were forced to join the labour force at an early age. And even worse, poverty led not only to the deprivation of childhood but of life itself, as infanticide was practised for economic reasons.[7] As early as in the Song, Chinese officials were aware of children in poverty and the then government "was the first ever in Chinese history to officially take on the responsibility to establish orphanages."[8] Yet the problem was not resolved from the Song through the Qing. Many local governments found it very hard to support such charitable institutions, as more and more poor parents abandoned their children to the charity organisations, thinking that would give their children an opportunity to survive. In fact few abandoned children survived, as the institutions were often short of resources, for example, one wet-nurse had to look after several infants and was not able to provide all of them with enough nutrition. Therefore, some scholar-officials, such as Peng Yunzhang of the Qing, advocated the reform of the system. He suggested that this kind of institution should be abolished and financial support should be offered to those poor parents who would then be able to nurse their own children instead of abandoning them to institutions. According to him, the number of abandoned children was increasing, even though some local organisations, such as the Baoying she (the organisation for infant protection) in the Wuxi area, had been established to protect infants and young children.[9]

The difference in the treatment of children between the rich and the poor can also be seen in the practice by wealthy families of employing wet-nurses to suckle infants. As discussed in Chapter One, both medical advisers and Confucian writers were very concerned about the impact that a wet-nurse could have on the child's physical growth and moral development. As early as in the Song, Confucian writers began to voice their criticism of the practice, as Hong Mai (1125–1202) recorded in his book. The critics maintained that employing wet-nurses was not a humanitarian practice, as mothers from poor families had to abandon their own children so as to suckle the babies of wealthy families in exchange for income.[10] From the Song to the Qing, similar criticism was raised from time to time. In this context, what the *Pictures of Tilling and Weaving* provided is perhaps a picture of an idealised life.

Nevertheless, in spite of the harsh realities of their existence, peasants still desired children, and children who survived against all the odds were highly valued by their parents. This relates to the notions of filiality as well as economic values. In her study of the traditional Chinese practice of adoption, Ann Waltner points to the importance of having an heir in the late Ming and early Qing period.[11] Like the elite, peasants needed heirs to continue the line of descent. In both elite circles and the peasantry, to have heirs was "a concrete expression of filial piety by the future father towards his ancestors" — this notion, as Fei observes, persisted from the late imperial period into the mid-twentieth century.[12]

The value of peasant children also lay in their early contribution to the family economy. Peasant children began helping in the fields at a very early age. In picture 6 of the section on tilling, a child is shown taking lunch to two adults sowing seeds in a field. Though the child is not portrayed as a major part of the picture as a whole, the painter does not neglect his characterisation, giving him a hairstyle appropriate to his age. A dog following the child adds a pleasant touch to the scene, suggesting that the child is not ill-treated as a hard labourer. Picture 15 of the section on tilling shows four children at harvest-time picking up the rice while adults are busy reaping (Figure 7.2). The youthfulness of the children in this picture is indicated not only by their hairstyles but also by a fight between two of the children. As he cries, kicks and lies on the ground, a younger boy tugs at the clothing of an older lad. Apparently, the younger boy

Figure 7.2 Picture 15 from the section on tilling, *Geng zhi tu*, 1696

is not counted as a serious helper, as the other three boys are each holding large sheaves of rice while he has nothing in his hands. It seems that, as a youngster, he knows he can get away with acting pettishly, a freedom unique to childhood. This also indicates that childhood in peasant families was unquestionably perceived as a distinct stage in human life. Thus, while children might have begun helping in the fields and at home at an early age, they were not treated as field-labourers. Starting at the age of seven and increasingly as they approached fifteen, children were required to take on the tasks and responsibilities of adulthood.[13]

The education for peasant children also differed from that for children of rich families. As mentioned earlier, farming and studying were the basic pattern of village schools, which were adjusted to the seasonal requirements of farming. Peasant children had their own educational courses: by and large, boys would learn farming skills from their fathers and girls the techniques of the silk industry, sewing and housework from their mothers. In this context, peasant children mingled with the adult world, and being taken into the fields where adults were working, for example, was not just so that their parents could keep an eye on them but also for practical instruction in the techniques of farming. Picture 7 in the section on tilling shows a child out walking with his father along the path through a field. Though the child is depicted as a small-scale adult, the little bird standing on his left hand indicates his youth. According to the poem which accompanies the picture, it is the time for spring sowing. As all peasants knew, sowing had to be done at the right time. The man is walking around his field in the evening to check if it is the right time to sow. Thus what appears only as a picture of a father and a son out walking together is also an educational tour through which the child could obtain knowledge vital to farming.[14]

Children in the section on weaving are often depicted with women, which suggests the pattern of child-rearing in peasant families. There were no such things as child-care centres or any other child-care agencies in pre-modern China. In a wealthy family, a wet-nurse or a helper could be employed to look after the young children. Peasants could not afford such luxuries and women had to care for the children and work in sericulture at the same time. The activities of children in these illustrations afford insights into parental care and the character of the parental role in peasant families. Picture 18 from the section on weaving shows two women in the evening busy spinning; beside them is a child in bed, watching them as they work (Figure 7.3). As it is dark outside another woman is walking towards the room with an oil lamp in her hands while a little boy tugs at her clothing and cries. The child seems tired and wants his mother to put him to bed; yet the mother has to join the other women in the room to work through the night. The poem tells us that it is already late autumn and winter is approaching. The women must work hard in order to earn enough to pay government taxes and to prepare winter clothing, because their husbands are soldiers and far away from home.[15] Neither the picture nor the poem suggests that children were treated with indifference in peasant

Figure 7.3 Picture 18 from the section on weaving, *Geng zhi tu*, 1696

families. They only expose unfortunate aspects of child-rearing which were unavoidable under those particular socio-economic conditions. It was these conditions which to a large extent determined whether peasant parents could give their own children adequate care and protection.

Picture 2 in the section on weaving tells the same story (Figure 7.4). Here three women work in a silkworm breeding room. One has two children with her. She lifts up one infant while another woman reaches across for the baby, which stretches out its arms as if ready to cling to her. While these women give their attention to the infant, an older child in the left-hand corner feels ignored and jealous. He is tugging at the back of his mother's clothing and crying for attention.

Figure 7.4 Picture 2 from the section on weaving, *Geng zhi tu*, 1696

According to the poem, it is in the middle of spring when silkworms undergo several moultings or so-called "pupations." This is a crucial stage in the growth of silkworms, so these women are worried about the threat of a cold snap which could do serious harm. The child cannot understand his mother's worries and just keeps on demanding attention. The need for maternal care is natural for children, because they are born helpless and totally dependent on adults not just for protection but also for socialisation and acculturation. The importance of parental care in child development was recognised in pre-modern China. However, burdened as they were with heavy taxes and the constant struggle for survival, peasant parents were not always able to devote much time and attention to their children. In these circumstances, children often seemed neglected.

Sometimes grandparents would help working mothers, as picture 21 from the section on weaving suggests. This is still a feature of early child care in China today. In this picture, two women are spinning in a spinning room. Outside a third woman carries a teatray in her right hand while holding a child's hand in the other. The child is drying its tears with its left hand. Behind the child is its grandmother who is attempting to coax a smile from the child with a toy — a peddler's drum (*bolanggu*).

Generally speaking, while peasant children had to join the labour force at an early age, youngsters from elite families received an education that aimed to implant Confucian moral values in children from an early age. However, such jobs as helping in the fields, collecting grass to feed sheep and attending to sheep or cows, were congenial to peasant children, as they could be free of any interference from adults, and could play with their companions while carrying out their duties.[16] "Freedom" of this kind may be described as "gay indifference," a term used by Aries to portray medieval attitudes to children in the West, namely that children at that time were allowed to grow up as they pleased. In his view, it was from the seventeenth century onward that the "solicitude" of family, church and moralists represented a new interest in children's education; but this also involved depriving children of the freedom they had enjoyed before and subjecting them to a severe regime of discipline.[17] Aries sees this shift as detrimental to childhood, preferring medieval "gay indifference" to modern discipline.[18] Applying this notion to the case of China, we may suggest that Chinese peasant children grew up in a wilder, rougher environment than would have been the case in school, so they were less restricted by Confucian norms. Within this context, we may contend that although Neo-Confucian ideas may have dominated formal education and child-raising in gentry families in the late imperial period, the daily life of illiterate peasants was guided by convention and custom (some of which is now known as "superstition") rather than scholarly opinions.

The Reform of Peasant Children and the Construction of a Confucian Ideal Society

The preceding discussion has shown that children in the peasantry were less constrained by Confucian norms than children in educated elite families. However, the Confucian endeavour to shape the ideal child and then to construct an ideal society was not only limited to the elite minority. Confucianists, especially those in Ming-Qing China, strove to extend education to children in lower layers of society, and to transfer Confucian ethics from scholarly classics to the realm of conventional beliefs. This intellectual effort can be attributed to the emergence of the Wang Yangming school in the late Ming and the interpenetration of Buddhism and Taoism with Confucian doctrines. In this section, an analysis of some primers will uncover the fact that elementary education in Ming-Qing China did not only serve the interests of the educated elite and the increasing demands for literacy skills. To a certain extent, it functioned more broadly as an essential means to construct a Confucian society.

Public Morality and Basic Education for Peasant Children

In Ming-Qing China, elementary education was more associated with public education than it had been before. "Public education" functioned as an instrument to improve public morality. In this sense, education on the level of the common people was not confined to formal institutions, and thus its content was not limited only to the rudiments of literacy. Furthermore, the association between elementary and public education also reflected many Confucian scholars' anxieties over public morality and the impact of corrupted customs on children. For example, in theory Chinese children were not permitted to gamble, and all games of chance were strenuously condemned. Not only Confucian educators but also many in the general community were convinced that gambling would harm young children. Cards and dice were thus not regarded as children's games. However, at times the line between gambling and harmless games was very ambiguous; it is doubtful that children could have been kept away from all types of gambling, since it was practised so widely in society.[19]

Take dice as an example. In one of the oldest children's primers, *Newly Compiled Illustrated Four Word Glossary* (*Xinbian duixiang siyan*), dice (*shaizi*) was listed with other everyday terms. According to L. Carrington Goodrich, the book is valuable for providing simple glimpses of contemporary material culture.[20] Although it is believed that the primer was at least a late Ming publication (1436), dice had a very long history associated with the *bo* and *yi* (chess) games. The original dice was the *touzi* used in the game *bo*. It was during the period of the Southern and Northern Dynasties that the game *bo* became *liubo*, which entirely changed the nature of the game. After that, *bo* was no longer a kind of chess game but a kind of gambling, in which *touzi* made of wood were used, so the game was also called *wumu* (five pieces of wood). During the Tang dice were formed as we see them today, and then many games using dice were created for both entertainment and gambling. In the regime of Song Huizong (1101–1125) dominoes were produced based on dice.[21] It can be safely assumed that the dice was regarded as a frequently-used article with which children must have been familiar. As the history of dice indicates, dice could be used for either a normal chess game or for a gambling game. So children were possibly given dice to play with, although theoretically they were not encouraged to participate in gambling.

Animal games could also be either seasonal pastimes or gambling. For example, cock-fighting and bull-fighting were very popular amusements after the fifth century or even earlier.[22] Originally, animal-fighting was for recreation among adults as well as children. Since animals were natural toys for children, playing with crickets, as picture 12 of the *Pictures of One Hundred Children* (*Baizi tu*)[23] shows, was not just a seasonal pastime for adults, but also a favourite amusement for children. However, this kind of game soon became a widely accepted vehicle for gambling — gamblers used to wage money on cricket fights.[24]

In the Ming-Qing period, gambling was popular right across society, although authorities at all levels strenuously condemned it. Anti-gambling campaigns, as one Ming document indicates, were enforced in the lower layers of society through village ordinances.[25] Meanwhile, Ming-Qing educators attempted to use education as an instrument to improve public morality. Traditionally, many scholar-officials regarded the establishing of schools as one of the most important issues in their official careers. Song Neo-Confucians had set up academies (*shuyuan*) to promote their educational ideas, but for these Ming-Qing educators, charity schools (*yixue*) and community schools were as important as academies,[26] because the promotion of basic education in villages and towns was part of their far reaching programme of social reform. This can be exemplified by the activities of Lü Kun in the late Ming.

Lü Kun saw education as a means to maintain social order, and used fairly plain language to persuade peasants to send their children to community school during the slack periods of farming. Perhaps it was the very nature of the community school that was appealing to Lü Kun, who determined to use this organisation to put his educational ideas into practice.

The "community school," as its name suggests, was not a separate educational institution but a part of the community. Its origin can be traced back to the Yuan dynasty, when the curriculum of the Imperial Academy was dominated by Confucian classics, and learning characters became affiliated with the study of the Classics.[27] Under these circumstances, literacy education was supposed to be conducted in community schools. At that time, the activities in the community mainly focused on farming, but every community was also required to set up a school for all children at a quiet time for farming. A qualified teacher in such a community school had to be well versed in the Confucian classics.[28] Schools as such continued into the beginning of the Ming. Children under fifteen were sent there to practise the ceremonies for such rites as marriage, worship and funerals. This kind of school did not last long.[29] However, some of them were also conducted as local schools. According to Quan Zuwang (1705–1755), every thirty-five households were supposed to set up a community school, and children who were willing to learn would be enrolled. Only a knowledgeable and respected person could be chosen as a teacher in such a school. Students at first learned characters and used textbooks such as *One Hundred Surnames* and *One Thousand Characters*. Then they started learning classics, historical works, astronomy and mathematics. Administration was under the supervision of local government, and students were expected to sit the civil service examinations.[30] This administrative arrangement suggests that the community schools in the Ming were not completely private schools, although they differed from official schools.

To Lü Kun, the community school was a place to teach peasant children both basic literacy skills and good manners. In his *Essential Points in Community School*, he maintained that learning characters (*shizi*) was related to understanding principles (*mingli*). Lü's principles were not identical to those in Neo-Confucianism, as he included law among the principles. The following is a message that Lü Kun sent to peasants in the community:

> Parents with [long term] ambitions send children to school and expect them to achieve a sound reputation and attain officialdom. Parents with a short-term aim send children to school and wish them to learn characters and then to know the laws. Sending children to school is the most wonderful thing in the world. However, some careless and stupid parents do not let children go to school. Without proper education to help their children to get rid of wicked ideas and to correct their children's wild nature, these children might become bad people, such as thieves and robbers, and might break laws. Who sees educated people who are thieves or robbers? Hence, as a local official, I instruct all people: your children of school age must be sent to a community school. Even if some families are very busy with their farming, children have to be in a community school after the tenth month of [the lunar calendar]; in the third month of [the lunar calendar], they can go home and help with the farming. Children study in a community school for three years and can go back to farming if they do not wish to sit the civil service examinations.[31]

Professor Woodside regards this device of education for children of the peasantry as Lü's attempt to divorce "the purpose of community schools from those of the examination system."[32] He also states that Chen Hongmou (1696–1771), an eminent Qing Confucian scholar and a devoted educator like Lü Kun, failed to carry on Lü's idea, as his "actual eighteenth-century charity schools in Yunnan" contained "two types of curricula": one "for ignorant children" and the other "for advanced pupils" who were preparing for the civil service examinations.[33] In fact, neither Lü nor Chen attempted to separate their popular schools from the main stream of education, which was divided into two stages: elementary and advanced levels. What Lü Kun said was that only if children in the peasantry did not wish to sit the civil examinations could they quit school after his proposed three-year compulsory education and return to their families.

Despite what Professor Woodside has suggested, Lü Kun's recommendation of community schools was perhaps not due to a hostile attitude toward family education.[34] As discussed in the previous section, peasants could not give their children adequate care because of their unfortunate economic situation, which also limited their children's opportunity to receive a proper education. Lü Kun was aware of this, as he acknowledged that peasant children were needed to help with farming or housework. At the same time, he was worried about peasant children's moral well-being which, in his opinion, was linked closely with social stability. Bearing these concerns in mind, Lü Kun made three-year schooling at a community school compulsory for children in the peasantry, hoping this would provide every child with a basic Confucian education, regardless of their family's financial situation. At the same time, these community schools were only operated during slack periods in farming, which addressed the need for labour in peasant families.

Furthermore, in Lü Kun's version of how to shape children into the ideal Confucian mould, priority was given to social order and law instead of sagehood in the Neo-Confucian sense. As discussed earlier, the civil examination system provided people of lower social status with opportunities to climb up the social ladder, which encouraged a programmatic attitude to learning. Song Neo-Confucian educators, with an emphasis on moral cultivation, attempted to steer the public away from this "learning for official emolument" approach and advocated "learning for the sake of one's self." In their view, elementary learning was a necessary step to reach sagehood. Yet sagehood for children in the peasantry seemed too far from their real life. Lü Kun had no intention of encouraging peasant children to pursue education at the advanced level just to be successful in the civil service examinations. On the other hand, however, he pointed out that discussion about the attainment of sagehood in Neo-Confucian writings was unlikely to benefit state affairs and the maintenance of law.[35] To him, it was more important and practical that peasant children learned how to abide by the law through the acquisition of basic literacy skills.

In reality, however, peasants did not see any financial gains from the basic education their children received, and few children could reach a level that would make them successful in the civil service examinations, due either to financial difficulties or to the lack of ability. This is why Lü Kun was worried that peasant parents would refuse to send their children to school, and that without a basic Confucian education the children of the poor would not be law-abiding subjects.

Lü Kun's concern was certainly shared by Tang Jian (1778–

1861), an eminent Neo-Confucianist in the middle of the Qing dynasty. Despite the Confucian ideal that children of all common people had to go to school, Tang Jian recognised that in reality people who had to earn a living by farming and trading at an early age were not able to attend school. Most children were thus unlikely to receive even a basic education because their parents could not afford a private tutor. In Ming-Qing China, there were a good number of commercial cities, such as Jinling (now Nanjing). According to Tang Jian, children from poor families in such cities, like most peasant children, had few educational opportunities. He was concerned that peasants' children were playing too much and youths in Jinling lacked basic education, and they could become juvenile delinquents (*e'shao*). Thus Tang Jian attempted to run charity schools as a kind of public institution, hoping that could help to maintain social order. To this effect, Tang challenged the conventional perception that elementary schools were intended for children under fifteen (*youtong*), and children above fifteen (*chengtong*) were supposed to study at an advanced level (*daxue*). In his proclamation he encouraged all youths who had not received the basic Confucian education but were willing to learn to enrol in school, regardless of their age. Like Lü Kun and Chen Hongmou, Tang founded schools for children from all kinds of backgrounds wherever he held official posts. When he had problems finding funds from his local government budget, Tang Jian persuaded local devotees of education to help found charity schools for poor people. For example, he organised the establishment of eight charity schools in Jinling when he was posted to Zhejiang province.[36]

Many scholar-officials in the Ming-Qing period, as Woodside's study shows, took *jiaohua*, or transformation through education, more seriously than ever before. For instance, within only five years (1733–1738), Chen Hongmou established or rehabilitated nearly 700 elementary schools in Yunnan. Besides this, his *Five Regulation Series* (*Wuzhong yigui*) was widely accepted as authorised material for moral education in the Qing.[37] Clearly, these scholars all attempted to convert poor children to Confucian norms through education, and then to create a Confucian uniformity among the people. From this perspective, Woodside is right to contend that Lü Kun's community schools and the charity schools of Tang Jian and Chen Hongmou all aimed "to detach poor children from the undesirable behavior of their everyday milieus, without necessarily promising to change their actual social positions."[38]

In order to achieve their objectives, both Lü Kun and Tang Jian chose their teaching materials carefully. From a pedagogical perspective, charity schools or community schools were, in a sense, primary schools, and the curricula in these institutions were very similar. For instance, in Lü Kun's curriculum for community schools, pupils under eight had to learn *The Trimetrical Classic, One Thousand Characters* and *One Hundred Surnames* first.[39] Then they were taught Zhu Xi's *Elementary Learning*, the *Classic of Filial Piety* and some basic knowledge of characters such as how they were structured.[40] In Tang Jian's scheme for charity schools, the *Four Books*, the *Five Classics*, the *Classic of Filial Piety* and Zhu Xi's *Elementary Learning* took precedence over all other books. For young beginners Tang Jian, like Lü Kun, recommended *The Trimetrical Classic, One Thousand Characters*, Lü Desheng's *Words for Children* (*Xiao'er yu*) and Lü Kun's *Song of Good People* (*Haoren ge*).[41] Evidently, both Lü Kun and Tang Jian paid attention to the nature of young children and advocated the use of popular primers instead of using the *Classic of Filial Piety* and Zhu Xi's *Elementary Learning* directly, as had their Song predecessors.

Their choice of the *San Bai Qian* series also reflected their determination to change the moral culture through popular education. Lü Kun outlined the functions of this series:

> *The Trimetrical Classic* is able to extend people's knowledge; *One Hundred Surnames* is convenient for people's daily life; and *One Thousand Characters* also includes some teachings of Confucianism.[42]

As mentioned at the beginning of Chapter Three, both Rawski and Woodside regard this series as elite primers. Their view is based on a comparison with *zazi* primers which, Professor Woodside concludes, "shared very little vocabulary with elite primers like *The Thousand Character Classic*, and made no attempt to introduce peasant children to the idiom of the idealized ancient world from which the elite drew so much of its imaginative energy."[43] The existence of the *zazi* books evidently points to the fact that there were traditional primers for practical use instead of indoctrination. Our earlier discussion has shown, however, that the origin of the *San Bai Qian* series was associated with the wordbooks and village books, and ironically the series was rejected by Neo-Confucian educators prior to the Ming. In their opinion, these primers were too vulgar in comparison with the Confucian classics.

More importantly, we also have to bear in mind that occupational education was excluded from the traditional Chinese educational system, that is, neither formal educational channels such as government schools and academies, nor grass-level organizations such as community and charity schools, incorporated craft education into their curricula. For instance, in the 1750s Chen Hongmou, "as governor of Shaanxi, launched a program of mass instruction in sericulture in the Wei River Valley." His aim was to make "peasants who were willing to learn" "be gradually enriched." This sericulture education, however, was not run in schools but in "silkworm bureaus" (*canju*), and the man who was hired to teach the peasants was not called "teacher" but "silkworm chief" (*canzhang*).[44] This illustrates that there was occupational education in pre-modern China, but such education was not carried out in schools, as traditional Chinese education segregated "schools from practical, mundane craft education in order to preserve such schools as uncontaminated laboratories for the future revival of the ancient ideal humanism."[45] For Lü Kun, Tang Jian and Chen Hongmou, the schools they established particularly for the poor did not aim to teach them practical skills but Confucian norms. This perhaps accounts for the fact that even popular schools in the Ming-Qing period rejected the use of *zazi* books but welcomed the *San Bai Qian* series.

The rejection of *zazi* books and the popularity of the *San Bai Qian* series in Ming-Qing elementary education can perhaps be better explained by David Johnson's theory of "the structure of dominance" in a society. In his view, education and access to the literacy tradition depended on wealth, which "in turn was closely related to position in the structure of dominance." Furthermore, "learning itself was an essential aspect of dominance," and "dominance was legitimated by learning."[46] In this sense, wealth and education constituted the attributes of the ruling class who were dominant in traditional Chinese society. These privileged men used the "magical potency" of the written word to popularise complex ideas and beliefs, to spread Confucian values and in the end to shape "non-elite consciousness."[47] This was exactly what Ming-Qing educators attempted to achieve through their promotion of mass education, and was also what Woodside calls "empowering literacy to the powerless."[48] From this perspective, we may say that the *San Bai Qian* series represented elite values but were not necessarily designed for elite pupils. This series can also be seen as an example of how the elite class tried to use the power of literacy to convert or shape the non-elite class, so as to ensure social stability and the safety of the empire. And they started with children.

Primers in the Form of Vernacular Literature

In order to succeed in the indoctrination of the poor, some Ming-Qing educators employed the vernacular to combine elementary education with their social reform programme. Some primers even appeared in the form of children's "songs."

Children's songs were a kind of vernacular literature. By the standards of formal literature, they were unrefined and were despised by most literati in ancient China. From the Song onward, vernacular literature emerged along with changes in the social structure and the invention of printing. Merchants, peasants and other people who were definitely outside the circle of literati directly participated in the creation of such literary works. The monopoly of the educated elite in cultural activities was thus broken,[49] and vernacular literature was adopted to promote public education. *Words for Children* and *Song of Good People* were two representative educational texts written in the vernacular.

Words for Children was written by Lü Desheng (fl. 1550), Lü Kun's father. The title of the book suggests that the manual was addressed to young children. Its contents, however, touched upon the essentials of social norms. Lü Desheng indicated he was aware that most literati would feel ashamed of writing a ballad in shallow and colloquial language, but he thought that moral instruction was more important than anything else. He said that the principles of self-cultivation (*yili shenxin*) could be contained in such songs, and children of the ordinary people loved these ballads dearly. In this sense, the ballads in the colloquial style had some merit in moral instruction, which literature in other forms lacked. Firstly, they were easily committed to children's memories. Secondly, children could learn them while they were jumping, shouting and laughing. Finally, these ballads would spread quickly. Therefore, said Lü Desheng, he did not care about the fact that he might have been regarded as shallow and ignorant.[50]

Lü Kun was more sensitive to what other people thought about his father's *Words for Children* because he held high government positions. In his revised version he tried to change the style of language, but his version seemed to be too colloquial for students in formal school and too formal for ordinary people. Eventually, he realised that his father's manual was close to the oral language and children enjoyed chanting his ballads. In contrast, his own more formal work was not as popular as his father's and was not suitable for children and other common people who did not have formal education. Thus, Lü Kun gave up his attempt to revise his father's work and retained his own work as *A Sequel to "Words for Children"* (*Xu xiao'er yu*).[51]

These two treatises were originally intended for children outside formal schooling. Hence, certain behaviour patterns were at the core of these treatises. For instance, the beginning of Lü Desheng's work says:

> [Children] must behave with great composure;
> All mistakes are made because of being flustered.
> Behave serenely and speak leisurely;
> Any frivolities will be despised by others.[52]

However, some of his instructions addressed the common people in general. For example, Lü Desheng seemed to be addressing parents when he wrote,

> Children who are pampered too much will disappoint their parents in the future;
> Hence parents will have their children as foes after innumerable hardships in raising them.[53]

In Lü Desheng's opinion, the proper upbringing of children was also for the parents' own good, because spoilt children would not return love to their parents when they were grown up.

The book also contained advice derived from conventional beliefs rather than from the Classics or any other scholars' works. This kind of advice was even closer to oral speech and not confined by rhymes or a specific number of characters in a sentence. It was called *zayan*, or miscellaneous words. For example, Lü Desheng tried to persuade parents to set good examples for their children:

If a father swims all day, his son might become a drowning ghost.
If a father steals fruit, his son might become a murderer or an arsonist.[54]

Lü Kun too combined Confucian values with popular conventions. For example,

If one wants one's son to be obedient, one should first be filial to one's own parents.[55]

By modern standards, Lü Kun's *Song of Good People* was an educational text for the following of conventions (*xunsu*) rather than a primer intended for school. The text exhorted all people to be good. Virtues like filial piety, respect for elder brothers, righteousness, loyalty and sincerity were outlined at the beginning of it. Then detailed rules were offered:

A good person should not be drunk; a good person should not be involved with prostitutes; a good person should not gamble; a good person should not quarrel with others.[56]

The emphasis on public education had also been a significant element of Song Neo-Confucian education. For example, as a local official, Zhu Xi had great interest in local schools and issued proclamations to maintain a high level of public morality.[57] Lü Kun did not object to Neo-Confucianism completely. He agreed with the opinion of the Cheng brothers and Zhu Xi that the *Four Books* and the *Six Classics* contained the essentials of Confucianism.[58] As well as this, the Lüs' treatises articulated the same concerns about public morality as Zhu Xi had expressed in his proclamations. One of Zhu Xi's instructions said:

All members should encourage and remind each other to be filial to parents, respectful to elders, cordial to clansmen and relatives and helpful to neighbours. Each should perform his assigned duty and engage in his primary occupation. None should commit vicious acts or theft, or indulge in drinking or gambling. They should not fight with or sue each other.[59]

Clearly, the difference between Zhu Xi and Lü Kun did not lie in their emphasis on ethical values and general moral precepts but in the means they chose to guide the common people.

At the same time as this scholarly effort to extend basic education to those of lower social status, colloquialism was gradually entering into elementary texts. Such factors as the growth of popular literature and the increasing number of tradespeople might also have encouraged the use of colloquial language in composing primers. Take Guan Fang's *Small Talk* (*Jiachang yu*) as an example.[60]

Guan's *Small Talk* is even bolder than Lü's *Words for Children* in its unusual acknowledgement in the title that his instruction for pupils was just like a nice chat. In the orthodox Confucian tradition, teachers and teaching were expected to be authoritative and serious; students were often regarded only as a kind of vessel to receive knowledge from teachers. Between teachers and pupils, there was no room for small talk. Using the term "small talk" as the title implies that the author challenged this sober tradition, and intended to treat students in a more liberal manner. This attitude was embodied in the colloquial style adopted in the primer. Although the text consisted of four-character phrases and was in rhyme, the phrasing did not have the refinement usual in poetry.

Nevertheless, its content was not new. Like other school regulations and instructions for children, Guan's *Small Talk* focused on proper behaviour in school and at home. For example, at the beginning of the instruction, it advised pupils that the premier purpose of going to school was to learn proper manners:

> Pupils going to school
> learn how to behave first:
> walking properly,
> talking softly.
> Respecting teachers
> once you enter the classroom.
> Flippant conduct
> is not appropriate for pupils.
> While talking with a low voice,
> you should read characters aloud.
> When you concentrate on learning,
> you will remember the teacher's instruction easily.[61]

Also like other primers, Guan's *Small Talk* contained teaching on filial piety, such as

> Your life was given by your parents,
> so you have to use it to repay them.

If your parents beat you,
it is for your well-being.
Don't blame your parents for beating you too much,
you should be worried if they don't beat you very often.[62]

To modern minds this instruction appears absurd, as it reads like a message that children should invite their parents to abuse them physically. But in ancient China, as discussed in Chapter Five, children were expected to obey their parents even under trying conditions. Bearing this in mind, the last pair of lines has two readings. The first is that by traditional Chinese standards, if parents did not beat children very often, this indicated that those parents did not discipline their children. This interpretation is consistent with an old Chinese saying: "The rod will produce a dutiful son" (*Bangtou dixia chu xiaozi*), which vividly reflected a conventional Chinese belief that corporal punishment would do children good.[63] The other explanation is that children should be alarmed if their parents stopped beating them, as this could be due to parents' failing health. This reading relates to the story about Boyu of the Han, one of the twenty-four examples of filial piety.[64] It was said that Boyu never defended himself or cried when his mother beat him; instead he often took his mother's punishment with a smile. But one day he cried, which surprised his mother. She asked him why. Boyu replied that he felt so sad that he could not help weeping, because his mother was too weak to hurt him.[65] No matter which reading the author originally intended here, it is evident that Guan's *Small Talk* successfully used colloquial speech to convey Confucian teachings.

In brief, peasant children and children from elite families lived in different worlds of childhood. Peasant children might have been deprived of childhood because of poverty, whilst children in rich families probably lost their childhood freedom under the restrictions of Confucian discipline. Theoretically, freedom from Confucian discipline can be seen as a "gay indifference" that peasant children enjoyed. To Ming-Qing scholar-officials, however, the "gay indifference" had the potential to produce juvenile delinquents that would threaten the social order. It was from this perspective that they tried to provide all children with a basic Confucian education. Their vision of the ideal child was first of all a law-abiding subject.

In attempting to achieve their goal, these scholar-officials sometimes combined popular education and elementary education, through which to promote public morality and to eliminate the "gay indifference" of peasant children. Manuals in the form of vernacular ballads, such as *A Song of Good People* and *Words for Children*, functioned as a medium between elementary education and the public. Children learned these ballads in school and chanted them at home or while they were playing. People heard them and thus received an education even if they did not go to school. Hence, they were also a kind of social treatise in popular education and nourished children's characters while following the conventions of morality. In addition, scholar-officials like Lü Kun and Tang Jian believed that elementary education should be compulsory for all, because it was the basis of a just society and the guarantee of the maintenance of laws. Probably it was from this perspective that Ming-Qing scholars adopted a much more flexible attitude towards both popular primers and the use of colloquialisms in the writing of them.

Western Influence and an Intellectual Search for a New Type of Primer

After the Opium War of the 1840s, many Chinese intellectuals were aware of the weakness of China's position in the world. Being well informed about education and political systems in the West and Japan, reformers inside and outside the late Qing court called for a re-appraisal of the system and the content of traditional education in order to meet the challenges posed by aggressive Western powers. At the same time, however, apologists for tradition strongly argued that the only way to save China from being destroyed by the Western powers was to defend the Confucian Way (*dao*) by embedding traditional values and principles in all layers of society through education. On the surface, this argument appeared to be a conflict between Western influence and Chinese tradition; but at a deeper level, it reflected a feeling of confusion, helplessness and panic among Chinese intellectuals who were not able to find a sound solution derived from the Confucian classics in the face of the economic, political and social crisis of the time.

In 1895, China's defeat in the Sino-Japanese War and the publication of Yan Fu's translation of Thomas Huxley's *Evolution and Ethics* stirred cries for reforms in education and institutional systems. It was within this setting that traditional views of children and childhood were re-interpreted, and the traditional practices of child-rearing and education were challenged. The education of children, argued the reformers, was critical to China's survival or extinction.

To explain this intellectual milieu and its impact on educational reform, this chapter first analyses *Songs for Educating Children* (*Xunmeng gejue*), a new type of primer written by Lin Shu. Then the chapter focuses on Liang Qichao's proposed reforms of children's education and the new curriculum he designed before the 1898 Reform. It first examines Liang's version of social Darwinism and the connection he saw between the education of children and China's fate. Then, taking into account his theoretical orientation and his criticism of traditional Chinese education, it looks in detail at Liang's curriculum, identifying the Western influence on his vision of modern education for a new China. Finally it analyses Liang's emphasis on the synthesis of Chinese-Western learning as reflected in his ideas on education, and discusses the impact of the educational reforms proposed by Liang and his associates on the establishment of a modern Chinese school system.

Lin Shu's Primer *Songs for Educating Children*

Lin Shu was born in 1852, a time at which China was having to face foreign aggression as well as the outbreak of the Taiping Rebellion. He grew up along with the emergence and development of the Self-strengthening Movement, which placed an emphasis on military modernisation between the 1860s and 1870s, and on the establishment of modern industrial enterprises in the 1870s and 1880s. Reformers in the Self-strengthening Movement sincerely believed that their efforts would help to close the gap between China and the Western powers, but the humiliating Treaty of Shimonoseki (Maguan tiaoyue), a result of China's defeat in the Sino-Japanese War, roused the whole nation to great indignation. A new generation of reformists realised that the reforms carried out in the previous decades were an inadequate response to Western aggression, and the only way to meet the challenge of the West and Japan was to reform China's educational system and political institutions. In 1898, Kang Youwei (1858–1927) and his associates, through the Guangxu Emperor, promulgated a series of reforms, including the abolition of the civil service examination system and the establishing of modern schools. The reform lasted only one hundred days, but in the aftermath of the Boxer Uprising of 1900 many changes were reinstated by the Qing court under Empress Dowager.

Lin Shu's *Songs for Educating Children*, containing thirty-two poems, was produced against this background. All the poems were written around 1895, and were published as his first collection of poetry under the title *New Folk Songs from Fujian* (*Minzhong xin yuefu*) in 1897. Qiu Weixuan (1874–1941), an overseas Chinese writer in Xingzhou (an earlier Chinese name for Singapore), perceived Lin's collection as "a precious primer," so in 1898 he changed its title to *Songs for Educating Children* and reprinted it as part of a series of primers entitled *Haiti zhi'ai.*[1] This primer, written as a reaction to the 1898 Reform, was the only text Lin Shu ever composed for children, and he was not known as an educator or a writer of primers but as a pioneer in introducing Western literature into China.

The term *yuefu* which Lin Shu used in the title of his collection literally means Music Bureau, which was established under Emperor Wu of Han (r. 140–87 B.C.) "to provide music for court rituals and feasts and to collect appropriate melodies." In later centuries, *yuefu,* as a general term, referred to either folk songs or hymns composed at court.[2] It was in the hands of Bai Juyi that *yuefu* became a type of political song in uncomplicated language, focusing basically on social criticism. Lin Shu deliberately imitated the style of Bai Juyi to convey his concerns for China's plight. The *yuefu* format made this tiny volume of poetry very similar to children's songs, suitable for children to chant and understand. But unlike the children's songs written by Lü Desheng and Lü Kun of the late Ming, Lin's primer did not contain any advice on moral norms for both children and parents. Instead, it stressed the fact that China's humiliation could only be eliminated by applying Western learning to political and social reforms.

To address this theme, Lin Shu first encouraged children to be aware of China's crisis and to be prepared to take responsibility to save China from being colonised by the Western powers and Japan. In his poem "Our Nation's Foes" (*Guochou*), Lin Shu wrote: "Where are our country's enemies? Britain, Russia, Germany, France and Japan."[3] He pointedly stated that these five countries had all attempted to occupy some parts of China. To avoid this fate, China had to reform her traditional education system, especially the civil service examinations. If all the talented youths were preoccupied with the examinations while armies in Europe were ready to invade China, he warned, China would soon be colonised just like Poland and India, and Chinese people would be captured and become slaves of the invaders.[4] Like many Chinese literati, Lin Shu and his associates protested against the Treaty of Shimonoseki by submitting a petition to the Qing court. The same anger and grief over China's defeat were clearly embodied in each line of this poem, suggesting that the event affected his outlook on the content of education for children.

However, Lin Shu did not intend simply to stir up hatred in children towards the West and Japan. Rather he called for the adoption of Western knowledge in order to make progress and improvements in China. He strongly expressed his disagreement with conservative scholars who regarded anything foreign or Western as barbarian (*yi*), according to an old Chinese concept of the world where China perceived herself as "central" in both the cultural and the geographical senses. He was also disgusted with the then government's insistence that foreign diplomats had to perform the ceremony of kowtow at the Qing court.[5] Lin said that the ritual was not important in China's relations with the West, and what was more important was to take anything from the West that would bring benefits to China. He acknowledged the superiority of Western polity as well as Western military power on which, Lin recommended, China should be modelling itself.[6]

Furthermore, the attitude to the adoption of Western learning, in Lin's opinion, was actually pertinent to China's survival. Lin's generation of intellectuals began to see the differences between China's two encounters with the West. In the late sixteenth and early seventeenth centuries, the Jesuits used Western scientific knowledge as a means to preach Christianity in China; but in the nineteenth century the Western powers and Japan forced China to open her doors by employing their military superiority. In such circumstances, Lin said, if China refused any changes and only adhered to past practices whilst the West was making progress everyday, then China would end up far behind the West, and a weak China could not resist Japanese and Western aggression.[7]

From this perspective, like many reformers of the time, Lin believed that the main task of education was to enlighten people so as to catch up with the Western powers and Japan. However, traditional Chinese education was deficient in undertaking this mission. Lin pointed out that under the traditional Chinese system of education, thousands of literati were trained to be familiar with Confucian classics and historical books, but they had no ability to deal with invaders, as their hands were tied by writing "eight-legged essay."[8] Even worse, these well trained literati did not even have the basic skills for their own survival. In his *Mouyi nan* (lit. "it is difficult to make a living"), Lin made a comparison between China and Western countries, noting that in the West much attention was given to the development of technology, but that the Chinese government did not consider it really important to the country's economy and people's lives, because the Confucian tradition only respected the literati and despised craftsmen and tradesmen. What the literati learned through traditional education was how to be a prime minister (*zaixiang*) and how to govern a country. However, how many of them could achieve this goal? Most literati could only govern the country through empty talk but not in actual practice. Thus, these literati were only bookworms who in the end had no skills at all, and so they were not even able to eke out a living. To change this situation, Lin Shu suggested that the literati should first learn how to support their families, and then they might dream of becoming a high-ranking official through the civil service examination system.[9]

What Lin Shu expressed here is very similar to the opinions held by educational reformers during the late Ming and early Qing. According to their views, traditional education only valued Confucian philosophy and overlooked practical crafts. It was said that this approach originated with Confucius himself. The *Analects* contained the phrase *junzi bu qi*. Literally, these four characters mean that "a superior man is not a utensil."[10] The *Analects* did not explain these four characters clearly. The story of Fan Chi, who asked for knowledge of farming but was scorned by Confucius,[11] may illustrate Confucius' negative attitude toward the practical crafts. However, Confucius did seem to accept the need to know the names of animals and plants.[12] It was Dong Zhongshu (179–104 B.C.), the eminent Han scholar, who interpreted *junzi bu qi* as to: "Illuminate the Way without pursuing mere utility; follow righteousness without calculating success."[13] He strongly stressed the Way (*dao*) and righteousness (*yi*), and thought of practical subjects and practical action as unimportant learning which would misdirect young people.[14]

As discussed in previous chapters, Neo-Confucianism in the Song and Ming developed the aspect of moral practice; and the curricula in schools were designed mainly as preparation for the civil service examinations in which Neo-Confucian texts had become enshrined. By the late Ming, the Jesuits who came to China observed that mathematics and medicine were not as important as Confucian philosophy in scholarly pursuits.[15] However, from the first encounter of the West and China, Western influence stimulated a few scholars to challenge traditional values. Before the collapse of the Ming, the introduction of the most up-to-date European instruments, such as the telescope, surprised Emperor Chongzhen as well as some Chinese scholars. As a result, these scholars challenged the idea that a superior man (*junzi*) should not be distracted by practical skills. They argued that the exquisite Western instruments persuasively demonstrated that "crafts" were also a branch of learning of the sages (*shengxue*). For example, Wang Zheng took the craft of instrument-making as his major academic interest, and in 1627 cooperated with Terrenz in writing *Illustrated Explanation of Rare Western Instruments* (*Yuanxi qiqi tushuo*), the first work on mechanics in Chinese. Wang Zheng did not feel ashamed of his artisan-like interest. On the contrary, he declared with pride that instrument-making "could benefit the people in their daily life (*minsheng riyong*) even though it was considered a craft and an insignificant affair (*mowu*) in traditional learning."[16]

Later, the collapse of the Ming made the Ming loyalists feel ashamed. Some of them joined military forces to fight the Manchu but failed; some took refuge in seclusion. They felt helpless when they witnessed the destruction of the Ming, although they were equipped with thousands of classics, historical books and poetry. Li Gong said that the learning of Neo-Confucianism had a fatal weakness: it ignored *minwu*. *Minwu* meant the responsibility for people and the nation. Li criticised Neo-Confucianists who were immersed in books and forgot other things. When they were pressed to undertake their responsibilities towards the people and the nation, he asserted, the only thing they could do was to kill themselves. Individually, suicide might indicate the virtue of loyalty, but it did not benefit the public at all.[17] Hence, thinkers of the time opposed a focus only on abstract morality, and advocated the learning of practical knowledge, especially its application to public affairs.

Yan Yuan revised Dong Zhongshu's explanation, claiming instead, "Follow righteousness in order to pursue utility; illuminate the Way in order to calculate success."[18] And Huang Zongxi stated in a similar vein, that "utility" (*li*) and "success" (*gong*) should thus not conflict with virtue and the Way.[19] Clearly, the unity of the Way and utility manifested the transformation of the conception of Confucian values in this intellectual movement.

Besides this, such thinkers made a further criticism of Neo-Confucianism. They said that if all the people indulged in empty discourse on human nature and the mind, and farmers did not cultivate the fields and artisans did not produce any goods, who would support their elder brothers and fathers? If people did not have the ability to feed their fathers and elder brothers, how could they practise the virtues of loyalty, filial piety and respect toward them?[20]

Yan Yuan strongly criticised Neo-Confucianism, claiming it even lacked the principle of survival (*shengli*).[21] This principle of survival required the use of practical skills, so the value of craft or skill (*yi*) should not be underestimated. Yuan Mei (1716–1797) said that in the Ming period, "out of a hundred, there were no distinguished doctors," but "'village scholars' (*cunru*) were everywhere."[22]

The collapse of the Ming dynasty seemed to illustrate this modified concept of values in a painful way for intellectuals in the early Qing, who saw that many dutiful sons were not able to prevent their fathers being killed by enemies; many younger brothers were unable to protect their elder brothers, and loyal officials were unable to save the life of their emperor.[23]

About two centuries later, history seemed about to repeat itself, only this time China did not face the collapse of a dynasty but the possible extinction of the whole nation. It was in this context that Lin Shu and his generation of scholars made the same criticisms of traditional Chinese education as the seventeenth-century thinkers had, arguing that the value of learning should lie in utility, and crafts were a branch of sagely learning; any virtue should be manifested in success, and without success there were no virtues.

Moreover, in Lin Shu's time more and more intellectuals were aware that the education young children received was responsible for their future uselessness as literati. For instance, in his preface to Lin's primer, Qiu Weixuan remarked that since, under the civil service examination system, children were driven to memorise the *Four Books*, and to learn how to compose "eight-legged essays," their elementary schooling was extremely limited, and rote memorisation was the basic method used in the whole teaching process. As long as a child was able to learn the *Four Books* by heart, he would be guaranteed to obtain the *xiucai* degree. This kind of education, Qiu pointed out sharply, "hindered the child's intellectual development," and nothing could be more harmful than that.[24] Qiu then criticised Chinese education further through a comparison with Western education. He believed that children under the Western education system were never forced to memorise anything but learnt how to read through understanding what they read first. He contended that children would obtain knowledge through understanding (*wuxing*) rather than mechanical memorisation.[25]

In his poem *Village Teachers* (*Cun xiansheng*) Lin Shu expressed the same opinion. The theme of *Village Teachers* was clearly indicated in a five-character note under the title: criticism of the faults of traditional education for children. Lin at first sketched a picture of Chinese elementary schooling: Confucian classics were the textbooks, and children were often taught the meaning of these Classics even before they had learned how to read. This teaching strategy was not in accordance with the stages of the child's development, and confused elementary schooling and advanced learning. Lin used a metaphor to describe this teaching method as "entering the room without reaching the gate first."[26] Consequently, Lin wrote, children all seemed to be able to talk about the *Great Learning* and the Way of the sages after three or four years in school, but they were actually not qualified to undertake any task involving basic reading and writing.[27]

Lin then proposed that children should be taught things they encountered daily instead of archaic knowledge, as archaic knowledge would not help but impede the child's intellectual development. He urged educators: "Don't let rotten stuff enter children's minds, enlighten children by using [new] knowledge."[28]

Lin's "new knowledge," as reflected in his *Songs for Educating Children*, touched upon almost all the socio-political issues of the time, such as defending the nation through reform of education and political institutions; the use of Western knowledge to change Chinese society; the abolition of foot-binding; and females' right to education. Lin Shu's primer presented all these serious issues for children as if they were "learned scholars." It appears that he treated children like adults. On the other hand, however, this was consistent with his idea that children encountered these socio-political problems everyday, so these issues should be part of their education. From this point of view, his primer was written to encourage children to prepare themselves for the mission of wiping out the nation's humiliation.[29]

In brief, Lin Shu's primer is an example of how seventeenth-century education theory was inherited and developed by the intellectuals of his generation in the context of China's struggle for survival. Their understanding of the functions of the human brain helped them to recognise the importance of children's intellectual development to China's modernisation, so they called for a reappraisal of the teaching methodology used in traditional education for children. These views, as a reflection of the intellectual milieu of the time, will be further elaborated in the following discussion of Liang Qichao's educational thought.

Liang Qichao on the Education of Children and the Fate of China

Liang Qichao had a more profound influence than Lin Shu on the course of reform and on the intelligentsia in this transitional era.[30] As early as 1896, Liang started to publish a series of articles entitled "On Reform" (*Bianfa tongyi*) in *Current Affairs* (*Shiwu bao*). In this series of articles he touched upon almost all the issues concerning education (such as schools in general, teachers' colleges, academic societies, and the education of women and children), concluding that education was the key to reform.

Liang's search for alternatives to traditional Chinese practice was partly stimulated by information about Western education in missionary writings.[31] For instance, he "specifically called upon the authority of [Timothy] Richard to argue for educational reform" in his "On Reform."[32] Of all the Western nations, Liang Qichao admired England most, as he saw England as the first nation that had a modern polity as well as national power,[33] so his term "Western education" often referred specifically to English education.

Before the 1898 Reform, Chinese intellectuals were still very much influenced by the thesis of "Chinese learning as substance (*ti*) and Western learning for practical use (*yong*)." This *ti-yong* formula was officially advocated by Zhang Zhidong (1837–1909),[34] one of the key figures in the modernisation of Chinese education. Both Zhang and Liang selected some elements of Western education in their attempts to create a new type of education for China, but their selections were made against their own academic background and their feelings towards religious practice in mission schools. Zhang was particularly enthusiastic about modelling on Japan which, in his opinion, had already succeeded in both adopting Western learning and preserving Confucianism. The Japanese model was very appealing to Liang Qichao as well, especially after he fled to Japan in the aftermath of the 1898 Reform. At the time he was writing "On Reform," however, his proposed curriculum was largely based on the model of Western education.[35]

The superiority of Western education systems, according to Liang's observation, was that (1) Westerners had thousands of new inventions each year, but nothing was invented in China; (2) in the West, thousands of new scholarly works were published to address new findings and theories, but none appeared in China; and (3) literacy rates in the West reached 80–90%, but in China less than 30–40% of the population could read and write. After listing these facts, Liang questioned if such huge differences between the Chinese and Western people resulted from different talents with which endowed by nature. If so, he continued, how could Chinese students overseas achieve so well and not be inferior to their Western peers? This suggested, Liang asserted, that the intellectual faculties of the Chinese were equal to those of Western people, but education for young children impeded the development of Chinese people's creativity.[36] In other words, the huge gap between China and the Western powers was not due to differences in race but to differences in educational systems, within which the education of children was a crucial factor affecting the fate of a nation.[37] To further buttress his argument, Liang then re-interpreted Darwin's theory of evolution by relating it to the traditional Chinese "foetal education."

Liang Qichao learned Darwin's theory of evolution from his acquaintance with Yan Fu (1853–1921), who translated Thomas Huxley's *Evolution and Ethics* and Western political theories[38] into Chinese. These translations circulated widely among Chinese intellectuals, who were particularly alerted after learning the ideas of "the survival of the fittest," and began to see the only two options for China as national extinction or reform.

According to Liang's own account, he read the draft of Yan's translation of Huxley's *Evolution and Ethics* in 1896,[39] and he immediately applied this new theory in his criticism and analysis of traditional Chinese education by arguing that the defence of China should start with the defence of the Chinese race, and the education of children is the key to improving the race.[40] Based on his interpretation of Darwin's theory of evolution, Liang made a close link between China's fate and the education of children. His "On Female Education" (*Lun nüxue*) and "On the Education of Children" (*Lun youxue*), two articles in the series "On Reform," systematically elaborated this idea.

In Liang's understanding of Darwin's theory, propagation was a gradual process of evolution, involving changes and improvements; this was how anthropoid apes evolved and became human beings, and barbarous nations became civilised people. At the beginning of evolution, changes and improvements seemed insignificant, but eventually they reached a great end. A person's intellect, physical form and personality were formed under the influence of both genetic factors and environmental forces. Liang said that his understanding of this idea came from Yan Fu, who in his letter explained:

> According to the rules of biology, man's mind, talent, physical form, and habits were formed many generations ago; and then were influenced by man's experience, such as what he saw and heard, as well as his surroundings, such as friends, teachers and environment.[41]

This explanation suggested that the genes parents inherited from their ancestors and then passed on to their offspring could affect the personalities of many generations, and would even have an impact on the formation of a nation's character. Liang then employed the traditional Chinese "foetal education" theory to argue further that inheritance was part of evolution and the mother's womb was where heredity and education combined.

To modern minds, it might be difficult to understand how "education could begin in the womb," and how this "early Chinese prejudice" could be used to introduce the theory of evolution.[42] But it was China's problems that made Liang Qichao, Yan Fu and Kang Youwei extremely interested in Darwin, and they deliberately interpreted his theory of evolution to serve their reform programmes.[43] This Chinese version of social Darwinism inevitably complied with traditional Chinese ideas in which education was highly valued for teaching people and transforming society. What interested these scholars more was not the original or real meanings of Darwin's theory of evolution but how it might help to explain

China's weakness and awaken the Chinese people to the grim reality of the situation. Under these circumstances, the traditional theory of "foetal education" was borrowed to interpret Darwin's theory of evolution in Chinese terms.

In Chapter One we saw that the traditional Chinese "foetal education" originally emphasised the influence of external forces on the child's physical and moral development. Foetal environment, as part of the "external forces," was believed by the ancient Chinese to have a significant impact not only on the developing foetus but also on the child's temperament and moral status after its birth and in its later life. Accordingly Chinese women were advised to avoid "evil encounters" and be careful about their body movements, emotions and diets during pregnancy. The theory also urged parents to carefully examine the physical and moral qualities of wet-nurses.

Liang Qichao translated these traditional concerns and practices into an emphasis on the importance of the mother's physical fitness and educational level in the making of a strong and intelligent child. To his knowledge, the Western powers were all trying to develop their military forces, so women in these countries were "ordered to engage in callisthenics" to ensure they would produce strong and healthy children.[44] Traditional "foetal education" advised Chinese women to be careful about the external phenomena they perceived. Liang advised physical exercise instead. The underlying principle, however, remained the same: the mother's fitness would be transmitted to the child through her life energy and blood. "Foetal education" in this context was interpreted as an urgent practice which, in social Darwinian terms, would contribute to the making of physically strong children who would then grow into the valiant soldiers that China so desperately needed. From this perspective, Liang argued for the significance of "foetal education" to China's survival.

Liang then further related women's education to the nation's evolution. He pointed to the fact that Chinese children before the age of ten were generally under the care of women, most of whom were uneducated and knew only trivial things. Under these circumstances, the only education children could receive from their mothers or their care-givers, he went on, was to be taught to achieve success in the civil service examinations, and then to obtain emolument, to inherit family property, and to start a family. As the

Chinese had been brought up in this way generation after generation, they cared about nothing but private gain, and had become shameless, stubborn and brutal. In this context, Liang argued that the education of children was not just about how children were brought up, but was about how the nation's character was formed, and how the nation's fate was decided.[45] He sincerely believed that the solution for China's crisis was to start with the defence of the Chinese race, and the defence of the Chinese race should start with resolving the problem of unqualified teachers.[46] Here the "unqualified teachers" were actually the epitome of traditional Chinese education which, like Lin Shu and Qiu Weixuan, Liang characterised as *zhinao* education.

The term *zhinao* means "blocking the development of one's brain." After drawing a sharp contrast between the rote learning central to traditional Chinese education and the emphasis on understanding in Western education, Liang Qichao, like many reformers before the 1898 Reform, argued that the existing education system failed to develop the child's brain power which, from his Darwinian perspective, was crucial to China's creative adaptation if it was to avoid extinction.

From the information he received, Liang was extremely impressed by the Western notion of education, in which the attributes of children were well considered and teaching did not proceed ahead of the stages in the child's intellectual and physical development. This basic principle, Liang noticed, was applied to all aspects of education for children. For instance, in the West the procedure of learning how to read and write was carried out step by step: first to recognise words connected to things which children encountered in daily life, then to understand the meaning of these words, and later to make sentences by using these words, and finally to write essays.[47] In China, Liang explained, children were forced to learn Confucian classics from the very beginning of schooling, chanting sentences such as "The Way of higher learning is to illustrate illustrious virtues" (*daxue zhi dao zai ming mingde*). Sentences like this were so abstract that even scholars from the Han to the Song could not clearly define the term *mingde* in all their writings. If so, Liang questioned, how could one expect young children to understand it? This kind of content, Liang remarked, discouraged children from study; even worse, it provoked hatred towards their teachers because of the hardship pupils suffered in the process of learning.[48]

Why did traditional Chinese education force young children to study Confucian classics rather than other useful subjects that related to daily life? The civil service examination system was the driving force, said Liang. The aim and content of education were very much affected by the temptation of the gains which flowed from success in the examinations.[49] Like Lin Shu, Liang argued that this existing education was *zhinao*, hindering children's intellectual development.[50]

Western textbooks, Liang pointed out, were written in the colloquial language and some were in the form of folk songs or ballads. Children would chant and understand textbooks of this kind easily. In the teaching process, much attention was given to children's ability to understand; astronomy and scientific subjects, for example, were taught through performing tricks,[51] and history was taught in the colloquial language in a style similar to that of Chinese popular entertainment.[52] These methods, Liang said, would attract children to the study of these subjects, and would make all these courses more enjoyable. In contrast, the content of Chinese elementary education was not in a form that children could understand easily, so teachers had to force children to memorise texts in order to meet the requirements of the civil service examinations.[53]

Liang's arguments represented the views of many late nineteenth-century reformers and educators. With a much better understanding of the human brain than their predecessors, they proposed changes to both content and teaching method in elementary education, so as to help develop children's brain power effectively, and then to improve the Chinese race.

The Chinese understanding of the functions of the human brain was associated with missionary publications on Western medicine, some of which introduced Western knowledge of the human body into China. Joannes Terrenz (1576–1630), with the help of a Chinese scholar called Bi Gongchen, published *A Western Account of the Human Body* (*Taixi renshen shuogai*) in 1643, stating that the human intellect was not stored in the heart but was connected with the development of the brain. As discussed in Chapter One, ancient Chinese thought that the heart was the organ for thinking, and the brain was one of the storing organs. Therefore, it was not surprising that Terrenz's idea initially shocked the Chinese literati,[54] although it was then gradually accepted by some Chinese medical practitioners such as Li Shizhen (1518–1593), an outstanding Chinese doctor of the time, and scholars such as Jin Sheng (1598–1644), who studied Western calendar making with Franciscus Sambiasi (1582–1649), one of the Jesuit missionaries in China. Fang Yizhi, as we have pointed out in earlier chapters, was also aware of this new idea, and recorded it in his writing. This recognition of brain power allowed some seventeenth-century thinkers, such as Wang Fuzhi, to re-interpret the early Chinese concept of man.

However, Wang Fuzhi and other educational reformers at that time did not yet perceive education as a significant means of developing brain power. Their better understanding of the human brain seemed only to enhance traditional beliefs in children's memory capacity and to confirm the use of rote memorisation in the teaching process. The traditional pedagogical approach was to encourage children under the age of fifteen to memorise as much as they could. Wang Yun's *Explanations of Characters for Children* can be seen as a reflection of the nineteenth-century teaching practice that memorising and reciting were still designed as the basic processes for elementary training.

Interestingly, before Wang Yun wrote his primer, Wang Qingren (1768–1831), who is regarded as the first Chinese anatomist, published the *Corrections of Errors in Chinese Medical Writings* (*Yilin gaicuo*) that corrected many Chinese misunderstandings of the human body, including the brain. In his *On the Human Brain* (*Naosui shuo*), Wang Qingren contended that the human capacity for memory was determined by the quality of the brain: infants and toddlers lacked good memory skills because their brains had not yet fully developed, and aged people gradually lost their memories because their brains shrank.[55]

What Wang Qingren said here was already, as mentioned earlier, accepted by some Chinese medical specialists and philosophers in the early seventeenth century. At that time, however, the idea did not spread. It was not until the nineteenth century that the knowledge of Western anatomy was systematically introduced to the Chinese. At the same time, more and more Chinese people in the treaty ports, such as Shanghai, Guangzhou and Ningbo, turned to Western medicine as an alternative to the traditional Chinese medicine. This trend then helped the promotion of missionary books on Western medicine, such as the *New Theory of the Human Body* (*Quanti xinlun*), written by Benjamin Hobson (1816–1873). In his book, Hobson particularly emphasised that the human brain, as the headquarters of the human body, was in charge of the functions of the whole bodily system. Hobson's book enjoyed greater popularity than Terrenz's, and Hobson was pleased that Chinese literati "all know this is a useful book."[56]

Within this context, we may see Wang Qingren's work as a marker of change: by the late nineteenth century more educators and scholars had understood the function of the human brain, and had begun to see the significance of developing brain power through education, and the harmfulness of rote learning used in the teaching process. So it is not surprising that Wang Yun, as we have pointed out in Chapter Six, stressed the necessity of mastering at least two thousand basic characters on the one hand, but on the other, was disgusted with any practice that forced children to memorise and recite books and characters all day.

Liang Qichao's criticism of mechanical memorisation was linked to his critique of China's backwardness in science and technology. He pointed out that in traditional Chinese learning, there were some branches of knowledge similar to subjects in Western learning: Chinese *dixue* was similar to Western geography, and names and knowledge of ancient *gongshi* were somewhat close to Western architecture. However, Chinese scholars only focused on searching for the original meanings of words in historical documents and Confucian classics. When this method was also employed in teaching children, young pupils were then required simply to learn all the archaic knowledge by heart, but were not encouraged to explore their visual experience and to master practical knowledge that would benefit their daily life. In this way, children's minds were developed for only one function: memorising mechanically, and their knowledge was limited to selected ancient books. This was why, Liang concluded, Westerners were able to invent so many new machines (e.g. the invention of the steam engine was inspired by observation of boiling water), and create new ideas (e.g. the theory of gravity was inspired by falling apples), but none of this happened in China.[57]

Liang's Proposed Curriculum: A Vision of Modern Education for Children

This section focuses on Liang's proposals for curriculum reform, including a school timetable he designed and teaching material he advocated. Liang mainly addressed two key issues in elementary education: literacy and the structure of knowledge.

Liang and like-minded intellectuals were very concerned about China's high rate of illiteracy. In order to catch up with Western nations in terms of literacy rates, Liang clearly identified the basic task of elementary education as teaching children literacy skills. For this purpose, he recommended the use of Wang Yun's *Explanations of Characters for Children* in teaching children two thousand basic characters, and the practice of calligraphy was part of the course.[58]

Liang also agreed with other scholars, such as Ma Jianzhong (?–1899), that the lack of grammar teaching made the Chinese language difficult to master and this contributed to a far lower literacy rate in China than in Western countries.[59] Therefore, Liang inserted grammar into his curriculum and advised the use of *The Ma Grammar* (*Mashi wentong*), the first Chinese work on grammar.[60] *The Ma Grammar* was written under Western influence, as grammar in its modern definition was new to the Chinese.[61] Both Liang and Ma believed that the study of *The Ma Grammar* would be beneficial to young students who were studying either classical Chinese or Western languages.

China's low rate of literacy was also related, in Liang's view, to rote learning. To find alternatives to traditional Chinese teaching methods, Liang advocated the adoption of a Western pedagogical approach. First he proposed the use of textbooks written in rhyme (*gejue shu*). This proposal was not new, as most traditional Chinese primers were in rhyme. However, Liang was dissatisfied with the content of these primers which, in his opinion, did not contain enough new knowledge. Therefore, he argued that new primers should include the essence of all kinds of knowledge — from classical learning, to history, to astronomy, to geography, and other scientific subjects such as botany and microbiology — and all the texts should be rhymed.[62] In his plan, books in rhyme would be taught in the first class every morning.[63]

Along with texts in the format of songs or ballads, Liang then promoted the use of the colloquial language (*baihua*)[64] in the writing of textbooks. According to his information about Western education, teaching material of this kind had a story-telling style which made learning more enjoyable.[65] Moreover, Liang held that the linguistic separation between written form and spoken language was responsible for China's high rate of illiteracy, as classical Chinese made literacy a monopoly for the elite, and had prevented many Chinese people from mastering literacy skills. This linguistic separation consequently had become an obstacle in improving the Chinese race through education. To change this situation and to extend literacy education to the majority of the population, Liang emphasised the use of colloquial language in elementary education,[66] and a late afternoon class was allocated for teaching textbooks in the colloquial language. In this class children would be allowed to read whatever they liked.[67]

Third, in order to place an emphasis on understanding instead of rote learning, Liang suggested adopting catechism as a teaching device. Catechism, the question-answer format, was originally used in Christian education for religious instruction. Liang probably knew of this format through reading missionary writings, some of which answered questions concerning the political system, history and technology in the West. Some missionary textbooks were also written in this question-answer format, such as *A Concise Geography for Children* (*Dili biantong lüezhuan*), by Walter Henry Medhurst (1796–1857)[68] and *Western Astronomy in the Format of Question-answer* (*Tianwen wenda*) published by Andrew Patton Happer (1818–1894) in Ningbo in 1849.[69] By 1896, when Liang wrote "On Reform," missionaries had published a great number of books which covered not only the Christian religion but almost all aspects of Western learning. Liang's *Bibliography of Western Learning* indicates that he was familiar with missionary publications, and appreciated those in question-answer format very much. He believed that by adopting this dialogue format all kinds of useful knowledge could be contained in about thirty books, which would then enable all children, even those who were unintelligent, to be equipped with sound and useful knowledge before they reached fifteen. Besides this, school teachers who were behind the times could use them to refresh their own knowledge.[70] So he arranged the study of texts in question-answer format as the second morning class, emphasising that it was not necessary for students to memorise, but to understand the meanings of the texts.[71]

Alongside his efforts to promote literacy education, Liang stressed the importance of broadening the content of education. He strongly recommended the study of foreign languages and mathematics, as he was informed that these were the two key subjects in Western elementary education. In his understanding, acquisition of languages at an early age would be easier than in the child's later life; and arithmetic would be useful for children's future careers, no matter what occupations they chose.[72]

At the end of the nineteenth century, learning Western languages was no longer new to Chinese society, and people's attitude toward Western languages and mission schools had changed dramatically. In the 1850s and the 1860s missionary schools had difficulty attracting Chinese students; those who enrolled in their schools usually came from poor families, and were by and large attracted by free food and accommodation. At that time, even students in the government schools, such as the Tongwen guan in Beijing (established in 1862) and Shanghai (established in 1863),[73] still focused only on knowledge useful to their success in the civil service examinations, and few were interested in foreign languages and technology.[74] In the 1870s and the 1880s, however, Western languages and other subjects gradually became fashionable, and mission schools in trading ports, such as Fuzhou and Shanghai, were very popular. In the 1880s, missionary schools no longer needed to provide their students with food and accommodation, and some even charged quite expensive tuition fees. Even so, there were still more applicants than the schools could actually accept, although those who were admitted to mission schools, such as Zhongxi shuyuan (Chinese-Western Academy), tended to come from wealthy families and were only interested in Western subjects.[75]

Although the study of foreign languages appeared fashionable at that time, Liang was dissatisfied with the situation that, for most learners, the purpose of mastering a foreign language was to participate in trade with overseas companies or to work for foreign firms in China. According to his ideal, a "new citizen" should be equipped with both Chinese and Western learning. But foreign language schools of the time were only interested in meeting the needs of the import-export trade. This, in Liang's words, was the

practice of tradesmen and Westerners' servants (*shijing yangyong*).
Liang despised this practice, and encouraged children to learn Latin
first. After mastery of Latin, he believed, children would find it much
easier to study English and French.[76] This proposal was a rejection of
the *Yangwu yundong* (Westernisation Movement), which only focused
on Western firearms, technology and material well-being which, in
Liang's opinion, were not the essence of Western learning. In his
later article "New Citizen" (*Xinmin shuo*), Liang further elucidated
this view, maintaining that new citizens ought to be versed in Western
learning and then use it to make China as "civilized" as the West. For
this purpose, his school timetable allocated a daily class for foreign
languages, and original foreign textbooks for children were
recommended for use in teaching.[77]

To teach arithmetic in elementary schooling was not a novelty in
curriculum reform, because as early as in the seventeenth century
Yan Yuan and Li Gong had made this suggestion. It was not new
either that Liang called upon the authority of the original Confucian
education to argue the necessity of teaching arithmetic at an
elementary level.[78] Liang's proposal, however, not only invoked this
tradition, but also emphasised the new knowledge from the West as
a significant part of this subject. In his proposed curriculum,
children over the age of eight should be taught how to count in their
head (*xinsuan*), and then should gradually learn written calculation,
and basic geometry, algebra, and calculus, and then they would be
able to claim to be specialists in the area (*chouren*)[79] before reaching
the age of fifteen.[80] Therefore, the third class in his daily school
timetable was to focus on mathematics and maps (i.e. the knowledge
of geography) — maths on the dates with an odd number and maps
on the dates with an even number.[81]

There was a correlation between Liang's efforts to broaden the
content of elementary education and his emphasis on the synthesis of
Western and Chinese learning. In his view, without the framework of
Chinese learning the pursuit of Western learning alone would only
lead to "the emergence of Chinese compradors and business go-
betweens working slavishly for the Westerners."[82] This view was
reflected in his argument for the continuing use of *menjing shu*, a
traditional Chinese format in which authors briefly introduced books
to readers according to the four categories.[83] Liang said that no one
could be exhaustive in book reading, but encyclopedic books might

be able to compensate for this as they could brief readers on books in all categories, including ancient and recent books as well as newly translated Western works. The most comprehensive work of this kind was *The Essentials of the Encyclopaedia* (*Siku tiyao*), but it was too large for young children. So Liang urged scholars to compile a new kind of introductory book especially for children and to provide them with a broader sweep of knowledge, covering traditional Chinese as well as Western learning, and ancient as well as contemporary scholarship.[84]

At the same time, Liang was particularly amazed at the comprehensive features of the Western-style dictionary (*mingwu shu*). He believed that books in this form could be extremely useful for anyone who, after learning some basic skills of reading and writing, could study all kinds of knowledge simply through reading the dictionary. In Liang's time the Western-style dictionary had already been introduced into China, and the term *zidian* had already been adopted to refer to this Western format,[85] but he preferred the term *mingwu shu*, as he saw the function of a dictionary as introducing things of the world to readers rather than only words.[86]

While emphasising the importance of broadening the content of education, Liang pointed to the necessity of taking children's physical development into account. In Western education, he noticed, daily teaching would not be more than three hours, and music and gymnastics were part of the curriculum.[87] Although Liang did not mention the curriculum of mission schools in China, he was perhaps aware of their practice, because popular mission schools of the time, such as the Zhenjiang Girls' School (Zhenjiang nüshu), taught music and gymnastics from the first year through the final year.[88] So he arranged gymnastic practice as the first afternoon class. He even allowed children to play freely after formal practice,[89] as he was informed that, after school, children in the West were encouraged to play together.[90]

Liang further related the issue of the child's physical development to the "survival of the fittest." He said that Western education aimed to help children grow up physically strong so that in future they could all be soldiers to defend their countries. This was why, he believed, gymnastics was part of their school curriculum.[91] In China, Liang complained, pupils were like the teachers' prisoners, who had to sit upright all day long in a room without fresh air. This was not only harmful to children's physical development but also prevented them from enjoying education, because they regarded school as a prison.[92] On this basis, Liang affirmed that traditional Chinese elementary education obstructed children's physical, intellectual, and psychological development instead of helping them grow up happily and healthily.

Liang's Synthesis of Chinese and Western Learning

Liang's proposed curriculum was a reflection of his emphasis on the synthesis of indigenous Chinese learning with Western ideas and practices. However, his synthesis was not a simple matter of "smuggling" Western learning into a traditional Chinese framework, but an important process of creating new Chinese thought which, he believed, was essential for China's progress, because "the lack of thought" in China resulted in the lack of inventions.[93] From this perspective, Liang insisted on the indivisible nature of the new structure of scholarship, in which neither Western knowledge nor traditional Chinese learning should be ignored. He expressed this idea consistently from 1896 (when he wrote "On Elementary Education") to the eve of the 1898 Reform (when he drafted the regulations for Jingshi Daxuetang — the early prototype of Beijing University).[94]

Liang's persistence in emphasising the synthesis of Western and Chinese learning related to the Chinese attitude to Western influence before the 1898 Reform. At that time there was no "outright opposition" to Western knowledge (such as Yang Guanxian's rejection in the 1600s),[95] as government schools, such as the Tongwen guan in both Beijing and Shanghai, had already been established to teach Western languages and subjects in science and technology. Chinese views on Western knowledge gradually changed along with the prevalence of missionary publications and education facilities over the period from the 1840s to the 1890s. For instance, early in the 1800s the Chinese used the word *yi* (barbarian) to denigrate anything not Chinese. Then the word *xi* (West, or western) was adopted to indicate that Western languages were like any other Chinese dialects (the Tongwen guan in Shanghai was called "Guang fangyan guan," literally meaning "the college of extending dialects"). Compared to the word *yi*, the word *xi* reflected progress in terms of the Chinese attitude to Western learning; on the other hand, it reflected a Chinese view of the world in which China was at the centre. Timothy Richard (1845–1919), one of the most outstanding missionary educators, in 1887 wrote a pamphlet entitled *Essential Information about Modern Education in Seven Countries* (*Qiguo xinxue beiyao*), introducing the educational systems of England, France, Germany, Russia, America, Japan and India to Chinese reformers and government officials such as Li Hongzhang (1823–1901) and Zhang Zhidong. Richard used the word *xin* (new) instead of *xi* (West) to refer to education and knowledge from the West. Then Zhang Zhidong followed suit in his *Exhortation to Learning* (*Quanxue pian*), advocating the study of both the old (including the *Four Books, Five Classics*, Chinese history, government and maps) and the new knowledge (including political systems, technology, and history of the West). Zhang then advocated "the old learning for substance (*ti*) and the new subjects for practical use (*yong*)."[96]

The substitution of the word *xin* for *xi* was not simply a linguistic exercise. The change actually allowed Western subjects to enter the framework of Chinese learning. For Zhang Zhidong, the preservation of traditional Chinese learning could be achieved, if it were supplemented by certain Western skills. For Liang Qichao and other like-minded reformers, this word "new" gave them a base for the integration of traditional Chinese learning with Western knowledge so as to create the new Chinese thought. This approach is evident in Liang's proposed curriculum.[97]

In order to create the new Chinese thought, Liang did not just repeat the *ti-yong* formula, but also carefully separated the Christian religion from Western secular learning. To Liang "even if there were definite grounds on which Chinese culture compared unfavorably with Western secular learning, this did not mean that similar grounds could also be found for denigrating Confucianism as a moral-religious system in comparison with Christianity."[98] Therefore, while integrating Western elements into his new curriculum, Liang modified many details of the Western education system. For example, he used the ten-day study period instead of the "week": on the tenth day students were allowed to have a day off and to bath themselves.[99] Evidently, this was Liang's subtle rejection of Christian practice, as the term "week" was introduced into China in connection with the Christian religion. Similarly, Sunday worship was changed in Liang's plan to a gathering to worship Confucius and to sing a song praising Confucianism.[100] He also proposed that every morning school should start with a ceremony where both children and teachers sang a song to praise Confucianism; every afternoon, classes formally ended with the holding of an assembly where both teachers and students sang a patriotic song. As well as this, students would annually have ten days holiday — five days for celebrating the birth of Confucius and the other five days for the Emperor's birthday.[101]

These modifications appeared, on the surface, to reflect Liang's attempt to preserve traditional Chinese practice, such as *xili*, or the practice of ritual or ceremony, which was a significant part of traditional Chinese education. At a deeper level, however, this is not a vestige of Chinese tradition but an indication that Liang Qichao, like his teacher Kang Youwei, was endeavouring to invent a religious practice that would parallel Christian worship. Liang's concept of *baojiao*, or "preserving the faith,"[102] and the modifications he made in his proposed curriculum coincided with Kang Youwei's intention to make "Confucianism a national religion, with its own holidays, empire-wide network of churches and missionaries."[103] Such intentions indicate their acceptance of the missionaries' view that religion might save China; on the other hand, they believed that China could still have progress without accepting the Western God. As Paul Cohen points out, during this period Chinese reformers were willing to "buy what the missionaries had to sell," but "were not willing to accept the conditions which the missionaries thought were implicit in the transaction."[104]

Another important factor that might have affected Liang's synthesis of Western and Chinese learning was the Protestant missionaries' involvement in secular education in late nineteenth-century China. Statistically, enrolment in Protestant mission schools was 6,000 in 1877, but by 1890 it had increased to 16,836.[105] And more significantly, after the first general conference of Protestant missionaries in China (1877), Protestant mission schools began to teach not only science, technology, religion, politics and the history of the West, but also a comprehensive range of Chinese subjects. In order to attract Chinese students, mission schools even directly adopted the popular Chinese primers *The Trimetrical Classic* and *One Thousand Characters* for beginners, and the format of *The Trimetrical Classic* was used to create new and suitable textbooks.[106] In short, while Western knowledge influenced Chinese reformers greatly, "Chinese perspectives and values shaped the form and content of the mission primary-school curriculum" in the late nineteenth century.[107]

This accommodation of Chinese models and values in mission schools suggests a "process of cognitive contamination"[108] in the encounters between East and West, and between the old and the new. This "cognitive contamination" gave the *ti-yong* formula a new dimension: it referred not only to the Chinese intellectual efforts at reconciling Chinese traditional learning and Western knowledge, but also to the mission schools' adaptation to the Chinese situation. Historically, this "cognitive contamination" first occurred during China's first encounter with the West — the Jesuits clothed Western influence in traditional Chinese dress, and Chinese intellectuals, such as Xu Guangqi and Mei Wending, cloaked Western concepts "in the name of traditional symbols."[109] However, this early "contamination" only allowed Xu and Mei to integrate some knowledge of Western mathematics and astronomy into the framework of traditional Chinese learning. After the Opium War, the Westernisation movement focused only on the adoption of Western technology. In the 1890s, Kang Youwei and Liang Qichao, as a new generation of reformers, demanded institutional changes. In so doing, they returned to the Confucian classics for "traditional symbols," arguing that the original Confucianism supported institutional reform. This argument was like a manifesto of the Modern Text School (*jinwen*), indicating that their study of Confucian classics was not for the sake of archaic knowledge or for success in the civil service examinations, but for the promotion of reform programmes.[110]

Meanwhile, the Protestant mission schools' adaptation to the Chinese situation, as part of the "cognitive contamination," directly or indirectly influenced the course of educational reform. Firstly, the teaching methods used in mission schools represented a sharp contrast to traditional Chinese education, which Liang Qichao, Lin Shu, and his associates referred to as *zhinao* education. In mission schools children were taught in accordance with the stages in the child's physical and intellectual development, and teachers paid much attention to their students' ability to understand, instead of forcing them to memorise anything abstract and irrelevant to daily life. In Liang's criticism of traditional Chinese education these factors were referred to as the characteristics of "Western education," and as alternatives to traditional Chinese teaching methods.

Secondly, the mission schools' curriculum contained "practical learning"(*shixue*) which, throughout the history of Chinese education, many thinkers and educators had been searching for. For instance, Mei Wending dreamed of establishing a school to study mathematics and astronomy only, and other early seventeenth-century reformers, as mentioned earlier, accused traditional education of being responsible for the collapse of the Ming dynasty, as it did not include practical learning. In the late nineteenth century, many subjects taught in mission schools appeared to resonate with the *shixue* tradition. Liang in his curriculum particularly emphasised the study of mathematics and English, which were already a standard part of the mission schools' curricula.

Thirdly, the mission schools' curricula accommodated both Western and Chinese learning, but rejected the practice of writing "eight-legged" essays. This also accorded with Liang's vision of modern education for children. Although Liang did not directly acknowledge the mission schools' curricula and practice in his proposal, his references to "Western education" and the similarities between his proposed curriculum and the mission primary-school's syllabus suggest that missionary practice in education was at least partly the source of his idea of Western education.[111]

As for new textbooks for children, among Liang's proposed teaching material only the *Explanations of Characters for Children* and *The Ma Grammar* already existed, and the others still had to be written.[112] At one stage, Liang, together with Kang Youwei, took the job into his own hands. Kang drafted a style sheet (*tili*), and Liang attempted to compile the new textbooks he advocated. But his political commitments did not allow him to achieve this goal, and after five years no books of this kind were close to completion.[113]

The task of producing new textbooks was carried out by both missionaries and Chinese reformers. By 1890 Protestant missionaries had already produced eighty-four books and forty maps and charts since the setting-up of a "School and Textbook Series Committee" in 1877. These books were mostly secular in content, and had a great impact on Chinese reformers before 1898. The first series of textbooks produced by the Chinese were three volumes of the *Readers for Elementary Learning* (*Mengxue duben*), published by the Nanyang gongxue (Nanyang Public School) in 1897. In 1898 Zhong Tianwei (1840–1901) completed twelve volumes of textbooks for the Sandeng

School he established in Shanghai, and in the same year the Sandeng School of Wuxi also had its own textbooks in seven volumes.[114] These Chinese productions paralleled the missionaries' efforts.

The new textbooks were produced at the same time as the reformers were endeavouring to establish new schools modelled on those of the West. Before the 1898 Reform, Liang Qichao and his associates were strongly intrigued by the practice of compulsory education in the West. They believed that what had made Germany and Japan powerful was their commitment to basic education. This idea was accepted not only by influential reformers such as Liang, but also by less famous scholars and educators such as Zhong Tianwei. As a graduate from Shanghai Gezhi shuyuan (Gezhi Academy, or Shanghai Polytechnic Institution and Reading Room),[115] Zhong devoted himself to establishing modern schools, while participating in the translation of Western books along with missionaries and other Chinese translators. The word "*sandeng*" which he used in his school's name meant "the third level of education," referring to elementary schooling — from the ages of seven to nine, children studied in Mengxue guan (junior primary school), focusing on basic literacy skills; and from the ages of ten to twelve they studied in Jingxue guan (division for the study of Classical learning), focusing on the study of the *Four Books* and other classics, science, and English. He emphasised that only those who mastered both Western and Chinese learning could be recognised as excellent students.[116] The curriculum he designed and the textbooks he composed all reflected his own training at Gezhi Academy.

Zhong Tianwei's case indicates that (1) Liang Qichao's proposed reform of education for children was not an isolated phenomenon but a reflection of the intellectual atmosphere in the 1890s, and (2) the 1898 Reform measures included ideas and practice that emerged during this period.[117] Although the Reform lasted only one hundred days, many reform measures were reinstated after the Boxer Uprising of 1900. In 1902 the first draft of the new regulations on education envisaged a modern Chinese school system; later Zhang Zhidong was summoned to revise the draft. In 1904 the regulations were announced, and in the following year the civil service examination system was officially abolished. The two events signalled the end of traditional Chinese education and the birth of a modern school system, to which the reformers' proposals and practice contributed greatly. For instance, the 1904 regulations endorsed compulsory education, which was viewed by Liang Qichao and like-minded reformers as the issue crucial to China's survival. Also, Liang's plans for worshipping Confucius and for school holidays, his emphasis on including arithmetic and gymnastics in the primary school curriculum, and his objection to treating students like prisoners were all part of or reflected in the regulations.[118]

The 1904 regulations opposed mechanical memorisation, stating that it would adversely affect the development of the students' brains. On the other hand, the memorisation of the Confucian classics was still recommended as a necessary part of learning. This was perhaps partly due to the context in which Liang and his associates criticised rote learning. They charged that rote learning was harmful to children's intellectual development in the context of traditional Chinese curricula, the civil service examination system and its by-product — the "eight-legged essays." For example, although the catechism format which Liang Qichao so much appreciated was actually rote learning, when it was used to introduce knowledge of science, Liang did not look on it as a teaching device similar to mechanical memorisation. In his proposal, a class to study texts in question-answer format did not require students to memorise but to understand. Similarly, in his instruction on teaching methods used in his Sandeng School, Zhong Tianwei clearly stated that Western methods should be applied to the teaching of Chinese subjects, so as to correct the old teaching method that required students to memorise texts without understanding them first, and that rote learning should be emphasised in teaching English, as spelling was important and required memorisation. Here Zhong pointed to a necessary balance between the emphases on the ability to understand and on memorisation, according to the subjects concerned.[119]

The emphasis on the memorising of Confucian classics in the 1904 regulations was associated with Zhang Zhidong's vision of a new Chinese education. In the course of revising the 1902 draft, Zhang adopted Western elements from Japanese sources which, in his understanding, had already resolved the *ti-yong* problem.[120] Although Liang claimed that his synthesis was different from Zhang's, as he aimed to create a new Chinese thought rather than only adopting some Western techniques, his approach, like that of other reformers before 1898, was limited by the second-hand nature of his information about the West. This limitation, as Sally Borthwick points out, in many cases inevitably led these reformers to "a simplistic and one-dimensional view of the operations of Western society." For instance, they were not able to analyse whether mass literacy was "the cause, concomitant, or production of industrialization." Nor could they see "flaws in nineteenth-century industrialization," such as "child labor in British factories."[121] However, China's problems at the time perhaps only allowed these reformers to pay attention to what they could use in their arguments for China's educational reform and to finding a resolution for China's crisis. The examples of Prussia and Japan convinced both reformers and policy makers (such as Zhang Zhidong) that universal education was essential to China's progress. Also, during his exile in Japan, Liang's admiration of Japanese achievements in modernisation grew. At this point, Liang's synthesis did not conflict with Zhang's borrowing from Japan in the making of the 1904 regulations. Perhaps both believed, or at least hoped, that a system combining Confucianism with Western elements would work for China, since it had already worked for Japan. Above all, the 1904 regulations bore the great imprints not only of Zhang Zhidong's ideas, but also of the intellectual efforts of the late nineteenth century, some of which were reflected in Liang's proposed reforms of education for children. Although the achievement of Protestant missionaries in the promotion of secular education in China was not acknowledged in the 1904 regulations, missionaries' science textbooks were directly adopted as some of the official teaching manuals for new schools.

ᐁ Conclusion ᐁ

Children in pre-modern China were valued because they symbolized the future. Many symbolic children in New Year's pictures and woodcuts were also indicative of the position of children in Chinese culture. The old saying, "More children will bring people more fortune" (*duozi duofu*), to a certain extent reveals both elite and conventional perceptions: symbolic children, characterised by youth, innocence, resilience and freshness, represented prosperity, good luck and people's aspirations.

In reality, children were indeed perceived in various ways, which were indicative of the adult world's expectations for them. To translate these expectations into reality, and to bridge the world of childhood and adulthood, education had became the sole means of achieving these goals. The significance of children to a family lay firstly in carrying on the family line, then in honouring their ancestors and finally in changing the social status of the family. No matter how poor a family was, poverty could never prevent parents from dreaming of a brilliant future for their children, and they were willing to labour hard to give their children an education — the only way, in a Confucian society, for poor families to climb the social ladder. Children were the future subjects of the empire, their obedience to the emperor was more important than anything else, and education was employed as an instrument to inculcate it. In Confucian idealism, the child was the adult of the future, and education for children therefore concentrated on preparation for becoming adult. The intellectual efforts made to shape the ideal child were actually an investment in the ideal adult, who would be the basic constitutent of an ideal society. The content of primers in late imperial China represented all these perspectives, and indicates that education was the only means adults could use to try to improve their prospects for the future in pre-modern China.

The notion that children symbolised the future originated in the early Chinese concept of man in which children's imperfection and incapability were not perceived as limitations but potential for developing into full human beings. However, ancient philosophers were deeply divided as to what human nature was. In Mencius' view, the imperfection and incapability of the child were related to innocence, so human nature was good. Xun Zi held the opposite opinion. Nevertheless, both schools believed that the power of *xi*, which was identified as environment and education, could transform the bad to the good, and allow human beings to grow out of their imperfections. This image of human potential was well expressed in primers, where children were instructed to achieve total moral purification in the process of growing to adulthood.

Ancient Chinese philosophers understood that moral cultivation involved a process of personal and social integration. It appears, however, that scholars before and during the Han had not constructed a theoretical framework to indicate how the biological child could be successfully transformed into the social child, although Han documents contained rich resources of ancient Chinese understanding of children and childhood. It was not until the Song that Neo-Confucianists began to work on a child-rearing formula. This fact may allow some historians plausibly to contend that Chinese childhood was first discovered in the Song. The discussions of the early Chinese concept of man and of Han primers in this study, however, have shown that the child and childhood were explained either in medical terms or from a philosophical perspective. Song Neo-Confucian contributions to the Chinese conceptions of children and childhood lay in their synthesis of the views of children expressed by their predecessors and the clear version they drew of what the ideal child ought to be. To put their version into practice, Neo-Confucian educators gave detailed instructions as to how to regulate the relationship between parents and children.

In Neo-Confucian metaphysics, the bond between the child and its parents was a natural one that could not be broken. This understanding originated from the *Xiaojing*, which says that the child owed its life to its parents, so it had no right to damage any part of its own body, not even skin and hair. More importantly, the child was obliged to do everything it could to repay its parents. This simple but fundamental principle was at the core of the virtue of filial piety. Examples of dutiful sons depicted in primers provided children with clear instruction about how to practise this virtue.

Song Neo-Confucian educators further elaborated on this system of filial piety. In their view, man, Heaven and Earth were integrated into one body in which a man was considered a son of Heaven and Earth, and thus the relationship between a father and a son, and between a ruler and a minister were both ruled by the Principle of Nature. It was under this principle that the child had no right to disobey its parents even if its parents were clearly in the wrong. Meanwhile, the authority of the father as the head of the family was seen as an echo of the sovereignty of the emperor. In this context, ritual behaviour in the service of parents was designed in accordance with the demands of the social system, and filial piety was actually the index of government authority and social order.

To modern minds, Confucian views of the relationship between children and parents gave too much emphasis to the power of the parents over their children, and children had no choice but to obey their parents. This, however, was only one perspective of Confucian approaches to human relationships. Unlike modern societies where children's rights are protected by laws, pre-modern Chinese employed the Principle of Nature to declare the rights and power of parents over their children on the one hand; but on the other hand, parents' responsibilities were also clearly stated to regulate the natural relation of children and parents.

Traditionally, Chinese childhood was divided into two phases: from conception to seven *sui* and then from eight *sui* to becoming an adult. The first period was closely associated with family education, and there the role of parents in the child's social and moral development was overwhelmingly decisive. The thesis of "foetal education" was promoted to urge the pregnant mother not to come into contact with evil forces, which were believed to affect the foetus in the womb. After the birth, since its parents and its family surroundings were the child's first social encounters, the parents were obliged to make sure that the child lived in a proper environment. The *xi* theory and illustrative stories, such as Mencius' mother moving house three times, highlight the significance of parental choice in ensuring the right environment for the child's development. Above all, it was parents themselves who had to set examples for their children, as in Confucian theory parents were the first teachers the child had in its life. Formal education centred on the second period of childhood. It was the parents' responsibility, as stipulated in *The Trimetrical Classic*, to provide children with a sound education.

Correlating with the conception that the child was the adult of the future, education in Neo-Confucian theory was divided into two stages: *xiaoxue* and *daxue*. But the lack of a clear definition between these two stages of learning pointed to the Song Neo-Confucian educators' eagerness to expedite the child's maturing process. According to their theory, adulthood was not marked by ages but by moral qualities which could only be achieved through practising Confucian rituals in self-cultivation. Although Neo-Confucian theory did not deny the existence of the child's traits, childish behaviour and characteristics were only acknowledged in order to support Neo-Confucian educators' anxiety about the child's moral well-being. In this context, education at elementary level was to help children to be rid of those childish traits, and the earlier the better. Under the shadow of this theory, the child's right to play was discouraged in formal education.

Song Neo-Confucian concerns about children and their views of the function of education were philosophical and conceptual. Ming-Qing educational theory was developed within this framework but seemed to be more practical and conventional. The school of Wang Yangming in particular represented a significant change in attitudes towards the child's traits. In Wang Yangming's approach, the recognition of children's special characteristics and acceptance of childish traits were an integral part of education. With this significant alteration, Wang Yangming also advocated the use of music and educational play in teaching practice. Although Wang Yangming's proposals did not change the basic features of traditional Chinese education in the late Ming and the Qing period, they at least signalled a relatively liberal attitude to children before Western ideas were introduced into China.

At the same time, Ming-Qing scholar-officials were concerned more about children and the well-being of the whole of society. As shown in Ming-Qing primers and scholarly writings, Confucian teachings were translated into conventional beliefs through the use of the colloquial language and popular literature. This can be seen as a Confucian endeavour to transmit Confucian teachings to a lower layer of society, and education in a broader sense became more accessible. In attempting to make basic education compulsory for everyone, Ming-Qing scholar-officials re-defined the concept of "children" on the basis of the education they received. In their theory and practice, the child's moral well-being was not a metaphysical discovery of the "true self" but was directly linked with the maintenance of social order.

The above outline of what the ideal child ought to be, how the ideal education could shape the ideal child and then construct a society of high moral standard was only a theoretical design, and education in practice appeared to be more complex and practical. From the Han to the Qing, elementary schooling basically followed the stages designated in the *Record of Rites*, and educators all agreed that the purpose of education was to transform the biological child into the social child. However, because of myths about the human body before and during the Han, fact and fiction became confused in historical documents, and precocious children described in the Han writings were a reflection of this confusion between man and divine power. Nevertheless, Han education, focusing on mastery of characters and Confucian classics, seemed very pragmatic, and most precocious children were measured against their educational achievements. Both Han primers and other documents indicate that Han children carried the burden of fulfillings their parents' aspirations by entering officialdom as early as possible. This also became one of the main tasks of Han elementary education. From this point we may argue that a child's precocity in the Han represented a utilitarian connection between children and the future.

The establishment of the civil service examination system in the Tang appeared to promote this connection, but the importance of literary composition broadened the definition of the concept of the *shi*, in which not only Confucian classics but also poetry became essential elements of education. Therefore, the criteria for a child's precocity altered along with this change; and instead of emphasising preternetural abilities, studying hard for earlier success in the examinations became the priority in parents' ambitions for their children.

Song Neo-Confucian educators launched a campaign for the

revival of the original Confucian education so as to shift the focus of education from the pursuit of literary composition to moral cultivation. Their view was that learning was for the sake of the self, and elementary education should nourish and mould children's personalities at an early age. Therefore, an essential component of Neo-Confucian primers was the prescription of ritualised behaviour patterns for children, who were encouraged to pursue moral transcendence rather than success in the civil service examinations. However, the temptations of officialdom and emolument were hard to resist. As is well reflected in the primers, the aim and content of education in late imperial China were characterised by a pursuit both of Neo-Confucian moral cultivation and of success in the civil service examinations.

In brief, this study has traced Chinese views of childhood through an analysis of primers circulated in the late imperial period. The term "a Confucian outlook on childhood," defined broadly, might be too generalised to characterise what was presented in these primers, but it at least indicates the elite perception of children and intellectual efforts to shape the ideal child through integrating literacy skills with moral instruction. The case of Qing evidential scholarship well illustrates this point.

By emphasising the Chinese written language as a medium to convey Confucian teaching, Qing evidential scholars inherited and developed both Han and Song scholarly traditions in which the meaning and the use of language were employed to transmit Confucian moral ethics, although these three schools of thought might have differed in their approaches to the understanding of the essentials of Confucianism. The integration of language teaching with moral instruction characterised the content of primers in late imperial China and underlay the main task of elementary education: basic training in literacy skills and "good manners." The continued dominance of this approach may account for the fact that the content of Chinese textbooks did not change greatly over the centuries.

It was not until the late nineteenth century that this time-honoured approach to the education of children was seriously challenged. This challenge was partly attributed to the legacy of the seventeenth-century thinkers, which strongly advocated a change of attitude towards the use of literacy and numeracy skills. Although some elements of Western knowledge were incorporated into the thesis of "practical learning," the seventeenth-century intellectual trends failed to cause a sharp break with tradition in China, and the structure of knowledge remained balanced between book-learning and self-cultivation and pre-occupied with the moral well-being of society. From the Opium War onward, Western military weapons, technology, practical learning, and economic and political systems became much stronger influences than the Western religious and scientific knowledge which had been introduced by the Jesuits in the late Ming and early Qing. In the face of the Western threat, forward-looking Chinese scholar-officials became aware of the necessity for reform as well as for borrowing Western technology. Lin Shu's primer and Liang Qichao's educational ideas on the eve of the 1898 Reform reflected the experiences of the generation of intellectuals who received a Confucian education as children, and then re-appraised this education by employing their newly acquired Western ideas and values. The year 1895 marked the start of this intellectual search for an alternative education for children. In both Lin Shu's primer and Liang's views of education, the significance of providing children with a modern education was highlighted in the context of China's struggle for survival in a social Darwinian sense; and the attributes of children were recognised through a better understanding of brain power and its potential for the improvement of the Chinese race. This is made clear in Liang Qichao's accusation that China ruined young children: "Both girls and boys were harmed at an early age. Girls were physically ruined as they were forced to bind their feet, while boys were intellectually ruined as their brains were injured by [mechanical memorisation]."[1] Children were ruined, and therefore so was China. Liang's charge may be too emotional, but the intellectual milieu reflected in his remarks signalled the imminent end of traditional Chinese education and the birth of a modern school system.

⌒ Notes ⌒

Foreword

1. William Theodore de Bary, "Education in Premodern East Asia," in *Confucian Traditions in East Asian Modernity*, edited by Tu Weiming (Cambridge, Mass.: Harvard University Press, 1996), pp. 28–29.
2. William Theodore de Bary, "Education in Premodern East Asia," p. 32.
3. Li Bingde, "A Brief Overview of Sino-Western Exchange Past and Present," in *Knowledge Across Cultures: A Contribution to Dialogue among Civiilzations*, edited by R. Hayhoe and J. Pan (Hong Kong: Comparative Education Research Centre, University of Hong Kong, 2001), p. 291.

Introduction

1. Aries's work, *L'Enfant et la vie familiale sous l'ancien régime* (Paris, 1960), was translated into English from French by R. Baldick, as *Centuries of Childhood* (London: Cape, 1962).
2. For a detailed and critical review of the literature on the history of childhood in the West, see Linda A. Pollock, *Forgotten Children: Parent-Child Relations from 1500 to 1900* (Cambridge, England and New York: Cambridge University Press, 1983), Chapters 1 and 2. Also A. Wilson, "The Infancy of the History of Childhood: An Appraisal of Philippe Aries," *History and Theory*, 19 (1980), pp. 132–154; and Shulamith Shahar, *Childhood in the Middle Ages* (London and New York: Routledge, 1990).
3. Chris Jenks, "Introduction" to *The Sociology of Childhood, Essential Readings*, edited by Chris Jenks (London: Batsford Academic and Educational Ltd., 1982), p. 23.
4. Such as Linda A. Pollock, *Forgotten Children*; David Hunt, *Parents and Children in History* (New York: Basic Books, 1970).
5. Such as Lawrence Stone, *The Family, Sex and Marriage in England 1500–1800* (London: Weidenfeld & Nicolson, 1977); Michael Anderson, *Approaches to the History of the Western Family, 1500–1914* (London: Macmillan Press, 1980).
6. Such as Nicholas Orme, *English Schools in the Middle Ages* (London: Methuen, 1973), and his *From Childhood to Chivalry: The Education of the English Kings and Aristocracy, 1066–1530* (London: Methuen, 1984). In Shahar's *Childhood*

in the Middle Ages, from Chapter Eight to Chapter Twelve, education in the
second stage of childhood, and education for specific purposes such as for
service in the secular church and in the monastery, and education in the
nobility, urban society and peasantry are all well discussed.

7. Lee made this claim in his review of *Chinese Views of Childhood*, edited by Ann
    Kinney (Honolulu: University of Hawaii Press, 1995). See Lee's review
    article, *China Review International*, 4.2 (1997), pp. 454–457. Lee's own article
    on Song children's education is a chapter in *Kultur, Begriff und Wort in China
    und Japan*, edited by Sigrid Paul (Berlin: Dieter Reimer, 1984), pp. 159–189.

8. Ann Kinney, "Dyed Silk: Han Notions of the Moral Development of
    Children," in *Chinese Views of Childhood*, p. 17.

9. Thomas Lee's book review of *Chinese Views of Childhood*, *China Review
    International*, pp. 457, 456.

10. David Johnson, "Communication, Class, and Consciousness in Late
    Imperial China," in *Popular Culture in Late Imperial China*, edited by David
    Johnson, Andrew Nathan and Evelyn Rawski (Berkeley: University of
    California Press, 1985), p. 46.

11. David Johnson, "Communication, Class, and Consciousness in Late
    Imperial China," p. 36; Evelyn Rawski, *Education and Popular Literacy in
    Ch'ing China* (Ann Arbor: The University of Michigan Press, 1979), p. 1.

12. David Johnson, "Communication, Class, and Consciousness in Late
    Imperial China," p. 36.

13. Evelyn Rawski, *Education and Popular Literacy in Ch'ing China*, pp. 2–3, 8–9,
    144.

14. David Johnson, "Communication, Class, and Consciousness in Late
    Imperial China," p. 47.

15. David Johnson, "Communication, Class, and Consciousness in Late
    Imperial China," pp. 46–47.

16. Girls in pre-modern China never had an opportunity to go to school, as
    formal education was not open to girls. A few girls did learn to read and
    write, but the educational channels for them differed and were separated
    from those for boys. The content of female education focused on ritual,
    virtues and various rules designed especially for women. In terms of
    textbooks, there was a series of special primers for females, such as *The
    Female Trimetrical Classic* (*Nü sanzi jing*) and *The Female Analects* (*Nü lunyu*). In
    this study the female role is mentioned in the discussion of the child from
    birth to maturity, yet female children and their education are not covered in
    depth as this is another research topic in itself, and there are research works
    focusing on female education in particular, such as Dorothy Ko's *Teachers of
    the Inner Chambers: Women and Culture in China, 1573–1722* (Stanford:
    Stanford University Press, 1994); Susan Mann, "The Education of Daughters
    in the Mid-Ch'ing Period," in *Education and Society in Late Imperial China*,

edited by Benjamin Elman and Alexander Woodside (Berkeley: University of California Press, 1994), pp. 19–49. Also in her work on women and virtue in the period of the Warring States and the Han dynasty, Lisa Raphals has a chapter focusing on instructional texts for women. See Lisa Raphals, *Sharing the Light* (New York: State University of New York Press, 1998), pp. 235–257.

17. See Evelyn Rawski, *Education and Popular Literacy in Ch'ing China*, Chapter Six.

18. For instance, in *Neo-Confucian Education: The Formative Stage* (edited by William Theodore de Bary and John Chaffee; Berkeley: University of California Press, 1989), scholars have analysed many important developments in aspects of educating children in the Tang and Song; the Song Neo-Confucian treatises are examined to demonstrate to what extent they had an impact on the basic format of education in the later imperial period. And Evelyn Rawski's *Education and Popular Literacy in Ch'ing China* studies Chinese elementary education in the Qing with a focus on the role of literacy in China's path to modernisation.

19. Zhang Zhigong, *Chuantong yuwen jiaoyu chutan* (A Preliminary Research on Traditional Language Teaching) (Shanghai: Shanghai jiaoyu chubanshe, 1962).

20. Nevertheless, the information supplied in Zhang's book is well absorbed in Evelyn Rawski's research.

21. Consequently, in China's current book market these reprinted primers overlap each other in different collections with such titles as the *Mengxue quanshu* (A Full Collection of Primers) and the *Chuantong mengxueshu jicheng* (A Comprehensive Collection of Traditional Primers).

22. Christine Nguyen Tri has a good bibliographical essay on the reprinting of Chinese primers. See C. N. Tri, "La Vogue des Manuels d'Enseignement Elementaire Traditionnels en RPC: naissance d'une recherche, retour de la morale confucéenne ou manipulation politique?" *Revue Bibliographique de Sinologie*, 13 (1995), pp. 35–46.

23. The foreword by C. John Sommerville to *Chinese Views of Childhood*, p. xi.

24. Thomas Lee's book review of *Chinese Views of Childhood*, pp. 454–455.

25. Lu Xun, *Selected Works*, translated by Yang Xianyi and Gladys Yang (Beijing: Foreign Language Press, 1980), vol. 2, pp. 26–28, 56–71. For a study of Lu Xun's criticism of traditional Chinese attitudes to children and his contribution to creating a new type of literature for children, see Mary Ann Farquhar, *Children's Literature in China: From Lu Xun to Mao Zedong* (Armonk, New York and London: M. E. Sharpe, 1999), Chapter Two.

26. See Chow Tse-tung, *The May Fourth Movement: Intellectual Revolution in Modern China* (Cambridge, Mass.: Harvard University Press, 1960).

27. See Jon Saari, *Legacies of Childhood: Growing up Chinese in a Time of Crisis, 1890–1920* (Cambridge, Mass. and London: Harvard University Press, 1990).

Chapter 1

1. L. C. Hopkins, "Archaic Sons and Grandsons, A Study of a Chinese Complication Complex," *The Journal of the Royal Asiatic Society*, 1934, p. 66.

2. In Chinese the word *qiang* stands for the baby carrier which was 1 *chi* 2 *cun* long and 8 *cun* wide — 1 Chinese *chi* is 1 foot or English measure, 0.3581 metres; *cun*, Chinese inches, 10 *cun* is 1 foot. The size quoted here is from the *Shiji zhengyi* (*Orthodox Interpretations of Records of the Historian*), ESWS, vol. 1, p. 323.

   The *bao* characters refer to clothes for wrapping and covering the newborn's body. Both characters bear either a radical *si* (silk) or *yi* (clothes in general). Yet these two *bao* characters can also be substituted by the word *bao* with a radical *ren* (person), which in its earlier form looks like an infant in its long skirt and jacket [see Dai Tong, *Liu shu gu* (Six Categories of Characters Elucidated) (Xishu: Li Dingyuan shizhu zhai edition, 1784), 9. 1b]; or its two side strokes can be seen as the indication of swaddling clothes. Based on this interpretation of its earlier form, the word *bao* with the radical *ren* appears to illustrate "the disguise of the infant in its protective wrappings" (L. C. Hopkins, "Archaic Sons and Grandsons," p. 60).

3. The word 抱 is also pronounced *bao* but with a different tone. The character with a radical indicating hands originally meant "carry" and "cuddle." The meaning of infancy was generated partly from its phonetic sharing with the *bao* characters (緥, 褓, 保) with the radicals of silk, cloth and person, so all these characters were often used interchangeably. For an example of the word 抱 used to refer to infancy, see *Hanshu* (History of the Former Han Dynasty), ESWS, vol. 1, p. 576.

4. Dai De, *Da Dai Liji jiegu* (*Record of Rites* by the elder Dai), commentated by Wang Pingzhen (Beijing: Zhonghua shuju, 1983), p. 251.

5. This was recorded in volume eight of the *Essentials of Family Health and Child Birth* (*Weisheng jiabao chanke bieyao*), by Zhu Duanzhang (fl. 1174–1189), a magistrate of Jiangxi in the Southen Song (1127–1278). According to the preface to the 1887 edition, Zhu Duanzhang was not a doctor but a magistrate devoted to charity work. He compiled several medical works which preserved many valuable earlier medical writings. See Zhu Duanzhang, *Weisheng jiabao chanke beiyao* (1184; 1887 reprint, CSJC), p. 113.

6. Ronald S. Illingworth, *The Development of the Infant and Young Child* (7th ed.; Edinburgh, London and New York: Churchill Livingstone, 1980), pp. 120–123.

7. This view was clearly expressed in the *Prescriptions for Children's Health* (*Xiao'er weisheng zongwei lunfang*), a medical work produced in the Song and collected in the *Siku quanshu*; yet its author is unknown. The other title of the book is *A Complete Work on Children's Health* (*Bao you daquan*). There is a paragraph about the stages of the development of the infant, which is exactly the same as

the quotation from Zhu Duanzhang's work, but with some extra words emphasising the importance of teaching infants these basic skills on time. See *Xiao'er weisheng zongwei fanglun* (*Siku quanshu* edition), p. 12.

8. *Qi* in traditional Chinese medical theory "named the original, primordial sources of life energy." See Charlotte Furth, *A Flourishing Yin: Gender in China's Medical History, 960–1665* (Berkeley and London: University of California Press, 1999), p. 28.

9. *Huangdi neijing, Suwen* (Basic Questions of The Yellow Emperor's Classic of Internal Medicine), ESEZ, p. 875.

10. *Huang Ti Nei Ching Su Wen, The Yellow Emperor's Classic of Internal Medicine*, translated with an introduction by Ilza Veith (Berkeley: University of California Press, 1966), p. 9. For a brief discussion of the authorship and the age of this medical classic, see pp. 4–9.

11. Ernest H. Watson and George H. Lowrey, *Growth and Development of Children* (2nd ed.; Chicago: The Year Book Publishers, 1958), p. 292.

12. The Chinese word for age is *sui*. Here one has to bear in mind that the Chinese way of calculating age differs from the Western method. The Chinese considered that the child entered its first year at the time of birth and thereafter each lunar new year added a year to its age. For example, seven *sui* was roughly between five and six in Western terms. For a brief explanation of *sui* in English, see Charlotte Furth, *A Flourishing Yin: Gender in China's Medical History, 960–1665*, p. 45 (ft. 18).

13. For instance, the terms *shengchi* referring to the eruption of primary teeth, and *huichi*, or *chen*, or *tiao* to the eruption of permanent teeth, were all used in literature or historical documents to stand for children at this age. See Dai De, *Da Dai Liji*, p. 251; Xu Shen, *Shuowen jiezi zhu* (Explanations of Words and Characters), commentated by Duan Yucai (1815; reprint, Shanghai: Guji chubanshe, 1981), p. 78; and Han Ying, *Hanshi waizhuan* (Han Ying's Exoteric Commentary on the *Book of Songs*), SBCK, 1.7.

14. Liu Xi, *Shiming* (Explaining Names), commentated by Wang Xianqian (1896; reprint, Shanghai: Guji chubanshe, 1984), p. 147.

15. See Chen Zizhan, *Shijing zhijie* (Commentaries on the *Book of Songs*) (Shanghai: Fudan University Press, 1983), vol. 2, pp. 986–987.

16. For a discussion of the medical rituals for newborns in ancient China, see Charlotte Furth, "Concepts of Pregnancy, Childbirth, and Infancy in Ch'ing Dynasty China," *Journal of Asian Studies*, 46.1 (1987), p. 20.

17. The earliest use of the term to refer to childhood is perhaps in the *Book of Songs* (*Shijing*), e.g. "How happy we were, our hair in tufts; how fondly we talked and laughed." See Chen Zizhan, *Shijing zhijie*, vol. 1, p. 183. English translation from *Selections from the "Book of Songs,"* translated by Yang Xianyi, Gladys Yang and Hu Shiguang (Beijing: Panda Books, 1983), p. 34.

18. For example the terms *danmao* and *tiao*, portraying the child's hair covering

its forehead and just above its eyebrows and ears. The unshaven hair in ancient times was called *duo*, and then the compounds *tiaoduo, duojian* and *tiaofa* were all created to refer to childhood. Since the growth of hair and appearance of teeth were seen as important indicators of the child's development, the words *tiao* and *chen* were combined into one word, meaning childhood.

19. Philippe Aries, *Centuries of Childhood*, pp. 33–49.

20. Linda A. Pollock, *Forgotten Children: Parent-Child Relations from 1500 to 1900*, pp. 46–49.

21. There is an old but well presented discussion about the different systems of perspective employed in Western and Chinese painting in *Chinese Painters*, by Raphael Petrucci, translated by Frances Seaver, with a biographical note by Laurence Binyon (New York: Brentano's Publishers, 1920), chapter II.

22. See Jia Yi, *Xinshu* (New Works), ESEZ, p. 754.

23. *Guoyu* (Discourses of the States), SBCK, p. 94.

24. Hong Mai, *Rongzhai suibi* (Jottings from Rongzhai Studio) (Jilin: Wenshi chubanshe, 1994), p. 87.

25. Liu An, *Huainan zi* (The Huainan Master), ESEZ, p. 1252.

26. For a discussion of the possibility of a unique trait in man in early Chinese philosophy, see Donald J. Munro, *The Concept of Man in Early China* (Stanford: Stanford University Press, 1969), pp. 14, 62–73.

27. *Xun Zi*, SBCK, 16.1b.

28. *Huangdi neijing, Suwen*, ESEZ., p. 889; Ilza Veith, *Huang Ti Nei Ching Su Wen, The Yellow Emperor's Classic of Internal Medicine*, p. 145.

29. *Meng Zi*, 2A:6; English translation from W. A. C. H. Dobson, *Mencius* (Toronto: University of Toronto Press, 1963), p. 132.

30. *Meng Zi*, 6A:6; Dobson, *Mencius*, p. 111.

31. *Xun Zi jianshi* (Commentaries on *Xun Zi*), commentated by Liang Qixiong (1955; reprint, Beijing: Zhonghua shuju, 1983), pp. 309–310; for English translation, see Burton Watson, *Hsün Tzu* (New York: Columbia University Press, 1963), p. 142.

32. *Xun Zi jianshi*, p. 313. Burton Watson, *Hsün Tzu*, pp. 142–143.

33. *Xun Zi jianshi*, p. 310. Burton Watson, *Hsün Tzu*, p. 140.

34. Fang Yizhi, *Wuli xiaoshi* (Small Encyclopedia of the Principles of Things) (1666; reprint, Yuzhai, 1884), 3.10b.

35. Wang Fuzhi, *Du Sishu daquan shuo* (On "The Complete Commentary on the Four Books") (Beijing: Zhonghua shuju, 1975), pp. 458–459.

36. Wang Fuzhi, *Shangshu yanyi* (Elaborating the Meaning of the *Book of Documents*) (Beijing: Zhonghua shuju, 1976), p. 63.

37. Dianne Nixon and Katy Gould, *Emerging: Child Development in the First Three Years* (Wentworth Falls, N.S.W.: Social Science Press, 1996), p. 13.

38. *Meng Zi*, 4B:12; Dobson, *Mencius*, p. 188.

39. *Meng Zi*, 6A:6; Dobson, *Mencius*, p. 113.
40. *Meng Zi*, 6A:2.; Dobson, *Mencius*, pp. 110–111.
41. *Xun Zi jianshi*, p. 327; Watson, *Hsün Tzu*, p. 157.
42. *Xun Zi jianshi*, p. 253; Watson, *Hsün Tzu*, p. 89.
43. *Xun Zi jianshi*, p. 2; Watson, *Hsün Tzu*, p. 15.
44. As the source of a perfume, this kind of root is supposed to have a pleasant smell, but in Xun Zi's metaphor, being soaked in urine results in an unpleasant smell.
45. *Xun Zi jianshi*, p. 3; Watson, *Hsün Tzu*, pp. 16–17.
46. For the story of the mother of King of Wen, see Liu Xiang (79–8 B.C.), *Lienü zhuan* (Biographies of Women), enlarged by Mao Kun and commentated by Peng Yang with the title *Gujin lienü zhuan pinglin* (Past and Present Commentaries on *Lienü zhuan*), 1.11b. Collected in *Zhongguo gudai banhua congkan erbian* (The Collection of Traditional Chinese Woodcuts, second series) (Shanghai: Guji chubanshe, 1994), vol. 4, p. 50. For the story of the mother of King of Cheng, see Jia Yi, *Xinshu*, ESEZ, p. 762. For the story of the mother of Mencius, see Han Ying, *Hanshi waizhuan*, SBCK, 9.2b.
47. *Huangdi neijing, Suwen*, ESEZ, p. 880.
48. They are the heart, the spleen, the lungs, the liver and the kidneys.
49. There are five mental functions: the divine spirit (*shen*), the animal spirits (*po*), the soul and the spiritual faculties (*hun*), ideas and opinions (*yi*), will power and ambition (*zhi*).
50. *Huangdi neijing, Suwen*, ESEZ, p. 881. Ilza Veith, *Huang Ti Nei Ching Su Wen, The Yellow Emperor's Classic of Internal Medicine*, pp. 117, 208.
51. Zhu Zhenheng, *Gezhi yulun* (More on "Natural Knowledge" of Phenomena), CSJC, p. 8. In present-day society, pregnant women are told of the possible impact on the foetus if they drink and smoke, or worst of all use drugs. At this point, the ancient Chinese advice on "foetal poison" is similar to this warning.
52. Zhang Hua (232–300), *Bo wu zhi* (An Encyclopaedic Book) (Shanghai: Guji chubanshe, 1990), pp. 34–35.
53. In her *Technology and Gender*, apart from some discussion of traditional Chinese theories of *qi*, the Five Elements, and *yin* and *yang* (e.g. pp. 302–303), Francesca Bray has a brief introduction to various ideas about physical heredity in late imperial China. Some of these ideas laid emphasis on the father's *qi* in the infant's make-up, while the mother's contribution to the child's constitution was well acknowledged. See Francesca Bray, *Technology and Gender* (Berkeley: University of California Press, 1997), pp. 344–345. For a discussion of breast milk, the mother's responsibility and the role of wet nurses in infant care, see Charlotte Furth, "Concepts of Pregnancy, Childbirth, and Infancy in Ch'ing Dynasty China," pp. 21–23.
54. Zhu Duanzhang, *Weisheng jiabao chanke beiyao*, p. 113.

55. For instance, *Zhulinsi nüke* (Medical Care for Women from the Bamboo Grove Temple) was first published in 1786 and contained exactly the same sentences. See "Zi yu" section, p. 29a.

56. See Charlotte Furth, "Concepts of Pregnancy, Childbirth, and Infancy in Ch'ing Dynasty China," p. 24.

57. Ronald S. Illingworth, *The Development of the Infant and Young Child*, p. 176.

58. Judith Rich Harris and Robert M. Liebert, *The Child: Development from Birth through Adolescence* (2nd ed.; Englewood Cliffs: Prentice-Hall, 1987), pp. 174–175.

59. J. Gavin Bremner, *Infancy* (2nd ed.; Oxford, UK; Cambridge, Mass.: Basil Blackwell, 1991), p. 42; also see Chapter 3 for a further discussion of perceptual development.

60. *Lunyu*, 17:2; English translation from James Legge, *The Chinese Classics* (Oxford: Clarendon Press, 1893), vol. 1, p. 318.

61. *Meng Zi*, 6A:7.

62. *Sanzi jing* (The Trimetrical Classic), collected in *Sanzi jing jikan* (Collected Versions of *The Trimetrical Classic*), edited by Lu Lin (Anhui: Jiaoyu chubanshe, 1994), p. 4.

63. *Huangdi Neijing, Lin Shu* (Mystical Gate), SBCK, 10.112.

64. *Meng Zi*, 6A:7; English translation is based on James Legge, *The Chinese Classics*, vol. 2, pp. 404–405.

65. Han Ying, *Hanshi waizhuan*, 3.24.

66. Han Ying, *Hanshi waizhuan*, 3.31.

67. Han Ying, *Hanshi waizhuan*, 5.45.

68. Han Ying, *Hanshi waizhuan*, 5.46.

69. See Wang Fuzhi, *Du Sishu daquan shuo*, section 7. For a thorough discussion of Wang Fuzhi's thought, see Alison Harley Black, *Man and Nature in the Philosophical Thought of Wang Fu-chih* (Seattle: University of Washington Press, 1989).

70. *Huang Zongxi quanji* (Complete Works of Huang Zongxi) (Zhejiang: Guji chubanshe, 1985), p. 138.

71. *Yan Yuan ji* (Collected Works of Yan Yuan) (Beijing: Zhonghua shuju, 1987), p. 29.

72. Han Ying, *Hanshi waizhuan*, 2.18–2.19.

73. Wang Fuzhi, *Du Sishu daquan shuo*, p. 469.

74. *Liji*, SSJZS, vol. 2, p. 1471.

75. *Liji*, SSJZS, vol. 2, p. 1471.

76. Liu Xi, *Shiming*, p. 146.

77. Liu Xi, *Shiming*, p. 146.

78. See Ann Waltner, "The Moral Status of the Child in Late Imperial China: Childhood in Ritual and in Law," *Social Research*, 53.4 (1986), pp. 679–680.

79. Liu Xi, *Shiming*, p. 146.
80. *Liji*, SSJZS, vol. 2, p. 1471.
81. *Huangdi neijing, Suwen*, ESEZ, p. 875.
82. Liu Xi, *Shiming*, p. 147.
83. Dai De, *Da Dai Liji jiegu*, p. 251.
84. Dai De, *Da Dai Liji jiegu*, p. 51.
85. *Jia Yi ji* (Collected Works of Jia Yi) (Shanghai: Renmin chubanshe, 1976), p. 91.
86. In the Zhou dynasty the imperial palace had *sanmu* or three mothers to nurture children. These "three mothers" actually referred to the concubines in the imperial palace who were selected either as *shi* or teachers who were in charge of the children's education, or as *cimu* or "kind mothers" who were supposed to take care of the children's needs, or as *baomu* whose duty was to nurse the children (*Liji*, SSJZS, vol. 2, p. 1469).

    However, *baomu* were not exclusive to the palace but were often hired by aristocratic families as early as in the Spring and Autumn Period. It was said that a young lady did not even try to escape from the house during a fire, as it was not proper for a lady to leave her inner chamber without the company of her *baomu* (See *Guliang zhuan*, SBCK, 9.65). Later the meaning of *baomu* was extended to refer to all women who nursed and looked after other people's children.
87. See Xu Shen, *Shuowen jiezi*, p. 763; and *Hanshu* (Beijing: Zhonghua Shuju, 1970), p. 1721.

Chapter 2

1. They were *Shizhou, Cangjie, Yuanli,* and *Boxue.* The *Shizhou* appeared in the Zhou dynasty while the other three emerged during the Qin dynasty. *Shizhou, cangjie, yuanli* and *boxue* were the first two characters in the books and were used as the titles, so it is impossible to translate these titles into English. The author of the *Shizhou* was unknown, but the others were said to have been composed by officials: the *Cangjie* in seven chapters was written by Li Si, the prime minister of the Qin; the *Yuanli* in six chapters was written by Zhao Gao, an official of the Qin; and the *Boxue* in seven chapters was written by Hu Mu, also an official of the Qin. See *Hanshu* (1970), p. 1721.
2. This new version of *Cangjie* had fifty-five chapters, each of which included sixty characters. In the regime of Emperor Wu (140–87 B.C.), Sima Xiangru (179–117 B.C.) compiled the *Fanjiang.* That no character appeared more than once differentiated this book from other books. The *Jijiu*, by Shi You, appeared in the reign of Emperor Yuan (49–33 B.C.). Later, Li Chang compiled the *Yuanshang* (32–7 B.C.). *Fanjiang* and *yuanshang*, as well as *xunzhuan, pangxi* in the following paragraphs, are all the first two characters in each book. See *Hanshu* (1970), p. 1721.

3. See Cheng Shunying, *Lianghan jiaoyu zhidu shi ziliao* (Documents of the Educational System in the Former and Later Han) (Beijing: Beijing Normal University Press, 1983), pp. 142–149.

4. Wang Chong, *Lunheng* (Doctrines Evaluated), with comments by Liu Pansui (Shanghai: Guji chubanshe, 1957), p. 580.

5. Cui Shi lived in the middle of the Later Han period. For details of his life, see Fan Ye, *Hou Hanshu* (History of the Later Han Dynasty) (Hong Kong: Zhonghua shuju, 1971), pp. 1725–1738.

6. See Cui Shi, *Simin yueling* (Monthly Calendar for the Four Classes of People) (Beijing: Zhonghua shuju, 1965), pp. 9, 60.

7. This was the figure given by Duan Yucai in his commentaries on the *Shuowen jiezi*, p. 760.

8. Xu Shen was said to have compiled the *Shuowen jiezi* in 100, yet the definite dates of Xu Shen's birth and death are unknown (see *Hou Hanshu*, p. 2588, for the detail of his life). The book was presented to Emperor An in 121 by Xu's son Xu Chong (dates unknown). See Xu Shen's "*Shuowen jiezi* xu" (Preface to *Shuowen jiezi*), and Xu Chong's "Shang *Shuowen jiezi* biao" (Memorial on the *Shuowen jiezi*) for further details. Some works on the history of Chinese philology and phonology also contain discussions about and introductions to this book, such as Hu Pu'an, *Zhongguo wenzixue shi* (A History of Chinese Philology) (1937; reprint, Shanghai: Shanghai shudian, 1984), vol. 1, pp. 39–43.

9. *Shuowen jiezi*, p. 760.

10. The eminent Han scholar Yang Xiong re-wrote the combined book *Cangjie* and retitled it *Xunzhuan*. Ban Gu recorded the implementation of this project, relating how in the middle of the Yuanshi reign-period (1–8) the emperor gathered together hundreds of scholars who were able to read and write characters, and ordered them to write down the characters which they knew. To comply with this order, Yang Xiong removed the repeated characters from the *Cangjie*, then adopted the characters which still had vitality and compiled the *Xunzhuan* as the continuation of the *Cangjie*, with eighty-nine chapters. Then Ban Gu himself added another thirteen chapters as the continuation of Yang's book. Thus, the book totals one hundred and two chapters, and no character appears more than once.

11. *Hanshu* (1970), p. 1721. Here the six Confucian classics referred to are the *Shi, Shu, Li, Yue, Yi* and *Chunqiu*. The *Lunyu* and the *Xiaojing* were not listed as Confucian classics in the Han, and the *Yue* did not survive. Therefore, in the Han dynasty there were only five Confucian classics. See *Hanshu* (1970), pp. 1720–1721; Pi Xirui, *Jingxue lishi* (A History of Classical Chinese Learning) (1907; reprint, Beijing: Zhonghua shuju, 1961), pp. 67–68; Wu Feng, *Zhongguo gudian wenxian xue* (Ancient Chinese Reference Books) (Jinan: Qilu shushe, 1982), pp. 52–53.

12. The term "archaic characters" here refers both to characters in archaic forms and those which were obsolete in everyday usage.

13. See *Hanshu* (1970), p. 1721.

14. See Cheng Shunying, *Liang Han jiaoyu zhidu shi ziliao*, pp. 149–150.

15. See Gu Yanwu, *Rizhi lu* (Daily Added Knowledge), with collation, punctuation and commentaries (Hunan: Yuelu shushe, 1994), p. 760.

16. See Ouyang Xiu and Song Qi, *Xin Tangshu* (New Tang History) (Beijing: Zhonghua shuju, 1975), p. 1162.

17. This connection can be seen in the Classics carved on stone (*shijing*), which first appeared at the end of the Han. In the Tang dynasty the process of officially establishing the nine Confucian classics also involved the process of editing and correcting each character in the canon. During the period 836–840, these nine Confucian classics were carved in stone as official publications. The intention was to standardize not only words, phrases and sentences, but also the style and the forms of characters in each classic; this was collectively named *shuxue*, and became part of an advanced level of education. See Liu Xu et al., *Jiu Tangshu* (Old Tang History) (Beijing: Zhonghua shuju, 1975), p. 571.

18. See *Da Tang liudian* (Six Groups of Statutes of the Great Tang Dynasty) (Guandong: Guangya shuju, 1893), 21.5a.

19. See Lu You, *Laoxue'an biji* (Jottings from Laoxue'an), CSJC, 2.20.

20. See Su Shi, *Dongpo zhilin* (Jottings of Su Shi) (Beijing: Zhonghua shuju, 1981), p. 47.

21. See Tuo Tuo, *Songshi* (Song History) (Beijing: Zhonghua shuju, 1982), vol. 11, pp. 3657–3663.

22. See Nai Deweng, *Ducheng jisheng* (Accounts of the Capital City) (Yangzhou: Yangzhou shiju, 1706), p. 14.

23. See Lu You, *Lu You ji* (Collected Works of Lu You) (Beijing: Zhonghua shuju, 1974), vol. 2, p. 632.

24. See Thomas H. C. Lee, "Life in the Schools of Sung China," *Journal of Asian Studies*, 37.1 (1977), p. 48.

25. See Cui Shi, *Simin yueling*, pp. 9, 60.

26. Hu Jizong, *Shuyan gushi* (Stories from Ancient Books) (1464; collected in *Hekeben leishu jichen*, or *Nako ku hon ruishi shusei* in Japanese, compiled by Nagasawa Kikuya; reprint, Shanghai: Guji chubanshe, 1990), vol. 11, p. 174.

27. See Wang Guowei (1877–1927), *Guantang jilin* (Collected Works of Wang Guowei) (Beijing: Zhonghua shuju, 1961), 21.4.

28. An incomplete copy of the preface to an early Tang (627–649) edition of the *Tuyuan ce*, by Du Sixian, was found in the Dunhuang caves. See Wang Guowei, *Guantang jilin*, 21.4.

29. See Chao Gongwu, *Junzhai dushu zhi* (Notes on Books from the Prefect's

Studio), (Haining, 1722), 14.16b–17a; and Lu You, *Jiannan shigao* (Poetry of Lu You) (Jigu ge edition), 25.7a–b.

30. The copies of the *Baijia xing* found at Dunhuang seem to suggest that the text was completed in the early Song. These earliest copies of the text are now kept in the Bibliothéque Nationale de France in Paris.

31. These popular texts are frequently mentioned and discussed in works on education, such as E. S. Rawski, *Education and Popular Literacy in Ch'ing China*, Chapter Six; Pei-yi Wu, "Education of Children in the Sung," and Thomas H. C. Lee, "Sung Schools and Education Before Chu Hsi," both in *Neo-Confucian Education*, edited by William Theodore de Bary and John W. Chaffee, pp. 307–324, 105–136.

32. In her study on the form and content of school education for children in the Lower Yangtze region in the late Ming and the early Qing periods, Angela Ki Che Leung interestingly provides detailed accounts of how young children were taught to learn basic characters by using various other means in addition to this series. See Angela Ki Che Leung, "Elementary Education in the Lower Yangtze Region in the Seventeenth and Eighteenth Centuries," in *Education and Society in Late Imperial China, 1600–1900*, edited by Benjamin Elman and Alexander Woodside (Berkeley: University of California Press, 1994), pp. 393–396.

33. Chinese scholars in the past all agreed that the author of *One Thousand Characters* was Zhou Xingsi. According to Gu Yanwu, however, there was another version of *One Thousand Characters* which was written by Xiao Zifan, although Xiao's version was lost long before the Sui dynasty. See Gu Yanwu's *Rizhi lu* (1994), p. 761.

34. Li Fang collected this story in his *Taiping guangji* (Wide Gleanings from the Taiping Era) (Beijing: Zhonghua shuju, 1961), but acknowledged that the story was originally recorded in Li Chuo's *Shangshu gushi*, CSJC, p. 13. For general information about Zhou's life, see Yao Silian, *Liang Shu* (Liang History) (Beijing: Zhonghua shuju, 1973), pp. 697–698; and Li Yanshou, *Nanshi* (History of the Southern Dynasties, 317–589) (Beijing: Zhonghua shuju, 1975), pp. 1779–1780.

35. See Lei Qiaoyun, *Dunhuang ertong wenxue* (Children's Literature in Dunhuang Materials) (Taiwan: Xuesheng shuju, 1985), p. 32.

36. See Wang Dingbao, *Tang zhiyan* (Collected Notes of the Tang Dynasty), SBBY, 10.10; also Yu Yue, *Chaxiangshi congchao* (Collected Works from the Fragrant-Teahouse) (Wuxia Chunzaitang, 1883), 9.5b.

37. Zhou Xingsi, *Qianzi wen*, collected in *Sanzi jing, Baijia xing, Qianzi wen* (hereafter cited as *San Bai Qian*) (Shanghai: Guji chubanshe, 1988), p. 127.

38. Zhou Xingsi, *Qianzi wen*, in *San Bai Qian*, p. 134.

39. See Yu Yue, *Chaxiangshi congchao*, 9.5b. James T. C. Liu, "The Classical Chinese Primer: Its Three-Characters Style and Authorship," *Journal of the*

American Oriental Society, 105.2 (1985), pp. 191–196. See also Pei-yi Wu, "Education of Children in the Sung," in *Neo-Confucian Education*, p. 321, n. 36.

40. See Zhang Binglin's preface to the revised *Sanzi jing*, in *San Bai Qian*, p. 97.

41. Nine of which now belong to the collection of the British Library in London while sixteen are held in the Bibliothéque Nationale de France in Paris.

42. For details of the text, see Lei Qiaoyun, *Dunhuang ertong wenxue*, pp. 44–55.

43. For details of authorship and editions of these four primers, see Xu Zi and Wang Xuemei, eds., *Mengxue yaoyi* (Essentials of Children's Books) (Shanxi: Jiaoyu chubanshe, 1991), p. 249.

44. Such as the *Zengding fameng sanzi jing* (Newly Enlarged and Edited *Trimetrical Classic*), written by Xu Yinfang (1832–1901) of the Qing.

45. Such as the *Sanzi jing jizhu yinshu* (*The Trimetrical Classic* with all Commentaries and Phonetic Guidance). The author of the book is unknown. According to Zhang Zhigong, there is a 1877 edition published by the Liushi Jiaojing Tang. See Zhang Zhigong, *Chuantong yuwen jiaoyu chutan*, p. 158.

46. Such as the *Sanzi jing zhutu* (*The Trimetrical Classic* with Illustrations and Commentaries) by Shang Zhaoyu of the late Qing. The primer was published by the Li Guangming zhuang in 1878.

47. There were the *Sanzi shijing Shangshu* (The *Book of Documents* in Three Characters and Carved on Stone) and the *Sanzi shijing Chunqiu* (*The Spring and Autumn Annals* in Three Characters and Carved on Stone). See Ma Guohan, *Yuhan shanfang jiyishu* (Lost Writings Restored in the Jade-Receptacle Studio) (Changsha: Langhuan guan, 1883), 63.1a–2a.

48. This primer will be further discussed in Chapter Three.

49. Such as *zhou* (a hat that soldiers wore in war in ancient times) and *wei* (stomach), *mu* (mother) and *wu* (do not).

50. See Zhang Zhigong, *Chuantong yuwen jiaoyu chutan*, p. 14.

51. *Zhouyi*, SSJZS, vol. 1, p. 20.

52. See Chao Gongwu, *Junzhai dushu zhi*, 14.26a.

53. The story originated in the *Jinshu* (History of the Jin), by Fang Xuanling, ESWS, pp. 1365, 1386–1387. For the original Chinese text, see *Mengqiu* composed by Li Han and commentated by Xu Ziguang (*Xuejin taoyuan* edition; Shanghai: Shangwu yinshuguan, 1922), p. 117. English translation, see Burton Watson, *Meng Ch'iu: Famous Episodes from Chinese History and Legend* (Tokyo, New York and San Francisco: Kodansha International, 1979), p. 19.

54. *Mengqiu*, p. 117; Burton Watson, *Meng Ch'iu: Famous Episodes from Chinese History and Legend*, p. 23.

55. Such as the phrase "Zhuge gulu," which tells the story of how, when Zhuge

Liang was a hermit in Nan Yang, Liu Bei visited his grass hut three times, consulting him on affairs of the time. *Mengqiu*, p. 120; Watson, *Meng Ch'iu: Famous Episodes from Chinese History and Legend*, p. 167.

56. Such as the phrase "Xiang Xiu wen di," which literally means "Xiang Xiu listens to a flute." Xiang Xiu (c. 227–272) was one of the ""Seven Sages of the Bamboo Grove." The four-character phrase actually refers to the story that Xiang Xiu wrote a *fu* (a form of rhyme-prose), entitled "Recalling Old Times" to express his recollection of his friendship with Ji Kang, who was particularly skilled at playing stringed instruments. See *Mengqiu*, p. 119; Watson, *Meng Ch'iu: Famous Episodes from Chinese History and Legend*, p. 87.

57. Burton Watson, *Meng Ch'iu: Famous Episodes from Chinese History and Legend*, p. 10.

58. See Chen Zhensun, *Zhizhai shulu jieti* (The Annotated Catalogue of the Upright-Studio) (Shanghai: Guji chubanshe, 1987), p. 427.

59. This type of book usually contains information about authors, publishers, editions and gives a brief introduction to the content of the book concerned.

60. Qian Zeng's record was re-documented by Ruan Yuan in his *Yanjingshi waiji* (Outer Collection of the Studying the Classics Studio) (*Wenxuan lou* edition, 1823), p. 13b.

61. Three other primers are: Fang Fengchen's *Mingwu mengqiu* (The Names and Descriptions of Things), Huang Jishan's *Shixue tiyao* (An Outline of Historiography), and Cheng Duanmeng and Cheng Ruoyong's *Xingli zixun* (Explanations of New-Confucian Terms). The title *Xiao sishu* indicates that it matches the *Four Classics*.

62. See *Songshi* (History of the Song), ESWS, p. 5811.

63. This primer is collected in *Yihai zhuchen* (Sea of Literature and Jewellery of the World), compiled by Wu Xinglan, supplemented by Qian Xifu (Jinshan: Qianshi shushixuan, 1850).

64. This textbook will be further discussed in Chapter Six.

65. Such as *Xu Mengqiu* which, according to Jiao Hong, was written by Shu Jin of the Song. See Jiao Hong, *Guoshi jingji zhi* (On Classics in Official History Books) (*Yueyatang congshu* edition, 1851), 2.64a.

66. This definition of *xiaoxue* and *daxue* originated from the *Book of Rites by the Elder Dai*, which reflected Han scholars' views on education. Some scholars of later generations used this documentary record as the ideal of Confucian education. See *Da Dai Liji jiegu*, p. 60. Also, see Wang Yinglin, *Kunxue jiwen* (Records of Knowledge Learned), SBCK, 5.11; and Wang Can (177–217), "Ru li lun" (On the Confucians and Officials), in *Wang Can jizhu* (Selected Works of Wang Can, with Commentaries) (Henan: Zhongzhou shuhuashe, 1984), p. 94.

67. The *shi* class in late imperial China consisted of people who had literary

qualifications, including those who participated and succeeded in the civil service examinations; those who failed to achieve any high degrees; and those who were not attracted by examination qualifications but were practitioners in teaching and academic activities. In the context of this book, the word *gentry* is used as one of translations of the Chinese term *shi*, but one has to bear in mind that this use of the term *gentry* differs from the concept and the usage of *gentry* in English history.

In seventeenth-century England, there were four orders of gentry. The first stratum was the baronets, the second the knights. Esquires were the third. These three ranks all had medieval and military origins. The lowest level of the gentry was a group which was distinguished from the yeomen or landowning farmers by the quality of gentility, "a distinction acquired principally by birth, education, and the wealth and leisure to follow gentlemen's pursuits" (Gordon Mingay, *The Gentry: The Rise and Fall of a Ruling Class*; London; New York: Longman, 1976, p. 3). The Chinese *shi* may have had some characteristics in common with this lowest level of English gentry, but it differed from the English gentry in many significant respects, such as its origins, methods of entry, links to land, and life style. Moreover, some of the English gentry were illiterate (see Franz Michael's introduction to Chang Chung-li's *The Chinese Gentry*; Seattle: University of Washington Press, 1955, p. xix), whereas a member of the Chinese *shi* class was unlikely to be illiterate. No matter whether a *shi* passed or failed in the civil service examinations, he had to be equipped with a high level of literacy skills.

68. D. Twitchett and John K. Fairbank, general eds., *The Cambridge History of China*, vol. 1: *The Ch'in and Han Empires, 221 B.C.–A.D. 220*, edited by D. Twitchett and Michael Loewe (Cambridge, England and New York: Cambridge University Press, 1986), p. 28.

69. Twitchett and Lowew, eds., *The Cambridge History of China*, vol. 1, p. 29.

70. For an explanation of "Six Confucian Classics" and "Five Classics," see note 11 above. For a further discussion, see Limin Bai, "Primers and Paradigms" (Ph.D. dissertation, La Trobe University, 1993), Chapter Four.

71. See Twitchett and Fairbank, general eds., *The Cambridge History of China*, vol. 3: *Sui and T'ang China, 589–906*, edited by D. Twitchett (Cambridge, England and New York: Cambridge University Press, 1979), pp. 8–22.

72. Twitchett, ed., *The Cambridge History of China*, vol. 3, p. 490.

73. See Zhu Xi, "*Daxue zhangju* xu" (Preface to "Commentary on *Great Learning*"), in *Zhuzi wenji* (Selected Works of Zhu Xi), CSJC, pp. 417–418.

74. See *Songshi*, p. 12769.

75. *Lunyu*, 19:12.

76. Tu Wei-ming has written a few papers on Confucian education, such as "The Sung Confucian Ideas of Education: A Background of Understanding," in *Neo-Confucian Education*, edited by W. T. de Bary and J. Chaffee, pp.

139–150; and "The Confucian Sage: Exemplar of Personal Knowledge," in *Saints and Virtues*, edited by John Stratton Hawley (University of California Press, 1987), pp. 73–86; also "The Confucian Perception of Adulthood," *Daedalus*, 105.2 (1976), pp. 109–123.

77. Zhu Xi, "*Daxue zhangju* xu," in *Zhuzi wenji*, CSJC, p. 417.

78. For a discussion of Zhu Xi's *Xiaoxue*, see M. Theress Kelleher, "Back to Basics: Chu Hsi's Elementary Learning (Hsiao-hsueh)," in *Neo-Confucian Education*, edited by W. T. de Bary and J. Chaffee, pp. 219–251.

79. *Xiaojing*, 1.

80. See *Er Cheng ji* (Collected Works of the Cheng Brothers) (Beijing: Zhonghua shuju, 1981), vol. 4, p. 183.

81. *Xiaojing*, 1.

82. *Lunyu*, 16:25.

83. *Quli*, SSJZS, p. 1233a; in Zhu Xi's *Xiaoxue jizhu* (Collected Commentaries on *Elementary Learning*), SBBY, 2.2b. Translation is based on James Legge's *Sacred Books of the East* (Delhi: Motilal Banarsidass, 1966), vol. xxvii, p. 67.

84. *Quli*, p. 1233a; *Xiaoxue jizhu*, SBBY, 2.12b; James Legge, *Sacred Books of the East*, vol. xxvii, p. 67.

85. *Quli*, p. 1238a; *Xiaoxue jizhu*, SBBY, 2.12b; James Legge, *Sacred Books of the East*, vol. xxvii, p. 70.

86. *Wangzhi*, SSJZS, p. 1347b; *Xiaoxue jizhu*, SBBY, 2.14a; James Legge, *Sacred Books of the East*, vol. vii, p. 244.

87. See Zhu Xi's preface to *Xiaoxue*, SBBY, p. 1.

88. Zhu Xi, "Dushu fa," in *Yangzheng yigui*, WZYG, 2.4a–2.6a.

89. The dates of his birth and death are unknown, but he received the degree of *jinshi* in 1177. Hence, it can be safely concluded that Cheng Ruoyong was a contemporary of Cheng Duanmeng. See Ji Yun et al., *Siku quanshu zongmu* (Annotated Catalogue of the Complete Collection in Four Treasuries, 1772–1789; reprint, Beijing: Zhonghua shuju, 1965), p. 805.

90. See *Xingli zixun* (Explanations of Neo-Confucian Terms), collected in *Xiao sishu* (Four Little Books), edited by Zhu Sheng (1637 edition), pp. 3b–7b. For a brief introduction to the text, see Mao Lirui et al., *Zhongguo gudai jiaoyu shi* (A History of Traditional Chinese Education) (2nd ed.; Beijing: Renmin jiaoyu chubanshe, 1982), pp. 427–428.

91. Cheng Duanli, "Dushu fennian richeng" (The Daily Schedule of Studies), collected in *Yangzheng yigui*, WZYG, 3.6b–3.7a.

92. See Cheng Duanli, "Dushu fennian richeng," in *Yangzheng yigui*, WZYG, 3.5a–3.15b. Also see Wm. Theodore de Bary, "Chu Hsi's Aims as an Educator," in *Neo-Confucian Education*, pp. 212–213, for a discussion of Cheng's schedule.

93. Zhi Yong was a monk and calligrapher of the Liang dynasty. For the story about his writing *One Thousand Characters*, see Li Fang, *Taiping guangji*, p. 1579.

94. Cheng Duanli, *Dushu fennian richeng*, in *Yangzheng yigui*, WZYG, 3.8b–3.9a.
95. See Lu Longqi's postscript to *Dushu fennian richeng*, in *Sanyutang wenji* (Collected Works from the Three-Fish Studio) (Jiahui Tang, 1694), 4.29b–4.32b.
96. See Ji Yun, *Siku quanshu zongmu*, p. 779.
97. See Lü Benzhong, *Tongmeng xun* (Instructions for Children) (*Wanyou Wenku* edition; reprint, Taiwan: Shangwu yinshu guan, 1966), p. 8.
98. Lü Benzhong, *Tongmeng xun*, p. 10.
99. The book lists words under topics. Perhaps it was composed between the third and the second centuries B.C.
100. See Wang Guowei, *Guantang jilin*, 4.6b–4.7a. It was in the early Song that the *Erya*, along with the *Lunyu*, *Xiaojing* and *Mengzi*, was established as one of the classics.
101. See *Tongmeng xun*, p. 25.
102. See *Siku quanshu zongmu*, p. 779.
103. Zhu Xi, *Tongmeng xuzhi* (Children Should Know) (hereafter cited as "TMXZ"), collected in *Yangzheng yigui*, WZYG, 1.6a.
104. Xiong Danian, ed., *Yangmeng daxun* (Great Instructions for Children), collected in *Yuyuan congshu* (Collectanea of Yuyuan), compiled by Huang Zhaoyi (Nanhai Huangshi, 1935).
105. They were Zhu Xi, Cheng Yi, Cheng Hao, Yang Shi (1053–1135) and Rao Lu. See Xiong Danian, *Yangmeng daxun*, p. 2a.
106. Apart from the above five scholars, the other five were: Hu Yin, Chen Chun, Wang Bai (1197–1274), Cheng Duanmeng and Rao Yingzi (1206–1262). Xiong Danian, *Yangmeng daxun*, pp. 1a–2a.
107. A *jueju* is a stanza of four lines, each line having five or seven characters. The whole text is in *Yangmeng daxun*, pp. 29a–44b.
108. Zhu Xi, "Xiaoxue," in Xiong Danian, *Yangmeng daxun*, p. 35b.
109. Xiong Danian, *Yangmeng daxun*, pp. 3b–4a.

Chapter 3

1. Evelyn Rawski, *Education and Popular Literacy in Ch'ing China*, p. 47.
2. Alexander Woodside, "Real and Imagined Continuities in the Chinese Struggle for Literacy," in *Education and Modernization: The Chinese Experience*, edited by Ruth Hayhoe (Oxford and New York: Pergamon Press, 1992), p. 37.
3. For a definition of *shidafu*, see Patricia Buckley Ebrey, *Family and Property in Sung China: Yuan Ts'ai's Precepts for Social Life* (Princeton, N.J.: Princeton University Press, 1984), pp. 3–10.
4. Wang Fuzhi, *Liji zhangju* (Commentary on Sentences of the *Record of Rites*), collected in *Chuanshan yishu* (Writings of Wang Fuzhi) (Shanghai: Taipingyang Shudian, 1935), 1.13a.
5. For a definition of *liangzhi*, see Tang Chun-i, "The Development of the

Concept of Moral Mind from Wang Yang-ming to Wang Chi," in *Self and Society in Ming Thought*, edited by Wm. Theodore de Bary et al. (New York: Columbia University Press, 1970), pp. 100–108.

6. See Wm. Theodore de Bary's introduction to *Self and Society in Ming Thought*, pp. 8–12.

7. See Wm. Theodore de Bary, "Individualism and Humanitarianism in Late Ming Thought," in *Self and Society in Ming Thought*, pp. 151–156.

8. Wing-tsit Chan, trans. *Instructions for Practical Living and Other Neo-Confucian Writings by Wang Yang-Ming* (New York: Columbia University Press, 1963), p. 182.

9. Wing-tsit Chan, *Instructions for Practical Living*, p. 185.

10. Wing-tsit Chan, *Instructions for Practical Living*, p. 184.

11. Wing-tsit Chan, *Instructions for Practical Living*, p. 184.

12. Wing-tsit Chan, *Instructions for Practical Living*, p. 183.

13. Wing-tsit Chan, *Instructions for Practical Living*, p. 184.

14. Wing-tsit Chan, *Instructions for Practical Living*, p. 183.

15. Wing-tsit Chan, *Instructions for Practical Living*, p. 183.

16. Wing-tsit Chan, *Instructions for Practical Living*, p. 185.

17. Wing-tsit Chan, *Instructions for Practical Living*, p. 183.

18. See Wm. Theodore de Bary, "Individualism and Humanitarianism in Late Ming Thought," in *Self and Society in Ming Thought*, pp. 171–173.

19. See Ping-ti Ho, *The Ladder of Success in Imperial China: Aspects of Social Mobility, 1368–1911* (2nd ed.; New York and London: Columbia University Press, 1967).

20. Lu Shiyi, "Lun xiaoxue" (On Elementary Education), in *Sibian lu jiyao* (Summary of Thinking and Differentiating), SBBY, 1.3b–1.4a.

21. See Zhu Weizheng, "Confucius and Traditional Chinese Education: An Assessment," in *Education and Modernization: The Chinese Experience*, edited by Ruth Hayhoe, p. 14.

22. Zhu Weizheng, "Confucius and Traditional Chinese Education: An Assessment," p. 16.

23. Zhu Weizheng, "Confucius and Traditional Chinese Education: An Assessment," p. 18.

24. Wm. Theodore de Bary, "Individualism and Humanitarianism in Late Ming Thought," in *Self and Society in Ming Thought*, p. 174.

25. See Tadao Sakai, "Popular Educational Works," in *Self and Society in Ming Thought*, pp. 332–362; and Judith Berling, *The Syncretic Religion of Lin Chao-en* (New York: Columbia University Press, 1980).

26. Here *mowen qiancheng* literally means "do not ask whether these good things will benefit your future." See *Mingxian ji* (Collection of Wise Sayings), collected in *Mengxue quanshu* (Complete Collection of Children's Primers), compiled by Song Hong and Qiao Sang (Jilin: Wenshi chubanshe, 1991), p. 86.

27. *Mingxian ji*, p. 97.
28. *Mingxian ji*, p. 103.
29. *Lienü* refers to a widow who prefers to die rather than re-marry.
30. *Mingxian ji*, p. 103.
31. *Mingxian ji*, p. 102.
32. *Mingxian ji*, p. 98.
33. *Mingxian ji*, p. 100.
34. This social and intellectual phenomenon has been well discussed by Cynthia J. Brokaw in her book *The Ledgers of Merit and Demerit: Social Change and Moral Order in Late Imperial China* (Princeton: Princeton University Press, 1991).
35. *Zengguang xianwen* (Enlarged Collection of Wise Words), in *Mengxue quanshu*, p. 107.
36. Eight copies of *Collection of Ancient Worthies' Deeds* were found in the Dunhuang Caves, six of which are in the Bibliothéque Nationale de France in Paris and the other two in the British Museum.
37. A form of literature in which stories about Buddha and from sutras (classic religious texts of Buddhism), as well as secular themes and historical events were narrated in the vernacular. For a definition and discussion of *bianwen*, see Zheng Zhenduo, *Zhongguo suwenxue shi* (History of Chinese Popular Literature) (Beijing: Wenxue guji kanxingshe, 1959), vol. 1, pp. 180–270.
38. Chapter Five discusses the twenty-four examples of filial piety in detail.
39. See Chen Zuolong, "Dunhuang xue zaji" (Notes on the Study of Dunhuang Materials), *Youshi yuekan* (Young-Lion Monthly), 40.5 (1974), pp. 56–61. For the full text of the *Guxian ji*, see Chen Qinghao, "Guxian ji jiaozhu" (A Textual Criticism and Commentary on the Ku-Hsien-chi), in *Dunhuang xue* (Dunhuang Scholarship), edited and published by Dunhuang xuehui (New Asia Institute of Advanced Chinese Studies), vol. 3 (1976), pp. 63–102.
40. Yuan Zhen, *Yuanshi Changqing ji* (Selected Works of Yuan Zhen) (Beijing: Wenxue guji kanxingshe, 1956), 51.1. "Weizhi" is the literary name of Yuan Zhen.
41. For an introduction to the origin of this book and its later versions, see Zhang Zhigong, *Chuantong yuwen jiaoyu chutan*, pp. 93–94.
42. See *Quan Tangshi* (Complete Tang Poetry) (Beijing: Zhonghua shuju, 1960), pp. 7419–7437.
43. See Zhang Zhigong, *Chuantong yuwen jiaoyu chutan*, p. 68.
44. See Su Shi, *Dongpo zhilin*, 1.7.
45. Hu Yin, *Xugu qianzi wen* (Ancient History in One Thousand Characters) (Dongtingyu tang edition, 1901).
46. See Chen Wanzhi's preface to *Shuyan gushi* (Stories from Ancient Books), collected in *Hekeben leishu jichen* (1464), vol. 11.
47. Chen Wanzhi's preface to *Shuyan gushi*.
48. Hu Jizong, *Shuyan gushi*, collected in *Hekeben leishu jichen*, vol. 11, p. 62.
49. Hu Jizong, *Shuyan gushi*, p. 67.

50. Hu Jizong, *Shuyan gushi*, p. 15.

51. Hu Jizong, *Shuyan gushi*, p. 200.

52. Hu Jizong, *Shuyan gushi*, p. 179. For the original poem, see Su Shi, *Su Dongpo quanji* (Complete Works of Su Shi) (reprint, Beijing: Zhongguo shudian, 1991), vol. 1, p. 54.

53. *Liezi* was allegedly written by a pre-Han Taoist but was probably a third century A.D. compilation based on earlier materials. SSBY edition. For English translation, see A. C. Graham, trans., *The Book of Lieh-tzu* (London: Murray, 1960).

54. Hu Jizong, *Shuyan gushi*, p. 156.

55. Hu Jizong, *Shuyan gushi*, p. 163.

56. Hu Jizong, *Shuyan gushi*, p. 126.

57. Hu Jizong, *Shuyan gushi*, p. 191.

58. Hu Jizong, *Shuyan gushi*, p. 178. For the use of the term *xiaoxi* in Du Fu's poem, see *Du Fu quanji* (Complete Works of Du Fu) (Shanghai: Guji chubanshe, 1996), p. 157.

59. Xiao was a *jijiu*, a position like that of a chancellor in a university today.

60. Xiao Liangyou, *Longwen bianying* (The Young Horse and the Shadow of a Whip) (reprint, Hunan: Yuelu shushe, 1986), p. 1.

61. See Yang Chenzheng's preface to *Longwen bianying*, pp. 12–13.

62. See Li Enshou's preface to *Longwen bianying*, p. 11.

63. Zheng Zhenduo, "Zhongguo gudai mukehua shilüe" (A Brief History of Traditional Chinese Woodcuts), vol. 9 of *Zhongguo gudai mukehua xuanji* (Selected Works of Traditional Chinese Woodcuts) (1956; reprint, Beijing: Renmin meishu chubanshe, 1985), p. 3.

64. For more information about illustrated books and publishing history in the late imperial period, see Robert E. Hegel, *Reading Illustrated Fiction in Late Imperial China* (Stanford: Stanford University Press, 1998).

65. Literally the title means "allusions for daily memorising," that is, the primer was intended for children to memorise one allusion a day.

66. *Riji gushi* (Stories for Daily Learning), originally composed by Yu Shao, was re-edited and produced by Xiong Damu in 1542. This 1542 version of the text is now collected in Zheng Zhenduo, *Zhongguo gudai mukehua xuanji*.

67. See Nagasawa Kikuya's explanation of the titles of texts collected in vol. 3 of *Hekeben leishu jichen*, pp. 4–5.

68. For a discussion of the changes of format and style in Chinese woodblock illustrations, see Hegel, *Reading Illustrated Fiction in Late Imperial China*, pp. 164–289.

Chapter 4

1. James H. S. Bossard and Eleanor S. Boll, *Ritual in Family Living* (Philadelphia: University of Pennsylvania Press, 1956), pp. 14, 16.

2. See Wm. Theodore de Bary, Wing-tsit Chan and Burton Watson, eds., *Sources of Chinese Tradition* (New York: Columbia University Press, 1966), p. 30; Denis Twitchett and John K. Fairbank, general eds., *The Cambridge History of China*, vol. 1: *The Ch'in and Han Empires, 221 B.C.–A.D. 220*, pp. 706–707.

3. Herbert Fingarette, *Confucius: The Secular as Sacred* (New York: Harper & Row, 1972), p. 3.

4. Herbert Fingarette, *Confucius: The Secular as Sacred*, p. 6.

5. Herbert Fingarette, *Confucius: The Secular as Sacred*, p. 76.

6. Wm. Theodore de Bary, *East Asian Civilizations* (Cambridge, Mass.: Harvard University Press, 1988), p. 6.

7. *Lunyu*, 15:38; translation is from James Legge, *The Four Books* (New York: Paragon Book Reprint Corp., 1969), p. 235.

8. See Zhu Xi, "*Daxue zhangju* xu" (Preface to the Commentaries on the Chapters and Sentences of the *Great Learning*), in *Zhuzi wenji*, pp. 417–418.

9. Patricia Ebrey sees the Song scholars' emphasis on ceremonial activities as markers in the dynamics of social inequality rather than as part of Neo-Confucian ideals for building a truly Confucian society. See Patricia Ebrey, "Education Through Ritual: Efforts to Formulate Family Rituals During the Sung Period," in *Neo-Confucian Education*, pp. 281–282.

10. See Patricia Buckley Ebrey, trans., *Chu Hsi's Family Rituals* (Princeton: Princeton University Press, 1991).

11. See M. Theress Kelleher, "Back to Basics: Chu Hsi's Elementary Learning (Hsiao-hsueh)," in *Neo-Confucian Education*, pp. 219–251.

12. See E. L. Jones, *Growth Recurring: Economic Change in World History* (Oxford: Clarendon Press; New York: Oxford University Press, 1988).

13. See Mark Elvin, *The Pattern of the Chinese Past* (London: Eyre Methuen, 1973).

14. See James T. Liu, "How Did a Neo-Confucian School Become the State Orthodoxy?" *Philosophy East and West*, 23.4 (1973), p. 484.

15. *Zhouyi*, 1:4; SSJZS, vol. 1, p. 20.

16. *Shangshu*, SSJZS, vol. 1, p. 169.

17. *Zhouyi*, SSJZS, vol. 1, p. 20.

18. For a discussion of the Principle of Nature and material force in terms of desires, see Chung-ying Cheng, "Reason, Substance, and Human Desires in Seventeenth-century Neo-Confucianism," in *The Unfolding of Neo-Confucianism*, edited by Wm. Theodore de Bary (New York: Columbia University Press, 1975), pp. 469–471; also Wing-tsit Chan's introduction to *Reflections on Things at Hand*, translated with notes by Wing-tsit Chan (New York: Columbia University Press, 1967), p. xxii.

19. *Mencius*, 7B:35.

20. *Laozi*, chaps. 3, 34, 37, 57.

21. See Wing-tsit Chan, *Reflections on Things at Hand*, p. 123; also *A Source Book in Chinese Philosophy*, translated and compiled by Wing-tsit Chan (Princeton: Princeton University Press, 1983), p. 473.
22. Wing-tsit Chan, *A Source Book in Chinese Philosophy*, p. 553.
23. Wing-tsit Chan, *Reflections on Things at Hand*, p. 155.
24. Wing-tsit Chan, *Reflections on Things at Hand*, p. 163.
25. Wing-tsit Chan, *Reflections on Things at Hand*, pp. 166–167.
26. Wing-tsit Chan, *Reflections on Things at Hand*, p. 167.
27. Wing-tsit Chan, *Reflections on Things at Hand*, p. 154.
28. Wing-tsit Chan, *Reflections on Things at Hand*, p. 155.
29. See *The Analects*, 12:1.
30. Wing-tsit Chan, *Reflections on Things at Hand*, p. 155.
31. Wing-tsit Chan, *Reflections on Things at Hand*, p. 155.
32. Mary Douglas, *Natural Symbols* (Harmondsworth: Penguin Books, 1973), p. 195.
33. Mary Douglas, *Natural Symbols*, p. 195.
34. Wing-tsit Chan, *Reflections on Things at Hand*, p. 155.
35. Mary Douglas, *Natural Symbols*, p. 193.
36. Mary Douglas, *Natural Symbols*, p. 195.
37. See *Zhuzi yulei* (Categorized Selections of Master Zhu's Analects), SBBY, 14:1.
38. For example, even in the early nineteenth century, Liao Jiheng (1803–1862) recorded:
   I was carried to a classroom (*shuguan*) when I was only four years old. I listened to other students reading classics such as the *Great Learning*, the *Doctrine of the Mean* and the *Analects* aloud and clearly. Gradually, I was able to learn some sentences by heart; and thus my grandfather began to teach me these classics. When I was seven years old, I was able to recite the *Four Books* and the *Book of Songs* edited by Mao Jin. [Liao Jiheng, "Qiuke tang ziji" (The Self-record of Qiuke Hall), in *Qiuke Tang liangshi yishu* (Liaos' Works of Qiuke Hall) (Yongding Liaoshi, 1875–1908), 1.1.]
39. See *Learning to be a Sage: Selections from the Conversations of Master Chu*, translated by Daniel K. Gardner (Berkeley: University of California Press, 1990), p. 94.
40. Zhu Xi, "TMXZ," in *Yangzheng yigui*, 1.6b.
41. Chen Chun, "Xiaoxue lishi" [hereafter cited as XXLS"], *Yangzheng yigui*, WZYG, 1.10b.
42. There is a similar notion in humanist ideas. For instance, according to Erasmus, the look of the eyes reveals the "character and appearance not only of the eyes but of the whole body as well." See Erasmus, "De Civilitate Morum Puerilium," in *Collected Works of Erasmus*, edited by J. K. Sowards (Toronto: University of Toronto Press, 1985), vol. 25, p. 274.

43. Zhu Xi, "TMXZ," 1.4a.
44. Zhu Xi, "TMXZ," 1.3b.
45. Chen Chun, "XXLS," 1.13a.
46. Zhu Xi, "TMXZ," 1.4a.
47. Zhu Xi, "TMXZ," 1.5a.
48. Chen Chun, "XXLS," 1.11b.
49. Chen Chun, "XXLS," 1.11b.
50. Chen Chun, "XXLS," 1.11a.
51. Zhu Xi, "TMXZ," 1.6b.
52. Chen Chun, "XXLS," 1.9b.
53. See Tu Wei-ming, "The Creative Tension between Ren and Li," *Philosophy East and West*, 18.1–2 (1968), pp. 29–39; and his "Li as Process of Humanization," in *Humanity and Self-Cultivation: Essays in Confucian Thought* (Berkeley: Asian Humanities Press, 1979), pp. 17–34.
54. *Lunyu*, 12:2. The translation is basically taken from *Sources of Chinese Tradition*, pp. 27–28.
55. For a discussion of some common characteristics in English humanist and Song Neo-Confucian textbooks, see Limin Bai's dissertation, "Primers and Paradigms," Chapter Three.
56. See Zhu Xi, *Sishu zhangju jizhu* (Collected Commentaries on the Chapters and Sentences of the *Four Books*) (Beijing: Zhonghua shuju, 1983), p. 3.
57. Wm. Theodore de Bary's introduction to *Principle and Practicality* (New York: Columbia University Press, 1979), p. 11.
58. Lü Kun, *Mengyang li* (Rituals for Nourishing Children), collected in *Mengxue yaoyi*, edited by Xu Zi and Wang Xuemei, pp. 44–52.
59. Cui Xuegu, *Youxun* (Instructions for Young Children) (*Tanji congshu* edition, 1695), p. 1.
60. Tu Xiying, *Tongzi li* (Rituals for Children), collected in *Yangzheng leibian* (Catalogued Collection of Documents on Nurturing Virtues) of *Zhengyi tang quanshu* (Complete Collection of Zhengyi Hall), edited by Zhang Boxing (Fuzhou: Zhengyi shuyuan, 1866), pp. 3.1–3.11.
61. Huang Zuo, *Xiaoxue guxun* (Elementary Learning in the Classics), collected in *Lingnan yishu* (Collected Works of Lingnan), compiled by Wu Yuanwei and Wu Chongyao (Nanhai: Yueya tang, 1850), vol. 3, p. 1b.
62. Li Yuxiu, *Dizi gui* (Regulations for Disciples), collected in *Xiao'ershu ji* (Collection of Children's Books), compiled by Zhang Chengxie (Dong tingyutang, 1901), p. 4a.
63. *Liji*, SSJZS, vol. 1, p. 1238.
64. *Liji*, SSJZS, vol. 1, p. 1240.
65. Chen Hu, *Xiaoxue richeng* (Daily Practice of Elementary Learning), collected in *Mengxue xuzhi*, edited by Xu Zi and Wang Xuemei (Shanxi: Jiaoyu chubanshe, 1991), p. 38.

66. Hu Yuan, *Mengyang shijiao* (Poetry for Nourishing Children) (*Zhaodai congshu* edition, 1697), p. 4a.
67. Hu Yuan, *Mengyang shijiao*, p. 4b.
68. Zhu Xi, *Bailudong shuyuan xuegui* (Regulations of Bailudong Academy), collected in *Mengxue xuzhi*, pp. 41–43.
69. Dong Zhu was a disciple of Zhu Xi, so he might have been active between the second half of the twelfth century and the beginning of the thirteenth century.
70. See Cheng Duanmeng and Dong Zhu, *Cheng Dong er xiansheng xueze* (School Regulations by Masters Cheng Duanmeng and Dong Zhu), collected in *Yangzheng yigui*, WZYG, pp. 11a–15a.
71. For Lü Kun's life and activities in politics, see Zhang Tingyu et al., *Mingshi* (Ming History) (Beijing: Zhonghua shuju, 1974), pp. 5937–5943; Huang Zongxi, *Mingru xue'an* (The Records of Ming Scholars) (Cixi, 1739), 54.9b–54.10a. For Lü Kun's views on Song Neo-Confucians, see *Lü Kun zhexue xuanji* (Selected Lü Kun's Works on Philosophy) (Beijing: Zhonghua shuju, 1962); and *Dictionary of Ming Biography, 1368–1644* (hereafter cited as *DMB*), edited by L. Carrington Goodrich and Chaoying Fang (New York: Columbia University Press, 1976), vol. 1, pp. 1006–1010. In Huang Zongxi's *Mingru xue'an*, Lü Kun is in the category of "Miscellaneous Scholars." See *The Records of Ming Scholars* (hereafter cited as *RMS*), edited by Julia Ching with the collaboration of Chaoying Fang (Honolulu: University of Hawaii Press, 1987), pp. 218–219. For a discussion of Lü Kun's thought, see Joanna F. Handlin, *Action in Late Ming Thought* (Berkeley: University of California Press, 1983).
72. See *DMB*, p. 1010.
73. See Lü Kun, *Shenyin yu* (Words of Moaning) (Taiwan: Zhengda yinshuguan, 1975), 2(1).53b; 2(2).17a–b.
74. Lü Kun, *Shenyin yu*, 1(4).41a–b.
75. Lü Kun, "Shexue yaolüe," in *Yangzheng yigui*, 3.30b.
76. Lü Kun, "Shexue yaolüe," 3.30b.
77. Lü Kun, "Shexue yaolüe," 3.30b–3.31a.
78. See *Liji*, SSJZS, p. 1233.
79. *Liji*, SSJZS, pp. 1467–1468.
80. *Liji*, SSJZS, p. 1598.
81. *Liji*, SSJZS, p. 1463.
82. Lü Kun, "Shexue yaolüe," 3.31a.
83. *Liji*, SSJZS, p. 1240. Translation is from James Legge, *Sacred Books of the East*, vol. xxvii, p. 76.
84. See Wang Mingqing (c. 1127–1197), *Yuzhao xinzhi* (*Xuejin taoyuan* edition, Shanghai: Shangwu, 1922), 3.20a–b. Also Wang Guowei, *Guantang jilin*, 21.3a–b.

85. See Xiang Anshi, *Xiangshi jiashuo* (Instructions for the Xiang Family), SBCK, 7.6.

86. See Wang Chongmin, *Dunhuang guji xulu* (Annotation and Records of Historical Documents in the Dunhuang Caves) (Beijing: Zhonghua shuju, 1979), p. 220.

87. See Wang Chongmin, *Dunhuang guji xulu*, pp. 221–222.

88. For an English version, see Teng Ssu-yü (trans.), *Family Instructions for the Yan Clan* (Leiden: E. J. Brill, 1968).

89. See Li Baiyao (565–648), *Beiqi shu* (History of the Qi Dynasty, 550–577) (Beijing: Zhonghua shuju, 1972), pp. 617–626; Li Yanshou, *Beishi* (History of the Northern Dynasty, 386–581) (Beijing: Zhonghua shuju, 1974), pp. 2794–2796.

90. See Yan Rurang's post-script to the *Yanshi jiaxun jijie* (Yan's Family Precepts, commentated by Wang Liqi) (Shanghai: Guji chubanshe, 1980), pp. 554–555.

91. See Huang Shulin, "*Yanshi jiaxun* jiechao xu" (Preface to the abridged edition of *Yanshi jiaxun*), in *Yanshi jiaxun jijie*, pp. 560–561.

92. See Lu Wenchao, "Zhu *Yanshi jiaxun* xu" (Preface to Commentaries on *Yan's Family Precepts*) and "Lie yan" (Notes on Style), in *Yanshi jiaxun jijie*, pp. 561–564.

93. See Ji Yun, *Siku quanshu zongmu*, pp. 779–781.

94. For a discussion and translation of this book, see Patricia Buckley Ebrey, *Family and Property in Sung China: Yuan Ts'ai's Precepts for Social Life*.

95. Zhen Dexiu, *Jiashu changyi* (Daily Rites in Family Schools), in *Mengxue xuzhi*, edited by Xu Zi and Wang Xuemei, pp. 50–55.

96. For Huo Tao's experience in officialdom, see Zhang Tingyu et al., *Mingshi*, pp. 5207–5215; also *DMB*, pp. 679–683.

97. See Huo Tao, *Huo Weiya jiaxun* (Family Rules by Huo Tao) (*Hanfenlou miji* edition, Shanghai: Shangwu yinshuguan, 1916–1926), p. 19a.

98. Huo Tao, *Huo Weiya jiaxun*, pp. 21b–22b.

99. *Liji*, SSJZS, pp. 1484–1485.

100. *Liji*, SSJZS, p. 1240.

101. Huo Tao, *Huo Weiya jiaxun*, p. 22b.

102. See *Liji*, SSJZS, p. 1234.

103. Wing-tsit Chan, *Reflections on Things at Hand*, p. 267.

104. Mary Douglas, *Natural Symbols*, p. 193.

105. See *Mingshi*, pp. 5181–5185.

106. See Zhao Erxun et al., *Qingshi gao* (Qing History) (Beijing: Zhonghua shuju, 1977), pp. 13169–13170.

107. Li Guojun et al., eds., *Qingdai qianqi jiaoyu lunzhu xuan* (Selected Writings on Education, 1664–1840) (Beijing: Renmin jiaoyu chubanshe, 1990), vol. 1, p. 220.

108. *Qingdai qianqi jiaoyu lunzhu xuan*, vol. 1, p. 220.
109. *Qingdai qianqi jiaoyu lunzhu xuan*, vol. 1, p. 220.
110. *Qingdai qianqi jiaoyu lunzhu xuan*, vol. 1, p. 220.
111. *Qingdai qianqi jiaoyu lunzhu xuan*, vol. 1, p. 220.
112. *Qingdai qianqi jiaoyu lunzhu xuan*, vol. 1, p. 220.

Chapter 5

1. John Dardess, "Childhood in Premodern China," in *Children in Historical and Comparative Perspective*, edited by Joseph M. Hawes and N. Ray Hiner (Westport: Greenwood Press, 1991), p. 75.
2. Anne Behnke Kinney, "The Theme of the Precocious Child in Early Chinese Literature," *T'oung Pao*, LXXXI (1995), p. 1.
3. Mark Golden, *Children and Childhood in Classical Athens* (Baltimore and London: The Johns Hopkins University Press, 1990), p. 1.
4. *Lunyu*, 16:9.
5. *Lunyu*, 5:28.
6. D. C. Lau, Introduction to *Confucius, The Analects (Lunyu)*, translated by D. C. Lau (2nd ed.; Hong Kong: The Chinese University Press, 1992), p. xliii.
7. Xiong Damu, *Riji gushi* (1542), 1.2b.
8. *Zhuazhou* refers to the test conducted at the end of the first year of a child's life. In this test a child is allowed to grab whatever he fancies from a selection of articles; his future career is believed to be indicated by what he grabs.
9. Anne Kinney, "The Theme of the Precocious Child in Early Chinese Literature," pp. 14–15.
10. For a discussion of the concept of *shi* and a definition of learning in the Tang, see Peter K. Bol's *"This Culture of Ours": Intellectual Transitions in T'ang and Sung China* (Stanford: Stanford University Press, 1992), pp. 15–16, 32–75.
11. See Zhu Guozhen, *Yongzhuang xiaopin* (Jottings from Yongzhuang) (Shanghai: Jinbu shuju, 1926), 24.7.
12. Wang Zhu, *Shentong shi* (Poetry by a Child Prodigy), in *Mengxue shipian* (Ten Primers), collated and commentated by Xia Chu and Hui Ling (Beijing: Beijing Normal University Press, 1990), p. 85.
13. Wang Zhu, *Shentong shi*, p. 85.
14. Wang Zhu, *Shentong shi*, p. 85. Here *fu kongxu* literally means "an empty belly," implying someone who has no knowledge of anything.
15. Wang Zhu, *Shentong shi*, p. 86.
16. Wang Zhu, *Shentong shi*, p. 86.
17. Wang Zhu, *Shentong shi*, p. 87.
18. Wang Zhu, *Shentong shi*, p. 88.

19. There was a Dragon Gate in He Jin County, Shanxi Province. It was said to have been built by the Great Yu, a legendary hero in the pre-historical period, so was also known as Yu Gate. Here the rapid current and the waves made it difficult for carp (*liyu*) to leap over the gate. According to the legend, however, once a carp did succeed in leaping over the Gate it would immediately turn into a dragon. Therefore, the phrase *li yue longmen* was used to refer to the success achieved by candidates in the civil service examinations.

20. Wang Zhu, *Shentong shi*, p. 88.

21. Wang Zhu, *Shentong shi*, p. 89.

22. Xiong Damu, *Riji gushi* (1542), 1.7a.

23. Xiong Damu, *Riji gushi* (1542), 1.2a.

24. See Hu Bingwen, *Chunzheng mengqiu* (Pure *Mengqiu*) (*Siku quanshu* edition), 952:23.

25. Xiong Damu, *Riji gushi* (1542), 1.7a–b.

26. Hu Bingwen, *Chunzheng mengqiu*, 952:23.

27. Hu Bingwen, *Chunzheng mengqiu*, 952:23.

28. See *Xiaojing*, 9.

29. See Hui-chen Wang Liu, *The Traditional Chinese Clan Rules* (Locust Valley, N.Y.: J. J. Augustin Incorporated Publisher, 1959), Chapter III and Table 3.

30. See Ji Yun, *Siku quanshu zongmu tiyao* (The Essentials of the Annotated Catalogue of the Complete Collection in Four Treasuries) (Shanghai: Shangwu yinshuguan, 1933), 31:75.

31. Lin Tong, *Xiaoshi* (The Poetry of Filial Piety), collected in *Xuehai leibian* (Catalogued Collection of the Sea of Learning), compiled by Cao Rong, enlarged by Tao Yue (Shanghai: Hanfen lou, 1920).

32. For discussions about Buddhism, morality books and popular education, see Daniel L. Overmyer, *Folk Buddhist Religion: Dissenting Sects in Late Traditional China* (Cambridge, Mass.: Harvard University Press, 1976), pp. 179–181; Sakai Tadao, *Chūgoku zensho no kenkyū* (The Study of Chinese Morality Books) (Tokyo: Kokusho kankou kai, 1960); and his "Confucianism and Popular Educational Works," in *Self and Society in Ming Thought*, edited by William Theodore de Bary et al., pp. 331–366.

33. See Lei Qiaoyun, *Dunhuang ertong wenxue*, pp. 86–87.

34. This translation is derived from *A Dictionary of Chinese Buddhist Terms*, compiled by W. Soothill and L. Hodous (1937; reprint, Taipei: Ch'eng-wen Publishing Company, 1970), p. 454.

35. Stephen F. Teiser presents a thorough study of the myth of Mu Lian and the Ghost Festival in his *The Ghost Festival in Medieval China* (Princeton: Princeton University Press, 1988). In this study, however, I have adopted a popular Chinese version of the story about Mu Lian, as it is found in much introductory literature on Buddhism, such as He Yun, *Wenhua baiwen —*

Fojiao (One Hundred Questions about Culture — Buddhism) (Beijing: Jinri Zhongguo chubanshe, 1992), p. 182.

36. For details of these three accounts, see Wang Bingzhao, "Ershisi xiao pingjie" (On Twenty-four Examples of Filial Piety), in *Mengxue shipian*, p. 186.

37. This perhaps became the later *Xinkan quanxiang ershisi xiaoshi xuan* (A New Illustrated Edition of the Twenty-four Examples of Filial Piety), collected in Japan's *Zhongguo xiaoshuo hanjian chaoben* (Rare copies of ancient Chinese fiction).

38. Tu Shixiang, *Mengyang tushuo* (Illustrations and Explanations for Children), collected in *Yunnan congshu chubian* (Yunnan Collectanea, first series), compiled by Zhao Fan and Chen Rongchang et al. (Yunnan, 1914).

39. See Yu Baozhen, *Baixiao tu* (One Hundred Illustrated Examples of Filial Piety) (Hejian Yu shi edition, 1871).

40. See *Xiaojing*, 10.

41. The first category includes stories in:

Elementary Learning

i. Yu Shun obeyed his parents although he was maltreated by his stepmother (4.2a).

ii. Min Sun stopped his father from divorcing his stepmother even though he suffered cold and hunger because of her (4.3b–4.4a).

iii. Lu Ji did not taste the oranges because he wished to present them to his mother first (5.1b–5.2a).

iv. Wang Xiang lay down on the ice to catch fish for his stepmother even though she did not show kindness to him (6.5a).

v. Zhu Shouchang refused to take a position in government as he wanted to find his natural mother, who went away early in his life (6.6b–6.7a).

Horse and Whip

i. The story of Yu Shun (p. 1).

ii. The story of Min Sun (p. 139).

iii. Huang Xiang cooled the bed in summer and warmed it in winter for his father (p. 140).

iv. The story of Wang Xiang (p. 134).

v. The story of Zhu Shouchang (p. 70).

The second category includes examples in:

Elementary Learning

i. Zi Lu, a disciple of Confucius, went more than a hundred *li* (1 *li* = 500m) to procure rice for his parents, because his family was poor and usually ate herbs and coarse pulses (5.1b).

ii. Lao Laizi pretended to be a little child to amuse his aged parents (4.4a).

iii. Jiang Ge hired himself out and supplied his mother with whatever she needed (6.1a–6.1b).

iv. Bo Yu had faults and his mother beat him. Bo Yu cried, not because he was hurt but because his mother was too weak to hurt him (4.4b).

v. Lady Tang of the Tang dynasty suckled her aged mother-in-law for years (6.5b–6.6a).

Horse and Whip

i. The story of Zi Lu (p. 194).

ii. The story of Guo Ju who was prepared to bury his only son to provide more food for his mother (p. 21).

iii. The story of Bo Yu (p. 23).

The third category includes examples in:

Elementary Learning

i. Yu Qianlou of the Southern Qi dynasty (479–502) tasted his father's excrement, because a doctor told him that sweet excrement was a sign of his father's illness becoming worse (6.6a).

The fourth category includes examples in:

Horse and Whip

i. In order to bury his father Dong Yong was obliged to sell his services as a long-term laborer (p. 70).

The fifth category includes examples in:

Horse and Whip

i. Ding Lian carved wooden images of his parents and served them as if they were alive (p. 123).

42. See *Xiaoxue*, SBBY, 4.4a.

43. See *Longwen bianying*, p. 21.

44. See *Longwen bianying*, p. 140. This was one of the most popular stories in the twenty-four examples, and appeared in many primers. Before Guo Jujing's poem appeared, it was in the *Xiaoshi*, p. 25. It can also be found in other popular primers such as *Sanzi jing*, p. 9; *Mengyang tushuo*, pp. 3b–4a.

45. *Lunyu*, 2:7.

46. *Meng Zi*, 4:19.

47. *Meng Zi*, 6A:6; see Wing-tsit Chan, trans. and comp., *A Source Book in Chinese Philosophy*, p. 54.

48. *Liji*, SSJZS, p. 1594; translation is based on Legge's work.

49. See *Neize*, SSJZS, p. 1467.

50. *Xiaoxue*, SBBY, 5.1b.

51. *Xiaoxue*, SBBY, 6.1a–b.

52. *Xiaoxue*, SBBY, 5.1b–2a.

53. *Lunyu*, 2:8.

54. See *Shangshu*, 1:1–2; *Zhongyong*, 6; *Meng Zi*, 4A:28.

55. Zhu Xi, *Xiaoxue*, SBBY, 4.2a–b; *Longwen bianying*, p. 1.

56. Wing-tsit Chan, *Reflections on Things at Hand*, p. 181.

57. *Longwen bianying*, p. 139; *Xiaoxue*, SBBY, pp. 4.3b–4.4a.
58. *Lunyu*, 11:4.
59. See *Longwen bianying*, p. 134; *Xiaoxue*, SBBY, p. 6.5a.
60. See Patricia B. Ebrey, *Family and Property in Sung China*, pp. 91–92.
61. Mary Douglas, *Natural Symbols*, p. 191.
62. Mary Douglas, *Natural Symbols*, pp. 100–101, 191–194.
63. *Lunyu*, 1:2. Translation is based on Legge's work.
64. *Lunyu*, 1:2. Translation is based on Legge's work.
65. Tu Wei-ming, "The Creative Tension Between Jen and Li," *Humanity and Self-Cultivation*, p. 9.
66. Zhang Zai, *Western Inscription*; the quotation is from W. T. de Bary, Wing-tsit Chan and Burton Watsons, eds., *Sources of Chinese Tradition*, p. 497.
67. Wing-tsit Chan, *Reflections on Things at Hand*, p. 77.
68. Wing-tsit Chan, *Reflections on Things at Hand*, pp. 53–54.
69. Wing-tsit Chan, *Reflections on Things at Hand*, p. 174.
70. Wing-tsit Chan, *Reflections on Things at Hand*, p. 77.
71. Wing-tsit Chan, *Reflections on Things at Hand*, p. 77.
72. Wing-tsit Chan, *Reflections on Things at Hand*, p. 58.
73. *Meng Zi*, 5B:1.
74. Wing-tsit Chan, *Reflections on Things at Hand*, p. 6.
75. Chen Chun, *Beixi ziyi*, translated by Wing-tsit Chan, with the title *Neo-Confucian Terms Explained* (New York: Columbia University Press, 1986), p. 128.
76. Anne B. Kinney, "The Theme of the Precocious Child in Early Chinese Literature," p. 22.
77. Xiong Damu, *Riji gushi* (1542), 1.4b; and Hu Bingwen, *Chunzheng mengqiu*, 952:23.
78. Anne B. Kinney, "The Theme of the Precocious Child in Early Chinese Literature," p. 22.
79. Xiong Damu, *Riji gushi* (1542), 1.4b.
80. Xiong Damu, *Riji gushi* (1542), 1.5a.
81. Anne B. Kinney, "The Theme of the Precocious Child in Early Chinese Literature," p. 23.
82. James Legge, *The Chinese Classics*, vol. 1, p. 196.
83. Arthur Waley, trans. and annotated, *The Analects of Confucius* (New York: Vintage Books, 1989), p. 124.
84. Zhu Xi, *Sishu zhangju jizhu*, p. 93.
85. *Bo* and *yi* were similar games, so the two words were often used together to refer to games similar to chess and draughts.
86. *Lunyu*, 17:22.
87. See Yan Zhitui, *Yanshi jiaxun*, p. 527.
88. Zhu Xi, *Sishu zhangju jizhu*, p. 181.

89. *Shangshu*, 13:7; SSJZS, vol. I, p. 195.
90. Xie Liangzuo, *Shang Cai xiansheng yulu* (Master Xie Liangzuo's Analects) (*Zhengyi tang quanshu* edition, 1866), 2.11.
91. Brian Sutton-Smith et al., eds., *Children's Folklore: A Source Book* (New York and London: Garland Publishing, Inc., 1995), pp. 64–65. Here I refer only to a similar attitude to play and games, and certainly appreciate that there is a fundamental difference in attitudes to science (such as mathematics) between Neo-Confucianism and Western epistemologies.
92. Sima Qian, *Shiji*, ESWS, vol. 1, p. 225.
93. Modern scholarship interprets Wang Yangming's view of children as allowing "for a child's desire to play and move about without restraint." Although Wang Yangming did acknowledge "the natural proclivities of children," it is doubtful that he really suggested that children be allowed to play and to act freely. In fact, singing and practising etiquette were Wang's ideas for restraining children. For a modern interpretation of Wang Yangming's view of children, see Pei-yi Wu, "Childhood Remembered: Parents and Children in China, 800 to 1700," in *Chinese Views of Childhood*, edited by Anne B. Kinney, pp. 145–148; and a summary of Wu's interpretation in Kinney's introduction to the book, pp. 5–6.
94. This story originated in Liu Xiang's *Lienü zhuan* (Biographies of Women), and became well known in every household. It was recorded in many primers, such as *The Trimetrical Classic*.
95. Friedrich Froebel (1782–1852), the founder of kindergartens, opened the first kindergarten at Keilhau in 1837. In his theory, kindergarten was an institution where the protective, garden-like atmosphere would guard children aged between three and six against the corrupting influence of society and the dangers of nature. Based on his educational theory, Froebel designed a simple educational apparatus as a series of six "gifts" for children to learn the elementary laws of physical science by experiment, and systematized a series of "occupations" for developing motor dexterity. The fundamental moral lessons, Froebel insisted, should be included in the songs and games of the kindergarten. For a discussion of how Froebel's idea of kindergarten was introduced into China, see Limin Bai, "The Chinese Kindergarten Movement, 1903–1927," in *Kindergartens and Cultures: The Global Diffusion of an Idea*, edited by Roberta Wollons (New Haven: Yale University Press, 2000), pp. 137–165.
96. See " Hunan mengyangyuan jiaoke shuolüe" (The Curriculum of Hunan mengyangyuan) (1905), in Shu Xincheng, *Zhongguo jindai jiaoyushi ziliao* (Materials on the History of Chinese Education, 1840–1919) (Beijing: Renmin jiaoyu chubanshe, 1980), vol. 2, pp. 393–395.
97. Xiong Damu, *Riji gushi* (1542), 1.4a.
98. Xiong Damu, *Riji gushi* (1542), 1.4a.

99. Wing-tsit Chan, *Reflections on Things at Hand*, p. 66.
100. *Liji*, SSJZS, p. 1233.
101. Daniel K. Gardner, *Learning to be a Sage*, p. 90.
102. Tu Wei-ming, *Humanity and Self-Cultivation*, p. 76.

Chapter 6

1. Dai Zhen, "*Liushu lun* xu" (The Preface to *On Six Rules*), in *Dai Zhen ji* (Selected Works of Dai Zhen) (Shanghai: Guji chubanshe, 1980), p. 77.
2. Ruan Yuan, *Yanjing shi ji* (Works of the Study-of-Classic Studio) (Taipei: Shijie shuju, 1964), 1.32.
3. Ruan Yuan, *Yanjing shi ji*, 1.32.
4. See C. M. Millward, *A Biography of the English Language* (New York: Holt, Rinehart and Winston, Inc. 1989), pp. 35, 78, 135–138, 202–204, 216–218.
5. See English textbooks in the sixteenth and seventeenth centuries, such as Richard Mulcaster, *Elementarie* (1582; reprint, Menston, England: Scolar Press, 1970); Francis Clement, *The Petie Schole* (1587; reprint, Menston, England: Scolar Press, 1967); John Brinsley, *Ludus Literarius* (1612; reprint, Menston, England: Scolar Press, 1968).
6. Bill Bryson, in his comparison of Chinese, Japanese and English, points out that Chinese has a pictographic-ideographic system; its symbols cannot guide its pronunciation as happens in alphabetic languages. Spellings in English are also very treacherous, but English as a body of spellings for the most part still reflects its pronunciation. See Bill Bryson, *Mother Tongue: The English Language* (London: Hamish Hamilton, 1990), pp. 108–124.
7. During the sixteenth and seventeenth centuries, there were only twenty-four letters.
8. For example, there is the *fanqie* system of syllabic transcription. *Fanqie* usually uses two characters to present the sound of a new character: the first one stands for the initial consonant, the second stands for the vowel(s). The problem is: if one is not able to read both these characters the *fanqie* system does not work. For further details about the history of the *fanqie* system, see Zhang Shilu, *Zhongguo yinyunxue shi* (A History of Chinese Phonology) (Hong Kong: Taixing shuju, 1963), pp. 8, 13, 126.
9. Wang Yun, "Jiao tongzi fa" (Methods of Teaching Children), in *Qingdai qianqi jiaoyu lunzhu xuan*, edited by Li Guojun et al., vol. 3, p. 485.
10. Wang Li, *Hanyu shigao* (A History of the Chinese Language) (Beijing: Kexue chubanshe, 1958), vol. 2, pp. 211–218.
11. Such as Brinsley's *Ludus Literarius* (1612), and Mulcaster's *Elementarie* (1582).
12. Han scholars had regarded *liushu* as the six rules for forming Chinese characters. Before Xu Shen, there were various explanations of the *liushu*. After the appearance of the *Explanations of Words and Characters*, Xu's statement became a final definition. The *liushu* referred to (1) the

pictographs, (2) the simple ideographs, (3) the compound ideographs, (4) the phonetic compounds, (5) borrowed characters and (6) extended characters used for new words by extension of meaning. Evidential scholars in the Qing accepted Xu's authority in palaeography and etymology. See Xu Shen, "*Shuowen jiezi* xu," in *Shuowen jiezi*, pp. 755–756. The English translation of the six types of characters is from Benjamin Elman's *From Philosophy to Philology* (Cambridge, Mass.: Harvard University Press, 1984), p. 213.

13. Wang Yun, *Wenzi mengqiu* (Explanations of Characters for Children) (1838; reprint, Taipei: Yiwen yinshuguan, 1971), pp. 1–5.

14. B. A. Elman, *From Philosophy to Philology*, pp. 215, 217.

15. For example, de Saussure says that language is a system of signs. The "signifier" is a form (sound image) which signifies; and the "signified" is an idea (or a concept) which is signified. They are not separate parts but the union of components of the sign. A particular combination of signifier and signified is an arbitrary entity.

      Ferdinand de Saussure (1857–1913) was the founder of modern linguistics. His *Course in General Linguistics* put together from notes taken by students who attended his various series of lectures. For an interpretation of "signifier" and "signified," see Jonathan Culler, *Ferdinand de Saussure* (2nd ed.; Ithaca, N.Y.: Cornell University Press, 1986), p. 28; David Holdcroft, *Saussure: Signs, System, and Arbitrariness* (Cambridge, England: Cambridge University Press, 1991), pp. 50–54.

16. Thomé H. Fang, *Chinese Philosophy: Its Spirit and Its Development* (Taipei: Linking, 1981), pp. 23–24.

17. Xu Shen, *Shuowen jiezi*, pp. 753–754.

18. Karlgren follows this opinion and stresses the significance of the phonetic element in Chinese characters. See Bernhard Karlgren, *Analytic Dictionary of Chinese and Sino-Japanese* (1923; reprint, Taipei: Ch'eng-wen Publishing Company, 1966), pp. 4–5; and his *Grammata Serica: Script and Phonetics in Chinese and Sino-Japanese* (1940; reprint, Taipei: Ch'eng-wen Publishing Company, 1966), pp. 1–14.

19. Wang Yun's preface to *Wenzi mengqiu*, p. 3.

20. Wang Yun, "Jiao tongzi fa," p. 485.

21. Wang Yun's preface to *Wenzi mengqiu*, pp. 1–4.

22. Wang Yun's preface to *Wenzi mengqiu*, pp. 1–4.

23. Zhang Zhigong, *Chuantong yuwen jiaoyu chutan*, p. 26.

24. The calculation and classification of the characters in this book is based on Herbert A. Giles' work, which analyses the structure of most Chinese characters in the *Sanzi jing* based on the *Shuowen jiezi*. See Herbert A. Giles, trans., *San Tzu Ching: Elementary Chinese* (Taipei: Ch'eng-wen Publishing Company, 1972).

25. Even those Western scholars who regard Chinese etymology as "the products of Chinese fancy and imagination" agree that it is helpful to use it to teach non-Chinese speakers Chinese characters through the mental associations it establishes. See G. D. Wilder and J. H. Ingram, *Analysis of Chinese Characters* (Taipei: Literature House, 1964), pp. iii–iv.

26. Wang Yun, *Wenzi mengqiu*, p. 11.

27. Wang Yun, *Wenzi mengqiu*, p. 127.

28. Wang Yun, *Wenzi mengqiu*, p. 66.

29. Wang Yun, *Wenzi mengqiu*, p. 66.

30. Wang Yun, *Wenzi mengqiu*, p. 66

31. Wang Yun, *Wenzi mengqiu*, p. 147.

32. *Lunyu*, 15:31.

33. Wang Yun, *Wenzi mengqiu*, p. 57.

34. Wang Yun, *Wenzi mengqiu*, p. 137.

35. *Lunyu* 19:13; James Legge, *The Chinese Classics* (Hong Kong: Hong Kong University Press, 1960), vol. 1, p. 344.

36. Wang Yun, *Wenzi mengqiu*, p. 11.

37. Wang Yun, *Wenzi mengqiu*, p. 71.

38. Wang Yun, *Wenzi mengqiu*, p. 65.

39. Western alphabetic writing, however, also originated in pictographs which were related to meaning as well as to sound. For example, the English letter "A" was originally the picture of the head of an ox. See John DeFrancis, *Visible Speech* (Honolulu: University of Hawaii Press, 1989), p. 230; and David Diringer, *Writing* (London: Thames and Hudson, 1962), pp. 104–178.

40. E. M. Field, *The Child and His Book: Some Account of the History and Progress of Children's Literature in England* (1892; reprint, Detroit: Singing Tree Press, Book Tower, 1968), p. 131.

41. *The A B C of Aristotle* (the author is unknown) might have been produced about 1430, and was printed by F. J. Furnivall in 1868; it was translated into modern English by Edith Rickert, in *The Babees' Book: Medieval Manners for the Young, Done into Modern English from Dr. Furnivall's Texts* (New York: Cooper Square Publishers, 1966), p. 10.

42. E. M. Field, *The Child and His Book*, p. 133.

43. In the mid-seventeenth century, there was a new interest in Chinese pictographs in England. Writers saw the connection between concepts and things through the pictorial status of Chinese pictographs. Some of them viewed picture writing and hieroglyphs as a useful metaphor in the transmission of knowledge. Ideographic scripts were often one of the main focuses in the search for a universal language. See Umberto Eco, *The Search for the Perfect Language* (Oxford: Blackwell, 1995); and Richard W. F. Kroll, *The Material Word: Literate Culture in the Restoration and Early Eighteenth Century* (Baltimore: The Johns Hopkins University Press, 1991), pp. 231–238.

44. As mentioned in Chapter Two, *Mingwu mengqiu* (*The Names and Descriptions of Things*) was one of a series of primers entitled *Four Little Books*. This series of primers must have met the needs of those teaching children as it was reprinted many times.
45. Fang Fengchen, *Mingwu mengqiu* (*Xiao sishu* edition), p. 2a.
46. An auxiliary word in classical Chinese.
47. A copula in classical Chinese.
48. Fang Fengchen, *Mingwu mengqiu*, p. 3a.
49. Fang Fengchen, *Mingwu mengqiu*, p. 5a.
50. See Huo Tao's *Jiaxun*, p. 25a.
51. The original term is "three *cun*." 1 *cun* = 3.3 cm or 1.3 inch.
52. T. C. Lai, *A Scholar in Imperial China* (Hong Kong: Kelly & Walsh Ltd., 1970), p. 9.
53. Wing-tsit Chan, *Reflections on Things at Hand*, p. 133.
54. Huo Tao, *Jiaxun*, p. 25b.
55. Lü Kun, "Shexue yaolüe," WZYG, 3.32a.
56. Huo Tao, *Jiaxun*, p. 1a.
57. J. A. Simpson et al., *The Oxford English Dictionary* (2nd edition; Oxford: Clarendon Press, 1989), vol. I, p. 631.
58. J. A. Simpson et al., *The Oxford English Dictionary*, vol. IX, p. 470.
59. J. A. Simpson et al., *The Oxford English Dictionary*, vol. IX, p. 470.
60. Joseph Needham, *Science and Civilisation in China* (Cambridge, England: Cambridge University Press, 1959), vol. III, p. 54.
61. There were ten heavenly stems (*tiangan*) and twelve earthly branches (*dizhi*).
62. Sixty is the smallest common multiple of 10 and 12.
63. A general description of a curriculum for elementary education in classical times usually originates from the *Record of Rites*. This can be seen, for instance, in Li Yan and Du Shiran, *Zhongguo gudai shuxue jianshi* (A Concise History of Chinese Mathematics) (Beijing: Zhonghua shuju, 1963), vol. I, pp. 30–31; or in its English version, *Chinese Mathematics: A Concise History*, translated by John N. Crossley and Anthony W. C. Lun (Oxford: Clarendon Press, 1987), pp. 22–23.
64. Limin Bai, "Primers and Paradigms," pp. 182–183.
65. *San Bai Qian*, p. 27.
66. *San Bai Qian*, p. 33.
67. *San Bai Qian*, p. 11.
68. *San Bai Qian*, p. 11.
69. See the commentary on the above sentence in the *Sanzi jing, San Bai Qian*, pp. 11–12; and Needham, *Science and Civilisation in China*, vol. III, pp. 55–56.
70. Zhong Ling, comp., *Yan Xizhai xiansheng yanxing lu* (A Biography of Master Yan Yuan) (*Yan-Li congshu* edition, 1923), 2.13b.

71. According to Feng Chen, the book was composed in 1700. See Feng Chen, *Li Shugu xiansheng nianpu* (A Chronicle of Master Li Gong) (*Guocui congshu* edition, 1908), 3.7b. Yet Li Gong's own preface to the book was dated 1705. See Li Gong, *Xiaoxue jiye* (An Elementary Text Collected from Classics), CSJC. Perhaps it was composed in 1700 and printed in 1705.

72. See Feng Chen, *Li Shugu xiansheng nianpu*, 3.7b.

73. In fact, this is multiplication, not addition, in modern terms. In traditional Chinese calculation, multiplication was an "'abridgement of addition,' a 'folding together' of many addends.'" For an explanation of *cheng*, see Needham, *Science and Civilisation in China*, vol. III, p. 63. This may be a reason why Li Gong regarded this example as addition instead of multiplication.

74. For more details about ancient and medieval Chinese numeral signs, see Needham, *Science and Civilisation in China*, vol. III, pp. 5–17.

75. According to Needham, in ancient China, counting rods were "six inches long, for calculating calendar and numbers"(p. 4). Before the appearance of the abacus, calculation was performed on the counting-board with its horizontal lines. For the detail and figures of the counting-board, see Needham, *Science and Civilisation in China*, vol. III, pp. 4–9, 63.

76. Needham, *Science and Civilisation in China*, vol. III, p. 152.

77. Literally the title "Tongwen suanzhi" means "method of calculating in common language," but Crossley and Lun translate it as "The Treatise on European Arithmetic." I adopt their translation in this study. For a brief introduction to the book, see John N. Crossley and Anthony W. C. Lun, *Chinese Mathematics, A Concise History*, pp. 196–199.

78. See E. G. R. Taylor, *The Mathematical Practitioners of Tudor & Stuart England* (Cambridge: Cambridge University Press, 1970), p. 167 for Recorde's biography, and p. 13 for a general introduction to this book.

79. See Robert Recorde, *The Grounde of Artes* (1542; reprint, New York: Da Capo Press and Amsterdam: Theatrvm Orbis Terrarvm Ltd., 1969).

80. See the full title of Francis Clement's *The Petie Schole*.

81. See the full title of Francis Clement's *The Petie Schole*.

82. Francis Clement, *The Petie Schole*, p. 63.

83. Francis Clement, *The Petie Schole*, p. 65.

84. This refers to small marks (e.g. commas) used in reckoning the great sum.

85. Clement, *The Petie Schole*, pp. 69–71.

86. Clement, *The Petie Schole*, p. 87.

87. John Brinsley, *Ludus Literarius*, p. 25.

88. John Brinsley, *Ludus Literarius*, pp. 25–26.

89. *San Bai Qian*, p. 6

90. *San Bai Qian*, p. 9. This is a well-known story about filial piety.

91. *San Bai Qian*, p. 10.

92. Edmund Coote, *The English Schoole-maister* (1596; reprint, Menston, England: Scolar Press, 1968), p. 65.

93. Edmund Coote, *The English Schoole-maister,* pp. 65–66.

94. For more information about mathematical study during the early and mid-Qing, see Limin Bai, "Mathematical Study and Intellectual Transition in the Early and Mid-Qing," *Late Imperial China,* 16.2 (1995), pp. 23–61; and Catherine Jami, "Learning Mathematical Sciences during the Early and Mid-Ch'ing," in *Education and Society in Late Imperial China, 1600–1900,* pp. 223–256.

95. Lu Shiyi, "Lun xiaoxue" (On Elementary Education), in *Qingdai qianqi jiaoyu lunzhu xuan,* vol. I, pp. 129–130.

96. Here, I translate *juan* as "section," because there is no equivalent term in English for *juan;* and in Li's book, each *juan* is an independent section separately paginated.

97. See Li Gong, *Xiaoxue jiye,* pp.1–4.

98. Li Gong, *Xiaoxue jiye,* pp. 5–18.

99. Li Gong, *Xiaoxue jiye,* pp. 19–46.

100. Li Gong, *Xiaoxue jiye,* pp. 49–53.

101. Li Gong, *Xiaoxue jiye,* pp. 54–84.

102. Li Gong, *Xiaoxue jiye,* p. 53.

103. See Feng Chen, *Li Shugu xiansheng nianpu,* 1.7b.

104. Feng Chen, *Li Shugu xiansheng nianpu,* 3.11b. Like other writers in the early Qing, Li Gong often used the phrases "to rescue the nation in crisis" or "to strengthen the nation," referring to the fall of the Ming and the responsibility of intellectuals for this tragedy.

105. Feng Chen, *Li Shugu xiansheng nianpu,* 1.7b.

106. Feng Chen, *Li Shugu xiansheng nianpu,* 3.18b.

107. Feng Chen, *Li Shugu xiansheng nianpu,* 3.19b.

108. Feng Chen, *Li Shugu xiansheng nianpu,* 3.19b.

109. The titles of these works are: *Rishi mengqiu* (Preliminary research on solar eclipses) and *Yueshi mengqiu* (Preliminary research on lunar eclipses).

110. See John N. Crossley and Anthony W. C. Lun, trans., *Chinese Mathematics: A Concise History,* p. 215. For a discussion of Mei Wending's contribution to the study of mathematics and astronomy in the early Qing period, see Limin Bai, "Mathematical Study and Intellectual Transition in the Early and Mid-Qing," pp. 23–61.

111. In *Mengxue yaoyi* (Essentials of Children's Books), there is a list of traditional Chinese elementary textbooks (*mengshu*), in which this kind of text is listed among the primers (see pp. 335–358). Perhaps this is attributed to the two editors who did not look into the contents of these texts and were perplexed by the use in the titles of terms, such as *mengqiu* and *fameng* (to enlighten the young or the dull).

Chapter 7

1. See Philip C. C. Huang, *The Peasant Economy and Social Change in North China* (Stanford: Stanford University Press, 1985), p. 33.
2. Philip C. C. Huang, *The Peasant Economy and Social Change in North China*, p. 33.
3. Hsiao-Tung Fei, *Peasant Life in China* (London: Routledge & Kegan Paul Ltd., 1939).
4. See *Wenwu* (Cultural Relics), 10 (1984), plates 2–4, and color plate 2.
5. Zheng Zhenduo, *Zhongguo gudai mukehua shilüe*. Vol. 9 of *Zhongguo gudai mukehua xuanji*, pp. 28, 95, n. 34.
6. The pictures and poems discussed in this chapter, if without specific footnotes, are all from the 1696 edition of the *Pictures of Tilling and Weaving*.
7. For instance, female infanticide was often associated with the dowry system. Throughout the late imperial period, many scholar-officials made efforts to forbid the killing of female infants, as indicated in official proclamations and educational materials. For some collections relating to this, see *Minjian quanshan shu* (Folk Morality Books), edited by Yuan Xiaobo (Shanghai: Guji chubanshe, 1995), pp. 57, 347–353. For a study of female infanticide in English, see Ann Waltner, "Infanticide and Dowry in Ming and Early Qing China," in *Chinese Views of Childhood*, pp. 193–218.
8. Thomas H. C. Lee, "The Discovery of Childhood: Children education in Sung China (960–1279)," in *Kultur, Begriff und Wort in China und Japan*, p. 168.
9. Peng Yunzhang, "Yu ying sanshan lun" (Three merits of rearing infants), in *Minjian quanshan shu*, p. 50. For a discussion of officially established welfare provision for destitute children in the Lower Yangtze area during the Qing period, see Angela Ki Che Leung, "Relief Institutions for Children in Nineteenth-Century China," in *Chinese Views of Childhood*, pp. 251–278.
10. Hong Mai, *Rongzhai suibi*, p. 691. For criticism from other Song scholars, see Pei-yi Wu, "Childhood Remembered: Parents and Children in China, 800 to 1700," in *Chinese Views of Childhood*, pp. 135–136.
11. See Ann Waltner, *Getting an Heir, Adoption and the Construction of Kinship in Late Imperial China* (Honolulu: University of Hawaii Press, 1990).
12. Hsiao-Tung Fei, *Peasant Life in China*, p. 31.
13. This kind of "economic value" of the child is also discussed in Fei's *Peasant Life in China*, p. 37.
14. Fei reveals the same information in his *Peasant Life in China*, p. 38.
15. For a description of the picture of women at work in a breeding room presented in the *Pictures of Tilling and Weaving*, see Dieter Kuhn, "Textile Technology: Spinning and Reeling," Part IX of Vol. 5 of *Science and Civilisation in China*, compiled and edited by Joseph Needham et al. (Cambridge, England: Cambridge University Press, 1988), pp. 314–315. For

a further discussion of women's work in traditional China, see Francesca Bray, *Technology and Gender*, part two.

16. This kind of child "freedom" is also reported in Fei's book *Peasant Life in China*, p. 37.

17. Philippe Aries, *Centuries of Childhood*, pp. 406, 413.

18. For a criticism of Aries's view, see David Hunt, *Parents and Children in History*, pp. 42–44.

19. One can easily find descriptions of gambling scenes in Ming-Qing fiction. There were also some manuals recording dice, dominoes and card games in detail. See Andrew Lo, "Dice, Dominoes and Card Games in Chinese Literature: A Preliminary Survey," in *Chinese Studies*, edited by Frances Wood (London: The British Library, 1988), pp. 127–135.

20. This book contains 306 drawings to illustrate 388 characters. See *15th Century Illustrated Chinese Primer, Hsin-pien Tui-hsiang Szu-yen*, facsimile reproduction with introduction and notes by L. Carrington Goodrich (Reprint; Hong Kong: Hong Kong University Press, 1990).

21. See Yang Yinshen, *Zhongguo youyi yanjiu* (The Study of Chinese Games) (1935; reprint, Shanghai: Wenyi chubanshe, 1990), pp. 7–8; Stewart Culin, *Korea Games, with Notes on the Corresponding games of China and Japan* (1895; reprint, New York: Dover Publications, Inc., 1991), pp. 102–122; also his article "Chinese Games with Dice and Dominoes," in *Report of U.S. National Museum*, 1893, pp. 491–537.

22. Yang Yinshen, *Zhongguo youyi yanjiu*, p. 6.

23. *Pictures of One Hundred Children* was said to be the work of Su Hanchen (fl. 1119–1125). The original edition of Su's work is not extant, and what we see today are copies made by later generations. Later the term "one hundred children" was used to refer to a whole genre of such paintings and woodblocks which present various dimensions of childhood.

    The copy of the *Pictures of One Hundred Children* discussed in this chapter was made by Qing artist Yu Zhisheng (fl. 1796–1820), who claimed that his sixteen pictures of children were copied from Su's original work. He said that he had yearned to see Su's original work for a long time. When he was eventually able to borrow a copy (which was believed to be Su's original work) from a collector, he marvelled at the life-like depiction of childhood, with children playing in gardens and courtyards, and behaving in a captivating manner. This is why he decided to copy Su's work. See Yu's note, written on the upper right-hand corner of the sixteenth picture of his copies (1814), collected in *Gujin mingren huagao* (Past and Present Prominent Paintings), photo-offset copy of Shanghai dianshi zhai edition (Beijing: Zhongguo shudian, 1984), vol. 2.

24. C. A. S. Williams has described this pursuit in detail, but he ignores the other, innocent side to cricket fighting, concluding simply that the common

cricket was caught and sold only for gambling. C. A. S. Williams, *Outlines of Chinese Symbolism and Art Motives* (1941; reprint, Rutland, Vermont and Tokyo: Charles E. Tuttle Company, 1974), p. 102.

25. The basic gambling described in this Ming document is that gamblers "either bet on card games or play with dice, vying to be the winner" (p. 137). Villagers were told that gambling was a disease "which is detrimental to social customs and ruins family fortunes." See Patricia Buckley Ebrey, ed., *Chinese Civilization and Society, A Sourcebook* (New York: The Free Press; London: Collier Macmillan Publishers, 1981), pp. 136–137.

26. For a study of academies in late imperial China, see John Meskill, *Academies in Ming China: A Historical Essay* (Tucson, Ariz.: The University of Arizona Press, 1982).

27. See Ke Shaomin, *Xin Yuanshi* (New History of the Yuan Dynasty) (Tianjin: Xushi Tuigeng- tang, 1919), 64.12a–b.

28. Ke Shaomin, *Xin Yuanshi*, 69.11a.

29. See Zhang Tingyu et al., *Mingshi*, p.1690.

30. See Quan Zuwang, *Jieqiting ji waibian* (Outer Collection of Jieqiting), SBCK, 22.113.

31. Lü Kun, "Shexue yaolüe," 3.30a.

32. Alexander Woodside, "Some Mid-Qing Theorists of Popular Schools, Their Innovations, Inhibitions, and Attitudes toward the Poor," *Modern China*, 9.1 (1983), pp. 12–13.

33. Alexander Woodside, "Some Mid-Qing Theorists of Popular Schools," p. 13.

34. Alexander Woodside, "Some Mid-Qing Theorists of Popular Schools," p. 17.

35. See *DMB*, p. 1007.

36. Tang Jian, *Tang Queshengong ji* (Collected Works of Master Tang Jian), SBBY, 5.10b–11a, 5.16b.

37. For an excellent study of Chen's project in Yunnan, see William T. Rowe, "Education and Empire in Southwest China, Ch'en Hung-mou in Yunnan, 1733–38," in *Education and Society in Late Imperial China, 1600–1900*, edited by Benjamin A. Elman and Alexander Woodside, pp. 417–457.

38. Alexander Woodside, "Some Mid-Qing Theorists of Popular Schools," p. 13.

39. Lü Kun, "Shexue yaolüe," 3.31b.

40. Lü Kun, "Shexue yaolüe," 3.30a.

41. Tang Jian, *Tang Queshengong ji*, 5.17b.

42. Lü Kun, "Shexue yaolüe," 3.31b.

43. Alexander Woodside, "Real and Imagined Continuities in the Chinese Struggle for Literacy," in *Education and Modernization: The Chinese Experience*, edited by Ruth Hayhoe, p. 37.

44. Alexander Woodside, "Some Mid-Qing Theorists of Popular Schools," pp. 26–27.

45. Alexander Woodside, "Some Mid-Qing Theorists of Popular Schools," p. 29.
46. David Johnson, "Communication, Class, and Consciousness in Late Imperial China," pp. 57–58.
47. David Johnson, "Communication, Class, and Consciousness in Late Imperial China," pp. 58–60.
48. Alexander Woodside, "Real and Imagined Continuities in the Chinese Struggle for Literacy," p. 32.
49. For a general history of Chinese vernacular literature, see Zheng Zhenduo, *Zhongguo suwenxue shi* (History of Chinese Popular Literature) (Shanghai: Shangwu yinshuguan, 1938). For a discussion of the relationship between popular literature and education, see Evelyn Sakakida Rawski, *Education and Popular Literacy in Ch'ing China*, pp. 109–124.
50. See Lü Desheng's preface to "Xiao'er yu" (1558), in *Yangzheng yigui*, 2.7b.
51. See Lü Kun's preface to "Xu xiao'er yu" (1593), 2.10b.
52. Lü Desheng, "Xiao'er yu," 2.8a.
53. Lü Desheng, "Xiao'er yu," 2.9a.
54. Lü Desheng, "Xiao'er yu," 2.9b.
55. Lü Kun, "Xu xiao'er yu," in *Yangzheng yigui*, 2.11a.
56. Lü Kun, "Haoren ge," in *Xunsu yigui*, WZYG, 2.16a.
57. See Ron-Guey Chu, "Chu Hsi and Public Instruction," in *Neo-Confucian Education*, pp. 252–273.
58. Lü Kun, *Shenyin yu*, 2(2).15b.
59. Here the quotation is from Ron-Guey Chu, "Chu Hsi and Public Instruction," p. 262.
60. Guan Fang was a Qing scholar, but the dates of his birth and death are unknown.
61. Guan Fang, *Jiachang yu* (Small Talk), in *Xiao'ershu ji bazhong* (A Collection of Eight Children's Books) (Dong tingyutang, 1901), p. 1a.
62. Guan Fang, *Jiachang yu*, p. 3a.
63. This belief perhaps existed in every traditional society, and similar expressions can also be found in other languages, such as "spare the rod, spoil the child" in English.
64. Some versions of the twenty-four examples of filial piety do not include this story, but the version discussed in Chapter Five does contain it.
65. Zhu Xi, *Xiaoxue*, 4.4b.

Chapter 8

1. Literally this title means "children know love." See Qiu's Preface to Lin's *Xunmeng gejue* (Songs for Educating Children) (Xingzhou, 1898), p. 3a.
2. Wilt Idema and Lloyd Haft, *A Guide to Chinese Literature* (Ann Arbor: The University of Michigan Press, 1997), p. 117.
3. Lin Shu, *Xunmeng gejue*, p. 1b

4. Lin Shu, *Xunmeng gejue*, p. 1b.
5. This controversy about the kowtow ritual started after the first formal British diplomatic mission arrived in China in 1793. See W. W. Rockhill, *Diplomatic Audiences at the Court of China* (London: Lusac, 1905).
6. Lin Shu, *Xunmeng gejue*, p. 2b.
7. Lin Shu, *Xunmeng gejue*, p. 2b.
8. Lin Shu, *Xunmeng gejue*, p. 11a–b.
9. Lin Shu, *Xunmeng gejue*, p. 13a–b.
10. *Lunyu*, 2:16; James Legge, *The Chinese Classics*, vol. I, p. 150.
11. See *Lunyu*, 13:4.
12. *Lunyu*, 17:9; James Legge, *The Chinese Classics*, vol. I, p. 323.
13. See *Hanshu*, p. 2524.
14. For a brief introduction and discussion of Dong's philosophy and political ideas, see Fung Yu-lan (Feng Youlan), *A Short History of Chinese Philosophy* (New York: The Free Press, 1966), pp. 191–203.
15. *China in the Sixteenth Century: The Journals of Matthew Ricci: 1583–1610*, translated by Louis J. Gallagher (New York: Random House, 1953), p. 32.
16. Wang Zheng, Preface to *Yuanxi qiqi tushuo* (Illustrated Western Machinery) (1627; reprint, CSJC), p. 11.
17. Feng Chen, *Li Shugu xiansheng nianpu*, 1.13b.
18. Yan Yuan, *Sishu zhengwu* (Critical Commentary on *Sishu*) (*Yan-Li Congshu* edition, 1923), 1.6a.
19. Huang Zongxi, *Huang Lizhou wenji* (Collected Works of Huang Zongxi), edited by Chen Naiqian (Beijing: Zhonghua shuju, 1959), p. 77.
20. See Limin Bai, *Xixue dongjian yu Ming-Qing zhi ji jiaoyu sichao* (Western Influence and Educational Thought in the Late Ming and Early Qing Period) (Beijing: Jiaoyu kexue chubanshe, 1989), p. 51.
21. See Zhong Ling, *Yan Xizhai xiansheng yanxing lu*, 2.28a.
22. Yuan Mei, *Xiaocangshan fang wenji* (Selected Works of Yuan Mei), SBBY, 19. 10a.
23. Tang Zhen, *Qian shu* (Shanghai: Guji chubanshe, 1955), p. 173.
24. See Qiu's Preface to Lin's *Xunmeng gejue*, p. 1a.
25. See Qiu's Preface to Lin's *Xunmeng gejue*, pp. 2b–3a.
26. Lin Shu, *Xunmeng gejue*, p. 4a.
27. Lin Shu, *Xunmeng gejue*, p. 4a
28. Lin Shu, *Xunmeng gejue*, p. 4a.
29. Lin Shu, *Xunmeng gejue*, p. 4b.
30. While much attention has been paid to Liang Qichao's political theories and activities in both Chinese and English literature, few researchers have focused solely on his educational ideas. For a study particularly focusing on Liang's educational thought in the period of the 1898 Reform, see Abe Yo, "Ryo Kei-cho no kyoku shiso to sono katsudo bojutsu hempoki o chushin to

shite" (Liang Qichao's Educational Thought and Activities in the Period of the 1898 Reform), *Kyushu daigaku kyoikubu kiyo* (Bulletin of the Department of Education of Kyushu University), 6 (1959), pp. 301–323.

31. This is evident in Liang's *Xixue shumubiao* (Bibliography of Western Learning), which he compiled in 1896.

32. P. C. Huang, *Liang Ch'i-ch'ao and Modern Chinese Liberalism* (Seattle and London: University of Washington Press, 1972), p. 33.

    Except for his personal contact with Timothy Richard, however, Liang seems not to have been involved with other missionaries. See Hao Chang, *Liang Ch'i-ch'ao and Intellectual Transition in China, 1890–1907* (Cambridge, Mass.: Harvard University Press, 1971), pp. 71–72.

33. This idea was well elaborated in his *Xinmin shuo* (New Citizen) and *Xin shixue* (New Historiography). For a further discussion, see Hao Chang, *Liang Ch'i-ch'ao and Intellectual Transition in China, 1890–1907*, p. 160.

34. For a study of Zhang Zhidong, see Daniel H. Bays, *China Enters the Twentieth Century: Chang Chih-tung and the Issues of a New Age, 1895–1909* (Ann Arbor: The University of Michigan Press, 1978).

35. For a discussion of Japanese influence on Liang, see Joseph R. Levenson, *Liang Ch'i-ch'ao and the Mind of Modern China* (Cambridge, Mass.: Harvard University Press, 1965), p. 50 (n. 30); and Hao Chang, *Liang Ch'i-ch'ao and Intellectual Transition in China, 1890–1907*, p. 148.

36. Liang Qichao, "Lun youxue" (On Elementary Education), in *Yinbingshi heji, wenji* (Collected Works and Essays from the Ice-drinker's Studio: Collected Essays) (Shanghai: Zhonghua shuju, 1941), vol. 1, p. 44.

37. Liang Qichao, "Lun nüxue" (On Female Education), in *Yinbingshi wenji*, vol. 1, p. 40.

38. They are presented in such works as John Stuart Mill's *On Liberty*, Montesquieu's *Defence of the Spirit of the Laws*, and Adam Smith's *Wealth of Nations*. For a study of Yan Fu, see Benjamin Schwartz, *In Search of Wealth and Power: Yan Fu and the West* (Cambridge, Mass.: Harvard University Press, 1964).

39. Liang Qichao, *Yinbingshi wenji*, vol. 11, p. 18. According to Hao Chang, Liang was not a close friend of Yan Fu, and their acquaintance was primarily an intellectual one. See Hao Chang, *Liang Ch'i-ch'ao and Intellectual Transition in China, 1890–1907*, p. 64.

40. Liang Qichao, "Lun nüxue," in *Yinbingshi wenji*, vol. 1, p. 41.

41. Liang Qichao, "Lun nüxue," in *Yinbingshi wenji*, vol. 1, p. 41.

42. See James Reeve Pusey, *China and Charles Darwin* (Cambridge, Mass.: Council on East Asian Studies, Harvard University, 1983), pp. 100–103.

43. For Yan Fu in this period, as Benjamin Schwartz points out, Western learning meant primarily social Darwinism: "It is the struggle for existence which leads to natural selection and survival of the fittest — and hence,

within the human realm, to the greatest realization of human capacities" (Benjamin Schwartz, *In Search of Wealth and Power: Yan Fu and the West*, pp. 52–59). As for Kang Youwei, his "espousal of Western concepts of historical progress and institutional reform naturally implied an acceptance of the ideal of wealth and power as the primary political goal of China at her present stage of history" (Hao Chang, *Liang Ch'i-ch'ao and Intellectual Transition in China, 1890–1907*, p. 52).

44. Liang Qichao, "Lun nüxue," in *Yinbingshi wenji*, vol. 1, p. 41.
45. Liang Qichao, "Lun nüxue," in *Yinbingshi wenji*, vol. 1, p. 40. For a discussion of Liang Qichao's interpretation of traditional Chinese "foetal education" in social Darwinian terms, see Pusey, *China and Charles Darwin*, pp. 102–103.
46. Liang Qichao, "Lun youxue," in *Yinbingshi wenji*, vol. 1, p. 45.
47. Liang Qichao, "Lun youxue," in *Yinbingshi wenji*, vol. 1, p. 45.
48. Liang Qichao, "Lun youxue," in *Yinbingshi wenji*, vol. 1, pp. 45–46.
49. Liang Qichao, "Lun youxue," in *Yinbingshi wenji*, vol. 1, p. 46.
50. Liang Qichao, "Lun youxue," in *Yinbingshi wenji*, vol. 1, pp. 46–47. For a brief history of intellectual efforts to reform the civil service examination system before and after 1898, see Benjamin A. Elman, *A Cultural History of Civil Examinations in Late Imperial China* (Berkeley: University of California Press, 2000), pp. 578–608.
51. The original phrase Liang used is *yan xifa* which perhaps referred to experiments used in teaching science in Western schools.
52. The original phrase Liang used is *shuogu ci* which is a type of story-telling consisting of talking, singing and playing instruments and drums.
53. Liang Qichao, "Lun Youxue," in *Yinbingshi wenji*, vol. 1, pp. 45–46.
54. In his preface to Terrenz's book, Bi Gongchen admitted that it was difficult to accept this theory. See Xu Zongze, *Ming-Qing jian yesuhuishi yizhu tiyao* (Synopsis of Works Translated by Missionaries during the Ming-Qing Period) (Shanghai: Zhonghua shuju, 1949), p. 304.
55. Wang Qingren, *Yilin gaicuo* (Corrections of Errors in Traditional Chinese Medical Writings) (Jinling: Wenying tang, 1849), p. 1.23.
56. Benjamin Hobson, "Xiyi lüelun xu" (Preface to *On Western Medicine*) (Shanghai, 1857), p. 1.
57. Liang Qichao, "Lun youxue," in *Yinbingshi wenji*, vol. 1, p. 47.
58. Liang Qichao, "Lun youxue," in *Yinbingshi wenji*, vol. 1, p. 58. The practice of calligraphy also included the writing of foreign languages.
59. Ma Jianzhong believed that grammar made it easy for Western children to master literacy skills in difficult Western languages; so in his *Ma Grammar* he followed Latin grammar step by step to elaborate the rules in classical Chinese, hoping this would help Chinese children to learn how to read and write more easily. See Ma Jianzhong, *Mashi wentong* (The Ma Grammar) (1898; reprint, Beijing: Shangwu yinshuguan, 1983), pp. 13–14.

60. Liang Qichao, "Lun youxue," in *Yinbingshi wenji*, vol. 1, p. 57.
61. Ma Jianzhong said that *wentong* meant "grammar" in Western terms. He acknowledged that the Chinese language had grammar, but no scholars before him had made efforts to systematically explicate the grammatical rules. See Ma Jianzhong, *Mashi wentong*, p. 14.
62. Liang Qichao, "Lun youxue," in *Yinbingshi wenji*, vol. 1, pp. 52–53.
63. Liang Qichao, "Lun youxue," in *Yinbingshi wenji*, vol. 1, p. 57.
64. *Baihua* was often used in folk literature which, however, was intellectually despised by intellectuals.
65. Liang Qichao, "Lun youxue," in *Yinbingshi wenji*, vol. 1, p. 54.
66. Liang Qichao, "Lun youxue," in *Yinbingshi wenji*, vol. 1, p. 54.
67. Liang Qichao, "Lun youxue," in *Yinbingshi wenji*, vol. 1, p. 58.
68. The book, published in Malacca in 1819, contains 60 questions and answers in eight sections about four continents — Asia, Europe, America and Africa, and countries such as China, England, Russia, Germany, America, India and Egypt. Xiong Yuezhi, *Xixue dongjian yu wan Qing shehui* (Western Learning and Late Qing Society) (Shanghai: Renmin chubanshe, 1994), pp. 115–116.
69. Ningbo by that time had become a publishing centre for American missionaries. Happer's book has twenty-two sections and each section contains ten to twenty questions, introducing a basic knowledge of Western astronomy to readers. Xiong Yuezhi, *Xixue dongjian yu wan Qing shehui*, pp. 173–175.
70. Liang Qichao, "Lun youxue," in *Yinbingshi wenji*, vol. 1, pp. 53–54.
71. Liang Qichao, "Lun youxue," in *Yinbingshi wenji*, vol. 1, p. 57.
72. Liang Qichao, "Lun youxue," in *Yinbingshi wenji*, vol. 1, p. 45.
73. Tongwen guan (or T'ung-wen Kuan) literally means "school of combined learning." W. A. P. Martin called it the Tung-wen College. See W. A. P. Martin, *A Cycle of Cathay* (New York; Chicago: F. H. Revell, 1897), p. 301. For an excellent study of the Tongwen guan in both Beijing and Shanghai, see K. Biggerstaff, *The Earliest Modern Government Schools in China* (Port Washington, N.Y.: Kennikat Press, 1961), pp. 94–165. Also, Xiong Yuezhi, *Xixue dongjian yu wan Qing shehui*, pp. 301–349.
74. M. J. O'Brien, one of the foreign instructors in the Beijing Tongwen guan, complained in 1869 of the poor quality of the students and of their lack of interest in their foreign studies: they gave their time and energy to Chinese learning, as it would give them "a status and position in the country" (K. Biggerstaff, *The Earliest Modern Government Schools in China*, pp. 145–146). The same complaints occurred in Shanghai: some students "had accustomed themselves to dictating their own scholarly ranking regardless of achievement" (K. Biggerstaff, *The Earliest Modern Government Schools in China*, p. 161).
75. Zhongxi shuyuan was established in Shanghai in 1881 by Young J. Allen

(1836–1907). For an introduction to Allen's life and his work in China, see W. A. Candler, *Young J. Allen, the Man Who Seeded China* (Nashvile: Cokesbury Press, 1931), pp. 108, 123, 148; for the Chinese-Western Academy, see Xiong Yuezhi, *Xixue dongjian yu wan Qing shehui*, pp. 616–620.

76. Liang Qichao, "Lun youxue," in *Yinbingshi wenji*, vol. 1, p. 56.

Perhaps Liang's suggestion of learning Latin was somewhat under the influence of Ma Xiangbo (1840–1939) and Ma Jianzhong, whom Liang became acquainted with in 1896. Although Liang and the Ma brothers regarded each other highly, Ma Xiangbo was very concerned about the young Liang, who only had a superficial knowledge of modern Western political philosophy. He thus advised Liang to study a European language. Liang took the advice and studied Latin under Ma Jianzhong in the Ma brothers' residence. See Ruth Hayhoe and Yongling Lu, *Ma Xiangbo and the Mind of Modern China, 1840–1939* (Armonk, N.Y.: M. E. Sharpe, 1996), pp. 35–36.

77. Liang Qichao, "Lun youxue," in *Yinbingshi wenji*, vol. 1, p. 58.

78. According to the *Record of Rites*, arithmetic was part of elementary education. However, as discussed in Chapter Six, no particular primers addressed instruction in arithmetic from the Tang through the Qing, and no more details of teaching and learning arithmetic can be found in later educational documents than are provided by the *Record of Rites*. Therefore, scholars attempting to promote arithmetic in elementary schooling usually quoted what had been written in this particular classic, and Liang was no exception. He claimed that in the original Confucian concept of education the knowledge of numerals and calculation was as important as the skills of reading and writing, but due to later changes which resulted in this kind of knowledge becoming insignificant, scholars no longer paid any attention to it. Because arithmetic and mathematics were not taught in school, they were seen as a kind of extraordinary learning (*juexue*) in the Qing. See Liang Qichao, "Lun youxue," in *Yinbingshi wenji*, vol. 1, p. 56.

79. "Chouren" referred to people who were knowledgeable in the areas of traditional Chinese mathematics and astronomy. For a further discussion of the concept of *chouren*, see Limin Bai, "Mathematical Study and Intellectual Transition in the Early and Mid-Qing," pp. 23–61.

80. Liang Qichao, "Lun youxue," in *Yinbingshi wenji*, vol. 1, p. 56.

81. Liang Qichao, "Lun youxue," in *Yinbingshi wenji*, vol. 1, p. 57.

82. See Hao Chang, *Liang Ch'i-ch'ao and Intellectual Transition in China, 1890–1907*, p. 119.

83. They are classics (*jing*), history (*shi*), scholarly works (*zi*) and literary writings (*ji*).

84. Liang Qichao, "Lun youxue," in *Yinbingshi wenji*, vol. 1, pp. 54–55.

85. The earliest Western-style dictionary was *Chinese-English Dictionary* (*Hua-Ying zidian*), compiled and published by Robert Morrison (1782–?) in 1822. In 1859 John Chalmers (1825–1899) published his *English-Cantonese Dictionary* (*Ying-Yue zidian*); between 1885 and 1890, John Fryer (1839–1928) published several dictionaries in his Gezhi shushi, or Gezhi Publishing House, which was established in 1885. See Xiong Yuezhi, *Xixue dongjian yu wan Qing shehui*, pp. 100, 147, 577–588.

86. Liang Qichao, "Lun youxue," in *Yinbingshi wenji*, vol. 1, p. 55.

87. Liang Qichao, "Lun youxue," in *Yinbingshi wenji*, vol. 1, p. 45.

88. For a list of subjects taught at Zhenjiang nüshu, see Xiong Yuezhi, *Xixue dongjian yu wan Qing shehui*, p. 298.

89. Liang Qichao, "Lun youxue," in *Yinbingshi wenji*, vol. 1, p. 57.

90. Liang Qichao, "Lun youxue," in *Yinbingshi wenji*, vol. 1, p. 48.

91. Liang Qichao, "Lun youxue," in *Yinbingshi wenji*, vol. 1, p. 45.

92. Liang Qichao, "Lun youxue," in *Yinbingshi wenji*, vol. 1, p. 49.

93. See Liang Qichao, *Yinbingshi heji, wenji*, vol. 4, pp. 41b–46.

94. Liang drafted the regulations for Jingshi Daxuetang in 1898. See Zhu Youhuan, *Zhongguo jindai xuezhi shiliao* (Materials on the Chinese Education System from the Late Qing to the Early Republican Period) (Shanghai: East China Normal University Press, 1983–1989), vol. 2, p. 656.

95. Yang Guangxian (1597–1669) attacked Christianity and the calendar devised by the Jesuit astronomer, Adam Schall (1591–1666). For a brief introduction to Yang's life and his conflict with the Jesuits, see A. W. Hummel, *Eminent Chinese of the Ch'ing Period* (Washington: U.S. Government Printing Office, 1943–1944), pp. 889–892; also Paul Rule, *K'ung-tzu or Confucius* (Sydney: Allen & Unwin, 1986), pp. 98–100; J. D. Young, *Confucianism and Christianity: The First Encounter* (Hong Kong: Hong Kong University Press, 1983), chapter 5.

96. Quoted from Shu Xincheng, *Zhongguo jindai jiaoyushi ziliao*, vol. 3, p. 977.

97. Liang in 1920 stated that the *ti-yong* formula was "regarded as a keynote" before the 1898 Reform, but there was a difference of opinion between men such as Li Hongzhang and Zhang Zhidong and men such as Kang Youwei, Liang Qichao and Tan Sitong (1866–1898): the former "positively would not admit that the Europeans and Americans, apart from their ability to make [guns], explore [terrain], sail [ships], and drill [troops], had any other kinds of knowledge," whereas the latter attempted to found "a new school of learning which would be neither Chinese nor Western but in fact both Chinese and Western." Liang Qichao, *Intellectual Trends in the Ch'ing Period* (*Ch'ing-tai hsüeh-shu kai-lun*), translated by Immanuel C. Y. Hsü (Cambridge, Mass.: Harvard University Press, 1959), p. 113.

98. See Hao Chang, *Liang Ch'i-ch'ao and Intellectual Transition in China, 1890–1907*, p. 117.

99. Liang Qichao, "Lun youxue," in *Yinbingshi wenji*, vol. 1, p. 58.
100. Liang Qichao, "Lun youxue," in *Yinbingshi wenji*, vol. 1, p. 58.
101. Liang Qichao, "Lun youxue," in *Yinbingshi wenji*, vol. 1, pp. 57–58.
102. For a discussion of Liang's concept of *baojiao*, see Hao Chang, *Liang Ch'i-ch'ao and Intellectual Transition in China, 1890–1907*, pp. 114–120.
103. Paul Cohen, "Christian Missions and Their Impact to 1900," in Part I of vol. 10 of *The Cambridge History of China*, edited by Denis Twitchett and John K. Fairbank et al. (Cambridge, [Eng.]; N.Y.: Cambridge University Press, 1978–1998), p. 588. Liang changed his view on the matter after the failure of the Reform. In 1902 and 1915 he expressed his disagreement with his teacher in *Xinmin congbao* (New People's Periodical) and *Guofeng bao* (Guofeng Newspaper). Later in his *Intellectual Trends in the Ch'ing Period*, Liang summarised the contrast between them, pointing out that Kang was enthusiastic about "the establishment of Confucianism as a state religion," and "the worship of Confucius together with Heaven," because he "mistakenly considered Christian worship in Europe as the basis of good government and state power," and "frequently attempted to equate Confucius with Christ by quoting a variety of apocryphal prognostications to support [his thesis]." This simplified analogy, Liang continued, would lead scholars to confine themselves to "their" Confucius instead of searching for the truth and having their own ideas. See Liang, *Intellectual Trends in the Ch'ing Period* (*Ch'ing-tai hsüeh-shu kai-lun*), pp. 95, 103, 104.
104. Paul Cohen, "Christian Missions and Their Impact to 1900," p. 589.
105. Paul Cohen, "Christian Missions and Their Impact to 1900," p. 577.
106. For a study of the missionaries' *Trimetrical Classic*, see E. S. Rawski, "Elementary Education in the Mission Enterprises," in *Christianity in China: Early Protestant Missionary Writings*, edited by S. W. Barnett and J. K. Fairbank (Cambridge, Mass.: Committee on American-East Asian Relations of the Dept. of History in collaboration with the Council on East Asian Studies, Harvard University , 1985), pp. 135–151.
107. E. S. Rawski, " Elementary Education in the Mission Enterprises," p. 151.
108. B. Berger, P. L. Berger, and H. Kellner, *The Homeless Mind: Modernization and Consciousness* (New York: Penguin Books, 1974), p. 149.
109. Berger, Berger, and Kellner, *The Homeless Mind*, p. 147.
110. Liang Qichao in 1920 summarised the political intention of the Modern Text School: "K'ang also used the *Kung-yang Commentary* to establish his doctrine of 'Confucius as a reformer,' in which he stated that the Six Classics were all created by Confucius, that both Yao and Shun were used by Confucius as disguises [for advocating reform], and that among the philosophers of the pre-Ch'in period there were none who did not 'use antiquity as a pretext for advocating reform.' This was certainly a very bold assertion which attempted to effect a sudden and profound liberation from

the classical works of the previous few thousand years, in order to open the door to free learning." And both Liang and Kang shared the idea of Gu Yanwu's "practical application," "using classical learning as a cloak for their political discussions. They departed from the original purpose of 'studying classics for the sake of classics,'" and their program therefore became "a prelude to the introduction of European and Western thought" (Liang, *Intellectual Trends in the Ch'ing Period*, p. 25). For a discussion of the New Text School and the scholarly origins of Kang Youwei and Liang Qichao, see Hao Chang, *Liang Ch'i-ch'ao and Intellectual Transition in China, 1890–1907*, pp. 7–34, 35–58.

111. Perhaps Liang's use of the term "Western education" was to avoid any clear reference to the works and activities of missionaries. This appeared to be the practice among reformers, only a few of whom in the 1890s directly acknowledged that their sources of information about the West originated in missionaries' writings and translated works, or were obtained through their personal contacts with missionaries. The only exception was perhaps Zheng Guanying who included many sections of Timothy Richard's *Qiguo xinxue beiyao* in his revised edition of *Shengshi weiyan* (Warning to a Prosperous Age) with a clear acknowledgment.

112. Liang began to publish his "On Reform" in 1896, the year he also became acquainted with Ma Jianzhong and his brother Ma Xiangbo (see n. 76). The *Ma Grammar* was published in 1898, so presumably Liang was informed about the book when he was writing his proposal, or he might even have seen the manuscript before it was published.

113. At the time he wrote "On Reform," a colleague in Macao raised the funds to set up a publishing house for children's books, and gathered other like-minded scholars to complete Liang's intended task. Liang was informed that four books were expected to be completed in a few months, and they would be printed by Guangshiwu Newspaper Ltd. in Macao. At the same time, these scholars started to compile a book similar to a Western-style dictionary. See Liang Qichao, "Lun youxue," in *Yinbingshi wenji*, vol. 1, p. 55.

114. One may argue that the first series of new Chinese textbooks was produced by Chen Qiu (1851–1904) in 1894. Chen's books, however, were not primers in a strict sense. Although all the books were in the format of *The Trimetrical Classic*, the content included both elementary education and medical knowledge, as Chen Qiu composed this series for his Liji Medical School. For a brief introduction to Zhong Tianwei's life and work, see Xiong Yuezhi, *Xixue dongjian yu wan Qing shehui*, pp. 535–536.

115. Gezhi shuyuan was established in the mid-1870s by a group of Chinese gentry and missionaries, such as John Fryer, to promote Western science and technology in China.

116. Zhu Youhuan, *Zhongguo jindai xuezhi shiliao*, vol. 2, pp. 578–579.

117. For a discussion of educational theories and experiments before the 1898 Reform, see Sally Borthwick, *Education and Social Change in China* (Stanford: Hoover Institution Press, 1983), pp. 38–64.

118. See both the 1902 and 1904 regulations for junior primary schools in Zhu Youhuan, *Zhongguo jindai xuezhi shiliao*, pp. 157–189.

119. Zhu Youhuan, *Zhongguo jindai xuezhi shiliao*, vol. 2, p. 587. For a discussion of memorisation in both Chinese and European classical education, see Alexander Woodside and Benjamin Elman, "Afterword: The Expansion of Education in Ch'ing China," in *Education and Society in Late Imperial China, 1600–1900*, edited by B. A. Elman and A. Woodside (Berkeley: University of California Press, 1994), pp. 533–534.

120. See Abe Yo, "Borrowing from Japan: China's First Modern Educational System," in *China's Education and the Industrialized World: Studies in Cultural Transfer*, edited by Ruth Hayhoe and Marianne Bastide (Armonk, N.Y.: M. E. Sharpe, 1987), pp. 57–80; Borthwick, *Education and Social Change in China*, pp. 66–68.

121. Borthwick, *Education and Social Change in China*, p. 49.

Conclusion

1.   Liang Qichao, "Lun youxue," in *Yinbingshi wenji*, vol. 1, p. 48.

Glossary

ai 愛
an 安

bagua 八卦
Baizi tu 百子圖
baihua 白話
Bai Juyi 白居易
Bailudong shuyuan xuegui 白鹿洞書院學規
Ban Gu 班固
Bangtou dixia chu xiaozi 棒頭底下出孝子
bao 保
baofu 保傅
baomu 保母
baojiao 保教
Baoying she 保嬰社
Baoyou daquan 保幼大全
bao 褓
bao 抱
Bi Gongchen 畢拱辰
bisuan 筆算
Bianfa tongyi 變法通議
Bianmin tuzuan 便民圖纂
bianwen 變文
Bingfu 餅賦
Boxue 博學
Bo Yü 伯俞
bolanggu 撥郎鼓
bu jian lü 不踐履

canju 蠶局
canzhang 蠶長
Can zhi tu 蠶織圖
Cangjie 蒼頡
ceyin zhi xin 惻隱之心
chen 齔
chen 臣
Chen Chun 陳淳
Chen Hongmou 陳宏謀
Chen Hu 陳瑚
Chen Li 陳櫟
Chen Qiu 陳虬
Chen Wanzhi 陳玩直
cheng 乘
Cheng Duanli 程端禮
Cheng Duanmeng 程端蒙
Cheng Hao 程灝
Cheng Juanzhi 程涓之
Cheng Ruoyong 程若庸
Cheng Yi 程頤
chengtong 成童
chi 尺
chizi zhi xin 赤子之心
chouren 疇人
chushi 處事
chuti ceyin 怵惕惻隱
Chuantong mengxueshu jicheng 傳統蒙學書集成
chunti 純體
cimu 慈母

congshu 叢書

Cui Shi 崔寔

Cui Xuegu 崔學古

cun 寸

cunru 村儒

cunshu 村書

Cun xiansheng 村先生

dafu 大夫

daxue 大學

daxue zhi dao zai ming mingde
　大學之道在明明德

dayi 大藝

Da Yu 大禹

Dai De 戴德

Dai Tong 戴侗

Dai Zhen 戴震

danmao 髧髦

dao 悼

dao 道

daotong 道統

de 德

di 弟

Dizi zhi 弟子職

Didu 帝都

Dili biantong lüezhuan 地理便童略傳

dixue 地學

dizhi 地支

diao 弔

Ding Lian 丁蓮

dongxue 冬學

Dong Yong 董永

Dong Zhongshu 董仲舒

Dou Yanshan 竇燕山

dudou 肚兜

Du Lin 杜林

Du Sixian 杜嗣先

Dushu minqiu ji 讀書敏求記

duanwu 端午

duanwu 端五

Duan Yucai 段玉裁

dui'ou 對偶

duizhang 對仗

Dunhuang 敦煌

duo 髻

duojian 髻剪

duozi duofu 多子多福

e 惡

e'shao 惡少

e'guidao 餓鬼道

enwu 恩物

ershisi xiao 二十四孝

Erya 爾雅

fameng 發蒙

Fan Chi 樊遲

fan 範

Fanjiang 凡將

fanqie 反切

Fang Fengchen 方逢辰

fangming 方名

fangtian 方田

Fang Yizhi 方以智

fenshu kengru 焚書坑儒

fengyi zushi, ersun raoxi 豐衣足
　食，兒孫繞膝

fu 賦

fu 婦

fu 傅

fu 腑

fu kongxu 腹空虛

fujing 負荊

fugu 復古

gejue 歌訣

gejue shu 歌訣書

gewu zhizhi 格物致知

Gezhi shuyuan 格致書院
gengdu 耕讀
Geng zhi tu 耕織圖
gong 弓
gong 功
gongjing zhi xin 恭敬之心
gongqing 公卿
gongshi 宮室
Gu Meng 顧蒙
Gu Rurang 顧汝讓
Gu Yanwu 顧炎武
gushi 故事
guayu 寡欲
guan 館
guanmeng 館蒙
Guan Fang 管汸
Guan Zhong 管仲
guanli 冠禮
Guang fangyan guan 廣方言館
Guang Sanzi jing 廣三字經
Guangshiwu baoguan 廣時務報館
Gui E 桂萼
Guo Ju 郭居
Guo Jujing 郭居敬
Guo Juye 郭居業
Guo Shoujing 郭守敬
Guo Shouzheng 郭守正
Guochou 國仇
Guofeng bao 國風報
guozi jian 國子監

Haiti zhi'ai 孩提知愛
Han Ying 韓嬰
Han Yu 韓愈
Hao'an xianhua 蒿庵閑話
Haoren ge 好人歌
Hetu 河圖
Hong Mai 洪邁
Hou Ji 后稷

Hu Mu 胡母
Hu Zeng 胡曾
hua 化
huagong 畫工
huajia 畫家
Hua-Ying zidian 華英字典
Huang Shulin 黃叔琳
Huang Xiang 黃香
Huang Zongxi 黃宗義
Huang Zuo 黃佐
Huang Xiang 皇象
huiyi 會意
huichi 毀齒
hun 魂

ji 激
Ji wei tan lai 激為灘瀨
ji 集
ji 計
ji 笄
Ji Kang 嵇康
jijiu 祭酒
Jijiu 急就
jiashu 家塾
Jiali 家禮
Jiaxun 家訓
Jiang Ge 江革
jiao 教
jiaohua 教化
jiaoyu 教育
jiao 角
jiaoshu 角黍
jiaolong 蛟龍
Jieyun youyi 節韻幼儀
Jinling 金陵
Jin Sheng 金聲
Jinsi lu 近思錄
jintui 進退
jinshi 進士

jinwen 今文
jing 經
jingmeng tongguan 經蒙同館
jingxue guan 經學館
jing 靜
jing 敬
jingshi 敬事
jingshen 敬身
Jingde chuandeng lu 景德傳燈錄
jingdu 競渡
Jingshi daxuetang 京師大學堂
jiu 九
jiujiu shu 九九數
Jiuzhang suanfa 九章算法
judou 句讀
jujing qiongli 居敬窮理
juan 卷
juanjuan zhe quan 涓涓者泉
juexue 絕學
jueju 絕句
jun 君
junzi 君子
junzi bu qi 君子不器

Kang Youwei 康有為
kaode 考德
kaogu zhunjin 考古准今
ke jin zhi neng 可盡之能
Kong Rong 孔融
koutou 叩頭
Kuang Heng 匡衡

Lao Laizi 老萊子
le 樂
Letian 樂天
leishu 類書
li 禮
li 里
li 理

li 利
Li Bai 李白
Li Chang 李長
Li Deng 李登
Li Enshou 李恩綬
Li Han 李瀚
Li Gong 李塨
Li Shizhen 李時珍
Li Si 李斯
Li Yuxiu 李毓秀
Li Zhizao 李之藻
Lishan 歷山
lishen 立身
li yue longmen 鯉躍龍門
Lian Po 廉頗
Liang Qichao 梁啟超
liangzhi 良知
liangzhi liangneng 良知良能
lienü 烈女
Lin Tong 林同
Lin Shu 林紓
Lin Xiangru 藺相如
Liu Bei 劉備
Liu Xi 劉熙
Liu Xiang 劉向
Liu Yan 劉彥
Liu Songnian 劉松年
Liu Zongdao 劉宗道
liu 六
liubo 六博
Liu shu 六書
Liu tao 六韜
liuyi 六藝
longzhou 龍舟
longwen 龍文
longshou 籠手
Lou Shu 樓璹
lu 祿
Lu Ji 陸績

Lu Jiuyuan 陸九淵
Lu Longqi 陸隴其
Lu Shiyi 陸世儀
Lu You 陸游
Lu Zishou 陸子壽
Lu Xun 魯迅
lü 慮
Lü Kun 呂坤
Lü Benzhong 呂本中
Lü Desheng 呂得勝
Lun nüxue 論女學
Lun youxue 論幼學
Lunyu 論語
Luoshu 洛書

Ma Renshou 馬仁壽
Ma Jianzhong 馬建中
Ma Xiangbo 馬相伯
Maguan tiaoyue 馬關條約
mantou 饅頭
maobi 毛筆
Mei Wending 梅文鼎
Menjing shu 門徑書
meng 蒙
Menggui 蒙規
Mengqiu 蒙求
mengxue 蒙學
mengxue guan 蒙學館
Mengxue duben 蒙學讀本
Mengxue quanshu 蒙學全書
mengshi 蒙師
mengshu 蒙書
meng yi yangzheng 蒙以養正
Miluo 汨羅
Mianhua tu 棉花圖
min 民
minwu 民物
minsheng riyong 民生日用
Min Sun 閔損

Minzhong xin yuefu 閩中新樂府
ming 命
ming jing 明經
ming renlun 明人倫
mingli 明理
Mingwu shu 名物書
mowu 末物
mo wen qiancheng 莫問前程
Mouyi nan 謀藝難
mu 母
Mu Lian 目蓮
Mudan ting 牡丹亭

nan geng nü zhi 男耕女織
Nanjing 南京
Nanyang gongxue 南洋公學
Naosui shuo 腦髓說
Neize 內則
nongshu 農書
Nongzheng quanshu 農政全書
nü 女
Nü sanzi jing 女三字經

Ouyang Xiu 歐陽修

Pangxi 湀熹
Pei Kai qingtong 裴楷清通
peng 朋
Peng Yunzhang 彭蘊章
ping'an 平安
Pingshui 平水
po 魄

Qi 齊
qi 氣
qizhi 氣質
qi sui xi yi 氣隨習移
Qiguo xinxue beiyao 七國新學備要
Qian Zeng 錢曾

Qianjia shi 千家詩
Qianqingtang shumu 千頃堂書目
qiang 繈 (or 襁)
qiongli 窮理
Qiu Weixuan 邱煒蔓
qing 情
Quli 曲禮
Qu Yuan 屈原
quan 泉
Quanxue 勸學
Quanxue pian 勸學篇
Quan Zuwang 全祖望
Quanti xinlun 全體新論

Rao Lu 饒魯
Rao Yingzi 饒應子
ren 仁
ren 人
renxin 人心
renyu 人慾
risheng richeng 日生日成
Rishi mengqiu 日食蒙求
ru 孺
Ruan Ji 阮籍
Ruan Yuan 阮元
rutong 儒童
ruxue 儒學
ruxue jiaoshou 儒學教授

sasao yingdui 灑掃應對
sandeng 三等
Sanguo zhi 三國志
sanmu 三母
Sanzi xun 三字訓
Sanzi jing jizhu yinshu 三字經集註音
　疏
Sanzi shijing Shangshu 三字石經尚書
Sanzi shijing Chunqiu 三字石經春秋
Sanzi xiaojing 三字孝經

shaizi 骰子
shan 善
shanshu 善書
shanzheng 善政
shangtu xiawen 上圖下文
shao 少
Shaoyi 少儀
shaonian laocheng 少年老成
Shao 勺
Shao Yong 邵雍
she 射
sheguan 舍館
shexue 社學
shen 深
Shen wei tan yuan 深為潭淵
shen 神
shentong 神童
Shentong shi 神童詩
sheng 生
shengchi 生齒
shengli 生理
shengzhi 生知
Shengshi weiyan 盛世危言
shengxue 聖學
shi 士
shidafu 士大夫
shi 仕
shi 師
shi 世
shi 史
Shi You 史游
Shizhou 史籀
shidao 適道
shijing 石經
shijing yangyong 市井洋佣
shifei zhi xin 是非之心
Shiwu bao 時務報
Shiwu sanzi jing 時務三字經
shixue 實學

shizi 識字

Shouyi guangxun 授衣廣訓

Shu Jin 舒津

shu 書

shuguan 書館

shuhui 書會

shulu 書錄

shumu 書目

shushi 書師

shushu 書數

shuxue 書學

shuyuan 書院

shuren 庶人

shu 數

shuji 數計

shuri 數日

shuxue 數學

Shu Xi 束皙

shui 水

shuike 説客

Shun 舜

shuochang wenxue 説唱文學

shuoguci 説鼓詞

si 糸

si 四

sibu 四部

Siku tiyao 四庫提要

Sixi 四喜

Siyan biandu 四言便讀

Sima Guang 司馬光

Sima Xiangru 司馬相如

Su Hanchen 蘇漢臣

Su Shi 蘇軾

suan 算

suanshu 算術

suanxue 算學

Songzhi 宋志

sui 歲

Suishi ji 歲時記

Sun Jing 孫敬

Tai Gong jiajiao 太公家教

taijiao 胎教

Taixi renshen shuogai 泰西人身説概

Tan Sitong 譚嗣同

Tang Jian 唐鑑

Tang Xianzu 湯顯祖

tanyuan 潭淵

tanlai 灘瀨

tao tao zhe shui 滔滔者水

ti 體

tili 體例

tian 天

tianli 天理

tianlun zhile 天倫之樂

Tianwen wenda 天文問答

tianzi 天子

tiao 齠

tiao 髫

tiaoduo 髫齔

tiaofa 髫髮

tong 童

tongmeng 童蒙

Tongmeng qiu wo 童蒙求我

Tongmeng xuzhi yunyu 童蒙須知韻語

Tongzi ke 童子科

tongjing 通經

Tongwen guan 同文館

Tongwen suanzhi 同文算指

tourong zhi 頭容直

touzi 投子

Tu Xiying 屠羲英

Tuiwei rangguo, youyu taotang 推位讓國，有虞陶唐

waidan neidan 外丹內丹

waixiang neigan 外象內感

Wan Huquan 萬斛泉

wanwu 玩物

wan wu sang zhi 玩物喪志

wan wu shi qing 玩物適情

wang 望

Wang Bai 王柏

Wang Chong 王充

Wang Fuzhi 王夫之

Wang Ling 王令

Wang Qinglin 王慶麟

Wang Qingren 王清任

Wang Rixiu 王日休

Wang Rong jianyao 王戎簡要

Wang Rui 王芮

Wang Sengru 王僧孺

Wang Shouren (Yangming) 王守仁 (陽明)

Wang Xizhi 王羲之

Wang Xiang 王祥

Wang Yinglin 王應麟

Wang Yun 王筠

Wang Zheng 王徵

Wang shentong shi 汪神童詩

Wang Zhu 汪洙

wei 為

wei 胃

Wei furen 衛夫人

Weizhi 微之

wenren huajia 文人畫家

Wen Yanbo 文彥博

wenzhang 文章

wo 臥

wu 五

wumu 五木

wuxing 五行

wu 毋

wu 物

wuxing 悟性

Wuxi 無錫

wufuwumu 無父無母

wuyu 無慾

Wu Hualong 吳化龍

Wu Meng 吳猛

Wuwang jiajiao 武王家教

xi 習

xili 習禮

Xici 繫辭

xi 西

xiwenxiyu 西文西語

Xixue shumubiao 西學書目表

xian 賢

Xiang 象

xiangxing 象形

xiangfu jiaozi 相夫教子

xiangxiao 鄉校

Xiang Xiu wendi 向秀聞笛

Xiang Anshi 項安世

xiao 孝

Xiao Liangyou 蕭良有

Xiao Zifan 蕭子範

Xiaosi 蕭寺

Xiao'er shi 小兒詩

Xiao'er yu 小兒語

xiaoxue 小學

xiaoxue jiaoshou 小學教授

Xiaoxue jiye 小學輯業

Xiaoxue shuxue 小學數學

xiaoxue zhi shu 小學之書

xiaozhuan 小篆

xiaoyi 小藝

xiaoxi 消息

Xie Liangzuo 謝良佐

xin 心

xinsuan 心算

xinxue 心學

xin 新

Xinbian duixiang siyan 新編對相四言

*Xinkan quanxiang ershisi xiaoshi
  xuan* 新刊全相二十四孝詩選
Xinmin shuo 新民說
Xinmin congbao 新民叢報
Xin shixue 新史學
xingbu 刑部
xingsheng 形聲
xing 性
xingren 杏仁
xiong 兄
Xiong Damu 熊大木
Xiong Danian 熊大年
xiu'e zhi xin 羞惡之心
xiucai 秀才
xu 續
Xu Chong 許沖
Xu Heng 許衡
Xu Naiji 許乃濟
Xu Shen 許慎
Xu Yinfang 許印芳
Xu Ziguang 徐子光
Xu Guangqi 徐光啟
xungu 訓詁
xunsu 訓俗
xue 學
xueliang 學糧
xuezhi 學知
Xunzhuan 訓篆
Xunmeng fa 訓蒙法
Xunmeng gejue 訓蒙歌訣

yaxi 雅戲
yayun 押韻
yazuowen 押座文
Yan zhong 言忠
yan xifa 演戲法
Yan Fu 嚴復
Yan Yuan 顏元
Yan Zhitui 顏之推

Yang 陽
yang 養
Yangmeng daxun 養蒙大訓
Yang Chenzheng 楊臣諍
Yang Guangxian 楊光先
Yang Guifei 楊貴妃
Yang Shi 楊時
Yang Xiong 楊雄
Yang Yanling 楊彥齡
Yangwu yundong 洋務運動
Yao 堯
yi 衣
yi 藝
yi 意
yi 夷
yi 義
yili shenxin 義理身心
yishu 義塾
yixue 義學
Yilin gaicuo 醫林改錯
Yi Luo yuanyuan lu 伊洛淵源錄
Yili 儀禮
yilei xiangxing 依類象形
Yin 陰
Yin Tieshi 殷鐵石
ying 嬰
Yingwen shushu 英文書塾
Ying-Yue zidian 英粵字典
yong 用
Yongle dadian 永樂大典
Yongshi shi 詠史詩
you 幼
youtong 幼童
youxue qidi zhizi 幼學啟迪之資
youyi 幼儀
you yu yi 游於藝
You Zi 由子
yu 育
yu 慾

yu 御

yu jiao yu le 寓教於樂

Yulan pen hui 盂蘭盆會

Yulan pen jing 盂蘭盆經

Yumen 禹門

Yu Shao 虞韶

Yu Shun 虞舜

Yü Qianlou 虞黔婁

Yu Zhisheng 于之勝

yuan 圓

Yuan Jian dashi 圓鑒大師

Yuanli 爰歷

Yuanshang 元尚

Yuan Zhen 元稹

Yuan Cai 袁采

Yuan Mei 袁枚

Yuan Shu 袁術

Yuanshi shifan 袁氏世範

Yuanxi qiqi tushuo 遠西奇器圖説

yue 樂

yuefu 樂府

Yueshi mengqiu 月食蒙求

za 雜

zaju 雜劇

zayan 雜言

zazi 雜字

zaixiang 宰相

zang 臟

Zeng Zi 曾子

Zengding fameng sanzi jing 增訂發蒙
   三字經

zongzi 粽子

Zhang Bi 張敝

Zhang Erqi 張爾歧

Zhang Ruitu 張瑞圖

Zhang Zai 張載

Zhang Zhidong 張之洞

Zhang Binglin 章炳麟

Zhao Gao 趙高

Zhao Jingfu 趙敬夫

zhe 者

Zhen Dexiu 真德秀

Zhenjiang nüshu 鎮江女塾

Zheng Deyu 鄭德與

Zheng Guanying 鄭觀應

Zheng Qiao 鄭樵

Zheng Zhensun 鄭振孫

zhengzi 正字

zhi 知

zhi 志

zhi 智

zhi 芷

zhi 質

zhinao 窒腦

zhishi 指事

zhixiao 至孝

zhiqi yangxin 治氣養心

Zhi Yong 智永

Zhongguo xiaoshuo hanjian chaoben
   中國小説罕見鈔本

Zhong Hui 鍾會

Zhong Ling 鍾鍰

Zhong Tianwei 鍾天緯

Zhong You 鍾繇

Zhongxi shuyuan 中西書院

Zhongyong 中庸

zhou 冑

Zhou Cheng Wang 周成王

Zhou Wen Wang 周文王

Zhou Dunyi 周敦頤

Zhou Xingsi 周興嗣

Zhu Duanzhang 朱端章

Zhu Sheng 朱升

Zhu Shouchang 朱壽昌

Zhu Xi 朱熹

Zhu Zhenheng 朱震亨

zhusheng 諸生

Zhuge gulu 諸葛顧廬

Zhuge Liang 諸葛亮

Zhulin qixian 竹林七賢

Zhulinsi nüke 竹林寺女科

zhuazhou 抓周

Zhuangyuan 狀元

zi 子

Zi Lu 子路

Zi Si 子思

Zi yu 子育

zidian 字典

Zizhi tongjian 資治通鑒

zongjiao 總角

Zuoshi mengqiu 左氏蒙求

❧ **References** ❧

Abbreviations

SSJZS — *Shisanjing zhushu* 十三經註疏 (The Thirteen Classics with Commentaries), 2 vols. Compiled by Ruan Yuan 阮元. Beijing 北京: Zhonghua shuju 中華書局, 1980.

SBBY — *Sibu beiyao* 四部備要 (Essentials of the Four Branches of Literature), 100 vols. Shanghai 上海: Zhonghua shuju 中華書局, 1935–1937.

SBCK — *Sibu congkan* 四部叢刊 (Four Libraries Series), 3,112 *ce.* Shanghai: Shangwu yinshuguan 商務印書館, 1919–1936.

CSJC — *Congshu jicheng chubian* 叢書集成初編 (Comprehensive Collectanea, first series), 3,467 vols. Shanghai: Shangwu yinshuguan 商務印書館, 1935–1937.

WZYG — *Wuzhong yigui* 五種遺規 (Five Regulatios Series). Edited by Chen Hongmou 陳宏謀. SBBY edition. Reprint. Taipei 臺北: Zhonghua shuju 中華書局, 1962.

ESEZ — *Ershier zi* 二十二子 (Twenty-two Works). Shanghai: Guji chubanshe 古籍出版社, 1986.

ESWS — *Ershiwu shi* 二十五史 (Twenty-five Histories), 12 vols. Shanghai: Shanghai shudian 上海書店 and Guji chubanshe 古籍出版社, 1986.

Selected Primers

Baijia xing 百家姓 (One Hundred Surnames). Author unknown. The text began to spread in China at the end of the Tang and the early Song. Collected in *Sanzi jing, Baijia xing, Qianzi wen* 三字經 百家姓 千字文 (abbreviated as *San Ban Qian* in the Ming-Qing period). Shanghai: Guji chubanshe 古籍出版社, 1988.

Baixiao tu 百孝圖 (One Hundred Illustrated Examples of Filial Piety), by Yü Baozhen 俞葆真. Hejian Yu shi 河間俞氏, 1871.

Cheng Dong er xiansheng xueze 程董二先生學則 (School Regulations by Masters Cheng Duanmeng 程端蒙 and Dong Zhu 董銖). In *Yangzheng yigui* 養正遺規 (Regulations for Nurturing Virtues). WZYG, 11a–15a.

Dizi gui 弟子規 (Regulations for Disciples), by Li Yuxiu 李毓秀 of the Qing. In *Xiao'ershu ji* 小兒書輯 (Collection of Children's Books), compiled by Zhang Chengxie 張承燮. Dong tingyutang 東聽雨堂, 1901.

Dushu zuowen pu 讀書作文譜 (The Methods of Reading and Writing), by Tang Biao 唐彪 of the Qing. Punctuated and collated by Bai Limin 白莉民. Hunan 湖南: Yuelu shushe 岳麓書社, 1989.

Ershisi xiaoshi 二十四孝詩 (The Poetry of Twenty-four Examples of Filial Piety), produced in the Yuan. There were different claims about its authorship.

Guxian ji 古賢集 (Collection of Ancient Worthies' Deeds). Author unknown. Probably circulated in the Dunhuang region in the late Tang period. For the full text, see Chen Qinghao 陳慶浩, "Guxian ji jiaozhu" 古賢集校註 (A Textual Critcism amd Commentary of Ku-Hsien-chi). In *Dunhuang xue* 敦煌學 (Dunhuang scholarship), vol. 3, pp. 63–102. Edited and published by Dunhuang xuehui 敦煌學會, New Asia Institute of Advanced Chinese Studies, 1976.

Jiachang yu 家常語 (Small Talk), by Guan Fang 管沴 (dates unknown). Collected in *Xiao'ershu ji bazhong* 小兒書輯八種 (A Collection of Eight Children's Books). Dong tingyutang 東聽雨堂, 1901.

Jiashu changyi 家塾常儀 (Daily Rites in Family School), by Zhen Dexiu 真德秀 (1178–1235). Collected in *Mengxue xuzhi* 蒙學須知 (Essential Primers). Edited by Xu Zi 徐梓 and Wang Xuemei 王雪梅, pp. 50–55. Shanxi 山西: Jiaoyu chubanshe 教育出版社, 1991.

Kaimeng yaoxun 開蒙要訓 (The Essentials for Beginners). It was said that the author was a person named Ma Renshou 馬仁壽, who lived in the region. The text was composed during the period of the Six Dynasties (222–589), but many copies were made by people of later generations. See Lei Qiaoyun 雷僑雲, *Dunhuang ertong wenxue* 敦煌兒童文學 (Children's Literature in Dunhuang), pp. 44–55. Taipei: Xuesheng shuju 學生書局, 1985.

Longwen bianying 龍文鞭影 (The Young Horse and the Shadow of a Whip). Originally under the title *Mengyang gushi* 蒙養故事 (Stories for Young Children), written by Xiao Liangyou 蕭良有 (1550–1602). Later, Yang Chenzheng 楊臣諍 (dates unknown) revised the book and changed the title to *Longwen bianying*. In 1883, Li Enshou 李恩綬 once again revised the book and changed the title to *Siyan biandu* 四言便讀 (Four Characters for Reading Convenience). Reprint. Hunan 湖南: Yuelu shushe 岳麓書社, 1986.

* Texts written by Lü Kun 呂坤 (1536–1618):
  • *Mengyang li* 蒙養禮 (Rituals for Nourishing Children), collected in *Mengxue yaoyi* 蒙學要義 (Essentials for the Education of Children), edited by Xu Zi 徐梓 and Wang Xuemei 王雪梅, pp. 44–52. Shanxi: Jiaoyu chubanshe 教育出版社, 1991.
  • *Haoren ge* 好人歌 (Song of Good People). Collected in *Xunsu yigui* 訓俗遺規 (Regulations for Public Morality). WZYG.

- *Shexue yaolüe* 社學要略 (Essential Points in Community School). Collected in *Yangzheng yigui*, WZYG.
- *Xu xiao'er yu* 續小兒語 (A Sequel to "Words for Children"). Collected in *Yangzheng yigui*, WZYG.

Lü Desheng 呂得勝 (fl. 1550), *Xiao'er yu* 小兒語 (Words for Children). Collected in *Yangzheng yigui*, WZYG.

Menggui 蒙規 (Regulations for Youngsters), by Huo Tao 霍韜 (1487–1540). Part of *Huo Weiya jiaxun* 霍渭崖家訓 (Family Rules by Huo Tao). Collected in *Hanfenlou miji* 涵芬樓秘笈 (Rare Collections of Hanfen Library), compiled by Sun Yuxiu 孫毓修. Shanghai: Shangwu yinshuguan 商務印書館, 1916–1926.

* *Mengqiu* 蒙求 and primers with the term *mengqiu* in their titles:
  - *Mengqiu* 蒙求, by Li Han 李瀚, a scholar who gained the *jinshi* 進士 degree in the Later Tang dynasty (923–936). Collected (with commentaries by Xu Ziguang 徐子光 of the Song dynasty) in *Xuejin taoyuan* 學津討源 (Bridges to the Origins of Learning). Cmpiled by Zhang Haipeng 張海鵬. Shanghai: Shangwu yinshuguan 商務印書館, 1922.
  - *Chunzheng mengqiu* 純正蒙求 (Pure *Mengqiu*), by Hu Bingwen 胡炳文 (dates unknown). *Siku quanshu* 四庫全書 edition.
  - *Lidai mengqiu* 歷代蒙求 (History of Past Dynasties), by Chen Li 陳櫟 of the Yuan . Collected in *Xiao sishu* 小四書 (Four Little Books). Compiled by Zhu Sheng 朱升, 1637.
  - *Mingwu mengqiu* 名物蒙求 (The Names and Descriptions of Things), by Fang Fengchen 方逢辰 (1211–1291). Collected in *Xiao sishu*.
  - *Shiqishi mengqiu* 十七史蒙求 (The History of Seventeen Dynasties), by Wang Ling 王令 (1032–1059). Collected in *Xiao sishu*.
  - *Wenzi mengqiu* 文字蒙求 (Explanations of Characters for Children), by Wang Yun 王筠. 1838. Reprint. Taipei 臺北: Yiwen yinshuguan 藝文印書館, 1971.
  - *Zuoshi mengqiu* 左史蒙求 (*Spring and Autumn* with Zuo's Commentary), by Wu Hualong 吳化龍. Collected in *Yihai zhuchen* 藝海珠塵 (Sea of Literature and Jewellery of the World). Compiled by Wu Xinglan 吳省蘭, supplemented by Qian Xifu 錢熙輔. Jinshan 金山: Qianshi shushixuan 錢氏漱石軒, 1850.

Mengyang shijiao 蒙養詩教 (Poetry for Nourishing Children), by Hu Yuan 胡淵 of the Qing. Collected in *Zhaodai congshu, bieji* 昭代叢書 · 別集 (Zhaodai Collectanea, a separate collection). Compiled by Zhang Chao 張潮 et al. Wujiang 吳江: Shenshi shikai tang 沈氏世楷堂, 1849.

Mengyang tushuo 蒙養圖説 (Illustrations and Explanations for Children), by Tu Shixiang 塗時相 of the Ming. Collected in *Yunnan congshu chubian* 雲南叢書初編 (Yunnan Collectanea, first series). Compiled by Zhao Fan 趙藩 and Chen Rongchang 陳榮昌 et al. Yunnan 雲南, 1914.

Mingxian ji 名賢集 (Collection of Wise Sayings). Author unknown. Allegedly produced before the Southern Song (1127–1278). Collected in *Mengxue quanshu* 蒙學全書 (Complete Collection of Children's Primers), compiled by Song Hong 宋洪 and Qiao Sang 喬桑, pp. 86–104. Jilin 吉林: Wenshi chubanshe 文史出版社, 1991.

* *Qianzi wen* 千字文 and primers in the genre:

- *Qianzi wen* 千字文 (One Thousand Characters), by Zhou Xingsi 周興嗣 (?–520). Collected in *Sanzi jing, Baijia xing, Qianzi wen*. Shanghai: Guji chubanshe 古籍出版社, 1988.
- *Xugu qianzi wen* 敘古千字文 (Ancient History in One Thousand Characters), by Hu Yin 胡寅 (1098–1156). Dong tingyutang 東聽雨堂, 1901.
- *Zhengzi qianzi wen* 正字千字文 (Rectifying One Thousand Characters), by Li Deng 李登 of the Ming. See Zhang Zhigong 張志公, *Chuantong yuwen jiaoyu chutan* 傳統語文教育初探 (A Preliminary Research on Traditional Chinese Language Teaching), p. 14. Shanghai: Shanghai jiaoyu chubanshe 上海教育出版社, 1962.

Riji gushi 日記故事 (Stories for Daily Learning), originally by Yu Shao 虞韶 of the Yuan. But the surviving versions were all produced in the Ming and afterwards, and each differed in content and illustrations. Two versions of the text are studied in this book: a 1542 edition and a 1669 Japanese version (based on a Ming edition). The 1542 edition, written and edited by Xiong Damu 熊大木, collected in Zheng Zhenduo 鄭振鐸, *Zhongguo gudai mukehua xuanji* 中國古代木刻畫選集 (Selected Works of Traditional Chinese Woodcuts), 9 vols. 1956. Reprint. Beijing: Renmin meishu chubanshe 人民美術出版社, 1985. The 1669 Japanese version is collected in *Hekeben leishu jichen* 和刻本類書集成 (or *Nako ku hon ruishi shusei* in Japanese), edited by Kikuya Nagasawa 長澤規矩也. Reprint. Shanghai: Guji chubanshe 古籍出版社, 1990.

* *Sanzi jing* 三字經 and the primers in the genre:

- *Sanzi jing* 三字經 (The Trimetrical Classic). Allegedly written by Wang Yinglin 王應麟 (1223–1296). Collected in *Sanzi jing, Baijia xing, Qianzi wen*. Also *Sanzi jing jikan* 三字經輯刊 (Collected Versions of *Sanzi jing*), edited by Lu Lin 陸林. Anhui 安徽: Jiaoyu chubanshe 教育出版社, 1994.
- *Sanzi jing zhutu* 三字經註圖 (*The Trimetrical Classic* with Illustrations and Commentaries), by Shang Zhaoyu 尚兆魚. Li Guangming zhuang 李光明莊, 1878.

Shentong shi 神童詩 (Poetry by a Child Prodigy), by Wang Zhu 汪洙 (fl. 1100). Collected in *Mengxue shipian* 蒙學十篇 (Ten Primers), collated and commentated by Xia Chu 夏初 and Hui Ling 惠玲, pp. 85–102. Beijing: Beijing Normal University Press, 1990.

Shuyan gushi 書言故事 (Stories from Ancient Books), by Hu Jizong 胡繼宗 of the Song. In *Hekeben leishu jichen* 和刻本類書集成 (based on a 1464 edition), compiled by Nagasawa Kikuya 長澤規矩也. Reprint. Shanghai: Guji chubanshe 古籍出版社, 1990, vol. 11.

Tai Gong jiajiao 太公家教 (Family Instruction by Tai Gong), a very popular teaching manual from 750 to 1000. For details, see *Yuzhao xinzhi* 玉照新志, by Wang Mingqing 王明清 (1127 ca–1197). *Xuejin taoyuan* 學津討源 edition, 3.20a–b.

Tongmeng xun 童蒙訓 (Instructions for Children), by Lü Benzhong 呂本中 of the Song. *Wanyou Wenku* 萬有文庫 edition. Reprint. Taiwan: Shangwu yinshuguan 商務印書館, 1966.

Tongzi li 童子禮 (Rituals for Children), by Tu Xiying 屠羲英 of the Ming. Collected in *Yangzheng leibian* 養正類編 (Catalogued Collection of Documents on Nurturing Virtues) of *Zhengyi tang quanshu* 正誼堂全書 (Complete Collection of Zhengyi Hall), edited by Zhang Boxing 張伯行, 3.1–3.11. Fuzhou 福州: Zhengyi shuyuan 正誼書院, 1866.

Tuyuan ce 兔園冊 (The Pamphlet of the Rabbit Garden). One of the earliest "village books" served as a popular textbook in the Five Dynasties (907–960). Opinions about its authorship and content varied. See Wang Guowei 王國維 (1877–1927), *Guantang jilin* 觀堂集林 (Collected Works of Wang Guowei), 21.4. Beijing: Zhonghua shuju 中華書局, 1961.

Xiao sishu 小四書 (Four Little Books), by Zhu Sheng 朱升 (1299–1370). 1637.

Xiaoxue guxun 小學古訓 (Elementary Learning in the Classics), by Huang Zuo 黃佐 (1490–1566). Collected in *Lingnan yishu* 嶺南遺書 (Collected Works of Lingnan), compiled by Wu Yuanwei 伍元薇 and Wu Chongyao 伍崇曜, vol. 3. Nanhai 南海: Yueya tang 粵雅堂, 1850.

Xiaoxue jiye 小學輯業 (An Elementary Text Collected From Classics), by Li Gong 李塨 (1659–1733). Possibly composed in 1700 and printed in 1705. CSJC.

Xiaoxue richeng 小學日程 (Daily Practice of Elementary Learning), by Chen Hu 陳瑚 (1613–1675). Collected in *Mengxue xuzhi* 蒙學須知, edited by Xu Zi 徐梓 and Wang Xuemei 王雪梅, p. 38. Taiyuan 太原: Shanxi jiaoyu chubanshe 山西教育出版社, 1991.

Xingli zixun 性理字訓 (Explanations of Neo-Confucian Terms). Compiled by Cheng Duanmeng 程端蒙 (1143–1191) and supplemented by Cheng Ruoyong 程若庸 (fl. 1177). Collected in *Xiao sishu* (Four Little Books), 3b–7b.

Xunmeng gejue 訓蒙歌訣 (Songs for Educating Children), by Lin Shu 林紓 (1852–1924). Initially published under the title *Minzhong xin yuefu* 閩中新樂府 (New Folk Songs from Fujian) in 1897. Qiu Weixuan 邱煒蔓 (fl. 1874–1941) changed its title to *Xunmeng gejue* and reprinted it as part of a series of primers entitled *Haiti zhiai* 孩提知愛 (lit. children know love). Xingzhou 星洲, 1898.

Yanshi jiaxun 顏氏家訓 (Yan's Family Precepts), by Yan Zhitui 顏之推 (531–

?595). Commentated by Wang Liqi 王利器 (titled *Yanshi jiaxun jijie* 顏氏家訓集解). Shanghai: Guji chubanshe 古籍出版社, 1980.

* *Yangmeng daxun* 養蒙大訓 (Great Instructions for Children), compiled and edited by Xiong Danian 熊大年 of the Yuan. Collected in *Yuyuan congshu* 芋園叢書 (Collectanea of Yuyuan), compiled by Huang Zhaoyi 黃肇沂. Nanhai Huangshi 南海黃氏, 1935.

The collection includes the following primers:

- *Jingxue qimeng* 經學啟蒙 (Classic Learning for Children), by Chen Chun 陳淳.
- *Jingxue xunyu* 經學訓語 (Instructions from Confucian Classics), by Chen Chun.
- *Yiluo jingyi* 伊洛精義 (The Essentials of Yi and Luo), by Wang Bai 王柏 (1197–1274).
- *Xingli zixun* 性理字訓 (Explanations of Neo-Confucian Terms), by Rao Ru 饒魯 (dates unknown).
- *Yumeng mingxun* 毓蒙明訓 (Clear Instruction for Children), by Cheng Duanmeng.
- *Xunmeng wuyan* 訓蒙五言 (Instruction for Children), by Rao Lu.
- *Xunmeng jueju* 訓蒙絕句 (Instructive Poetry for children), by Zhu Xi 朱熹.
- *Xiaoxue lishi* 小學禮詩 (Rituals for Children in Rhythm), by Chen Chun. (Another edition of *Xiaoxue lishi* collected in *Yangzheng yigui*, WZYG, 1. 9b–1.13a. The study of Chen Chun's *Xiaoxue lishi* in this book is based on WZYG edition.)

Youxun 幼訓 (Instructions for Young Children), by Cui Xuegu 崔學古 of the Qing. Collected in *Tanji congshu* 檀几叢書 (Collectanea of Tanji), compiled by Wang Zhuo 王啅 and Zhang Chao 張潮. Xin'an 新安: Zhangshi xiajutang 張氏霞舉堂, 1695.

Zazi 雜字 (Miscellaneous Characters). Primers under this title often differ in authorship and content. For an example of primers in this genre, see *15th Century Illustrated Chinese Primer, Hsin-pien Tui-hsiang Szu-yen*, facsimile reproduction with introduction and notes by L. Carrington Goodrich. 1967. Reprint. Hong Kong: Hong Kong University Press, 1990.

Zengguang xianwen 增廣賢文 (Enlarged Collection of Wise Words). Also entitled *Xishi xianwen* 昔時賢文 (Wise Words from the Past) and the *Gujin xianwen* 古今賢文 (Wise Words from Both the Past and Present). Author unknown. Believed to be first mentioned in a well-known Ming drama *Peony Pavilion* (*Mudan ting* 牡丹亭), by Tang Xianzu 湯顯祖 (1550–1616). Collected in *Mengxue quanshu*, compiled by Song Hong and Qiao Sang, pp. 105–151. Jilin: Wenshi chubanshe 文史出版社, 1991.

* Primers by Zhu Xi 朱熹:

- *Xiaoxue* 小學 (Elementary Learning). See *Xiaoxue jizhu* 小學集註. SBBY.

- *Dushu fa* 讀書法 (Methods of Study). In *Yangzheng yigui*, WZYG, 2.4a–2.6a.
- *Tongmeng xuzhi* 童蒙須知 (Children Should Know). In *Yangzheng yigui*, WZYG, 1.3a–1.6b.

Primary Sources

Chinese:

Ban Gu 班固. *Hanshu* 漢書 (History of the Former Han Dynasty), 8 vols. Beijing 北京: Zhonghua shuju 中華書局, 1970.

———. *Hanshu.* ESWS.

Chao Gongwu 晁公武 (ca. 1105–1180). *Junzhai dushu zhi* 郡齋讀書志 (Notes on Books from the Prefect's Studio). Haining 海寧, 1722

Chen Chun. See under "Xiaoxue lishi," 1962.

Chen Hu. See under "Xiaoxue richeng," 1991.

Chen Menglei 陳夢雷 et al. *Gujin tushu jicheng* 古今圖書集成 (The Imperial Encyclopedia). 1726–1728. Reprint. Shanghai: Zhonghua shuju 中華書局, 1934.

Chen Shou 陳壽. *Sanguo zhi* 三國志 (The Records of the Three Kingdoms). 5 vols. Beijing: Zhonghua shuju 中華書局, 1959.

Chen Zhensun 陳振孫. *Zhizhai shulu jieti* 直齋書錄解題 (The Annotated Catalogue of the Upright-Studio). Shanghai: Guji chubanshe 古籍出版社, 1987.

Chen Zizhan 陳子展. *Shijing zhijie* 詩經直解 (Commentaries on the *Book of Songs*), 2 vols. Shanghai: Fudan University Press, 1983.

Cheng Duanli 程端禮 (1271–1345). *Dushu fennian richeng* 讀書分年日程 (The Daily Schedule of Studies). Collected in *Yangzheng yigui*, WZYG, 3.6b–3.7a.

Cheng Duanmeng (1143–1191). See *Xingli zixun*, 1637.

Cheng Duanmeng, and Dong Zhu. See *Cheng Dong er xiansheng xueze*, 1962.

Cheng Yi 程頤, and Cheng Hao 程顥. *Er Cheng ji* 二程集 (Collected Works of the Cheng Brothers), 4 vols. Beijing: Zhonghua shuju 中華書局, 1981.

Cui Shi 崔寔. *Simin yueling* 四民月令 (Monthly Calendar for the Four Classes of People). Beijing: Zhonghua shuju 中華書局, 1965.

Cui Xuegu. See *Youxun*, 1695.

Da Tang liudian 大唐六典 (Six Groups of Statutes of the Great Tang Dynasty). Guangdong 廣東: Guangya shuju 廣雅書局, 1893.

Dai De 戴德. *Da Dai Liji jiegu* 大戴禮記解詁 (*Record of Rites* by the Elder Dai), commentated by Wang Pingzhen 王聘珍. Beijing: Zhonghua shuju 中華書局, 1983.

Dai Tong 戴侗. *Liu shu gu* 六書故 (Six Categories of Characters Elucidated). Xishu 西蜀: Li Dingyuan shizhuzhai 李定元石竹齋, 1784.

Dai Zhen 戴震. *Dai Zhen ji* 戴震集 (Selected Works of Dai Zhen). Shanghai: Guji chubanshe 古籍出版社, 1980.

Dong Gao 董誥. *Shouyi guangxun* 授衣廣訓 (Instructions on Cotton Planting and Manufacture) [1808]. Collected in *Zhongguo gudai banhua congkan* 中國古代版畫叢刊 (Collection of Traditional Chinese Woodcuts). Shanghai: Zhonghua shuju 中華書局, 1960.

Du Fu 杜甫. *Du Fu quanji* 杜甫全集 (Complete Works of Du Fu). Shanghai: Guji Chubanshe 古籍出版社, 1996.

Duan Yucai 段玉裁. *Jingyunlou ji* 經韻樓集 (Collected Works on Classics and Phonology), 12 *juan*. Qiyeyanxiang tang 七葉衍祥堂, 1821.

Fan Ye 范曄. *Hou Hanshu* 後漢書 (History of the Later Han Dynasty), 6 vols. Hong Kong: Zhonghua shuju 中華書局, 1971.

Fang Fengchen. See *Mingwu mengqiu*, 1637.

Fang Xuanling 房玄齡. *Jinshu* 晉書 (History of Jin). Beijing: Zhonghua shuju 中華書局, 1974.

———. *Jinshu*, ESWS.

Fang Yizhi 方以智. *Wuli xiaoshi* 物理小識 (Small Encyclopedia of the Principles of Things). 1666. Reprint. Yuzhai 愚齋, 1884.

Feng Chen 馮辰. *Li Shugu xiansheng nianpu* 李恕谷先生年譜 (A Chronicle of Master Li Gong). Guocui congshu 國粹叢書 edition, 1908.

Gao Cheng 高承. *Shiwu jiyuan* 事物紀原 (The Origins of Things). Collected in *Hekeben leishu jichen*, vol. 2. 1994.

Geng zhi tu 耕織圖 (Pictures of Tilling and Weaving). 1696 (Kangxi edition).

Gu Yanwu 顧炎武. *Rizhi lu* 日知錄 (Daily Added Knowledge). Shanghai: Guji chubanshe, 古籍出版社, 1982.

———. *Rizhi lu*, with collation, punctuation and commentaries. Hunan 湖南: Yuelu shushe 岳麓書社, 1994.

Guan Fang. See *Jiachang yu*, 1901.

Gujin mingren huagao 古今名人畫稿 (Past and Present Prominent Paintings), photo-offset copy of Shanghai dianshi zhai 上海點石齋 edition, 2 vols. Beijing: Zhongguo shudian 中國書店, 1984.

Guliang zhuan 谷梁傳 (Guliang Commentary). SBCK.

Guo yu 國語 (Discourses of the States). SBCK.

Han Ying 韓嬰. *Hanshi waizhuan* 韓詩外傳 (Han Ying's Exoteric Commentary on the *Book of Songs*). SBCK.

Han Yu 韓愈. *Dongyatang Changli ji zhu* 東雅堂昌黎集注 (Collected Works of Han Yu, with commentary). Shanghai: Guji chubanshe 古籍出版社, 1992.

Hao Yixing 郝懿行. *Erya yishu* 爾雅義疏 (Commentary on *Literary Expositor*), 3 vols. Beijing: Zhongguo shudian 中國書店, 1982.

Hong Mai 洪邁. *Rongzhai suibi* 容齋隨筆 (Jotting from Rongzhai Studio). Jilin 吉林: Wenshi chubanshe 文史出版社, 1994.

Hu Bingwen. See *Chunzheng mengqiu*, 1766.

Hu Jizong. See *Shuyan gushi*, 1990.

Hu Yin. See *Xugu qianzi wen*, 1901.

Hu Yuan. See *Mengyang shijiao*, 1697.

Huang Zongxi 黃宗羲. *Mingru xue'an* 明儒學案 (The Records of Ming Scholars). Cixi 慈溪, 1739.

———. *Huang Lizhou wenji* 黃梨洲文集 (Collected Works of Huang Zongxi). Edited by Chen Naiqian 陳乃乾. Beijing: Zhonghua shuju 中華書局, 1959.

———. *Huang Zongxi quanji* 黃宗羲全集 (Complete Works of Huang Zongxi). Zhejiang 浙江: Guji chubanshe 古籍出版社, 1985.

Huang Zuo. See *Xiaoxue guxun*, 1850.

Huangdi neijing, Suwen 黃帝內經・素問 (Basic Questions of The Yellow Emperor's Classic of Internal Medicine). ESEZ.

Huangdi neijing, Lingshu 黃帝內經・靈樞 (Mystical Gate of The Yellow Emperor's Classic of Internal Medicine). SBCK.

Huo Tao 霍韜. *Huo Weiya jiaxun* 霍渭崖家訓 (Family Rules by Huo Tao). *Hanfenlou miji* edition. Shanghai: Shangwu yinshuguan 商務印書館, 1916–1926.

Ji Yun 紀昀 et al. *Siku quanshu zongmu* 四庫全書總目 (Annotated Catalogue of the Complete Collection in Four Treasuries). 1772–1789. Reprint. Beijing: Zhonghua shuju 中華書局, 1965.

———. *Siku quanshu zongmu tiyao* 四庫全書總目提要 (The Essentials of the Annotated Catalogue of the Complete Collection in Four Treasuries). Shanghai: Shangwu yinshuguan 商務印書館, 1933.

Jia Yi 賈誼. *Jia Yi ji* 賈誼集 (Collected Works of Jia Yi). Shanghai: Renmin chubanshe 人民出版社, 1976.

———. *Xinshu* 新書 (New Works). ESEZ.

Jiao Hong 焦竑. *Guoshi jingji zhi* 國史經籍志 (On Classics in Official History Book). *Yueyatang congshu* 粵雅堂叢書 edition. Nanhai 南海: Wushi kanben 伍氏刊本, 1851.

Ke Shaomin 柯劭忞. *Xin Yuanshi* 新元史 (New History of the Yuan Dynasty), 60 vols. Tianjin 天津: Xushi Tuigengtang 徐氏退耕堂, 1919.

Li Baiyao 李百藥. *Beiqi shu* 北齊書 (History of the Qi Dynasty, 550–577), 2 vols. Beijing: Zhonghua shuju 中華書局, 1972.

Li Chuo 李綽. 1935–1937. *Shangshu gushi* 尚書故實. CSJC.

Li Fang 李昉. *Taiping guangji* 太平廣記 (Wide Gleanings Made in the Taiping Era), 10 vols. Beijing: Zhonghua shuju 中華書局, 1961.

Li Gong. See *Xiaoxue jiye*, 1935–1937.

Li Han. See *Mengqiu*, 1922.

Li Yanshou 李延壽. *Beishi* 北史 (History of the Northern Dynasty, 386–581). 10 vols. Beijing: Zhonghua shuju 中華書局, 1974.

———. *Nanshi* 南史 (History of the Southern Dynasty, 426–589). 6 vols. Beijing: Zhonghua shuju 中華書局, 1975.

Li Yuxiu. See *Dizi gui*, 1901.

Liang Qichao 梁啟超. *Intellectual Trends in the Ch'ing Period (Ch'ing-tai hsüehshu kai-lun)*. Translated by Immanuel C. Y. Hsü. Cambridge, Mass.: Harvard University Press, 1959.

———. *Xinmin shuo* 新民説 (New Citizen). Collected in *Yinbingshi quanji* 飲冰室全集 (Complete Works of Liang Qichao), 103 vols, 24 ce. Shanghai, 1932.

———. *Xixue shumubiao* (Bibliography on Western Learning), 3 *juan*. Shanghai: Shiwubao guan 實務報館, 1896.

———. *Yinbingshi heji, wenji* 飲冰室合集 • 文集 (Selected Works and Essays from the Ice-drinker's Studio: Selected Essays), 16 *ce*. Shanghai: Zhonghua shuju 中華書局, 1941.

———. *Zhongguo jin sanbainian xueshu shi* 中國近三百年學術史 (The Chinese Scholarship in Recent Three-Hundred Years). Taiwan: Zhonghua shuju 中華書局, 1963.

Liao Jiheng 廖冀亨. "Qiuke tang zij" 求可堂自記 (The Self -record of Qiuke Hall). In *Qiuke Tang liangshi yishu* 求可堂兩世遺書 (Liaos' Works of Qiuke Hall). Yongding Liaoshi 永定廖氏, 1875–1908.

Lin Shu. See *Xunmeng gejue*, 1898.

Lin Tong 林同. *Xiaoshi* 孝詩 (The Poetry of Filial Piety). Collected in *Xuehai leibian* 學海類編 (Catalogued Collection of the Sea of Learning), compiled by Cao Rong 曹溶, enlarged by Tao Yue 陶越. Shanghai: Hanfen lou 涵芬樓, 1920.

Liu An 劉安. *Huainan zi* 淮南子 (The Huainan Master). ESEZ.

Liu Xi 劉熙. *Shiming* 釋名 (Explaining Names). Commentated by Wang Xianqian 王先謙. 1896. Reprint. Shanghai: Guji chubanshe 古籍出版社, 1984.

Liu Xiang 劉向. *Lienü zhuan* 列女傳 (Biographies of Women). Enlarged by Mao Kun 茅坤 and commentated by Peng Yang 彭烊 under the title *Gujin lienü zhuan pinglin* 古今列女傳評林 (Past and Present Commentaries on *Lienü zhuan*). Collected in *Zhongguo gudai banhua congkan erbian* 中國古代版畫叢刊 • 二編 (The Collection of Traditional Chinese Woodcuts, second series), vol. 4. Shanghai: Guji chubanshe 古籍出版社, 1994.

Liu Xu 劉昫 et al. *Jiu Tangshu* 舊唐書 (Old Tang History). Beijing: Zhonghua shuju 中華書局, 1975.

Lu Lin 陸林, ed. *Sanzi jing jikan* 三字經輯刊 (Collected Versions of *The Trimetrical Classic*). Anhui 安徽: Jiaoyu chubanshe 教育出版社, 1994.

Lu Longqi 陸隴其. *Sanyutang wenji* 三魚堂文集 (Collected Works from the Three-Fish Studio). Jiahui tang 嘉彙堂, 1694.

Lu Shiyi 陸世儀. *Sibian lu jiyao* 思辨錄輯要 (Summary of Thinking and Differentaiting). SBBY.

Lu You 陸游. *Jiannan shigao* 劍南詩稿 (Poetry of Lu You). Jigu ge 汲古閣 edition.

——. *Laoxue'an biji* 老學庵筆記 (Jottings from Lao-xue-an). CSJC.

——. *Lu You ji* 陸游集 (Collected Works of Lu You), 5 vols. Beijing: Zhonghua shuju 中華書局, 1974.

Lü Benzhong. See *Tongmeng xun*, 1966.

Lü Desheng. See *Xiao'er yu* (1558), 1962

Lü Kun. *Lü Kun zhexue xuanji* 呂坤哲學選集 (Selected Lü Kun's Works on Philosophy). Beijing: Zhonghua shuju, 1962.

——. *Shenyin yu* 呻吟語 (Words of Moaning). Taiwan: Zhengda yinshuguan 正大印書館, 1975.

——. See *Haoren ge*, 1962.

——. See *Mengyang li*, 1991.

——. See *Shexue yaolüe*, 1962.

——. See *Xu Xiao'er yu* (1593), 1962.

Ma Guohan 馬國翰. *Yuhan shanfang jiyishu* 玉函山房輯佚書 (Lost Writings Restored in the Jade-Receptacle Studio). Changsha 長沙: Langhuan guan 瑯環館, 1883.

Ma Jianzhong 馬建忠. *Mashi wentong* 馬氏文通 (The Ma Grammar). 1898. Reprint. Beijing: Shangwu yinshuguan 商務印書館, 1983.

Nagasawa Kikuya 長澤規矩也, ed. *Hekeben leishu jichen* (or *Nako ku hon ruishi shusei* in Japanese) 和刻本類書集成 (Japanese Collection of Chinese Encyclopaedias). Shanghai: Guji chubanshe 古籍出版社, 1990.

Nai Deweng 耐得翁. *Ducheng jisheng* 都城紀勝 (Accounts of the Capital City). Yangzhou 揚州: Yangzhou shiju 揚州詩局, 1706.

Ouyang Xiu 歐陽修. *Ouyang Xiu quanji* 歐陽修全集 (Complete Works of Ouyang Xiu), 2 vols. Taipei: Shijie shuju 世界書局, 1963.

——, and Song Qi 宋祈. *Xin Tangshu* 新唐書 (New Tang History), 20 vols. Beijing: Zhonghua shuju 中華書局, 1975.

Peng Yunzhang 彭蘊章. "Yu ying sanshan lun" 育嬰三善論 (Three Merits of Rearing Infants), in *Minjian quanshan shu* 民間勸善書 (Folk Morality Books), edited by Yuan Xiaobo 袁嘯波, p. 50. Shanghai: Guji chubanshe 古籍出版社, 1995.

Quan Tangshi 全唐詩 (Complete Tang Poetry). 25 vols. Beijing: Zhonghua shuju 中華書局, 1960.

Quan Zuwang 全祖望. *Jieqiting ji waibian* 鮚奇亭集外編 (Outer Collection of Jieqiting), SBCK.

Ruan Yuan 阮元. *Yanjingshi ji* 揅經室集 (Works of the Study-of-Classic Studio). Taipei: Shijie shuju 世界書局, 1964.

——. *Yanjingshi waiji* 揅經室外集 (Outer Collection of the Study-of-Classic Studio). Wenxuan lou 文選樓 edition, 1823.

Sanzi jing, Baijia xing, Qianzi wen 三字經 百家姓 千字文 (*San Ban Qian*). Shanghai: Guji chubanshe 古籍出版社, 1988.

Shang Zhaoyu. See *Sanzi jing zhutu*, 1878.

Sima Qian 司馬遷. *Shiji* 史記 (Records of the Historian). Beijing: Zhonghua shuju 中華書局, 1976.

———. *Shiji zhengyi* 史記正義 (Orthodox Interpretations of *Records of the Historian*). ESWS, vol. 1.

Song Hong 宋洪, and Qiao Sang 喬桑, compl. *Mengxue quanshu* 蒙學全書 (Complete Collection of Children's Primers). Jilin: Wenshi chubanshe 文史出版社, 1991.

Song Lian 宋濂 et al. *Yuanshi* 元史 (Yuan History). Beijing: Zhonghua shuju 中華書局, 1976.

Su Shi 蘇軾. *Dongpo zhilin* 東坡志林 (Jottings of Su Shi). Beijing: Zhonghua shuju 中華書局, 1981.

———. *Su Dongpo quanji* 蘇東坡全集 (Complete Works of Su Shi). Reprint. Beijing: Zhongguo shudian 中國書店, 1991.

Tang Biao. See *Dushu zuowen pu*, 1989.

Tang Jian 唐鑑. *Tang Queshengong ji* 唐確慎公集 (Collected Works of Master Tang Jian). SBBY.

Tang Zhen 唐甄. *Qian shu* 潛書. Shanghai: Guji chubanshe 古籍出版社, 1955.

Tao Yuanming 陶淵明. *Tao Yuanming ji* 陶淵明集 (Selected Works of Tao Yuanming). Beijing: Zhonghua shuju 中華書局, 1979.

Tu Shixiang. See *Mengyang tushuo*, 1914.

Tu Xiying. See *Tongzi li*, 1866.

Tuo Tuo 脫脫. *Songshi* 宋史 (Song History), 20 vols. Bejing: Zhonghua shuju 中華書局, 1982.

Wang Can 王粲. *Wang Can jizhu* 王粲集註 (Selected Works of Wang Can, with Commentaries). Henan 河南: Zhongzhou shuhuashe 中州書畫社, 1984.

Wang Chong 王充. *Lunheng* 論衡 (Doctrines Evaluated). Commentated by Liu Pansui 劉盼遂. Shanghai: Guji chubanshe 古籍出版社, 1957.

Wang Dingbao 王定保. *Tang zhiyan* 唐摭言 (Collected Notes of the Tang Dynasty). SBBY.

Wang Fuzhi 王夫之. *Du Sishu daquan shuo* 讀四書大全説 (On "Complete Commentary on the *Four Books*"). Beijing: Zhonghua shuju 中華書局, 1975.

———. *Liji zhangju* 禮記章句 (Commentary on Sentences of the *Record of Rites*). Collected in *Chuanshan yishu* 船山遺書 (Writings of Wang Fuzhi). Shanghai: Taipingyang shudian 太平洋書店, 1935.

———. *Shangshu yanyi* 尚書衍義 (Elaborating the Meaning of the *Book of Documents*). Beijing: Zhonghua shuju 中華書局, 1976.

Wang Guowei 王國維. *Guantang jilin* 觀堂集林 (Collected Works of Wang Guowei). Beijing: Zhonghua shuju 中華書局, 1961.

Wang Mingqing 王明清. *Yuzhao xinzhi* 玉照新志. Collected in *Xuejin taoyuan*, compiled by Zhang Haipeng. Shanghai: Shangwu yinshuguan 商務印書館, 1922.

Wang Qingren 王清任. *Yilin gaicuo* 醫林改錯 (Corrections of Errors in Traditional Chinese Medical Writings). Jinling 金陵: Wenying tang 文英堂, 1849.

Wang Yinglin 王應麟. *Kunxue jiwen* 困學紀聞 (Records of Knowledge Learned). SBCK.

———. *Yuhai* 玉海 (Ocean of Jade). Taipei: Huawen chubanshe 華文出版社, 1964.

Wang Yun. See *Wenzi mengqiu*, 1971.

———. "Jiao tongzi fa" 教童子法 (Methods of Teaching Children). In *Qingdai qianqi jiaoyu lunzhu xuan* 清代前期教育論著選 (Selected Works on Education, 1644–1848), edited by Li guojun 李國鈞 et al., vol. III, p. 485. Beijing: Renmin jiaoyu chubanshe 人民教育出版社, 1990.

Wang Zheng 王徵. *Yuanxi qiqi tushuo* 遠西奇器圖説 (Illustrated Explanation of Rare Western Instruments). 1627. Reprint. CSJC.

Wang Zhu. See *Shentong shi*, 1991.

Wu Hualong. See *Zuoshi mengqiu*, 1850.

Xia Chu 夏初 and Hui Lin 惠林. *Mengxue shipian* 蒙學十篇 (Ten Primers). Beijing: Beijing Normal University Press, 1991.

Xiang Anshi 項安世. *Xiangshi jiashuo* 項氏家説 (Instructions for the Xiang Family). SBCK.

Xiao Liangyou. See *Longwen bianying*, 1986.

Xiao'er weisheng zongwei lunfang 小兒衛生總微論方 (Prescriptions for Children's Health). *Siku quanshu* edition.

Xie Liangzuo 謝良佐. *Shang Cai xiansheng yulu* 上蔡先生語錄 (Master Xie Liangzuo's Analects). *Zhengyi tang quanshu* 正誼堂全書 edition, 1866.

Xiong Damu. See *Riji gushi* (1542). 1985.

Xiong Danian. See *Yangmeng daxun*, 1935.

Xu Shen 許慎. *Shuowen jiezi zhu* 説文解字注 (Explanations of Words and Characters), commentated by Duan Yucai 段玉裁. 1815. Reprint, Shanghai: Guji chubanshe 古籍出版社, 1981.

Xu Zi 徐梓, and Wang Xuemei 王雪梅, eds. *Mengxue yaoyi* 蒙學要義 (Essentials of Children's Books). Taiyuan 太原: Shanxi jiaoyu chubanshe 山西教育出版社, 1991.

Xun Kuang 荀況. *Xun Zi* 荀子. SBCK.

———. *Xun Zi jianshi* 荀子簡釋 (Commentaries on *Xun Zi*), commentated by Liang Qixiong 梁啟雄. 1955. Reprint. Beijing: Zhonghua shuju 中華書局, 1983.

Yan Yuan 顏元. *Sishu zhengwu* 四書正誤 (Critical Commentary on *Sishu*). Yan-Li congshu 顏李叢書 edition, 1923.

———. *Yan Yuan ji* 顏元集 (Collected Works of Yan Yuan). Beijing: Zhonghua shuju 中華書局, 1987.

Yan Zhitui. See *Yanshi jiaxun jijie*, 1980.

Yao Silian 姚思廉. *Liang Shu* 梁書 (Liang History). Beijing: Zhonghua shuju 中華書局, 1973.

Yü Baozhen. See *Baixiao tu*, 1871.

Yu Yue 俞樾. *Chaxiangshi congchao* 茶香室叢鈔 (Collected Works from the Fragrant-Teahouse). Wuxia Chunzaitang 吳下春在堂 edition, 1883.

Yuan Mei 袁枚. *Xiaocangshan fang wenji* 小倉山房文集 (Selected Works of Yuan Mei). SBBY.

Yuan Xiaobo 袁嘯波, ed. *Minjian quanshan shu* 民間勸善書 (Folk Morality Books). Shanghai: Guji chubanshe 古籍出版社, 1995.

Yuan Zhen 元縝. *Yuanshi Changqing ji* 元氏長慶集 (Selected Works of Yuan Zhen). Beijing: Wenxue guji kanxingshe 文學古籍刊行社, 1956.

Zeng Gong 曾鞏. *Zeng Gong sanwen quanji* 曾鞏散文全集 (Complete Collection of Zeng Gong's Prose). Beijing: Jinri zhongguo chubanshe 今日中國出版社, 1996.

Zhang Hua 張華. *Bo wu zhi* 博物志 (An Encyclopaedic Book). Shanghai: Guji chubanshe 古籍出版社, 1990.

Zhang Tingyu 張廷玉 et al. *Mingshi* 明史 (Ming History), 28 vols. Beijing: Zhonghua shuju 中華書局, 1974.

Zhao Erxun 趙爾巽 et al. *Qingshi gao* 清史稿 (Qing History), 48 vols. Beijing: Zhonghua shuju 中華書局, 1977.

Zhen Dexiu. See *Jiashu changyi*, 1991

Zhong Ling 鍾錂. *Yan Xizhai xiansheng yanxing lu* 顏習齋先生言行錄 (A Biography of Master Yan Yuan). Yan-Li congshu 顏李叢書 edition, 1923.

Zhou Mi 周密. *Wulin jiushi.* 武林舊事 (Old Stories from Hangzhou). Hangzhou 杭州: Xihu shushe 西湖書社, 1981.

Zhou Xingsi. See *Qianzi wen*, 1988.

Zhu Duanzhang 朱端章. *Weisheng jiabao chanke beiyao* 衛生家保產科備要 (Essentials of Family Health and Child Birth). 1184; 1887 reprint. CSJC.

Zhu Guozhen 朱國禎. *Yongzhuang xiaopin* 涌幢小品 (Jottings from Yongzhuang). Shanghai: Jinbu shuju 進步書局, 1926.

Zhu Sheng 朱升. See *Xiao sishu*, 1637.

Zhu Xi 朱熹. *Bailudong shuyuan xuegui* 白鹿洞書院學規 (Regulations of the Bailudong Academy). Collected in *Mengxue xuzhi* 蒙學須知 (Essential Primers), edited by by Xu Zi 徐梓 and Wang Xuemei 王雪梅, pp. 41–43. Taiyuan 太原: Shanxi jiaoyu chubanshe 山西教育出版社, 1991.

———. *Sishu jizhu* 四書集註 (Collected Commentaries on the *Four Books*). Taipei: Qiming shuju 啟明書局, 1959.

———. *Sishu zhangju jizhu* 四書章句集註 (Collected Commentaries on the Chapters and Sentences of the *Four Books*). Beijing: Zhonghua shuju 中華書局, 1983.

———. *Xiaoxue jizhu* 小學集註 (Collected Commentaries on *Elementary Learning*). SBBY.

———. *Zhuzi wenji* 朱子文集 (Selected Works of Zhu Xi). CSJC.

———. *Zhuzi yulei* 朱子語類 (Categorized Selections of Master Zhu's Analects), 8 vols. Taipei: Zhengzhong shuju 正中書局, 1973.

———. *Zhuzi yulei.* SBBY.

———. See *Dushu fa*, 1962.

———. See *Tongmeng xuzhi*, 1962.

Zhu Zhenheng 朱震亨. *Gezhi yulun* 格致餘論 (More on "Natural Knowledge" of Phenomena). CSJC.

English:

Brinsley, John. *Ludus Literarius, or the Grammar Schoole.* 1612. Reprint. Menston, England: Scolar Press, 1968.

Clement, Francis. *The Petie Schole.* 1587. Reprint. Menston, England: Scolar Press, 1967.

Coote, Edmund. *The English Schoole-maister.* 1596. Reprint. Menston, England: Scolar Press, 1968.

Furnivall, F., ed. *The Babees Book.* 1868. Reprint. New York: Greenwood Press, 1969.

Mulcaster, Richard. *Elementarie.* 1582. Reprint. Menston, England: Scolar Press, 1970.

———. *Positions.* 1581. Reprint. New York, 1971.

Recorde, Robert. *The Grounde of Artes.* 1542. Reprint. New York: Da Capo Press and Amsterdam: Theatrum Orbis Terrarum Ltd, 1969.

Secondary Sources

Abe Yo. "Ryo kei-cho no kyoku shiso to sono katsudo bojutsu hempoki o chushin to shite" (Liang Qichao's Educational Thought and Activities in the Period of the 1898 Reform). *Kyushu daigaku kyoikubu kiyo* (Bulletin of the Department of Education of Kyushu University), 6 (1959), pp. 301–323.

———. "Borrowing from Japan: China's First Modern Educational System." In *China's Education and the Industrialized World: Studies in Cultural Transfer*, edited by Ruth Hayhoe and Marianne Bastid, pp. 57–80. Armonk, N.Y.: M.E. Sharpe, 1987.

Anderson, Michael. *Approaches to the History of the Western Family, 1500–1914.* London: Macmillan Press, 1980.

Aries, Philippe. *Centuries of Childhood.* Translated from French by R. Baldick. London: Cape, 1962.

Ayers, William. *Chang Chih-tung and Education Reform in China.* Cambridge, Mass.: Harvard University Press, 1971.

Bai Limin. "The Chinese Kindergarten Movement, 1903–1927." In *Kindergartens and Culture: The Global Diffusion of an Idea*, edited by Roberta Wollons, pp. 137–165. New Haven: Yale University Press, 2000.

——. "Mathematical Study and Intellectual Transition in the Early and Mid-Qing." *Late Imperial China*, 16.2 (1995), pp. 23–61.

——. "Primers and Paradigms." Ph.D dissertation. La Trobe University, 1993.

——. *Xixue dongjian yu Ming-Qing zhi ji jiaoyu sichao* 西學東漸與明清之際教育思潮 (Western Influence and Educational Thought in the Late Ming and Early Qing Period). Beijing: Jiaoyu kexue chubanshe 教育科學出版社, 1989.

Barnett, S. W., and J. K. Fairbank, eds. *Christianity in China: Early Protestant Missionary Writings.* Cambridge, Mass.: The Committee on American-East Asian Relations of the Dept. of History, in collaboration with the Council on East Asian Studies/Harvard University, 1985.

Bays, Daniel H. *China Enters the Twentieth Century, Chang Chih-tung and the Issues of a New Age, 1895–1909.* Ann Arbor: The University of Michigan Press, 1978.

Berger, B., P. L. Berger, and H. Kellner. *The Homeless Mind: Modernization and Consciousness.* New York: Penguin Books, 1974.

Berling, Judith. *The Syncretic Religion of Lin Chao-en.* New York: Columbia University Press, 1980.

Biggerstaff, K. *The Earliest Modern Government Schools in China.* Port Washington, N.Y.: Kennikat Press, 1961.

Black, Alison Harley. *Man and Nature in the Philosophical Thought of Wang Fu-chih.* Seattle: University of Washington Press, 1989.

Bol, Peter K. *"This Culture of Ours": Intellectual Transitions in T'ang and Sung China.* Stanford: Stanford University Press, 1992.

Borthwick, Sally. *Education and Social Change in China.* Stanford: Hoover Institution Press, 1983.

Bossard, James H. S., and Eleanor S. Boll. *Ritual in Family Living.* Philadelphia: University of Pennsylvania Press, 1956.

Bray, Francesca. *Technology and Gender.* Berkeley: University of California Press, 1997.

Bremner, J. Gavin. *Infancy.* 2nd edition. Oxford, England and Cambridge, Mass.: Basil Blackwell, 1991.

Brokaw, Cynthia J. *The Ledgers of Merit and Demerit: Social Change and Moral Order in Late Imperial China.* Princeton: Princeton University Press, 1991.

——. "Tai Chen and Learning in the Confucian Tradition." In *Education and Society in Late Imperial China*, edited by B. A. Elman and A. Woodside, pp. 257–291. Berkeley: University of California Press, 1994.

Bryson, Bill. *Mother Tongue: The English Language.* London: Hamish Hamilton, 1990.

Candler, W. A. *Young J. Allen, the Man Who Seeded China.* Nashvile: Cokesbury Press, 1931.

Chan, Wing-tsit, ed. *Chu Hsi and Neo-Confucianism.* Honolulu: University of Hawaii Press, 1986.

———, trans. *Instructions for Practical Living and Other Neo-Confucian Writings by Wang Yang-Ming.* New York: Columbia University Press, 1963.

———, trans. *Neo-Confucian Terms Explained.* New York: Columbia University Press, 1986.

———, trans. *Reflections on Things at Hand.* New York: Columbia University Press, 1967.

———, trans. and comp. *A Source Book in Chinese Philosophy.* Princeton: Princeton University Press, 1983.

Chang Chung-li. *The Chinese Gentry.* Seattle: University of Washington Press, 1955.

Chang Hao. *Liang Ch'i-ch'ao and Intellectual Transition in China, 1890–1907.* Cambridge, Mass.: Harvard University Press, 1971.

Chen Qinghao 陳慶浩. "Guxian ji jiaozhu" 古賢集校註 (A Textual Critcism and Commentary of Ku-Hsien-chi). In *Dunhuang xue* 敦煌學 (Dunhuang Scholarship), edited and published by Dunhuang xuehui 敦煌學會 (New Asia Institute of Advanced Chinese Studies), vol. 3 (1976), pp. 63–102.

Chen Zuolong 陳祚龍. "Dunhuang xue zaji" 敦煌學雜記 (Notes on the Study of Dunhuang Materials). *Youshi yuekan* 幼獅月刊 (Young-Lion Monthly), 40.5 (1974), pp. 56–61.

Cheng Chung-ying. "Reason, Substance, and Human Desires in Seventeenth-century Neo-Confucianism." In *The Unfolding of Neo-Confucianism,* edited by William Theodore de Bary, pp. 469–510. New York: Columbia University Press, 1975.

Cheng Shunying 程舜英. *Lianghan jiaoyu zhidu shi ziliao* 兩漢教育制度史資料 (Documents of the Educational System in the Former and Later Han). Beijing: Beijing Normal University Press, 1983.

Ching, Julia and Fang Chaoying, eds. *The Records of Ming Scholars.* Honolulu: University of Hawaii Press, 1987.

Chow Tse-tung. *The May Fourth Movement: Intellectual Revolution in Modern China.* Cambridge, Mass.: Harvard University Press, 1960.

Chu Ron-Guey. "Chu Hsi and Public Instruction." In *Neo-Confucian Education,* edited by William Theodore de Bary and John Chaffee, pp. 252–273. Berkeley: University of California Press, 1989.

Ci hai 辭海. 3 vols. Shanghai: Shanghai cishu chubanshe 上海辭書出版社, 1980.

Ci yuan 辭源. Beijing: Shangwu yinshuguan 商務印書館, 1979.

Cohen, Paul. "Christian Missions and Their Impact to 1900." In *The Cambridge History of China,* edited by Denis Twitchett and John K. Fairbank et al., Part I of vol. 10, pp. 543–590. Cambridge, England and New York: Cambridge University Press, 1978–1998.

Crossley, John N., and Anthony W. C. Lun, trans. *Chinese Mathematics: A Concise History*. Oxford: Clarendon Press, 1987.

Culin, Steward. *Korean Games, with Notes on the Corresponding Games of China and Japan*. 1895. Reprint. New York: Dover Publications, Inc., 1991.

———. "Chinese Games with Dice and Dominoes." In *Report of U.S. National Museum*, 1893, pp. 491–537.

Culler, Jonathan. *Ferdinand de Saussure*. 2nd edition. Ithaca: Cornell University Press, 1986.

Dardess, John. "Childhood in Premodern China." In *Children in Historical and Comparatie Perspective*, edited by Joseph M. Hawes and N. Ray Hiner, pp. 71–94. Westport: Greenwood Press, 1991.

de Bary, William Theodore. *East Asian Civilizations*. Cambridge, Mass.: Harvard University Press, 1988.

———, ed. *The Unfolding of Neo-Confucianism*. New York: Columbia University Press, 1975.

———, and Irene Bloom, eds. *Principle and Practicality*. New York: Columbia University Press, 1979.

———, and John Chaffee, eds. *Neo-Confucian Education: The Formative Stage*. Berkeley: University of California Press, 1989.

———, Wing-tsit Chan, and Burton Watson, eds. *Sources of Chinese Tradition*. New York: Columbia University Press, 1966.

——— et al., eds. *Self and Society in Ming Thought*. New York: Columbia University Press, 1970.

DeFrancis, John. *Visible Speech*. Honolulu: University of Hawaii Press, 1989.

Diringer, David. *Writing*. London: Thames and Hudson, 1962.

Dobson, W. A. C. H. *Mencius*. Toronto: University of Toronto Press, 1963.

Douglas, Mary. *Natural Symbols*. Harmondsworth: Penguin Books, 1973.

Ebrey, Patricia Buckley, ed. *Chinese Civilization and Society, A Sourcebook*. New York: The Free Press; London: Collier Macmillan Publishers, 1981.

———, trans. *Chu Hsi's Family Rituals*. Princeton: Princeton University Press, 1991.

———. "Education Through Ritual: Efforts to Formulate Family Rituals During the Sung Period." In *Neo-Confucian Education*, edited by William Theodore de Bary and John Chaffee, pp. 277–306. University of California Press, 1989.

———. *Family and Property in Sung China: Yuan Ts'ai's Precepts for Social Life*. Princeton: Princeton University Press, 1984.

Eco, Umberto. *The Search for the Perfect Language*. Oxford: Blackwell, 1995.

Elman, Benjamin A. *A Cultural History of Civil Examinations in Late Imperial China*. Berkeley: University of California Press, 2000.

————. *From Philosophy to Philology*. Cambridge, Mass.: Harvard University Press, 1984.

————, and Alexander Woodside, eds. *Education and Society in Late Imperial China*. Berkeley: University of California Press, 1994.

Elvin, Mark. *The Pattern of the Chinese Past*. London: Eyre Methuen, 1973.

Fang, Thome H. *Chinese Philosophy: Its Spirit and Its Development*. Taipei: Linking, 1981.

Farquhar, Mary Ann. *Children's Literature in China: From Lu Xun to Mao Zedong*. Armonk, New York and London: M. E. Sharpe, 1999.

Fei, Hsiao-Tung. *Peasant Life in China*. London: Routledge & Kegan Paul Ltd., 1939.

Feng Yu-lan (Feng Youlan) 馮友蘭. *Zhongguo zhexue shi* 中國哲學史 (A History of Chinese Philosophy). Hong Kong: Taipingyang tushu gongsi 太平洋圖書公司, 1961.

————. *A Short History of Chinese Philosophy*. New York: The Free Press, 1966.

Field, E. M. *The Child and His Book: Some Account of the History and Progress of Children's Literature in England*. 1892. Reprint. Detroit: Singing Tree Press, Book Tower, 1968.

Fingarette, Herbert. *Confucius: The Secular as Sacred*. New York: Harper & Row, 1972.

Furth, Charlotte. "Concepts of Pregnancy, Childbirth, and Infancy in Ch'ing Dynasty China." *Journal of Asian Studies*, 46.1 (1987), pp. 7–35.

————. *A Flourishing Yin: Gender in China's Medical History, 960–1665*. Berkeley and London: University of California Press, 1999.

Gallagher, Louis J., trans. *China in the Sixteenth Century: The Journals of Matthew Ricci: 1583–1610*. New York: Random House, 1953.

Gardner, Daniel K., trans. *Learning to be a Sage: Selections from the Conversations of Master Chu*. Berkeley: University of California Press, 1990.

Giles, Herbert A., trans. *San Tzu Ching: Elementary Chinese*. Taipei: Ch'eng-wen publishing company, 1972.

Goodrich, L. Carrington. *15th Century Illustrated Chinese Primer, Hsin-pien Tui-hsiang Szu-yen* (Facsimile reproduction with introduction and notes). 1967. Reprint. Hong Kong: Hong Kong University Press, 1990.

————, and Fang Chaoying, eds. *Dictionary of Ming Biography, 1368–1644*, 2 vols. New York: Columbia University Press, 1976.

Golden, Mark. *Children and Childhood in Classical Athens*. Baltimore and London: The Johns Hopkins University Press, 1990.

Graham, Angus Charles. *The Book of Lieh-tzu*. London: Murray, 1960.

Handlin, Joanna F. *Action in Late Ming Thought*. Berkeley: University of California Press, 1983.

Harris, Judith Rich, and Robert M. Liebert. *The Child: Development from Birth Through Adolescence*. 2nd edition. Englewood Cliffs: Prentice-Hall, 1987.

Hayhoe, Ruth, ed. *Education and Modernization, The Chinese Experience.* Oxford, New York, Seoul, Tokyo: Pergamon Press, 1992.

———, and Marianne Bastid, eds. *China's Education and the Industrialized World, Studies in Cultural Transfer.* Armonk, N.Y.: M.E. Sharpe, 1987.

———, and Yongling Lu. *Ma Xiangbo and the Mind of Modern China, 1840–1939.* Armonk, N.Y.: M.E. Sharpe, 1996.

He Yun 何雲. *Wenhua baiwen — Fojiao* 文化百問 —— 佛教 (One Hundred Questions about Culture — Buddhism). Beijing: Jinri zhongguo chuban-she 今日中國出版社, 1992.

Hegel, Robert E. *Reading Illustrated Fiction in Late Imperial China.* Stanford: Stanford University Press, 1998.

Ho, Ping-ti. *The Ladder of Success in Imperial China: Aspects of Social Mobility, 1368–1911.* 2nd edition. New York and London: Columbia University Press, 1967.

Hobson, Benjamin. "Xiyi lüelun xu" 西醫略論序 (Preface to *On Western Medicine*). Shanghai, 1857.

Holdcroft, David. *Saussure: Signs, System, and Arbitrariness.* Cambridge, England: Cambridge University Press, 1991.

Hopkins, L. C. "Archaic Sons and Grandsons, A Study of a Chinese Complication Complex." *The Journal of Royal Asiatic Society*, 1934, pp. 57–84.

Hu Pu'an 胡樸安. *Zhongguo wenzixue shi* 中國文字學史 (A History of Chinese Philology). 2 vols. 1937. Reprint. Shanghai: Shanghai shudian 上海書店, 1984.

Huang, Philip C. C. *The Peasant Economy and Social Change in North China.* Stanford: Stanford University Press, 1985.

———. *Liang Ch'i-ch'ao and Modern Chinese Liberalism.* Seattle and London: University of Washington Press, 1972.

Hummel, A. W. *Eminent Chinese of the Ch'ing Period.* Washington: U.S. Government Printing Office, 1943–1944.

Hunt, David. *Parents and Children in History.* New York: Basic Books, 1970.

Idema, Wilt, and Lloyd Haft. *A Guide to Chinese Literature.* Ann Arbor: The University of Michigan Press, 1997.

Illingworth, Ronald S. *The Development of the Infant and Young Child.* 7th edition. Edinburgh, London and New York: Churchill Livingstone, 1980.

Jami, Catherine. "Learning Mathematical Sciences During the Early and Mid-Ch'ing." In *Education and Society in Late Imperial China, 1600–1900,* edited by B. A. Elman and Alexander Woodside, pp. 223–256. Berkeley: University of California Press, 1994.

Jenks, Chris, ed. *The Sociology of Childhood, Essential Readings.* London: Batsford Academic and Educational Ltd., 1982.

Johnson, David. "Communication, Class, and Consciousness in Late Imperial China." In *Popular Culture in Late Imperial China,* edited by David

Johnson, Andrew Nathan and Evelyn Rawski, pp. 35–72. Berkeley: University of California Press, 1985.

Jones, Eric L. *Growth Recurring: Economic Change in World History.* Oxford: Clarendon Press; New York: Oxford University Press, 1988.

Karlgren, Bernhard. *Analytic Dictionary of Chinese and Sino-Japanese.* 1923. Reprint. Taipei: Ch'eng-wen Publishing Company, 1966.

———. *Grammata Serica: Script and Phonetics in Chinese and Sino-Japanese.* 1940. Reprint. Taipei: Ch'eng-wen Publishing Company, 1966.

Kelleher, M. Theress. "Back to Basics: Chu Hsi's Elementary Learning (Hsiao-hsueh)." In *Neo-Confucian Education: The Formative Stage,* edited by William Theodore de Bary and John Chaffee, pp. 219–251. Berkeley: University of California Press, 1989.

Kinney, Anne B., ed. *Chinese Views of Childhood.* Honolulu: University of Hawaii Press, 1995.

———. "Dyed Silk: Han Notions of the Moral Development of Children." In *Chinese Views of Childhood,* edited by Anne B Kinney, pp. 17–56. Honolulu: University of Hawaii Press, 1995.

———. "The Theme of the Precocious Child in Early Chinese Literature." *T'oung Pao,* LXXXI (1995), pp. 1–24.

Ko, Dorothy. *Teachers of the Inner Chambers: Women and Culture in China, 1573– 1722.* Stanford: Stanford University Press, 1994.

Kroll, Richard W. F. *The Material Word: Literate Culture in the Restoration and Early Eighteenth Century.* Baltimore: The Johns Hopkins University Press, 1991.

Kuhn, Dieter. "Textile Technology: Spinning and Reeling." In *Science and Civilisation in China,* vol. 5, part IX, edited by Joseph Needham et al. Cambridge, England: Cambridge University Press, 1988.

Lai, T. C. *A Scholar in Imperial China.* Hong Kong: Kelly & Walsh Ltd., 1970.

Lau, D. C., trans. *Confucius, The Analects (Lun yü).* 2nd edition. Hong Kong: The Chinese University Press, 1992.

Lee, Thomas H. C. Book review of *Chinese Views of Childhood. China Review International,* 4.2 (1997), pp. 454–457.

———. "The Discovery of Childhood: Children Education in Sung China (960–1279)." In *Kultur, Begriff und Wort in China und Japan,* edited by Sigrid Paul, pp. 159–189. Berlin: Dieter Reimer, 1984.

———. "Life in the Schools of Sung China." *Journal of Asian Studies,* 37.1 (1977), pp. 45–60.

———. "Sung Schools and Education Before Chu Hsi." In *Neo-Confucian Education,* edited by William Theodore De Bary and John Chaffee, pp. 105–136. Berkeley: University of California Press, 1989.

Legge, James, trans. *The Chinese Classics,* 5 vols in 8. Oxford: Clarendon Press, 1893; and 5 vols. Hong Kong: Hong Kong University Press, 1960.

——, trans. *The Four Books*. New York: Paragon Book Reprint Corp., 1969.

——, trans. *Sacred Books of the East*, vol. xxvii. Delhi: Motilal Banarsidass, 1966.

Lei Qiaoyun 雷僑雲. *Dunhuang ertong wenxue* 敦煌兒童文學 (Children's Literature in Dunhuang Materials). Taiwan: Xuesheng shuju 學生書局, 1985.

Leung, Angela Ki Che. "Relief Institutions for Children in Nineteenth-Century China." In *Chinese Views of Childhood*, edited by Anne B. Kinney, pp. 251–278. Honolulu: University of Hawaii Press, 1995.

——. "Elementary Education in the Lower Yangtze Region in the Seventeenth and Eighteenth Centuries." In *Education and Society in Late Imperial China, 1600–1900*, edited by B. A. Elman and A. Woodside, pp. 381–416. Berkeley: University of California Press, 1994.

Levenson, Joseph R. *Liang Ch'i-ch'ao and the Mind of Modern China*. Cambridge, Mass.: Harvard University Press, 1965.

Li Guojun 李國鈞 et al., eds. *Qingdai qianqi jiaoyu lunzhu xuan* 清代前期教育論著選 (Selected Writings on Education, 1664–1840), 3 vols. Beijing: Renmin jiaoyu chubanshe 人民教育出版社, 1990.

Li Yan 李儼, and Du Shiran 杜石然. *Zhongguo gudai shuxue jianshi* 中國古代數學簡史 (A Concise History of Chinese Mathematics), 2 vols. Beijing: Zhonghua shuju 中華書局, 1963.

Liu, James T. C. "The Classical Chinese Primer: Its Three-Characters Style and Authorship." *Journal of the American Oriental Society*, 105.2 (1985), pp. 191–196.

——. "How Did a Neo-Confucian School Become the State Orthodoxy?" *Philosophy East and West*, 23.4 (1973), pp. 483–505.

Lo, Andrew. "Dice, Dominoes and Card Games in Chinese Literature: A Preliminary Survey." In *Chinese Studies*, edited by Frances Wood, pp. 127–135. London: The British Library, 1988.

Lu Xun. *Selected Works*, 4 vols. Translated by Yang Xianyi and Gladys Yang. Beijing: Foreign Languages Press, 1980.

Mann, Susan. "The Education of Daughters in the Mid-Ch'ing Period." In *Education and Society in Late Imperial China*, edited by Benjamin Elman and Alexander Woodside, pp. 19–49. Berkeley: University of California Press, 1994.

Mao Lirui 毛禮鋭 et al. *Zhongguo gudai jiaoyu shi* 中國古代教育史 (A History of Traditional Chinese Education). 2nd edition. Beijing: Renmin jiaoyu chubanshe 人民教育出版社, 1982.

Martin, W. A. P. *A Cycle of Cathay*. New York and Chicago: F. H. Revell, 1897.

Meskill, John. *Academies in Ming China: A Historical Essay*. Tueson: The University of Arizona Press, 1982.

Millward, C. M. *A Biography of the English Language.* New York: Holt, Rinehart and Winston, Inc., 1989.

Mingay, Gordon. *The Gentry: The Rise and Fall of a Ruling Class.* London and New York: Longman, 1976.

Munro, Donald J. *The Concept of Man in Early China.* Stanford: Stanford University Press, 1969.

Needham, Joseph. *Science and Civilisation in China.* Cambridge, England: Cambridge University Press, 1954– .

Nixon, Dianne, and Katy Gould. *Emerging: Child Development in the First Three Years.* Wentworth Falls, N.S.W.: Social Science Press, 1996.

Orme, Nicholas. *English School in the Middle Ages.* London: Methuen, 1973.

———. *From Childhood to Chivalry: The Education of the English Kings and Aristocracy, 1066–1530.* London: Methuen, 1984.

Overmyer, Daniel L. *Folk Buddhist Religion: Dissenting Sects in Late Traditional China.* Cambridge, Mass.: Harvard University Press, 1976.

Paul, Sigrid, ed. *Kultur, Begriff und Wort in China und Japan.* Berlin: Dieter Reimer, 1984.

Petrucci, Raphael. *Chinese Painters.* Translated by Frances Seaver, with a biographical note by Laurence Binyon. New York: Brentano's Publishers, 1920.

Pi Xirui 皮錫瑞. *Jingxue lishi* 經學歷史 (A History of Classical Chinese Learning). 1907. Reprint. Beijing: Zhonghua shuju 中華書局, 1961.

Pollock, Linda A. *Forgotten Children: Parent-Child Relations from 1500 to 1900.* Cambridge, England and New York: Cambridge University Press, 1983.

Pusey, James Reeve. *China and Charles Darwin.* Harvard East Asian Monographs 100. Cambridge, Mass.: Council on East Asian Studies, Harvard University, 1983.

Raphals, Lisa. *Sharing the Light.* New York: State University of New York Press, 1998.

Rawski, Evelyn S. *Education and Popular Literacy in Ch'ing China.* Ann Arbor: The University of Michigan Press, 1979.

———. "Elementary Education in the Mission Enterprises." In *Christianity in China: Early Protestant Missionary Writings,* edited by S. W. Barnett and J. K. Fairbank, pp. 135–151. Cambridge, Mass.: Committee on American-East Asian Relations of the Dept. of History in collaboration with the Council on East Asian Studies, Harvard University, 1985.

Rickert, Edith. *The Babees' Book: Medieval Manners for the Young, Done into Modern English from Dr. Furnivall's Texts.* New York: Cooper Square Publishers, 1966.

Rockhill, W. W. *Diplomatic Audiences at the Court of China.* London: Lusac, 1905.

Rowe, William T. "Education and Empire in Southwest China, Ch'en Hung-mou in Yunnan, 1733–38." In *Education and Society in Late Imperial China, 1600–1900,* edited by B. A. Elman and A. Woodside, pp. 417–457. Berkeley: University of California Press, 1994.

Rule, Paul. *K'ung-tzu or Confucius.* Sydney: Allen & Unwin, 1986.

Saari, Jon. *Legacies of Childhood, Growing up Chinese in a Time of Crisis, 1890–1920.* Cambridge, Mass. and London: Harvard University Press, 1990.

Sakai, Tadao 酒井忠夫. *Chūgoku zensho no kenkyū* 中国善書の研究 (The Study of Chinese Morality Books). Tokyo: Kokusho kankou kai, 1960.

———. "Confucianism and Popular Educational Works." In *Self and Society in Ming Thought,* edited by William Theodore de Bary et al., pp. 331–366. New York: Columbia University Press, 1970.

Schwartz, Benjamin. *In Search of Wealth and Power: Yan Fu and the West.* Cambridge, Mass.: Harvard University Press, 1964.

Shahar, Shulamith. *Childhood in the Middle Ages.* London and New York: Routledge, 1990.

Shu Xincheng 舒新城. *Zhongguo jindai jiaoyushi ziliao* 中國近代教育史資料 (Materials on the History of Chinese Education, 1840–1919), 3 vols. Beijing: Renmin jiaoyu chubanshe 人民教育出版社, 1980.

Simpson, J. A. et al. *The Oxford English Dictionary.* 20 vols. 2nd edition. Oxford: Clarendon Press, 1989.

Sommerville, C. John. Foreword to *Chinese Views of Childhood,* edited by Anne B Kinney, p. xi. Honolulu: University of Hawaii Press, 1995.

Soothill, W., and L. Hodous. *A Dictionary of Chinese Buddhist Terms.* 1937. Reprint. Taipei: Ch'eng-wen publishing company, 1970.

Sowards, J. K. *Collected Works of Erasmus.* Toronto: University of Toronto Press, 1985.

Stone, Lawrence. *The Family, Sex and Marriage in England 1500–1800.* London: Weidenfeld & Nicolson, 1977.

Sutton-Smith, Brian et al., eds. *Children's Folklore: A Source Book.* New York and London: Garland Publishing, Inc., 1995.

———. "A Developmental Psychology of Play and Arts." *Perspectives on Education,* Spring (1971), pp. 8–17.

Tang, Chun-i. "The Development of the Concept of Moral Mind from Wang Yang-ming to Wang Chi." In *Self and Society in Ming Thought,* edited by William Theodore de Bary et al., pp. 100–108. New York: Columbia University Press, 1970.

Taylor, E. G. R. *The Mathematical Practitioners of Tudor & Stuart England.* Cambridge, England: Cambridge University Press, 1970.

Teiser, Stephen F. *The Ghost Festival in Medieval China.* Princeton: Princeton University Press, 1988.

Teng Ssu-yü. *Family Instructions for the Yan Clan*. Leiden: E.J. Brill, 1968.

Tri, C. N. "La Vogue Des Manuels D'enseignement Elementaire Traditionnels en RPC: naissance d'une recherche, retour de la morale confuceenne ou manipulation politique?" *Revue Bibliographique de Sinologie*, 13 (1995), pp. 35–46.

Tu, Wei-ming. "The Confucian Perception of Adulthood." *Daedalus*, 105.2 (1976), pp. 109–123.

———. "The Confucian Sage: Exampler of Personal Knowledge." In *Saints and Virtues*, edited by John Stratton Hawley, pp. 73–86. Berkeley: University of Califonia Press, 1987.

———. "The Creative Tension between Ren and Li." *Philosophy East and West*, 18.1–2 (1968), pp. 29–39.

———. *Humanity and Self-Cultivation: Essays in Confucian Thought*. Berkeley: Asian Humanities Press, 1979.

———. "The Sung Confucian Ideas of Education: A Background of Understanding." In *Neo-Confucian Education: The Formative Stage*, edited by William Theodore de Bary and J. Chaffee, pp. 139–150. Berkeley: University of California Press, 1989.

Twitchett, Denis, and John K. Fairbank, general eds. *The Cambridge History of China*, 15 vols. Cambridge, England and New York: Cambridge University Press, 1978–2002.

Veith, Ilza, trans. *Nei Ching Su Wen, The Yellow Emperor's Classic of Internal Medicine*. Berkeley: University of California Press, 1966.

Waley, Arthur, trans. and annotated. *The Analects of Confucius*. New York: Vintage Books, 1989.

Waltner, Ann. *Getting an Heir, Adoption and the Construction of Kinship in Late Imperial China*. Honolulu: University of Hawaii Press, 1990.

———. "Infanticide and Dowry in Ming and Early Qing China." In *Chinese Views of Childhood*, edited by Anne B. Kinney, pp. 193–218. Honolulu: University of Hawaii Press, 1996.

———. "The Moral Status of the Child in Late Imperial China: Childhood in Ritual and in Law." *Social Research*, 53.4 (1986), pp. 667–687.

Wang Bingzhao 王炳照. "Ershisi xiao pingjie" 二十四孝評介 (On Twenty-four Examples of Filial Piety). In *Mengxue shipian*, edited by Xia Chu and Hui Ling, pp. 1–16. Beijing: Beijing Normal University Press, 1990.

Wang Chongmin 王重民. *Dunhuang guji xulu* 敦煌古籍敘錄 (Annotation and Records of Historical Documents in Dunhuang Caves). Beijing: Zhonghua shuju 中華書局, 1979.

Wang Li 王力. *Hanyu shigao* 漢語史稿 (A History of the Chinese Language), 3 vols. Beijing: Kexue chubanshe 科學出版社, 1958.

Wang Liu Hui-chen. *The Traditional Chinese Clan Rules*. Locust Valley, N.Y.: J. J. Augustin Incorporated Publisher, 1959.

Watson, Burton, trans. *Hsün Tzu.* New York: Columbia University Press, 1963.

————, trans. *Meng Ch'iu: Famous Episodes from Chinese History and Legend.* Tokyo, New York and San Francisco: Kodansha International, 1979.

Watson, Ernest H., and George H. Lowrey. *Growth and Development of Children.* 2nd edition. Chicago: The Year Book Publishers, 1958.

Wenwu 文物 (Cultural Relics), 10 (1984), pls 2–4, and color pl 2.

Wilder, G. D., and J. H. Ingram. *Analysis of Chinese Characters.* Taipei: Literature House, 1964.

Williams, C. A. S. *Outlines of Chinese Symbolism and Art Motives.* 1941. Reprint. Rutland, Vermont and Tokyo: Charles E. Tuttle Company, 1974.

Wilson, A. "The Infancy of the History of Childhood: An Appraisal of Philippe Aries." *History and Theory,* 19 (1980), pp. 132–154.

Woodside, Alexander. "Real and Imagined Continuities in the Chinese Struggle for Literacy." In *Education and Modernization: The Chinese Experience,* edited by Ruth Hayhoe, pp. 23–45. Oxford and New York: Pergamon Press, 1992.

————. "Some Mid-Qing Theorists of Popular Schools, Their Innovations, Inhibitions, and Attitudes toward the Poor." *Modern China,* 9.1 (1983), pp. 3–35.

————, and Benjamin Elman. "Afterword: The Expension of Education in Ch'ing China." In *Education and Society in Late Imperial China, 1600–1900,* edited by B. A. Elman and A. Woodside, pp. 525–560. Berkeley: University of California Press, 1994.

Wu Feng 吳楓. *Zhongguo gudian wenxian xue* 中國古典文獻學 (Ancient Chinese Reference Books). Jinan 濟南: Qilu shushe 齊魯書社, 1982.

Wu Pei-yi. "Childhood Remembered: Parents and Children in China, 800 to 1700." In *Chinese Views of Childhood,* edited by Anne B. Kinney, pp. 129–156. Honolulu: University of Hawaii Press, 1995.

————. "Education of Children in the Sung." In *Neo-Confucian Education,* edited by William Theodore de Bary and J. Chaffee, pp. 307–324. Berkeley: University of California Press, 1989.

Xiong Yuezhi 熊月之. *Xixue dongjian yu wan Qing shehui* 西學東漸與晚清社會 (Western Learning and Late Qing Society). Shanghai: Renmin chubanshe 人民出版社, 1994.

Xu Zongze 徐宗澤. *Ming-Qing jian yesuhuishi yizhu tiyao* 明清間耶穌會士譯著提要 (Synopsis of Missionary's Translated Works during the Ming-Qing Period). Shanghai: Zhonghua shuju 中華書局, 1949.

Yang Xianyi, Gladys Yang, and Hu Shiguang, trans. *Selections from the "Book of Songs."* Beijing: Panda Books, 1983.

Yang Yinshen 楊蔭深. *Zhongguo youyi yanjiu* 中國游藝研究 (The Study of Chinese Games). 1935. Reprint. Shanghai: Wenyi chubanshe 文藝出版社, 1990.

Young, J. D. *Confucianism and Christianity: The First Encounter*. Hong Kong: Hong Kong University Press, 1983.

Yu Yingshi 余英時. *Lishi yu sixiang* 歷史與思想 (History and Thought). Taipei: Lianjing chuban shiye gongsi 聯經出版事業公司, 1976.

Zhang Shilu 張世祿. *Zhongguo yinyunxue shi* 中國音韻學史 (A History of Chinese Phonology). Hong Kong: Taixing shuju 泰興書局, 1963.

Zhang Zhigong 張志公. *Chuantong yuwen jiaoyu chutan* 傳統語文教育初探 (A Preliminary Research on Traditional Chinese Language Teaching). Shanghai: Shanghai jiaoyu chubanshe 上海教育出版社, 1962.

Zheng Zhenduo 鄭振鐸. *Zhongguo gudai mukehua shilüe* 中國古代木刻畫史略 (A Brief History of Traditional Chinese Woodcuts). Vol. 9 of *Zhongguo gudai mukehua xuanji* 中國古代木刻畫選集 (Selected Works of Traditional Chinese Woodcuts), 9 vols. 1956. Reprint. Beijing: Renmin meishu chubanshe 人民美術出版社, 1985.

——. *Zhongguo suwenxue shi* 中國俗文學史 (History of Chinese Popular Literature), 2 vols. Beijing: Wenxue guji kanxingshe 文學古籍刊行社, 1959.

——. *Zhongguo suwenxue shi*. Shanghai: Shangwu yinshuguan 商務印書館, 1938.

Zhu Weizheng. "Confucius and Traditional Chinese Education: An Assessment." In *Education and Modernization: The Chinese Experience*, edited by Ruth Hayhoe, pp. 3–21. Oxford and New York: Pergamon Press, 1992.

Zhu Youhuan 朱有瓛. *Zhongguo jindai xuezhi shiliao* 中國近代學制史料 (Materials on the Chinese Education System from the Late Qing to the Early Republic Period). Shanghai: The Press of East China Normal University, 1983–89.

ᔥ Index ᔥ